The Rhetoric of Oil in the Twenty-First Century

This book examines mass communication and civic participation in the age of oil, analyzing the rhetorical and discursive ways that governments and corporations shape public opinion and public policy and that activists reframe public debates to resist corporate framing.

In the twenty-first century, oil has become a subject of civic deliberation. Environmental concerns have intensified; questions of indigenous rights have arisen; and private and public investment in energy companies has become open to deliberation. International contributors use local events as a starting point to explore larger issues associated with oil-dependent societies and cultures. This interdisciplinary collection analyzes the global discourse of oil from the start of the twentieth century into the era of transnational corporations of the twenty-first century.

This book will be a vital text for scholars in communication studies, energy humanities, and environmental studies. Case studies are framed accessibly, and the theoretical lenses are across disciplines, making it ideal for a postgraduate and advanced undergraduate audience in these fields.

Heather Graves is Professor of English and Film Studies at the University of Alberta in Edmonton, AB, Canada, where she does research on argument in academic disciplines, the rhetoric of oil, the rhetoric of science, visual rhetoric, and the gamification of writing instruction.

David Beard is Associate Professor of Rhetoric in the Department of English, Linguistics, and Writing Studies at the University of Minnesota Duluth, where he researches rhetoric at the intersection of oral and written communication, popular and professional discourses.

Routledge Studies in Rhetoric and Communication

29 **Vernacular Christian Rhetoric and Civil Discourse**
The Religious Creativity of Evangelical Student Writers
Jeffrey M. Ringer

30 **The Aboutness of Writing Center Talk**
A Corpus-Driven and Discourse Analysis
Jo Mackiewicz

31 **Rhetorical Realism**
Rhetoric, Ethics, and the Ontology of Things
Scot Barnett

32 **American Political Discourse on China**
Michelle Murray Yang

33 **Professional Communication and Network Interaction**
A Rhetorical and Ethical Approach
Heidi A. McKee and James E. Porter

34 **The Rhetoric of Videogames as Embodied Practice**
Procedural Habits
Steve Holmes

35 **Orwell's "Politics and the English Language" in the Age of Pseudocracy**
Hans Ostrom and William Haltom

36 **The Rhetoric of Oil in the Twenty-First Century**
Government, Corporate, and Activist Discourses
Edited by Heather Graves and David Beard

For more information about this series, please visit: https://www.routledge.com

The Rhetoric of Oil in the Twenty-First Century

Government, Corporate, and Activist Discourses

Edited by Heather Graves
and David Beard

Routledge
Taylor & Francis Group
LONDON AND NEW YORK

First published 2019 by Routledge

2 Park Square, Milton Park, Abingdon, Oxon OX14 4RN
605 Third Avenue, New York, NY 10017

Routledge is an imprint of the Taylor & Francis Group, an informa business

First issued in paperback 2021

Publisher's Note

The publisher has gone to great lengths to ensure the quality of this reprint but points out that some imperfections in the original copies may be apparent.

Library of Congress Cataloging-in-Publication Data
CIP data has been applied for.

ISBN: 978-1-138-48437-5 (hbk)
ISBN: 978-1-03-217828-8 (pbk)
DOI: 10.4324/9781351052146

Typeset in Sabon
by codeMantra

Contents

Notes on Contributors

Gretchen Bakke is author of *The Grid* (2016), which brings anthropological sensibilities to a study of the immense infrastructural, historical, technological, legislative, and fiscal complexity of the U.S. electric grid. She is currently a guest professor at Humboldt University in Berlin.

Natalia Barrionuevo is teaching Assistant and Researcher in Instituto de Estudios Sociales y Políticos de la Patagonia - Facultad de Humanidades y Ciencias Sociales at Universidad Nacional de la Patagonia San Juan Bosco (Comodoro Rivadavia, Chubut, Argentina). She teaches social sciences, environmental sociology, and culture and communication. Her research interests include social effects of oil work, legitimation of class and gender inequalities, and social identities.

David Beard is Associate Professor of Rhetoric in the Department of English, Linguistics, and Writing Studies at the University of Minnesota Duluth, where he researches rhetoric at the intersection of oral and written communication, popular and professional discourses.

Sibo Chen is SSHRC Vanier Scholar in the School of Communication at Simon Fraser University. His research interests include environmental communication, energy-society relationship, political economy, and critical discourse analysis.

Heather Graves is Professor of English and Film Studies at the University of Alberta in Edmonton, AB, Canada, where she does research on argument in academic disciplines, the rhetoric of oil, the rhetoric of science, visual rhetoric, and the gamification of writing instruction.

Juliette Lapeyrouse-Cherry is a PhD candidate in Rhetoric and Scientific and Technical Communication in the Department of Writing Studies at the University of Minnesota-Twin Cities. Her research focuses on rhetorics of energy extraction and environment along the U.S. Gulf Coast.

Roberta Laurie teaches Sustainability Communication, Rhetoric, and Creative Non-Fiction in the Bachelor of Communications Studies Program at MacEwan University. She wrote her master's thesis on the framing of "ethical oil" and has been following the phenomenon since.

T.R. Kover, Environmental Studies and Science Technology and Society, Office of Interdisciplinary Studies, University of Alberta, earned his doctorate in philosophy at the H.I.W., K.U. Leuven and currently writes on issues in Environmental philosophy and the Energy Humanities.

John Moffatt holds a PhD from Queen's University and has been teaching rhetorical theory, leadership as communication, and rhetorical editing at the Ron and Jane Graham School of Professional Development at the University of Saskatchewan since 2007.

Corey Owen, a happily shipwrecked medievalist, has taught rhetoric and communication since 2007 at the Ron and Jane Graham School of Professional Development at the University of Saskatchewan.

Stefan Peters (Justus-Liebig-University Gießen /Instituto Colombo-Alemán para la Paz-CAPAZ) Chair for Peace Studies at the Justus-Liebig-University Gießen and Director of the CAPAZ, works on Development, Natural Resources, Social Inequalities, Peace Studies, Memory and Transitional Justice with a focus on Latin America.

Penélope Plaza is a Venezuelan architect, researcher and urban artivist. She is Lecturer in Architecture at the School of Architecture, University of Reading.

Debora Rolfes is a faculty member in the Graham School of Professional Development, College of Engineering, University of Saskatchewan, where she teaches professional communication.

Manuel Silva-Ferrer is a cultural and media theorist and research associate at the Latin-American Institute of the Free University of Berlin, Germany.

Ross Singer is Associate Professor of Communication at Saginaw Valley State University, MI, USA. Dr. Singer has published essays on various issues in contemporary environmental rhetoric in the United States.

Adam Thomlison is a PhD candidate at Carleton University; however, his chapter began as part of the Mediatoil.ca project at the University of Ottawa.

Ian Wereley is a Postdoctoral Fellow at the Calgary Institute for the Humanities, and Adjunct Curator of the History of Energy at the Canadian Science and Technology Museum.

Jeanie Wills, Graham School of Professional Development, College of Engineering, University of Saskatchewan, studies rhetorical theory and history and has published in feminist studies and the history of professional women in male-dominated industries.

Josh Wodak, Lecturer, Art and Design at the University of New South Wales, Australia. His work explores the ethics and efficacy of techno-scientific means to mitigate species extinction and biodiversity loss in the Anthropocene.

Sean Zwagerman is Associate Professor, Department of English, Simon Fraser University. He is interested broadly in rhetoric and writing—in the compositional relationship among the word, the self, and the world—and more narrowly in the intersections of analytic philosophy and rhetorical theory.

1 Introduction

Rhetoric in the Age of Oil: Energy Humanities and the Discourses of the Petrochemical Industry

Heather Graves and David Beard

A double-trailer oil tanker waits to turn across the Yellowhead Highway in front of me to go north to Josephburg, Alberta. Experienced westbound drivers know to slow down here because that tanker is going to pull out across their path even though the oncoming traffic is doing at least 110 km/hour and there is insufficient distance for the tanker to cross the westbound lane. Sure enough, the tanker starts its turn, but I and the other drivers have already braked to 90 km: we brake further to 60 km/hour. The tanker clears the crossing, and we continue safely over the rise. As I descend the hills leading into the city, the Edmonton and Sherwood Park skylines spread out in front of me. The tall high-rises of downtown are visible from 15 kilometers away, and off to the right the refineries are marked by mechano-like structures and plumes of smoke that fill the sky. Tongues of flame surge up from towering smoke stacks that burn off by-products from the refining processes. As my car skirts the refineries on my way to the University of Alberta campus, acrid smoke fills my nose. I wonder idly whether something I'm breathing right now triggered the allergic eczema that I have developed since moving east of Sherwood Park. Massive storage tanks flank the intersections where the Yellowhead crosses the Henday. Each tank is sunk into a deep, dry moat, guarding the surrounding city against potential leaks. Eventually the air clears as I cross into Edmonton and the industrial landscape gives way to residential neighborhoods and outdoor strip malls.

Unless they live in proximity to 'oil country,' most citizens living in the age of oil in the twenty-first century do not recognize how the fabric of their lives is constructed in, around, and through oil. They understand that oil heats or cools their houses and runs their cars, SUVs, and flights to academic conferences or exotic vacations, but they may not realize that it also makes possible a thousand other details of contemporary life—from plastic measuring cups in the kitchen to indestructible fabrics and floor coverings in the living room to shoes and household appliances. Even those elements of our lives that are not made from oil are produced using equipment fueled directly or indirectly by oil. Industrial farming depends on diesel-fed equipment and electricity or natural-gas powered feeding and milking "systems." Our construction industry also uses oil-based components transported by oil-fueled vehicles. Our manufacturing industries depend on oil and gas to keep their plants open and their products moving to markets around the world. In some ways, life in the twenty-first century is, at least initially, unimaginable if we remove oil from it.

What if we do remove oil from our daily lives in the twenty-first century? What will our existence look like? We only need look back about a century to acquaint ourselves with life pre-oil. Returning to life pre-twentieth century will require a new mind-set for those of us living in modern first world nations. But burning peat or wood to heat houses for those of us living in northern climates is not the answer either. We do need alternative sources to meet our contemporary energy needs. But what replaces our ubiquitous plastic-based items? Oil is a low-cost alternative to natural fibers (polyester versus cotton or wool), in household items (plastic versus wood or metal), in tools and equipment (plastics versus wood or metal), and so on. We will have to ramp up development of alternatives, e.g., cellulose-based plastics, and/or return to expensive and labor intensive materials (e.g., silk, wool).

When we exhort each other to "break our addiction to oil," who is this "we"? Not all human beings use oil equally; many of us living in modern first world nations consume oil disproportionately. We buy the latest devices, own multiple vehicles, multiple houses, and travel the world for work and pleasure: we carve a large carbon footprint. Some of us are less affluent but live in geographical locations with extremes in climate (north towards the Arctic, in mountainous or desert areas, for example) or sparse populations: we see heating (or cooling) and gasoline as essential to our survival; we carve a smaller but still significant carbon footprint. Still others of us are inspired by media depictions of the affluent, and we direct our efforts towards obtaining some of these symbols of this life. Can we be happy to learn that while others have reveled in these luxuries their whole lives they are now off-limits to us? The exhortation to "break our addiction to oil" seems to call on all of us to reject not just the symbols but the realities of contemporary life. Can we do this? Are we ready and willing (those of us in North America, for example) to *not* take that vacation, to *not* own a car (let alone several), to move to a temperate global region that doesn't require heating or cooling, to buy and eat only food grown locally, to own many fewer possessions, and all the other changes that removing oil from our daily lives would entail? And to do all this while others around the globe, for various reasons, do not?

When we, as a species, speak of breaking our "addiction to oil" we simplify the problem; in fact, as Gretchen Bakke concludes in this volume, we obscure elements of the problem that must be solved before we can envision human life post-oil in the twenty-first century. At the very least, we need a different metaphor that facilitates finding realistic solutions to the problems that we have, in part, created.

In calling for a new metaphor, we invoke rhetoric. Rhetoric has been and will continue to be central to discussions of oil because rhetoric *is* public debate—that is, debate about humanity's appropriate course of action on a complex, contentious issue with an uncertain outcome. Rhetoric is our only means to discuss such topics to achieve even partial agreement on how to proceed. Whatever stance participants take, they engage in rhetoric to present their perspective. However, not all participants are aware that in making an argument they are using rhetoric. In fact, some of the existing research on the rhetoric of oil published by energy humanities scholars co-opts the term rhetoric without fully acknowledging what rhetoric is, as evidenced by authors who present their analysis as The Truth and label the opposing viewpoint as *rhetoric*. But if rhetoric is "the faculty of observing in any given case the available means of persuasion" (Aristotle, 1984), then all participants must use rhetoric (effectively or poorly) if they advance an argument on the topic. This includes scientists who publish their findings from research. They interpret their results and present an argument that is judged valid or not. When their peers find those arguments compelling, the explanation can achieve the status of *fact*; however, further research may present new results that contradict that fact (Bazerman, 1994; Fahnestock, 2000; Gross, 1990, 2006; Myers, 1990; and many others). Scientists tend to be pragmatists who move forward based on their understanding of the facts but try to remain open to new research that might require rethinking their facts (Graves, 2005). On this basis, scientists are rhetoricians, yet the results of their research are often treated by nonscientists as unequivocal truth about the natural phenomenon. Admittedly, this impression is often fostered by scientific style, the point of which is to facilitate scientists in presenting their interpretations (subjective) as explanations (objective).

As noted, oil shapes popular and political discourses. It has also shaped academic discourse in the energy humanities, so much so that Jones (2016, p. 16) has branded the focus on oil "petromyopia" and called on scholars to focus on "non-oil topics" including coal, natural gas, and electricity. While the title of this book emphasizes its focus on oil, in fact, several of the authors in this volume have responded to Jones' call to action, writing chapters that place oil within a narrative and a continuum with coal and natural gas. However, the discourse surrounding oil is by no means exhausted through the scholarship published to date. And exploration into the *rhetoric* of oil is relatively underdeveloped.

Many of the authors in this volume connect their scholarship on the rhetoric of oil to climate change and related environmental issues, obvious connections for this discussion. They also highlight how rhetoric contributes to such discussions by providing means to move forward in the face of uncertainty about the *facts* as well as the outcome of myriad possible actions (i.e., Aristotle's deliberative rhetoric). In complex and confusing situations—for example, the contradictory positions and *factual* evidence advanced in mass communication about climate change—rhetoric provides ways to analyze, understand, and navigate the perhaps incommensurate discursive positions proposed. Analysis allows us to identify the writer's underlying assumptions about the audience, the subject, and the goal. Similarly, we can detect the perspective's primary values. In understanding the specific basis for the writer's position, we can perceive the broader context of values into which it fits. Major disagreements—how (or if) humanity should address the problem of climate change—cannot be resolved unless discussants find common ground in shared values, assumptions about, and understandings of the problem. Once we identify others' values, it becomes possible to create common ground. Granted, once we do understand each other's positions, we may still disagree on a common course of action—but without understanding action becomes impossible. The authors here offer fascinating analyses of energy and climate change discourse that illustrate that this discourse is not, in fact, neutral, factual, or straightforward.

Another theme in this collection is the multimodal nature of discourse about oil. Numerous authors use visual rhetorical theory to analyze and interpret video, film, and images with text. This multimodal focus reflects trends in humanities research to move beyond text to emphasize how visual/aural components contribute in contemporary mass communication. Contemporary discourse about oil is highly visual, from the images of bitumen mining in the Canadian oil sands in advertisements by environmental activist NGOs to the petro-state sponsored ad campaign in Venezuela depicting giant oil workers manipulating works of public art; historical discourse about oil is also visual, as Ian Wereley demonstrates in his analysis of political cartoons in early twentieth-century England.

This book takes a global perspective on what it means to live in the age of oil in the twenty-first century, with contributions from scholars contributing vantage points from North America, South America, Europe, and Australia. Our contributing authors use local events as starting points for exploring larger issues associated with oil-dependent societies and cultures. They highlight the assumptions underlying the positions they study to show how the arguments are constructed and how they position audience members politically, economically, or ideologically. These perspectives also help us to understand ways in which people around the globe, in fact, may share experiences despite their divergent circumstances.

This collection is organized into three large geographical sections: U.S. and European case studies, case studies in South America, and then in Canada. Section I presents a historical chapter on the transition from coal to oil in Britain at the turn of the twentieth century. The second chapter documents how efforts of citizens in the United States to free themselves from "fossil fuel addiction" are hampered because such metaphors rely on the logic of oil in their imaginings about fuel alternatives in the future. The remaining chapters in this section focus on the United States.

Euro-American Case Studies

In Chapter 2, "King Coal versus Prince Petroleo: Imagining Oil, Energy, and Transition in Early Twentieth-Century Britain," Ian Wereley notes that energy humanities scholarship lacks historical analyses of oil. Drawing on the concept of "oil spectacle" (using invented stories, images, and symbols to render oil comprehensible), Wereley analyzes two political cartoons from *Punch* to illustrate how the characters of King Coal and Prince Petroleo serve as rhetorical tools to understand the transition from coal to oil in Britain in the early 1900s. He argues that these cartoons act as cultural mirrors that both reflect and influence the society in which they were produced, affording valuable entry points into the discourse on oil and energy transition at that time that may shed light on contemporary society's effort to transition away from oil. He notes that oil, the proposed alternative energy source, is characterized as supporting traditional applications while also enabling entirely new technologies (aircraft and automobiles). Wereley concludes that oil discourse in Britain in that period reveals that the petrocultures of the past are alive "constantly shaping how oil is thought and talked about today."

In Chapter 3, "Crude Thinking," Gretchen Bakke analyzes an advertisement featuring Neil deGrasse Tyson exhorting viewers to "break our addiction" to oil in favor of solar energy. She analyzes the metaphor of "addiction" that deGrasse Tyson uses, noting that it characterizes the problem as cultural not technological: viewers lack the will to change. She argues that oil has twisted beyond all recognition the relationship between the necessary labor-time for its production and the energetic potential of the oil itself. To aid readers in reframing the future, Bakke quantifies how oil energy revolutionized the quality of human life and propelled us to, as deGrasse Tyson characterizes it, the brink of climate change disaster. She argues that he characterizes solar power as infinite, tacitly giving us license to increase our already excessive power consumption, and she emphasizes that this characterization perpetuates our imaginaries of oil: "a post fossil-fueled world . . . continues to be premised *even in the imagination* upon . . . thinking with the logics of oil."

In Chapter 4, "Rhetorics of Toxicity, Racism, and Religion on the Gulf Coast: Oil and Environmental Justice in the BP Spill Documentary

Films," Juliette Lapeyrouse-Cherry analyzes three documentaries about the effects of the Deepwater Horizon oil spill in 2010 on the Gulf Coast of Louisiana, USA: *The Big Fix*, *Vanishing Pearls*, and *The Great Invisible*. She links energy humanities with new materialist ecocriticism, drawing on transcorporeal understandings of the body to explore how the films implicitly and explicitly foreground the impact of the spill specifically and petroleum culture in general, on human and animal bodies along the Gulf Coast. Lapeyrouse-Cherry examines how the films link animal suffering and human physical experiences of the oil spill to illuminate the concept of transcorporeality. She contends that the films' success in conveying this concept hinges upon filmmakers' use of imagery to depict toxic action. She then applies an environmental justice lens to the films to assess their treatments of race and religion. She argues that when all public and academic discussions of the spill ignore issues of race and religion, we can never fully understand its impact on Louisiana's oil culture.

In Chapter 5, "When Water Meets Oil: Rupturing Rhetoric and Reality in Energy Policy and Climate Change," Josh Wodak analyzes the presence of oil extraction in the Gulf of México to explore the potential for the act of rupturing—both physical (pipelines/drilling rigs) and symbolic (climate change science's effect on our sense of the 'real')—to interrupt the climate science/energy policy impasse that he identifies between facts/values and is/ought during Barack Obama's tenure as president. In his discussion, Wodak links the discovery and extraction of oil in the Gulf, the American Space Program, and the decommissioning of military/industrial equipment into Artificial Reefs in the Gulf to illustrate the stark contrast in Obama's climate science and energy policy in his first and second presidential terms. Wodak examines how various ruptures challenge Obama's contradictory energy policy that, he argues, simultaneously facilitates and decimates the marine ecosystems in the Gulf. He argues that Obama's promotion of oil as innocuous and necessary was undermined by oil-related 'natural' and human-caused disasters during his presidency. Wodak then argues that repurposing booster rockets from the space program into artificial reefs in the Gulf has created the unlikely scenario of marine ecosystems relying on oil infrastructure and thus creates a responsibility to scale up rigs to reef conversion in general.

In Chapter 6, "The Flaming Faucet as Fracking's Ideographic Synecdoche: Tracking its Emergence in the Rhetorics of *Gasland* and the U.S. Natural Gas Industry," Ross Singer examines how the film, *Gasland*, which investigated the link between hydraulic fracturing ("fracking") and contaminated groundwater in the United States, galvanized environmental activists to oppose natural gas production in the United States starting in 2010. He shows how rhetorical devices and practices explain the film's impact, how they shaped the natural gas industry's response, and how these practices were appropriated and used against anti-frackers. He catalogs the ways that fracking uses and potentially contaminates water to explore its discursive meaning as proposed by both activists and industry. He proposes that the initial exchange between *Gasland*'s director, Josh Fox, and the U.S. natural gas industry took shape through contrasting articulations of synecdochic meanings ascribed to the flaming water faucet, creating a "representational ideograph." Singer argues that the flaming faucet became a shorthand political symbol that condensed and refuted broader ideological discourse: *Gasland* characterized the flaming faucet as a threat to "life," while the industry characterized it as a threat to "science." Singer shows how the flaming faucet became a focal point that shaped the entire conflict. He concludes that ideographic analysis can contribute productively to inquiry in environmental disputes, prompting attention to how ill-defined but widely validated terms and slogans that connect symbols to complex arguments are selected, arranged, and enacted.

Case Studies in the Global South

The second major section of this volume presents three discussions of oil culture in South America: two from Venezuela and one from Argentina. Given the political and social unrest in Venezuela, the scholars who contributed these chapters are potentially exposing themselves to considerable personal risk by commenting on and, in some cases, critiquing current and historical events in their homeland. We appreciate their courage in making these important contributions.

In Chapter 7, "The Birth of a Myth: The Latin American Modern Oil Nation," Manuel Silva-Ferrer explores the political and historical moments that laid the groundwork for Venezuela to be transformed from a physical location, a "non-existing country" into the narrative of a "modern oil nation." He identifies four pillars that supported the transformation: (1) the need for a discourse that legitimized the dictatorship's existence on the Venezuelan and international political scenes; (2) the United States' desire to consolidate the status quo in Latin America as a defense against Communism (even if it meant allying with dictatorial regimes); (3) the political and financial aid granted by transnational oil companies interested in expanding their production in Venezuela; and (4) the popular imaginary woven by mass culture mediators who spread the narratives of progress set in the Latin American landscape at a global scale. Silva-Ferrer elaborates each of these pillars in some detail, tying his discussion into a historical and cultural analysis of Venezuelan society. He argues that Venezuelan dictatorships constructed opulent visible symbols of progress without developing the cultural, political, industrial, and educational infrastructure that would have achieved genuine status as a modern oil nation. He concludes that the desired progress in Venezuela was an illusion, a costly narrative barely sustained by the colossal resources provided by the oil industry.

In Chapter 8, "Untangling the Myth of 'Culture as Renewable Oil': A Barthesian Exploration of PDVSA La Estancia's Visual Campaign *Transformamos el petróleo en un recurso renovable para tí*," Penélope Plaza explores a different Venezuelan myth: that oil is a renewable resource. She starts by explaining that, historically, Venezuela has drawn an analogy between the arts/culture and oil. Venezuela's national oil company, PDVSA La Estancia, has organizational and legal autonomy and follows its own agenda; thus, it has come to view culture as a natural resource. She analyzes an advertising campaign that ran 2005 to 2012 illustrating numerous city spaces and iconic public works of art in Venezuela that were restored by PDVSA La Estancia. The campaign featured photographs with images of giant oil workers inserted into the public space, showing them manipulating the artwork. Plaza analyzes the advertisements' visual rhetoric to elucidate the intended meanings behind its slogan, "We Transform oil into a renewable resource for you," and to define the idea of culture that PDVSA La Estancia mobilizes when they represent the city of Caracas as an oil field. She argues that the advertisements coalesce culture, oil, and the city into one entity, drawing an analogy between culture and renewable oil: "PDVSA La Estancia becomes the sorcerer that makes possible the impossible by transforming oil into a renewable resource." She concludes that this advertising campaign is a symbol of PDVSA's discursive power, that it subliminally communicates that the urban spaces and the city itself are contained within the oil industry's realm.

In Chapter 9, "Against all Odds: Oil Culture and the Commodity Consensus in Argentine's Patagonia," Natalia Barrionuevo and Stefan Peters counter the prevailing theory that raw materials extraction, especially oil, entails negative economic, social, and political consequences in resource dependent societies of the Global South. In their case study of the oil city, Comodoro Rivadavia, in the Patagonian province of Chubut in southern Argentina, they explore the harmonious coexistence of the perceivable negative effects of extraction in daily life and the equally perceptible support for the oil-based local development in this oil-centered society. They note that the importance of oil for the city and the province generates a broad social consensus on oil that permeates the local society and that this consensus strengthens in times of crisis. They argue that this broad support for the oil industry can be explained by a combination of material issues (rent distribution, employment, and economic dependency) and the construction and resignification of historical social imaginaries and collective identities. They use qualitative data from extensive fieldwork in Comodoro Rivadavia to explore its status as a rentier society with ambivalent development outcomes. They demonstrate how the "commodity consensus" on oil in the city and province is built on the ways that sociohistorical imaginaries constitute and redefine extraction. As common sense, these ideas pervade the local society and help to explain why, even in times of crisis, no critical voices promote a categorical transformation of the local oil-based development model.

A Closer Look at the Oil Sands in Alberta

In the third section we focus on oil extraction in the Canadian oil sands. Canada's oil sands have become a global target for environmental activists for various reasons, including the fact that they are conveniently geographically located within a benign democratic country where demonstrators can be assured of their personal safety. As Plaza notes in Chapter 7, Venezuela boasts the largest unconventional oil deposits in the world, yet global environmental activists have not targeted them nor organized protests to hinder extraction there. In fact, mass communication and public discourse about the oil sands in Canada provided the motivation for this volume. The marketing campaigns over the past decade by the oil industry, activist environmentalists, environmental organizations, governments, and non-profit organizations in support and against the oil sands offer captivating material for study and analysis. These essays offer perspectives on this public discourse ranging from how argumentative frames can become cognitive frames to analysis of multimodal messages that create powerful emotional appeals and textual arguments that seek to prohibit reasonable discussion of the issues, and in some cases, aims to achieve goals at odds with those stated.

In Chapter 10, "Still Ethical Oil: Framing the Alberta Oil Sands," Roberta Laurie examines the framing around arguments by Ezra Levant, a controversial conservative commentator, that stable, democratic government in Canada means that the Alberta Oil Sands constitutes 'ethical oil' compared to the brutal political regimes in African and Middle Eastern countries that produce 'conflict oil.' She traces the movement of the phrase "ethical oil" from Levant's polemic in *Ethical Oil* (2010) into the lexicon of Canadian political and resource-related discourse. She notes that while this term fell out of favor as an overt framing device in the discussion, it has joined the Canadian consciousness as a cognitive frame. She unpacks this term to explore how language users, once they accept the 'ethical oil' frame and accept that the Alberta oil sands are 'ethical,' begin to believe that those who oppose development of the oil sands are somehow unethical. She then explores how the frame continues to enable public discourse about the oil sands, noting that 'ethical oil' offers a narrative that lets Canadians maintain conventional norms: continuous economic growth, increased wealth, plentiful jobs, limitless energy, and the established order. Laurie argues that this frame forces Canadians to discuss where to source their oil rather than the significant social and environmental costs of its extraction.

In Chapter 11, "From Pipeline to Plate: The Domestication of Oil Sands through Visual Food Analogies," Adam Thomlison explores the trend in the promotional material of companies working in the oil sands to compare the bitumen to food, including yogurt, cupcakes, coffee, and peanut butter. He combines multimodal and semiotic analysis to develop a theoretical framework to analyze the visual rhetoric used in four sample ads. He identifies two figures of speech that perform rhetorical work in the sample, each with the intended aim of producing positive emotional associations with oil sands products. Since the associations are related to food, the goal is seemingly to domesticate the oil sands in the eyes of a public still weighing the benefits of extraction. Thomlison concludes that domestication is a rhetorical strategy within visual environmental communication and that food is a 'nature' image that can be co-opted for the purposes of greenwashing.

In Chapter 12, "Everything You Ever Wanted to Know about the Alberta Oil Sands (But Were Afraid to Ask Jacques Lacan)," T.R. Kover examines the pro-oil sands' public relations campaign from the theoretical perspective of Lacanian psychoanalysis. Although supporters of oil sands' development claim that such campaigns are motivated solely by the need to fight misinformation and "get the facts out there," Kover argues that their rhetorical appeal is less factual than emotive and symbolic. Drawing upon print and televisual examples from the current pro-oil sands' public relations campaign, Kover examines how oil is presented in these ads as a fantastic object, or what Lacan terms the "petit objet a," whose possession promises to heal all personal, social, and environmental ills and bring about an ecstatic state of wholeness. Kover concludes that countering the pro-oil sands rhetorical discourse may rest less in factual rebuttal than in what Lacan called "traversing the fantasy" by disclosing the symbolic and libidinal frameworks upon which they rest.

In Chapter 13, "'Know-Nothing Foreign Celebrity Millionaires': Celebrity, Authenticity, and the Sabotage of Civil Discourse in the Controversy of the Alberta Oil Sands," John Moffatt, Corey Owen, Debora Rolfes, and Jeanie Wills engage a debate initiated by celebrity comments on oil extraction in the oil sands. Moffatt et al analyze the tactic used to stifle public discourse over the oil sands, that is, the branding of outsiders who attempt to engage the issues of extraction and climate change as "know-nothing foreign celebrity millionaires." The authors argue that this tactic constructs oppositional categories that preclude the possibility of productive discussion, resulting in discursive gridlock. They note that both sides engage in rhetorical activity that primarily attacks opponents as inauthentic; this inauthenticity is presented as framing opponents' arguments as invalid, which, in turn, makes debate unnecessary, and thus renders undesirable the ideal of creating a public space for the solving of problems. Drawing on Burke, Moffat et al show how both sides construct an ethos that allows them to speak on behalf of "ordinary" citizens who are constructed as unreflective supporters for their respective "heroic" combatants rather than as engaged participants capable of contributing to a constructive solution. Moffatt et al conclude that when both sides discursively reduce their audiences to immature, pre-forensic states where adult problem-solving strategies are denied to them, genuine rhetorical activity is effectively removed from the agenda.

In Chapter 14, "From Persuasion to Manipulation: Tracing Oil Sands Narratives in the *Calgary Herald*," Sibo Chen examines the discursive presentation of the bitumen industry in the local Calgary newspaper in 2015. He notes that the media texts assume a defensive stance towards this industry and aggressively attack environmentalism. Using a corpus of 168 texts, Chen investigates how the *Herald* constructs the concept "oil sands" and its associated bitumen industry through a series of semantic prosodies and discursive tactics. He finds that (1) at the phrasal level, the newspaper tends to understate the fact that oil sands are a type of unconventional and toxic fossil fuel and define the bitumen industry as an indispensable component for economic stability in Alberta and Canada; (2) at the discursive level, the strategies of "binary construction" and "appeal to inevitability" have been implemented to ideologically enclose viable alternatives that might challenge the bitumen industry's dominance. These two strategies reinforce the idea that the governments of both Alberta and Canada should function as petro-states to ensure further expansion of the bitumen industry. Chen argues that the bitumen industry in Alberta has sought discursive legitimation by shifting from trying to persuade readers to trying to manipulate them.

In the last essay, Chapter 15, "How Not to Stop a Pipeline: A Critique of Activism in the Burnaby Mountain Protests," Sean Zwagerman analyzes published statements by four environmental activists about their participation in the protests against construction of the Kinder Morgan Trans Mountain pipeline in Burnaby, BC, in 2013–2014. Zwagerman uses Burke and Searle to analyze the activists' discourse to determine why the protests were not effective in changing the decisions around approving construction of the pipeline. He analyzes what the Burnaby Mountain activists were doing and saying and explores how the god terms of contemporary activism promote some attitudes towards and forms of protest and deflect others. He investigates how the attitudes that participants take towards a collective, linguistically constructed, social phenomenon largely determine its ontology. He notes that the concept of perlocution does not logically apply to *persuasion*: "one can argue by saying 'I argue that,' but cannot persuade by saying 'I persuade you that.'" In making this point, Zwagerman highlights that consideration of audience is lacking in the activists' conceptions of protest. He argues that the civil disobedience promoted by the activists is "expressive" protest that privileges the beliefs of the speaker and ignores the audience.

He concludes that the protests did not have, as a goal, persuading the public; instead they were acts of self-expression by the activists designed to appeal to an ideology.

Final Notes on the Age of Oil

Taken together, these essays describe the rhetorical dynamics of the age of oil. We want to end with the significance of reimagining rhetoric in the age of oil—the significance of reimagining the contemporary world as the age of oil.

We've divided human history into ages nearly as long as we've been writing histories. Hesiod offered us five ages (golden, silver, bronze, heroic, and iron); Ovid omitted the heroic age and reduced humanity to four ages. Hesiod and Ovid, broadly, use metals to establish the tenor and values of the ages metaphorically. Later scholars would use metals and other materials more literally: for example, the stone age, the bronze age, the iron age, as established by C.J. Thomsen, director of the Royal Museum of Nordic Antiquities, Copenhagen, as a curatorial sorting tool for the artifacts in the museum.

Scientists have long divided history into ages. Geologists and social scientists are struggling with mapping a kind of geological history for the contemporary world: from the *Pleistocene* (the ice age) to the *Holocene* (from the last ice age to about 200 years ago) to the *Anthropocene* (the period where human activity has had a defining impact on the environment, from the industrial revolution through today).

Scholars in the *energy humanities* attempt to reframe human history away from artistic or intellectual periodization (e.g., the Age of Exploration, the Romantic period, the Modern period, and so on) into an energy periodization. Human history can be divided into a wood age, a coal age, an oil age, a natural gas age, a nuclear age, and, perhaps, a renewable (solar, wind, geothermal) age, if we have the collective will to shift away from our addiction to fossil fuels.

Within the energy humanities, the age of oil is the age in which a central part of our energy needs is met by petroleum refined into fuels: gasoline, kerosene, heating oil, and more. But different from natural gas, coal, or nuclear energy, oil is not only a fuel source; we also use it to build our toys, our Tupperware, our clothing, our carpets, our soaps, our automobiles, and our pesticides. In this way, oil defines our material culture as well as our energy culture.

This collection, then, often addresses the moments when the oil becomes visible. It becomes visible, of course, in ecological disasters (like spills). It becomes visible, too, when oil companies become visible in political and civic life (for example, as advocates for public policy, such as changes in environmental legislation).

If our anthology is of use to public relations professionals working within the oil industry, or of use to policy advocates seeking to resist the expansion of oil, we think an increasing consciousness of oil's omnipresence matters. We began and now want to end, briefly, with a discussion of oil's place in the material life of the coeditors of this collection.

Duluth and Alberta sit at opposite ends of the Alberta Clipper pipeline, operated by Enbridge energy, connecting the oil sands of Alberta with a refinery on the shores of Lake Superior (across the bay from Duluth in Superior, WI). The Clipper pipeline is capable of sending a half million barrels of oil, in its crude state, daily from the tar sands (discussed so richly in the third section of this book) to the Husky refinery in Superior. The refinery employs a few hundred people, enough to be a significant employer but few enough to be part of the background noise in the Twin Ports, compared to the major employers (five colleges and universities, two hospitals, and one of the most active shipping ports in the United States). As a port town, then, Superior is connected to a vast network of shipping—boats, trains, trucking—that can send that oil to market.

Lake Superior is the largest freshwater lake in the world, and so subject to frequent environmental testing. In April of 2018, a set of those tests found microplastics in Lake Superior water as well as in beer brewed with Lake Superior water. Microplastics are small beads of plastic that used to be found in soaps; they are also shed from certain forms of fleece. Microplastics are oil suspended in our water and, no doubt, the reason the story received so much press, suspended in our gourmet beers.

In May of 2018, the Husky refinery caught fire, forcing an evacuation of thirty square miles of Superior, WI as toxic smoke spread with the wind. The precipitates from that smoke have settled into the soil, and experts have asked individuals within the area to test the soil before gardening this year; the vegetables will absorb the toxins from the soil. The fire produced very vivid images of oil in our air, our soil, and our food.

Taken together, these two events made us aware of what has been true for the last century: there is no part of our economy, our politics, our environment, our diet, that isn't touched by oil. The case studies in this anthology give us the tools to assess the impact of oil on our rhetorical environment and to enter into fruitful dialogue with each other at what might be the end of the age of oil.

References

Aristotle. 1984. *The Rhetoric and Poetics of Aristotle*. Trans. R. Roberts & I. Bywater. Modern Library College Ed. New York: McGraw-Hill.

Bazerman, C. 1994. *Shaping Written Knowledge*. Madison, WI: University of Wisconsin

Fahnestock, J. 2000. *Figurative Language in Science*. New York: Oxford University Press.
Graves, H. 2005. *Rhetoric in(to) Science: Style as Invention in Inquiry*. Cresskill, NJ: Hampton Press.
Gross, A.G. 1990. *The Rhetoric of Science*. Cambridge, MA: Harvard University Press.
Gross, A.G. 2006. *Starring the Text: The Place of Rhetoric in Science Studies*. Carbondale, IL: Southern Illinois University Press.
Jones, C. 2016. "Petromyopia: Oil and the Energy Humanities." *Humanities*, 5, 36; doi:10.3390/h5020036
Myers, G. 1990. *Writing Biology: Texts in the Social Construction of Scientific Knowledge*. Madison, WI: University of Wisconsin Press.

Section I

Euro-American Case Studies

2 King Coal versus Prince Petroleo

Imagining Oil, Energy, and Transition in Early Twentieth-Century Britain

Ian Wereley

Fossil Fuel Duel: Imagining Energy in Transition

On April 10, 1912, the conservative, highbrow, satirical weekly British magazine, *Punch*, published a full-page cartoon entitled "A Second String" [see Figure 2.1]. Created by Leonard Raven-Hill, *Punch*'s deputy political cartoonist, this image superbly illustrates his creative and imaginative mind. The pen and ink drawing depicted three characters in a ballroom with highly polished floors, decorated walls, and fluted columns. At the center of the image was the figure of Britannia, attired as the Greek goddess, Athena. Wearing an ornately decorated, floor-length robe, strapped sandals, and a Corinthian war helmet adorned by a lion, Britannia sat on a *curule*, a judgement seat that Consuls used in the ancient Roman Senate where they administered the Empire. On her right, in the place of honor, stands the youthful clean-cut figure of Prince Petroleo, in Roman dress, wearing a bright white, knee-length tunic, strapped sandals, and a diadem around his head, marked with the word "OIL." On Britannia's left stands the middle-aged, taller, bearded figure of King Coal, dressed as an Anglo-Saxon warrior in the style of Alfred the Great. In stark contrast to his bright and clean counterpart, the King is generously layered in coal dust. Across the King's strong chest and shoulders is a heavy cloak, fastened at his left shoulder with a brooch. Beneath this blackened outer layer, the King wears a tunic, loose trousers cross-gartered up to the knee, and heavy boots. Around his neck hangs a necklace fashioned from black lumps of coal. Attached to the King's waist, barely visible through the many layers of clothing, are the outlines of a large, circular shield and the tip of a broadsword. A black crown, billowing clouds of smoke, sits atop the King's head.

King Coal is a powerful figure, in the prime of life, proud and self-assured. "[J]auntily," he informs Britannia, "Afraid I've cut one or two of our dances." Seated on her chair of judgment, Britannia appears almost unfazed by the grievous social slight. Her unsmiling face and the coolness of her reply ("Oh, don't apologise! It has given me the opportunity of making the better acquaintance of Prince Petroleo – Very nice and

A SECOND STRING.

KING COAL (*jauntily, to Britannia*). "AFRAID I'VE CUT ONE OR TWO OF OUR DANCES."

BRITANNIA. "OH, DON'T APOLOGISE! IT'S GIVEN ME THE OPPORTUNITY OF MAKING THE BETTER ACQUAINTANCE OF PRINCE PETROLEO—VERY NICE AND GUSHING. YOU MUSTN'T THINK YOU'LL ALWAYS BE INDISPENSABLE."

Figure 2.1 Leonard Raven-Hill's provocative cartoon depicting energy in transition, "A Second String." Reproduced with permission from *Punch* magazine, April 10, 1912.

gushing"), exposes a moment that passes unnoticed by the overconfident King. And, in a gesture that also appears to escape the King's notice, Britannia casually holds a small posy of flowers, with which she nonchalantly points towards Prince Petroleo, as if to underscore the younger man's more agreeable company. As conceited as he is self-assured, King Coal twirls his moustache, apparently deaf to the warning uttered by Britannia: "You mustn't think you'll always be indispensable." In Prince Petroleo, Britannia has discovered a possible second string to her bow, a dancing partner who was younger, cleaner, more biddable, and refined.

"A Second String" is a historical document produced at the dawning of Britain's early twentieth-century transition from a predominantly coal-fueled way of life to one increasingly powered by oil. The cartoon represents, in a single image, the emergence of oil as an exciting new source of fuel, heat, and power and, at the same time, the frustration and anxiety that many Britons felt about the British coal industry. The figures of Britannia, King Coal, and Prince Petroleo are inscribed with multiple layers of meaning, serving as motifs that channel the complexity of Britain's changing energy landscape into characters and narratives that were familiar to contemporary readers. "A Second String" offers an allegory of the ebb and flow of fossil fuels in Britain during this period, and the ways in which foreign oil was rapidly emerging to rival British coal. In this concentrated frame, Raven-Hill conveys his perception of an energy transition waiting in the wings. Britannia, representing the British energy consumer and appearing as the fulcrum of power in the cartoon, is situated between the end of an old regime and the beginning of a new—metaphorically sitting at the intersection of the Age of Coal and the Age of Oil.

What stories and ideas about oil does "A Second String" convey? How does this cartoon fit into larger British discourses of oil and energy in transition during the early twentieth century? What do such documents tell energy historians about the past, and how might they be used to reconstruct previous experiences and interpretations of oil? This chapter engages with such questions by investigating examples of British discourses on oil during the first third of the twentieth century. Using Raven-Hill's 1912 *Punch* cartoon as a point of departure, it explores the anthropomorphosis of energy into imaginary characters such as King Coal and Prince Petroleo, focusing on the ways in which these figures were used as rhetorical tools for interpreting the transition from coal to oil. Cartoons, in particular, are rich and densely packed sources. They offer an artist's point of view of an event or moment while, at the same time, they act as a cultural mirror, both reflecting and influencing the society in which they are produced. As communicative devices that both create and disseminate information for public consumption, cartoons can provide important clues about how a society thought about oil, and how a range of people were conditioned to think about the resource (Williams 2013). "A Second String" therefore affords a valuable window onto the discourse on oil and energy transition in early twentieth century Britain. By the time it was published in 1912, oil was already being used in Britain in ever growing quantities and applications (Warde 2007, 14). Many Britons believed they were on the verge of an oil age—sitting, like Britannia, on the precipice of a revolutionary shift in energy regimes.

Oil scholars working in the field of Energy Humanities have noted, however, that oil is paradoxical, everywhere in the life of its consumers and yet far away from them (Logar 2011; Szeman and Whiteman 2012).

In the early twentieth century, oil was also an elusive substance, rarely seen and even less sensorially encountered. In Ross Barrett and Daniel Worden's edited collection, *Oil Cultures* (2014), Ruth Salvaggio argued that oil has always been "curiously concealed" in our daily lives, trapped beneath the ground or hidden inside pipelines, storage containers, rolling stock, and car engines. Oil, she notes, has always been a "spectral substance," difficult to see and impossible to fully grasp (386). To overcome the spectrality of oil, these scholars argue that consumers must compensate through their imaginations. Thus, Barrett and Worden have demonstrated how oil is made comprehensible through "imaginative representations" and "creative accounts," which convert the inert black substance into something familiar, relatable, and often magical (xxiii). This collective project of interpreting and representing oil through a constellation of invented stories, images, and symbols produces what Barrett and Worden conceive of as an "oil spectacle"—an imaginative petro-drama that plays out in the minds of everyday consumers when they think and talk about oil (xxv). What is currently missing from this literature is research that explores the imaginative constructions of oil in Britain during the late nineteenth and early twentieth centuries.

"A Second String" is a vivid historical example of Barrett and Worden's "oil spectacle." Raven-Hill's anthropomorphized energy characters helped to envisage the opening scene of an epic and impossibly complex petro-drama which was to pitch Prince Petroleo against Britain's traditional energy monarch, King Coal. In demonstrating the messages conveyed by Raven-Hill's imaginary energy characters, this chapter works to elucidate one way in which Britons made sense of their changing energy world. It aims to establish some of the historical antecedents of present-day oil discourses and petrocultures, and to suggest how Britons' experiences of the transition toward oil might be used to shed light on our current efforts to transition away from oil.

King Coal's Kingdom in Chaos

Raven-Hill's career as an illustrator began in London in 1890. In 1895, he published his first cartoon in *Punch* and, in 1901, the magazine hired him as a full-time cartoonist and caricaturist. Frank Palmeri (2009) has commented that, "[p]olitical cartoons, like satire and caricature generally, work by means of exaggeration . . ." (32). Raven-Hill's cartoons, however, were notable exceptions. His illustrations were superbly drawn and showcased his attention to detail and appreciation of subtlety and nuance. As Price (1957) has observed, "[e]very part of a Raven Hill cartoon was there for the purpose of some effect. As feeling rose, he rose with it" (217). He was expert at portraying complex emotions and attitudes convincingly, often in simple, uncluttered scenes featuring one or two central characters, which were realistic, relatable, and inscribed with layers of meaning. An intelligent critic of British daily life, Raven-Hill's "dour, biting political cartoons" (Graves 1922, 202) earned him the post of Deputy Political Cartoonist for *Punch* in 1910 (a position he held for 25 years) and a seat at the magazine's brainstorming space, the Mahogany Table. Raven-Hill was "one of the most celebrated black-and-white artists of the period" (Bryant and Heneage 1994, 111).

Raven-Hill was fascinated by energy. Many of his illustrations in *Punch* during the 1910s featured scenes of motor-vehicle crashes, dangerously crowded city streets, and the acute differences between those who could afford oil and those who could not (see, for example, June 12, 1901, 438; December 3, 1919, 463; December 14, 1932, 647). Several particularly striking themes used by Raven-Hill during this period addressed ideas of change, transition, and revolution in Britons' use of energy. One of the most chaotic and uncertain moments in British industrial history, characterized by a surge in labor unrest and strike actions, occurred the same year that Raven-Hill became deputy political cartoonist at *Punch*.

The period 1910–1920 has been described as "The Great Unrest" (McCord and Purdue 2007, 487), a radical and, at times, revolutionary period in Britain defined by immense social, cultural, economic, political, and industrial transformation, particularly in the country's large and historic coal mining industry. After years of unprecedented and seemingly limitless success and high profits, the coal industry had become not only outmoded, but moribund: British miners were roughly half as productive as their American and German counterparts, yet they worked more hours and for less pay (McCord and Purdue 2007, 493). In 1910, tensions boiled over in the coalfields of South Wales, where strikes and violent riots spread quickly, posing a threat to the stability of the national economy. Though ultimately unsuccessful, the Welsh miners' actions marked the start of two years of unprecedented labor turbulence that, at its peak, involved nearly one million British workers.

Many in Britain, particularly those who were geographically and socially removed from the plight of coal mining communities, imagined themselves caught in the middle of a revolution. In January 1912, *The Times* newspaper anxiously warned its readers that "if no improvement takes place in the mining situation, the public must be prepared for a conflict between Labor and Capital, or between employers and employed, upon a scale as has never occurred before" (January 6, 1912, 7). Later, in February, a *Times* editorial rather fantastically imagined that the coal strike represented "the greatest catastrophe that has threatened the country since the Spanish Armada . . ." (February 26, 1912, 9). After 37 days, and the loss of over 40 million working days, the government (also fearing civil unrest) finally intervened and passed emergency legislation to resolve the crisis ("Coal Mines [Minimum Wage] Bill," 1912). Dissatisfied with the terms of the bill, however, the miners rejected its adoption, but their leaders, in no small part fearing for the unity of the Miners Federation, prevailed upon the membership to return to work. The strike officially ended on April 6, 1912. Four days later, Raven-Hill's "A Second String" appeared in the pages of *Punch* magazine.

Placed in this historical context, "A Second String" can be viewed as an artist's interpretation of the chaotic events occurring in Britain's coal mining industry during the early 1910s, and a mirror onto the changing attitudes towards energy that formed following the strike. The cartoon is a signature Raven-Hill creation. Using simple, clean lines, he captures in the facial expressions and demeanor of the three characters the multi-faceted ills besetting the coal industry and the problems facing the Government, while at the same time expressing Britons' growing fascination with oil. Beyond the drawing itself, Raven-Hill uses several other clever techniques to convey the story of the emerging rivalry of King Coal and Prince Petroleo. The title of the piece, for example, alludes to the English expression to have "a second string to one's bow." Most vitally for the cartoon, the phrase carries the meaning that "a second resource [is] available if the first should fail" (Oxford English Dictionary, 2016). In more subliminal ways, the title also suggests a replacement "beau" for Britannia.

The cartoon relies on King Coal's grave social *faux pas* of "cutting" dances—failing to honor all of his entries on Britannia's dance card, an allegory for the coal strike that practically shut down the country in early 1912. The King acknowledges the slight, but his half-hearted apology is unequal to the insult, while his body language exudes an air of arrogant self-entitlement. Britannia appears coolly polite toward King Coal, and her languid posture conveys her assessment of his unpredictable behavior. She acknowledges his apology, but her words reveal an important truth. His absence had afforded her "the opportunity of making the better acquaintance of Prince Petroleo," and she found his company most agreeable: "very nice and gushing." The sting follows as Raven-Hill's Britannia warns the King: "You mustn't think you'll always be indispensable." King Coal was in her service; he was replaceable.

Prince Petroleo Appears on the Horizon

Raven-Hill captures Britannia's growing awareness of oil as an alternative to coal. The young, clean, and handsome Prince Petroleo strikes a confident pose: chin up, chest forward, one hand on hip, and the other at his heart. He is Britannia's "second string"—newly minted and prepared to replace his rival on the dance floor.

Obviously, Raven-Hill wanted his viewers to imagine Prince Petroleo as fundamentally opposite to King Coal. The shading divides the scene into two uneven parts: on the left are the characters of Petroleo and Britannia, bathed in light, while King Coal—unaware that he is set apart from the group—is distinguished by dark, heavy shading. The figure placement underscores the difference between coal and oil, while also reinforcing the narrative that Britannia and Petroleo are akin. The characters are also distinguished by their different heights, physical sizes and, perhaps most noticeably, by their age. Petroleo's youth suggests that he is not a boy, but not quite a man, untested but possessed of great potential. Petroleo is shorter and slighter than the King, but he also stands much closer to Britannia, nearly touching her and seemingly comfortable in her presence. These elements of the cartoon convey the message that oil was discrete from coal: something different and new, a younger, cleaner, leaner, and more reliable source of energy. Thus, Petroleo projects attentiveness, brightness, freshness and longevity—he seems to belong in the ballroom with Britannia—while King Coal is shown to be sooty, swarthy, self-absorbed, and fickle.

More subtle clues indicate how Raven-Hill imagined coal and oil as being diametrically different. Around the King's waist, beneath his cloak, are a shield and a broadsword: weapons of war that had no place in a ballroom. Around Prince Petroleo's waist, tied like a belt, is a ribbed gasoline hose with a pointed spout. The Prince's tunic is subtly bordered by a motif of two-gallon portable gas cans, evoking the classical Roman meander pattern. Thus, where King Coal is clothed in the garb of war, Prince Petroleo is identified with symbols of advanced technology, modernity, and the future.

As Raven-Hill uses King Coal to represent the troubled British coal industry, he uses Prince Petroleo to represent the simultaneous emergence of oil as an alternative energy source during the same period. Just as Petroleo offered Britannia an alternative dancing partner in "A Second String," in real life oil provided both the Government and the wealthy British consumer with a fascinating new energy source that could be used in customary ways like cooking and heating. However, oil could also go beyond coal, allowing novel technologies, such as aircraft and automobiles (Divall 2009). In 1912, Britons purchased 20,000 new motor vehicles (United Kingdom Parliamentary Papers [Cd. 3080] 1906, 11; Prest 1954, 142), and a 250-acre aerodrome was scheduled for construction near Harrow to accommodate the rapid growth of flight in Britain (*The Times*, February 3, 1912, 6).

By 1910, even in places where coal was formerly considered sacrosanct, oil was gaining a foothold. In 1911, one of the largest and most reliable consumers of British coal, the Royal Navy, began to investigate oil as a primary means of motive power (Lewes 1913). Less than a year later on April 9, 1912, three days after the "Great Unrest" ended and the day before "A Second String" was published, construction began on its first exclusively oil-powered battleship. The development of military aviation also occurred during this period. In spring 1912, the Army and Navy held the first open competition to procure new military aircraft (United

Kingdom Parliamentary Papers [Cd. 6286] 1912). Two days after "A Second String" appeared, the Royal Flying Corps was born (*The Times*, April 13, 1912, 7; United Kingdom Parliamentary Papers [Cd. 6067] 1912). Thus, 1912 was a crucial year for oil in Britain, marking the start of what many believed was a new "Age of Oil." Indeed, as one historian has written, during 1912 and 1913 "the Age of Coal first encountered head-on the Age of Oil" (Fletcher 1975, 5). Raven-Hill sought to express precisely this notion of potential revolution in "A Second String."

Creative Conversions: Bodies, Spirits, Minds

Imre Szeman (2014) has observed that "Despite being a concrete thing, oil animates and enables all manner of abstract categories, including freedom, mobility, growth, entrepreneurship, and the future in an essential way" (146). Certainly, this dictum holds true in the analysis of "A Second String," where oil is, quite literally, animated through imaginary characters that channel Szeman's abstract concepts. The spectral nature of oil enabled Raven-Hill to construct an image and narrative that could explain the tides of British energy consumption. In "A Second String," he created an "oil spectacle," using Prince Petroleo and King Coal to tell the story of the arrival of oil and to hint at the petro-drama that would follow.

Although Raven-Hill was one of the first to make accessible the emerging rivalry between coal and oil, he was only one of many Britons during the early twentieth century whose imagination was ignited by the prospects of a new "Age of Oil." In their efforts to conceptualize the new emerging energy source, British commentators frequently used anthropomorphosis and metaphors related to the body. Oil was "feed" or "juice" for motor vehicles and, in more abstract ways, "food" for individual consumers and British society writ large (Antrobus 1913, 7, 36, 39; Lockhart 1926, 36). John Cadman, Chair of the British Petroleum Company (BP), extended the metaphor of food in a 1927 lecture to the Royal Colonial Institute in London, when he asked his audience to "perhaps choose to call oil the 'milk' of industry" (Cadman 1927, 14). The nutritional comparison was apt, Cadman asserted, because "milk is quite a perfect human food and, like oil, is a highly organized, well balanced storage of heat and power" (14).

The metaphor of oil as blood also appeared frequently in British debates about petroleum during the early twentieth century and, in ways similar to food, this form of representation often framed the fuel as a life-sustaining source of power and nourishment. On November 21, 1918, for example, French Oil Commissioner Henri Bérenger stated at a banquet in London for the Inter-Allied Petroleum Conference that oil represented "the blood of the earth," and that "As oil had been the blood of war, so it would be the blood of the peace" (Peyton-Smith 1971).

In 1925, a series of advertisements for BP described the company's network of Persian oil pipelines as a "vein of steel" that carried "rich crude" over vast distances to British consumers (*Illustrated London News*, May 16, 1925, 985), while a British travel author, writing in 1927, imagined the Persian pipeline to be "the main artery through which flows the liquid stream on which the very life of the Company depends" (Williamson 1927, 89).

In the early 1930s, British commentators on the transition to oil continued to draw upon the bodily metaphors popular in the 1920s. Oil was frequently conceived of as a life-sustaining substance that had become an integral part of the British body politic. Often, the imagined rivalry between coal and oil was employed as a narrative framework for explaining the continued "rise" of oil and the perceived "downfall" of coal. As Sir John Cadman remarked in 1931 on the competition between the two sources of energy in Britain, "coal kept on at a jog-trot pace, whilst petroleum was running" (Cadman 1931, 11).

To many observers in the early 1930s, the transition to oil, begun less than a generation earlier, was complete, and the likelihood of King Coal returning to power seemed bleak. Oil consumption in Britain rose steadily during the start of the decade, often at coal's expense. Millions of tons of oil products and billions of gallons of motor spirit were consumed annually, over 90% of which was imported from abroad (Ferrier 1982, 683; United Kingdom Department of Energy and Climate Change 2015). This unabated flood of oil into Britain starkly contrasted the troubled coal industry, which then was experiencing some of its history's most difficult years (Supple 1987). Wales' largest local newspaper, the *Western Mail*, concluded that the widespread use of oil had been "a grave national blunder" that had turned Britain's coal industry into a "pathetic disaster" engaged in a "desperate fight for life" (April 1, 1931, 6). Indeed, the economic situation was so severe in Britain's coal mining communities that the editors of the *Colliery Guardian*, the industry's national trade magazine, questioned whether the country could ever "emerge from the imbroglio intact" (January 2, 1931, 47).

Confronted by an existential crisis of unprecedented magnitude, the British coal mining industry began to explore ways to promote the use of coal. One of the most promising means at that time involved, paradoxically, chemically treating coal to convert it *into* oil. Since the mid-1920s, British scientists had experimented with ways to produce oil from coal, but only in the early 1930s did the British Government and the coal mining industry begin to consider the large-scale production of hydrogenated or liquefied coal (Slade 1926; United Kingdom House of Commons Debate, July 26, 1933). The process was inefficient and expensive, but Britain had both untapped coal resources and unemployed miners. In the eyes of many proponents of coal, money expended on imported oil would be better spent "at home." Sir John Latta (October 25, 1933), for example, argued that producing oil from coal would alleviate "British Bondage to Alien Oil," while another author noted that hydrogenated coal could offer "a means of recovering our freedom from foreign control and of killing unemployment" (Acworth 1933, 508).

The dream of supplying Britons' insatiable appetite for oil from locally produced coal sparked a wellspring of creativity in the early 1930s. Like traditional crude oil extracted from deep below the ground, this new type of hybridized, synthetic fuel was spectral and difficult to comprehend: it was not quite coal, not quite oil, and consumers rarely saw or encountered it. British commentators debated vigorously the nature and characteristics of synthetic oil from coal, and questioned what its use meant to Britain and its coal industry (Jones 1930; Gordon 1932). Many proponents viewed coal's conversion into oil as a waste of public money and natural resources and, more abstractly, as a betrayal of traditional British livelihoods and ways of life. Thus, the *Western Mail* frequently framed its oil coverage during this period with adversarial headlines such as "Coal v. Oil Fight" (July 3, 1931, 11) and "Oil's March on Coal" (March 16, 1932, 12). In one particularly evocative editorial entitled "Coal's Battle Against Oil Fuel" (March 23, 1932, 12), the author called to arms the South Wales coal mining community, claiming it "was time to fight" for coal—"Protect your homes and your families from this insidious oil aggression, which . . . portends the eventual downfall of Great Britain" (March 23, 1932, 12).

Many of the same techniques used to disseminate ideas about oil in the 1910s and 1920s were employed in British discourses of oil from coal during the early 1930s. Anthropomorphosis and metaphors related to the body remained favorite tools for talking about fossil fuels, as did stories of rivalry, jealousy, usurpation, and dethronement between imaginary energy characters. However, debates about oil from coal in the 1930s were divisive and extremist. In Britain's struggling coal mining regions, foreign oil was maligned as a marauding invader that threatened to usurp King Coal and destroy his kingdom. At a Trafalgar Day Dinner in October 1933, for example, the Bishop of Llandaff rendered a spectacular image of oil as the "hated rival [to coal], smooth-tongued, suave, gushing, alien and oily" (*Western Mail*, October 28, 1933, 2). On the other hand, in places closer to London, far removed from coal mining communities and where petroleum products could be found everywhere and in everything, there existed entirely different attitudes toward oil—a powerful, magical, almost supernatural resource that had overtaken coal to become Britain's new energy lifeblood (Brame 1931; Cadman 1932). To many such observers, the development of the technology signaled an important signpost in the history of oil. In the summer of 1933, twenty-one years after publishing "A Second String," Leonard Raven-Hill once again turned to his pen and the pages of *Punch* magazine to give his interpretation of this crucial moment in the British transition from coal to oil.

A King Conquered, His Body Corrupted

"Black Magic; or the New King Coal" appeared in *Punch* magazine on July 26, 1933 [see Figure 2.2]. The cartoon offers a fascinating "second act" to the imaginative petro-drama that Raven-Hill envisioned two decades earlier in "A Second String." The cartoon centers on the by-now familiar King Coal, who is drawn with black shading. The King sits on a throne that seems to be made of laboratory parts, perhaps those from a coal hydrogenation plant. On top of the King's head is a crown labeled "COAL," with a peak like a traditional working man's cloth cap that spews black smoke. His face is dark and lacks the thick beard and moustache of "A Second String." His expression is resolute and confident, but his eyes are strangely unfocused, and a faintly maniacal grin lingers at the upturned corners of his mouth.

Unlike "A Second String," King Coal's dress is simple: a jet-black tunic conceals his torso, leaving only his left leg exposed, resting on a petrol drum. Around his waist, tied like a belt and reminiscent of Prince

BLACK MAGIC;
OR, THE NEW KING COAL.

Figure 2.2 Leonard Raven-Hill's dramatic cartoon depicting the rise of synthetic oil, "Black Magic; Or, the New King Coal." Reproduced with permission from Punch magazine, July 26, 1933.

Petroleo's hose belt, are three strips of fabric labeled "CHEMICAL INDUSTRIES PLAN." His arms are fashioned as oil pipes: a flanged pipe connection forms his shoulders, ball and tap joints create his elbows, and pointed pouring nozzles resemble hands, a detail that echoes the nozzle appearing on Prince Petroleo's belt. Coming out of the nozzles are streams of liquid like blood from King Coal's body, filling a collection of containers labeled "PETROL" and "OIL" that fill the foreground. These include two of the familiar rectangular, two-gallon gasoline cans that appeared on Prince Petroleo's tunic. In the bottom right hand corner, resting upside down as if discarded, is a coal scuttle.

"Black Magic" resumes the energy narrative introduced by Raven-Hill in his "Second String" cartoon, notably the struggle between King Coal and his rival, Oil. Its style links to other cartoons in Raven-Hill's corpus, including the use of anthropomorphic characters, simple compositions, and highly dramatic line work (see for example *Punch* 1915, 131; *Punch* 1926, 451). More specifically, King Coal's smoke-billowing crown, and the motor spirit hoses, pouring nozzles, and two-gallon oil cans in the foreground directly link to "A Second String." These similarities immediately establish it as a sequel to the "King Coal versus Prince Petroleo" drama begun over two decades earlier, updated to reflect the technical and political advancements in the production of oil from coal in Britain. Yet, by subtitling his cartoon "the New King Coal," Raven-Hill asserts that this version of the character is radically different from the King in "A Second String." He has remade himself through hydrogenation and lives to fight another day. But he has also been conquered by Oil; his body and blood are corrupted.

In "Black Magic," Raven-Hill invokes several familiar stories and images from his previous work, including the themes of rivalry, confrontation, and controversy that saturated "A Second String." But he also conveys new messages about oil in ways that reflect the culture and discursive context in which it was produced. In particular, it employs the rhetorical techniques common in British energy discourses of the 1920s and 1930s. Like other commentators during the period, Raven-Hill portrayed oil as an essential, life-sustaining corporeal fluid, closely resembling blood, which seems to "course" through King Coal's body and "gush" out of his arms. The cartoon suggested that oil had become as necessary to King Coal's survival as it was for the individual consumer and British society at large. Synthetic oil from coal was presented as a magical elixir that could grant King Coal new vitality, albeit with an entirely different demeanor.

In this cartoon, Raven-Hill produces a spectacular petro-drama: once again capturing a tipping point in the ongoing struggle between Coal and Oil. The central message that "Black Magic" delivers is that the shift from coal to oil in Britain was well in train, and that the overthrow of King Coal portended in "A Second String" was coming to pass. In 1933, Britain had fully entered the "Age of Oil."

Conclusion: King Coal's Kingdom Relinquished

This chapter has focused on Britons' mixed emotions about oil during 1912–1933, their excitement about its possibilities and their anxiety about the coal industry. Based on two *Punch* cartoons, "A Second String" (1912) and "Black Magic; or the New King Coal" (1933) by Raven-Hill, the chapter explored the anthropomorphosis of energy into the characters of King Coal and Prince Petroleo to reveal how they function as rhetorical tools to interpret the transition from coal to oil. Employing "oil spectacle" as an analytical frame, this chapter highlighted how King Coal and Prince Petroleo are inscribed with multiple meanings, and how they became motifs for channeling oil's cultural dimensions. As spectacle, the cartoons function as signposts in the making of British petroculture during the early twentieth century.

From 1912 to 1933, British coal consumption fell by nearly 20%, while over the same period, oil consumption rose by 400% (UK Dept. for Business, Energy & Industrial Strategy, 2016a, 2016b). Raven-Hill's goal in "Black Magic" was to explain the shift from coal to oil in Britain, and to narrate the overthrow of King Coal implied in "A Second String." In 1912, Prince Petroleo was depicted as a youthful and inexperienced potential challenger; by 1933, he had evolved into something far more powerful, something that had changed the body and mind of King Coal forever. In fact, synthetic fuels only delayed the inevitable transition to oil. For better or for worse, Britain was fully committed to the Age of Oil. Britannia and Petroleo had become intimate dancing partners.

In highlighting the use of bodily metaphors and anthropomorphic characters associated with the changing energy worlds in Britain in the early twentieth century, this chapter has illuminated some ways that coal, oil, and energy transitions have been imagined historically. Analyzing cartoons allows historians to elucidate early British interpretations of oil and to reveal how Britons creatively converted a complex, elusive, and often invisible natural resource into a spectacle that was familiar, relatable and, most importantly, comprehensible.

In undertaking a deconstructivist approach to British discourses of energy transition, this chapter also offers insight into early twenty-first century ways of envisioning energy in transition. Indeed, as Daniel Yergin (1992) has observed, "there has often been a 'oneness' to the story of oil, a contemporary feel even to events that happened long ago" (xvii). The astuteness of this reflection becomes even clearer in light of the analysis presented above. Early twentieth-century British oil discourses constitute a continuum with present-day petrocultures. Today, food metaphors continue to reveal the significance of petroleum. Motor spirit is still referred to as "juice" in Britain. Varieties of crude oil are measured by their "sweetness," "lightness," or "aroma," as if they were diet soft drinks. A group of cylindrical oil storage containers is called a "tank farm." In Canada's bituminous oil sands, experimental new projects have been referred to as "bite-sized" opportunities offering companies the "lowest hanging fruit" (*Calgary Herald*, 1 June 2016).

The metaphor of blood also remains a commonly used tool for disseminating ideas about oil today. Books and articles associating oil with blood are abundant, and their titles are often as creative and thought-provoking as Raven-Hill's—*Blood of the Earth* (Hiro 2007), *Lifeblood* (Huber 2013), and *Blood Oil* (Wernar 2015) are notable examples. Hematic metaphors are also popular in film and television representations of oil, such as the recent ABC television series "Blood and Oil" (2015) or the Hollywood film *There Will be Blood* (2007). As they did in early twentieth-century Britain, these types of narratives are often undergirded by notions of oil as an essential, life-sustaining commodity that consumers *need* to survive. In this vein, oil has been conceived of as *Living Oil* (LeMenager 2013), or the "lifeblood of suburban communities" and the "very nature of civilization" (Yergin 1992, xiv). Oil today, as it was in Britain in the 1930s, seems to be everywhere and in everything—even inside our bodies (Sandwell 2016, 3). As Stoekl (2014) has suggested of modern-day petro-societies, "in some ways we *are* oil" (xiii).

Animated cartoons also remain an important medium for sharing new ideas about energy in transition. In ways remarkably similar to Raven-Hill's "A Second String" and "Black Magic," twenty-first century cartoons condense into familiar and recognizable forms the murky and often invisible qualities of oil, creating three-dimensional and colorful versions of Barrett and Worden's oil spectacle. For example, in the popular British video game, *Banjo-Tooie* (Rare 2000), players encounter a "grubby boiler monarch" named Old King Coal, a black, sooty character described on a fan website as "a gigantic living pile of coal" (Wikia 2001). More recently, a January 2014 episode of *The Simpsons* depicted a band of energy characters called the Fossil Fuel Four: The Frakker, Femme Fatale Charcoal Briquette, Old King Coal, and Petroleus Rex (S.25, E.10, "Married to the Blob"). The troupe engages in an epic battle against the nuclear-powered Radioactive Man and his two bumbling sidekicks, Citizen Solar and Sidekick Windlad. One of the boss characters, Petroleus Rex, is redolent of the "New King Coal." His arms fashioned from motor spirit hoses and pouring nozzles, spewing jets of oil.

Similarities between the social and cultural contexts of energy in the early twentieth and early twenty-first centuries are also fascinating and demand further study. Today, energy consumers find themselves grappling with many of the same issues that British consumers faced a century ago. The traditional energy landscape is in a state of flux, shifting in response to global events and new scientific and technological developments. With the growth of alternative energy sources like wind, solar, wave, and geothermal power—our current day "second strings" to outmoded and dirty fossil fuels—the world is on the brink of transition to a new energy regime. Thus, the transition from coal to oil that Raven-Hill imagined in 1912 resembles the low-carbon, electrified future anticipated now. Indeed, the international oil industry has had to "cut a few dances" in recent years, slighting several partners, particularly in Canada. Yet, paradoxically, through the rise in production of unconventional oils (like bitumen sands and tight oil from hydraulic fracturing), the oil industry has been granted new life through still more "Black Magic"—a temporary revival that cannot endure. Present-day consumers and artists must determine the future of oil and envision the final chapters of the petro-drama crafted by Raven-Hill and others nearly a century ago.

References

Primary Sources

Official and Archival Sources

'Back to Coal Movement'. 1931. "The Navy's Fuel. A Petition to the Lords Commissioners of the Admiralty, June 26, 1931." National Library of Wales. Monmouthshire and South Wales Coal Owners Association Records. A4/3/1.

British Petroleum (BP). January 21, 1926. *Minutes of the 166th Meeting of the Board*. BP Archives, ARC 104206.

British Petroleum (BP). July 22, 1925. *Minutes of the 161st Meeting of the Board*. BP Archives, ARC 104206.

United Kingdom Department for Business, Energy & Industrial Strategy. 2016a. *Crude Oil and Petroleum: Production, Imports and Exports 1890 to 2015.*

United Kingdom Department for Business, Energy & Industrial Strategy. 2016b. *Crude Oil and Petroleum Products: Imports by Product 1920–2015.*

United Kingdom Department of Energy and Climate Change. 2015. *Historical Coal Data: Coal Production, Availability and Consumption 1853–2014.*

United Kingdom House of Commons Debate. July 26, 1933. "Economic Situation." Vol. 280, cc. 2621–2718.

United Kingdom House of Commons Debate. March 29, 1912. "Coal Mines (Minimum Wage) Bill." Vol. 36, c. 758.

United Kingdom House of Commons Debate. March 18, 1912. "Navy Estimates, 1912–1913." Vol. 35, cc. 1549–1618.

United Kingdom Parliamentary Papers. 1912. *Army. Memorandum on Naval and Military Aviation*. Cd. 6067.

United Kingdom Parliamentary Papers. 1912. *Army. Military Aeroplane Competition, 1912. Report of Judges Committee*. Cd. 6286.

United Kingdom Parliamentary Papers. 1906. *Royal Commission on Motor Cars. Report*. Cd. 3080.

Published Materials

Acworth, B. 1933. "The Navy's Fuel." *Naval Review* 21 (3): 504–508.

Antrobus, W. 1913. *Oil*. London: John Heywood.

Brame, J. 1931. "Power Fuel for the Services." *RUSI Journal* 76 (501): 64–81.
Cadman, J. 1932. "The British Fuel Problem – Oil." *Naft* 8 (1): 11–14.
Cadman, J. 1931. "Problems of Coal and Oil." *Naft* 7 (1): 11–13.
Cadman, J. 1927. "The Oil Era and the British Empire." *Naft* 3 (2): 11–18.
Coal Utilisation Council. 1933. *Aims and Policies*. London: The Council.
Gordon, K. 1932. "Coal Products and National Defence." *RUSI Journal* 77: 547–558.
Graves, C. 1922. *Mr. Punch's History of Modern England*, Vol. 4, 1892–1914. London: Cassell.
Jones, J. 1930. "The Present Position of the British Coal Trade." *Journal of the Royal Statistical Society* 93 (1): 1–63.
Latta, J. 1933. "British Bondage to Alien Oil." *Morning Post*, 25 October.
Lewes, V. 1913. "Liquid Fuel." *Journal of the Royal Society of Arts* 61: 666–673.
Lockhart, L. 1926. "B.P. by O.K." *Naft* 2 (6): 36–37.
Slade, E. 1926. "Oil Supplies in War." *RUSI Journal* 71 (481): 119–142.
Williamson, J. 1927. *In a Persian Oil Field: A Study in Scientific and Industrial Development*. London: Ernest Benn.

Secondary Sources

Barrett, R., and D. Worden, eds. 2014. *Oil Culture*. Minneapolis: University of Minnesota Press.
Bryant, M., and S. Heneage, eds. 1994. *Dictionary of British Cartoonists and Caricaturists 1730–1980*. Aldershot: Scolar.
Divall, C. 2009. "Transport, 1900–1939." In *Companion to Early Twentieth Century Britain*, edited by Chris Wrigley. London: Wiley-Blackwell.
Ferrier, R. 1982. *The History of the British Petroleum Company*, Vol. 1. Cambridge: Cambridge University Press.
Fletcher, M. 1975. "From Coal to Oil in British Shipping." *Journal of Transport History* 3 (1): 1–19.
Hiro, D. 2007. *Blood of the Earth: The Battle for the World's Vanishing Oil Resources*. New York: Nation.
Huber, M. 2013. *Lifeblood: Oil, Freedom, and the Forces of Capital*. Minneapolis: University of Minnesota Press.
'hqanon.' 2016. "Elon Musk Just Declared War on Big Oil and Fossil Fuels." *Anonymous*. www.anonhq.com/elon-musk-just-declared-war-fossil-fuels-big-oil/.
Jones, G. 1978. "The Oil-Fuel Market in Britain 1900–1914: A Lost Cause Revisited." *Business History* 20 (2): 131–152.
LeMenager, S. 2013. *Living Oil: Petroleum and Culture in the American Century*. Oxford: Oxford University Press.
Logar, E. 2011. *Invisible Oil*. Berlin: Springer-Verlag.
McCord, N., and B. Purdue, 2007. *British History 1815–1914*. Oxford: Oxford University Press.
Palmeri, F. 2009. "The Cartoon: the Image as Critique." In *History Beyond the Text*, edited by Sarah Barber and Corinna Peniston-Bird. London: Routledge.
Peyton-Smith, D. 1971. *Oil: A Study of War-Time Policy and Administration*. London: Her Majesty's Stationery Office.
Prest, A. 1954. *Consumers' Expenditure in the United Kingdom, 1900–1919*. Cambridge: Cambridge University Press.

Price, R. 1957. *A History of Punch*. London: Collins.
Salvaggio, R. 2014. "Imagining Angels on the Gulf." In *Oil Culture*, edited by Ross Barrett and Daniel Worden. Minneapolis: University of Minnesota Press.
Sandwell, R., ed. 2016. Powering Up Canada: A History of Power, Fuel, and Energy from 1600. Kingston/Montreal: McGill-Queen's.
Stoekl, A. 2014. "Foreword." In *Oil Culture*, edited by Ross Barrett and Daniel Worden. Minneapolis: University of Minnesota Press.
Supple, B. 1987. *The History of the British Coal Industry*, Vol. 4, 1913–1946. Oxford: Clarendon.
Szeman, I. 2014. "How to Know About Oil: Energy Epistemologies and Political Futures." *Journal of Canadian Studies* 47 (3): 145–168.
Szeman, I., and M. Whiteman. 2012. "Oil Imag(e)inaries: Critical Realism and the Oil Sands." *Imaginations* 3 (2): 46–67.
Warde, P. 2007. *Energy Consumption in England and Wales, 1560–2000*. Rome: Consiglio Nazionale delle Ricerche.
Williams, C. 2013. "'Our War History in Cartoons Is Unique': J.M. Staniforth, British Public Opinion, and the South African War, 1899–1902." *War in History* 20 (4): 491–525.
Yergin, D. 1992. *The Prize: The Epic Quest for Oil, Money and Power*. New York: Simon.

3 Crude Thinking

Gretchen Bakke

In mid-May of 2015, a picture, Neil deGrasse Tyson with his words typed neatly in black beside him, appeared on my Facebook feed.[1] Like many things that find their way there, it was unbidden, but unlike many it was not unwelcome. deGrasse Tyson is relaxed, all stone washed denim and kindly eyes above gently pursed lips. It's that sort of meme meant to evoke sensations of getting in trouble by your favorite 7th grade science teacher. You should feel bad, but only a little. It says:

> We're dumping carbon dioxide into the atmosphere at a rate the Earth hasn't seen since the great climate catastrophes of the past, the ones that led to mass extinctions. We just **can't seem to break our addiction to the kinds of fuel that will bring back a climate last seen by the dinosaurs, a climate that will drown our coastal cities and wreak havoc on the environment and our ability to feed ourselves.** All the while, the glorious sun pours immaculate free energy down upon us, more than we will ever need," says Tyson. **"Why can't we summon the ingenuity and courage of the generations that came before us?**
>
> **The dinosaurs never saw that asteroid coming.**
> **What's our excuse?** [2]

What Mr. deGrasse Tyson has so nicely captured here, is a pattern that pervades conversations about the energy transition in the U.S., which are cast with surprising frequency in terms of moving America away from its "addiction" to fossil fuels and ushering in a transition to an Edenic paradise where the wind and the sun provide all the power we need, plus some. All that is necessary in this scenario is that we harvest this sun and reap this wind. Bucolic pastoral verbs motivated for deeply industrial processes. As we see in this admittedly punchy excerpt, a wholesale swap of a fossil-fuel modernity for a renewably powered (alter-)modernity is rarely figured as a technological problem. Rather the transition is cast as a cultural one: why can't *we* break our addiction to oil? Why can't *we* summon the necessary ingenuity and courage? "What's *our* excuse?" The sun, immaculate and free, the wind, immaculate and free, pour down upon us and yet we remain committed to something else: an addiction to fossil fuels that will bring back the climate of the dinosaurs, will drown our coastal cities, and wreak havoc on our ability to feed ourselves. In this story, the dinosaurs are not the slow-thinking, lumbering beasts doomed to extinction by their own failings. We are.

There is something similar in the story told by Georges Bataille in the first volume of his magnum opus, *The Accursed Share* (1988 [1949])—a work of political economy that considers not "the production and use of wealth" (20) of classical economics but the wise expenditure (or consumption) of that wealth (9).

Completed in 1949 after 18 years of research and writing, Bataille, like deGrasse Tyson, is concerned with the excess energy of the sun.[3] He, too, is worried about the social and political ramifications of *not* taking seriously the unceasing flood of energy it provides to the planet; he too is bombastic:

> The living organism in a situation determined by the play of energy on the surface of the globe, ordinarily receives more energy than is necessary for maintaining life; the excess energy (wealth) can be used for the growth of the system (e.g., an organism); if the system can no longer grow, or if the excess cannot be completely absorbed in its growth, it must necessarily be lost without profit; it must be spent, willingly or not, gloriously or catastrophically. (21)

For Bataille, then, the real problem is not producing or accumulating wealth—that comes about naturally by virtue of the sun's own shining[4]—the problem is, rather, how to dispense with the accumulated money, things, power, and fat (all subcategories for him of "excess energy," to which we might add CO_2 and CH_4) in a way that is not destructive to social and political worlds. How, he wanted to know, might humans waste more wisely? How, we might now ask, might humans avoid anthropogenic climate change wrought from a careless wastefulness and geologic in impact?

In this chapter, following inspiration from Kenneth Burke (Burke 1984, 1968), I appose (not oppose) the excesses of the sun as solution to (in deGrasse Tyson's case) and source of (in Bataille's) climate change. To do this, I focus on the energetic excess of fossil fuels, and oil most especially, as rhetorical, which is to say as a habit of thought made evident in the unfolding logic of persuasive arguments. My larger claim here is that both Bataille and deGrasse Tyson *think* and thus *argue* the sun, its potentials, and its powers, in terms of a logic borrowed from oil.[5] I make this case slowly, by layering strata of data, from section-to-section of this chapter. Each stratum might stand alone but when pressed into the others each helps not so much to build an argument as to sediment one.

Or, to put it in less obsequiously geologic terms, when speaking of the energy transition I have tired of the "oppositional strategies [that] are . . . so ably suited to convincing the convinced, and so thoroughly unsuited to anything else" (Burke quoted in Crusius 358). Such arguments proliferate on both sides of the green divide. Burke's solution to (his own) boredom with the questionable efficacy of opposition was to turn toward what he calls "perspective by incongruity" or the eerie, slightly jarring sense of seeing the same thing from two angles, simultaneously. At the sentence level apposition creates this layering of frames by placing two terms of the same order—usually a noun and a noun phrase—side by side, e.g., "My sister, the king," or, "Arrhenius, the thoughtful Swede." Rather than producing a sensation of depth (stereoscopically) or complexity (via opposition), apposition argues its case straightforwardly, by presenting the same thing from competing, and often disjunctive, vantage points (see also Long 1997).

One might think of the classic story of the five blind men arguing over the nature of the elephant, each only touching a piece of the beast. Apposition is the sense one makes by taking all these impossible competing stories together ("it is long and flexible and covered in hairs" argues the man handling the trunk) and building up from them. Each section of this chapter thus hinges on a single claim: the energetic excesses of oil, which are unique in human history, have ground a normative sense of how energy works down into the very fundament of the way we[6] now talk about and conceptualize energy (potential and actual). This normative sense shapes much of how those who live in energy intensive economies (including Bataille and deGrasse Tyson, Burke and myself) imagine what they are and what their world might profitably become.

First then, to Battelle's counterintuitive accounting of energy and economy.

"The Turbulence of the Bull"[7]

Because economic theories do not generally treat excess as a problem, but rather as a solution—poverty for example is assuaged by wealth, worse situations are bettered by further growth—the issue of how one dissipates or "exudates" excess energy (wealth) is not, Georges Bataille argues, given the consideration it deserves. In focusing our attentions on the endless increase of wealth as the solution to poverty his contemporaries (and our own) fail to see that "*it is not necessity but its contrary "luxury" that presents living matter and mankind with their fundamental problems*"(12):

> Minds accustomed to seeing the development of productive forces as the ideal end of activity refuse to recognize that energy, which constitutes wealth, must ultimately be spent lavishly (without return),

> and that a series of profitable operations has absolutely no other effect than the squandering of profits. To affirm that it is necessary to dissipate a substantial portion of energy produced, sending it up in smoke, is to go against judgments that form the basis of a rational economy. (22)

In effect, Bataille reverses the commonsensical notion of profit as hard-won and worthy of careful management to propose instead that increase-until-die-off is the natural order of things, and that humans need to be far more attentive to ethical modes of wanton wastefulness. This reversal of the order of things leads to two major (and, from Bataille's point of view, underappreciated) problems for human society. First, economic theories attend to the wrong activities—the furtherance of wealth, for example, rather than a more effective dissipation of the excess we have.[8] Worse, war and other forms of thoughtless waste, or "involuntary destruction" emerge because "our ignorance . . . causes us to *undergo* what we could *bring about* in our own way, if we understood"(23):

> It [ignorance] deprives us of the choice of an exudation that might suit us. Above all, [it] consigns men and their work to catastrophic destructions. For if we do not have the force to destroy the surplus energy ourselves, it cannot be used, and like an unbroken animal that cannot be trained, it is this energy that destroys us; it is we who pay the price of this inevitable explosion. (23–24)

Bataille is writing in the wake of World War II. He lived through the first as well. During the first half of the twentieth century, Europe might well have seemed a machine for turning the riches of industrialization into epic, bloody wastefulness. Its wars generated the horrors of unplanned exudation that gave rise to Bataille's theory, such that by the end of World War II he was certain of the link. "It is sometimes denied," he writes, "that the industrial plethora was at the origin of these recent wars, particularly the first. Yet it was this plethora that both wars exuded; its size was what gave them their exceptional intensity" (25).[9]

Allan Stoekl, who has written extensively about Bataille's work on energy and economy brings this point to its logical extreme—annihilation at a species level—saying:[10]

> A steady state, can be attained by devoting large numbers of people and huge quantiles of wealth and labor to useless activity [. . .] most notably, one can waste wealth in military buildup and constant warfare: no doubt this kept populations stable in the past [. . .] but in the present (i.e., 1949) the huge amounts of wealth devoted to military armament, worldwide, can lead only to nuclear holocaust. (2007: 37)

One might see four decades of unwinnable war in Afghanistan in this light or the waste that now goes by the name of Syria.

For Bataille, the law of general economy is thus that organisms must expend or find a way to waste—rather than guard or reinvest or render productive—what classical economics terms "luxury." The ethical move that he enjoins us to consider, given the inevitability of squander, is of finding ways to expend the accursed share without destroying worlds and lives with it. Plowing excess back into existing systems, by recycling it (for example) or rendering it otherwise and once-again productive do not count for Bataille as forms of expenditure. This is because such processes continue to recognize only what is recoupable. Nothing changes when waste is rendered fodder for the same blind excess-producing system, just as nothing is learned when waste is cast thoughtlessly aside and hidden from view (in a dump or a bank, for example). Industrialization has made this project harder and more necessary as the factory system's capacity to both produce wealth and process raw (and recycled) materials is unparalleled in the history of human and natural economies.[11] (The exception might be, as Bataille often mentions, the unrelenting growth of plants).

It is difficult, for those of us steeped in neoliberal accounting of all things, to even conceive of a systematized support for pure dissipation (what Bataille terms "the turbulence of the bull") given the amount of excess energy now available to us. Much of that excess comes from the particular capacity of oil to twist beyond all recognition the relationship between the necessary labor-time for its production and the energetic potential, or capacity to "do work," of the oil itself, a relationship that deGrasse Tyson replicates in his argument about the benefits of solar power subsisting in its capacity to "pour energy down upon us, more than we will ever need."

In making this call, deGrasse Tyson is thinking with the logic of oil: he is using crude thinking to motivate a discussion about a different sort of entity—the sun. Simply embracing the golden shower of infinite solar power as a solution to planetary fossil-fueled problems fails to clarify that solar power is *different* from oil.[12] This difference is not in terms of the electrons each can be made to make, but in the ways in which we harness their energetic capacities: the who, what, where, when, how, and how much of power (and with it, money) production. Such is my presumption here, that once the rhetorical grounds of crude thinking are made evident, new questions of the future might be asked. Foremost among these is: what happens to discussions of an energy transition if these are made to include Bataillian concerns for the proper and inevitable dissipation of unused energies? How, in other words, might we approach the intensification of the greenhouse effect as a direct consequence of disregarding plentitude?

So Much Hot Air

The greenhouse effect, first sketched out in 1896 by the Swede, Svante Arrhenius, is not in and of itself a bad thing. It is what makes the earth supportive of life in all its diversity. It happens because the atmosphere traps about 90% of the heat, *not* of the sun directly but that which bounces back up from the earth after it has been first touched by the sun. The planetary environment becomes warm not just in one spot—where the sun's actual rays originally hit—but all over. Indeed, rather like a greenhouse, the air around us holds a kind of averaged (if uneven and turbulent) blanket of reradiated heat.

The composition of the atmosphere changes how much heat is trapped, giving rise, Arrhenius pointed out, to the occasional ice-age. He also suggested that the increase in carbon in the atmosphere that came from burning fossil fuels in all our newly (in the 1890s) ubiquitous heat engines could alter, and increase, the amount of radiated heat that got trapped by the atmosphere. Arrhenius, though not credited with inventing the concept of global warming, had already posited in the closing years of the nineteenth century that it was a plausible effect of fossil fuel use, a thing to watch, a thing to worry over.

As we now know well enough, the gases worth keeping a keen eye on are carbon dioxide (CO_2), methane (CH_4), and nitrous oxide (N_2O).[13] All are released when coal, oil, and natural gas are combusted, and they also put in a fair appearance when oil and natural gas are extracted, transported, and stored. There are other sources for all of them: bogs, cow farts, volcanoes, and animals exhaling. All were present before mass industrialization (when we had more bogs and fewer cows), and there was something like an equilibrium in our skies; the planet stayed more or less regularly warm.

Today, we use a lot of all of these fuels, and as deGrasse Tyson rightly points out, we have built up industrial, agricultural, energy, and transport infrastructures that depend deeply upon their bounty. The lightness of what remains when they are burned, the odorless, colorless remnant of their plenteousness—their invisible excess—is weirdly hard to panic about. Unlike the accreting coal dust, acid rain, urban smog, and chemical leaks that gave rise to environmental movements in Europe and the United States in the 1950s and 1960s, greenhouse gases produce little sense of propinquity because cause and effect are so seemingly *unlinked* in the immediacy of experience. Use a gas lawn mower, and there is no freak ice storm taking down your power lines later that afternoon, though there might be an unusually destructive monsoon in 11 years in Bangkok.[14] The problem is planetary, which is a scale hard to get used to, and although the sun may be the solution, according to deGrasse Tyson, it is also the root cause of our fossil-fueled problem. This is because fossil fuels are also of the sun, congealed into the muck of earth, plants that grew and decomposed, animal bodies that grew and decomposed, carbon and methane that could have been released in the moment of death but were trapped instead in ice and rock-pockets, intensified by time and geologic pressures.[15] Global warming is thus a sort of radical time-shift of carbon emissions. What should have taken millennia to seep slowly upward into the air we've thoughtlessly released in little more than a century. It's been a good run, the effects of which stretch far beyond industrialization, factory capitalism, extractive capitalism, neocolonialism, neoliberalism, and war to include basically everything known and normal to contemporary life.

Muscular Economies

To understand how deeply contemporary figurations of abundance rely rhetorically upon congealed, rotted, compressed, and thusly stored (to become coal, oil, and gas) solar energy, it is worth considering ideas about economy that predate Arrhenius, the thoughtful Swede. So much of what feels natural (and I will concretize this "feeling" in the end) to people living in thoroughly industrialized economies today is, relatively speaking, new. Indeed, over the last two thousand years—or most of human history until about 1820—human economies grew very little, if at all. Growth for this period is figured at about 0.05% every year.[16] This means that people living in 1820 were only negligibly more prosperous than those living in 1020. By negligibly, I mean that they had things like a fireplace with a chimney rather than a fire on the floor in the center of the house. I mean also that they had a horse or a slave to pull a plow rather than having to do it themselves. Wealth was measured by the control of muscle power other than your own. "As late as 1750," Isaac Asimov writes, "man's use of energy was still largely that of muscles—his own and those of animals—and the heat given off by wood fires" (1972: 8). Over a century later, in 1870 in New York City, draft animals accounted for more than half the total horsepower produced by prime movers.[17] Today, the term "prime mover" usually refers to an oil or steam fed engine. A hundred and fifty years ago it still referred largely to calorie-fed muscle. For the most part, in the United States, this consisted of horse muscle and human muscle.

Here is a picture: It's spring, 1882 in Lower Manhattan, the streets are crowded with horses—draft horses pulling carts, the leaner harness horses pulling buggies and carriages, while teams of huge drays pull the streetcars. Vast piles of dung steam in the cool morning air. Hosts of English sparrows flit through the channels between buildings, a plague upon the city streets; they stop to feed on the seeds that the horses' bellies have left undigested (Yaeger 2011: 308). Horses, piles of horseshit, hundreds of sparrows. This was New York 150 years ago. The horses, as well as most of the people, crapped outside.

In a month's time when summer's heat and humidity hit, the city will stink. Every breath will smell of horse and sweat and backyard privies and the trenches alongside apartment buildings into which chamber pots are emptied; every step will sully the shoe and muddy the skirts of those who rush across streets or who have just stepped out lightly from a carriage. It was into this morass that Edison began the task of building America's first DC electric grid, a smallish thing by today's standards, about a square mile around Wall Street in lower Manhattan.[18] It took years before the first bulbs were set aglow in the offices of America's richest men (and those of *The New York Times*, and by luck or plan, those of Edison's own lawyer) but for the most part these years were spent not in the lab perfecting the various components to make this grid function, though that is how the story is usually told—the genius inventor hard at work with brain and hands far from the thick stink of urban life. Another narrative runs parallel to this: that of mucking about in the streets, that of laying the lines. For in this first-square mile given over to electrification, *men* were pulling up cobbles to dig a long straight channel through the dirt and rocks beneath. Into these ditches they laid wires, each carefully wrapped in an unproven insulator. They then piled the dirt back on and relaid the cobbles on top.

In the spring of 1882, they'd been at the task for over a year. Some streets had been dug two or three times. The wires laid were encased in conduits and these were given to leakage—they were after all the first of their kind—causing small fires and big shorts. Every short meant pulling the cobbles back up, re-digging down to extract the faulty elements and relaying the electrical conductor. It was not a thankless job, though it might sound so to modern ears. This is just how it was in the 1880s; this is how America's electric grid, like many modern conveniences, was built, whether in New York or Muncie or Los Angeles. Muscle built, dug, and pulled; muscle ate, muscle sweated, and muscle shat. Human muscle and horse muscle, mostly (Figure 3.1).

Between the mid-1800s and the present day, world per capita income has increased 20 times faster than it had in the preceding eight centuries (see esp. Broadberry et al. 2015). In 1820, a chimney was a good thing to have, and burning charcoal was a nice but dirty alternative to wood; in 1970—a mere 150 years later—the vast majority of Americans had centralized heating or cooling (or both) depending on where they lived. In some regions, like the Pacific Northwest, this heating and hot water were supplied by hydroelectric dams; in others, like the Northeast, it was oil that fed the basement boilers that warmed people's homes (Figures 3.2 and 3.3).[19]

And if calorie-fed muscle still provided most of the power that moved our world in 1880, a mere 30 years later, the horses, their crap, and the sparrows that had fed upon it had disappeared from New York City's streets. Oil-fed motorcars had replaced horse drawn carts and carriages, while electric streetcars had replaced their muscle-driven precursors (Figure 3.4).

Figure 3.1 A horse team hauling the first generator to the Mill Creek #3 Hydroelectric plant, California ca. 1903. Reprinted courtesy of The Huntington Library and the papers of Southern California Edison.

Figure 3.2 Line crew with horse drawn wagon erecting a transmission pole in the desert with a derrick and gin pole, California ca. 1903. Reprinted courtesy of The Huntington Library and the papers of Southern California Edison.

Figure 3.3 A construction crew making cement at the Mill Creek #3 generating station, California ca. 1903. Note the man with no shovel, who directs (and presumably also pays) the muscle. Reprinted courtesy of The Huntington Library and the papers of Southern California Edison.

Figure 3.4 Enter the internal combustion engine. Big Creek Transmission Line, California 1922. Reprinted courtesy of The Huntington Library and the papers of Southern California Edison.

By the late 1920s *very* rich people in every urban metropolis in the nation had electric refrigerators, electric lights, electric irons, and a car.[20] By the late 1950s almost *everyone* had these things.

A report in the Edison Electric bulletin of 1942, when America was entering the seventh decade of electric power, points out that the horsepower available to factory workers had increased from three horses' worth in 1914 to the equivalent of 6.5 horses in 1942. Still an imaginable quantity of horses. The difference was that by 1942 electricity was supplying most of this horsepower. When the bulletin switches its unit of measure from horsepower to manpower, electricity made it seem that 6 billion more sweating, pushing, pulling workers had entered the economy—"equivalent to 50 slaves for each man, woman, and child."[21]

Different energetic regimes give rise not only to different material worlds and economies but to different rhetorical imaginaries. Horsepower as a measure of potential energy use might still be a term in circulation for everything from vacuum cleaners (at 4 horses) to mac trucks (at 425 horses), but slave power, equally common in everyday parlance until the mid-twentieth century, thankfully no longer has any place in conversation. Notable, however, is that both horses and slaves are ways of speaking about energy and its mastery that predate fossil fuels. Both harken back to an era *before* growth was an economic norm and when bodies did most of the work. Both became figures of speech—or energetic *imaginaries*—as the combustion of fossil fuels became the principle way of making power. Gas moves that mac truck; electricity runs that vacuum cleaner. Even odds, even today (2018), that that electricity is made from coal or natural gas. The power of 6 billion human-equivalents might have entered the American economy by means of fossil fuel-powered heat engines, but the power they contributed was distinct from that of a human (or a horse) because they didn't consume anything. "They" (these figurative 6 billion) produced, but they did not expend. One might see here a perfect figuration of Bataille's complaint: increased productivity from fossil fuels means that *making* has gone all out of whack with exudation. Who, after all, will do the work of wasting what those 6 billion people would have gifted and sexed and gobbled up just by being alive?

Horses, Slaves, Oil

According to physicist, Jacob Lund Fisker (who is now an early retirement activist): "There are various ways to do work. The most 'primitive' method is to eat food, which contains energy stored in the chemical bonds of fat, protein, and carbohydrates, and then use muscle power" (2005: 82).[22] "The rate of biological energy use (or the metabolic rate) of a human is about 100 watts, equivalent to 2,000 kilocalories per day."[23] Though this is expandable by eating more food, it cannot be increased indefinitely, since "human physiology restricts the amount of work which can be done to about a maximum of 180 watts, making it impossible to do more work just by eating more food" (Fisker 2005: 82).

Let's put this hypothetical human to work, for 10 hours a day at somewhere between resting and maximum wattage. This gives us something like 140 watts or, if we round up slightly, 1.5 kilowatts. That is the energy usage of a hardworking human. 50 men digging (see Figure 3.3) at this rate brings the total to 75 kilowatts of manpower, which was what electricity made available to "each man, woman, and child" in 1942.

In 2015, according to biologist James Brown, in "the most developed countries, our average per capita energy use is on the order of 10,000 watts [or 100 kilowatts] or 100 times greater than what we need biologically."[24] The total energy usage of "an average person in the United States, Canada, the Eurozone, or Japan is equivalent to the biological metabolic rate of a 30-ton primate. About 80 per cent of this extra-biological energy consumption comes from burning fossil fuels" (Brown et al. 2015).

Muscle is still a part of the imaginary how much potential-for-work (what laymen call 'power') is available to the "average person" but the metaphor of choice has changed. Rather than conceptualizing energy consumers as hypothetical slave owners—as was still the case in the 1940s, a shocking *eighty years* after abolition (in 1865)—with 67 hardworking slaves' (or 99 if they sit in front of computers) energy consumption is conceptualized as a correlate to body mass. To articulate the impact that fossil fuels have had on our consumption patterns, we can thus say that by means of fossil fuels we have increased our own putative mass. We no longer control the labor of others; we are now integrated, if obscenely big, selves; we are fossil fuel-consuming monsters, equivalent in energy consumption to the largest land-based mammal ever to have lived—the *Baluchitherium* (Figure 3.5).[25]

This is not, for Brown, merely a metaphor. We are, in point of fact, plottable on a metabolic chart that continues the "canonical" relationship between the metabolic rate of animals (i.e., the correlation between the calories that an animal consumes and the watts it produces) and their mass. Even Brown seems to have been surprised by this. Originally, his curiosity drove him to investigate whether there was a correlation at the level of national economies between GDP and fuel consumption, taking into account the caloric intake of a population on average and its energy consumption from other sources, like electricity and gas. He posited that "Just as a body has a metabolism that burns food energy to survive and grow a city, a national economy has a metabolism that must burn fuel in order to sustain itself and grow" (Brown et al. 2011: 22).

What Brown found when he plotted per capita energy consumption in watts versus per capita GDP was that the "slope or exponent 0.76 is close to three quarters, which is the canonical value of the exponent for

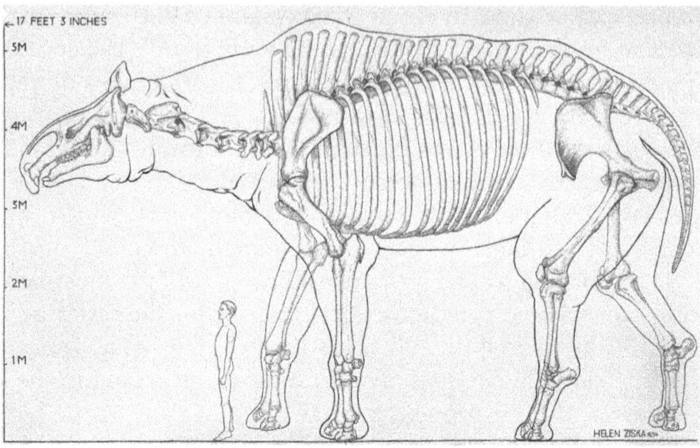

Figure 3.5 "The largest land mammal that has ever lived, the Baluchitherium, was a relative of the modern rhinoceros. Its body weight has been estimated at about 30 tons." From Schmidt-Nielsen 1984: 5, reproduced here with courtesy of the Library Services Department, American Museum of Natural history.

the scaling of metabolic rate with body mass in animals" (2011: 20). In other words, a contemporary American man, woman, or child really is calorically speaking a *Baluchitherium*. We are no longer a 2000-calorie per day (or 100 watt) being. We are a 10,000 watt being, but since we do not each weigh 30 tons, that extra wattage is not, indeed cannot be, supplied by food. It is not energy from calories. It appears, in fact, to be energy from fossil fuels (oil, gas, coal—not just essential to making electricity and heat; not just there to get a car to go, but also critical to manufacturing, to building materials, plastics, fabrics, polymers and getting food stuffs from one place to another) (Figure 3.6).

Brown's formulation is instructive not only because it demonstrates that the imagination has finally abandoned slavery as the truest metaphor for harnessing the work of others, but also because it acknowledges that fossil fuels are a great enabler (Brown et al. 2015). It is not that we control the labor of others, the energy, or—to slip quietly into Karl Marx's terminology—"the labor-time" of between 75 and 100 other humans; it is that we have, with oil most especially but fossil fuels more generally, happened upon what Marx in volume three of *Capital* calls "A Free Gift of Nature to Capital."

Although Bataille roots the causes of excess in industrialization and the 100 years of peace [1820–1914] that came with using excess energy to make factory capitalism work, with Marx we can take the source of excess back a step, to the extravagancy of fossil fuels, a free gift of

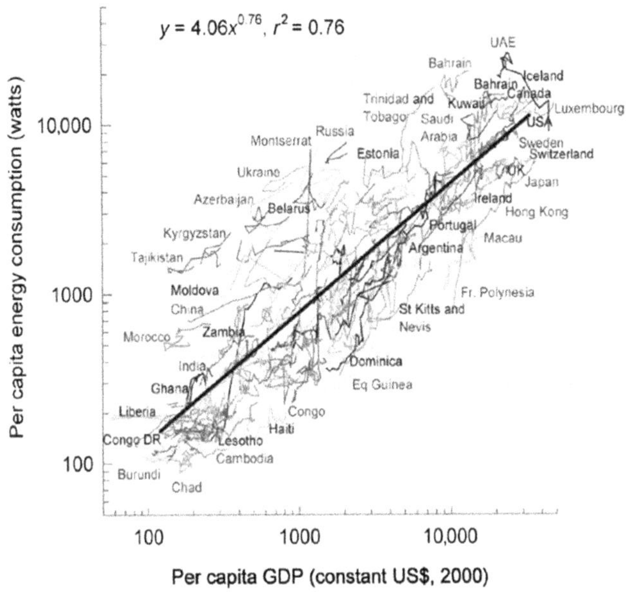

Figure 3.6 "If we were to expand this chart to include species of animals measuring energy consumption in watts converted to calories and body mass (in place of GDP), the slope, or exponent, would remain constant." From Brown et al. 2011. Reproduced with permission of Oxford University Press.

nature beyond human conception in the late 1800s, when Marx was penning his tome (1863–1883):

> Natural elements entering as agents into production, and which cost nothing, no matter what role they play in production, do not enter as components of capital, but as a free gift of Nature to capital, that is, as a free gift of Nature's productive power to labour, which, however, appears as the productiveness of capital, as all other productivity under the capitalist mode of production (Marx 1993).

This free gift as it relates to oil, spectacular even among fossil fuels, is explained by Michael Ziser, an English Professor in California:

> The mining of coal, which must be brought by brute force from seams buried far below ground epitomizes the zero degree of labor [. . .] and underscores the ultimate dependence of even an advanced industrial society on the input of *human* energy [. . .] Oil by contrast [to coal], is a liquid that in the classic scenario flows to the surface almost of its own accord, gushing out in all directions and

> proposing an entirely different relation among labor, consumption, and the body. Once struck, oil returns so much more energy than is required to produce it that it becomes an effectively costless substitute for human and animal labor. [One that] far exceed[s] what Marx [. . .] thought possible for a raw material to contribute to economic production. (Ziser, 321)

Following Ziser, it can be said with accuracy that the phenomenal—indeed, excessive—growth of human economies and capacities between 1860 and 1970 was due to the difference between the labor it took to extract and refine oil and the BTUs (heat) it produces.[26]

The "free gift" can be quantified by working out the difference between how much energy flows up of its own accord from a well and how much muscle power as a unit of energy (or Marx's labor-time) it takes to manage the process.[27] What is more, this relationship, or more properly speaking "ratio," between invested labor versus extracted energy has, since 1860, become a "natural" or commonsensical way for people (qua *Baluchitheria*) around the 10,000 watt mark on Brown's chart to understand first, the potential productivity of energy systems (like solar) and second, themselves and their weighty capacity to have an impact on the world (By which I should mean the wise deployment of their labor-power as the largest land animal ever to walk the earth, but the image I have instead (à la Bataille) is of the (impact) crater a 30-ton *Baluchitheria* would make when dropped from a great height).

As oil goes out of vogue because of the geopolitical complexities related to its movement around the globe and environmental catastrophes linked to its extraction and combustion, we can see in Bataille's work and the green energy dreams of deGrasse Tyson, that the magic of this "ratio" remains lodged in the imagination as we, *Baluchitheria* move forward to newer forms of sustaining our bulk—like the wind, the sun, and even natural gas. The excess of oil has, in other words, been naturalized as a conversation about growth and about the maximization of profits.

The easy question, to which most green energy dreamers set themselves, is: how might the energy needed to sustain, indeed grow, this non-negligible 10,000-watt beast be newly made? We might also wonder following Bataille: how might the feculence and lustiness of such 30-ton creatures be included into postulates for new society—one that not only changes how it makes power but also how it deals with waste.

Math

The numbers for operative oil wells are hard to find. The number of barrels of oil that are produced per day, for example, and the number of people involved in the production process are—while not exactly secret—not exactly public either. The explosion of the Deepwater Horizon in 2010 changed this. A lot of facts leaked out in the public domain together with all that crude. We know, for example, that when the Deepwater Horizon blew up, there were 126 people aboard the platform, and that before the well was capped, it was leaking the equivalent of 63,000 barrels of oil per day.

There are between 125 and 140 kilos of oil (or 132.5 kilos on average) in a single barrel, depending on the type of oil. Multiply this by 2.2 to convert the number from kilos to pounds and we get 291.5 lbs of oil per barrel. For the purpose of argument let's round it up to 300 lbs of oil per barrel. Multiplying this by 5.8 kilowatt-hours per pound gives us about 1,700 kilowatt-hours per barrel; if we multiply this, in turn, by 63,000 barrels of oil released per day by the Deepwater Horizon, we can deduce that the well was producing the equivalent of approximately 107,100,000 kilowatt-hours of potential energy per day. So that's the oil side of the equation. One hundred and seven million potential kilowatt-hours per day (or roughly the output per day of 100 nuclear reactors)[28]

Here is the human side. 150 watts of human labor per hour multiplied by 126 people and 10 hours of work per day equals 189,000 watt-workdays. Then, we add 14 hours resting at 100 watts per hour and we get 1,400 watts per day per person, or 176,500 for everyone living aboard the platform. The energy output of the men who work the well is thus equal to 189,000 working watts plus 176,500 resting watts which comes to 365,500 watts or 365.5 kilowatts per day.

The free gift of nature to capital is thus 107,100,000 kWh minus 365.5 kWh, or 107,099,634.5 kWh.

Or, to make the scale of things maximally clear, the necessary labor-time to produce 63,000 barrels of oil a day is the equivalent (in watt-hours) of the potential energy of just *one quarter of one barrel* of that oil per day. The free gift is the energy equivalent of 62,999.75 barrels of oil per day. Or 250,000 times the labor energy per day is necessary to extract it.

For this ratio to be fully accurate one would also have to take into consideration the non-negligible labor costs of extracting the raw materials for the platform as well as the labor that was used to build it, move it into place, and govern it. Even so, drilling for oil is clearly a winning game in classical economic thought precisely because of the radical imbalance between labor-power in (measured in watts) and potential power out (also measured in watts).[29] Oil produces luxury almost as a side effect. This luxury enters an economic system premised upon a sort of capitalist accumulation (following Marx(1993)) or self-interested activity (following Smith(2000)) designed to maximize and centralize wealth among the few. Wealth that even before the excesses of oil found its way into industrial systems in the 1860s must (according to both theorists) be dealt with by government-mandated systems of redistribution—radical gifting forced by law upon the rich. There was, in other words, already a dissipation problem before oil. And then oil magnified this problem two hundred fifty thousandfold without a concomitantly radical plan for the squander of this excess.

How to get rid of so much? Bataille's endorsement of nonproductive activities, like the arts, sex without procreation (a delicious recuperation of what Freud had called simply "perversion"), potlatch-style gifting, spectacle, and other "sumptuous moments," are hard to operationalize at this scale. Vicious war, he saw, was an outcome. Global warming, I suggest, is another.

Crude Thinking

I am certain the numbers presented above have been figured out before, and more accurately, and that I could have zipped down a ratio from the Internet and pasted it in here with much less fanfare. What I wanted to get at, though, was the stakes of such figures for the ways in which we talk about renewable energy as *more* capable of excess even than the system we currently have.

The naturalized excess matters to questions of how one might best govern an economy, but it also matters to the imagination and after 150 years of oil, a free gift of nature beyond any assumed by classical economics (though I suspect that it is not an accident that Marx arrived at this concept just as oil was changing capitalism in entirely unanticipated ways). The once inconceivable excesses of oil have established as normal a particular relationship between necessary labor-time and available energy. It seems impossible that 126 men can produce over 250,000 times their calorie-driven energy per day, yet the minor excesses of everyday life (like disposable coffee cups of which Starbucks alone produces 4 billion per year; or incandescent light bulbs which use only 5% of the electricity it takes to run them to make light, the other 95% is given off as waste heat) attest to a certain facility in the modern dissipation of excess energy. It seems similarly possible that the wind blowing, the tide moving, the sun shining might do the same with no men, with no muscle much at all involved in the daily operation of things.

Here we might remember Burke for a moment as oil shape-shifts to suit one discourse and then another, providing inspiration here, fodder there, and then energetic capacities to power economies, and also impossible-to-imagine (but true) ratios, as it (in yet another way) contributes to a felt self-concept of modern man (woman, and child) as equally impossibly humongous beasts of the rhino family—raised from extinction as fossils are from their beds of stone, to walk/power the earth once again. Its apposition, not of two terms but five or seven, each set next to the rest to constitute a world of oil, a world harder to leave behind than deGrasse Tyson might imagine because it is so impossibly thorough.

One route, then, to understanding the appeal of the energy transition that is currently underway is to acknowledge that oil helped to put in place and grind down into consciousness the "naturalness" of the free gift. And now, in an odd way, oil has not become "free enough"—still too linked to the terrestrial, the bellicose, and the dirty. It has lost a lot of its appeal culturally, while still maintaining all of it chemically, all of it rhetorically. Even the charm of renewables is driven by a desire to return to fuels that might maintain the excesses of oil coupled with a further reduction in (accidental or unavoidable) waste. This includes the waste and pollution from oil spills, from internal combustion engines, particulates, and carbon and methane emissions. Renewables command cultural appeal because they demand even less muscle than oil for (hopefully) even greater return. The fear, of course, is that the ratio of invested to extracted energy that applies to renewables will be nowhere as favorably disproportionate as that of oil. The promise is that with time and earnest pursuit it will come close to or (as dreamers inevitably dream) exceed the favorable ratio presented by oil extraction, thereby allowing us to consume power at an even more accelerated rate than the largest land animal ever to have walked the earth. James Brown's curve extending endlessly upward and to the right, a forty-five-degree angle without end and without limit. With renewables, we dreaming 10,000-watt beings might become as large as the dinosaurs deGrasse Tyson uses to threaten us with—increasing not only the wattage available to us, but also the majesty of the free gift. Not 250,000 times the power out for every unit of human labor invested, but an infinite multiplication of what man can do with very close to nothing at all. In other words, we don't want 10,000 watts, the top of Brown's chart in 2011 to be the end of the story of growth.

In this I wager that we don't see that there is a story that continues to be told, a story of a natural "energetic" order of things that proceeds from oil, that relies upon crude thinking, and is perpetuated in imaginaries of an oil-free future in which the social values of the late twentieth century are left untouched by as radical a transition of energy regimes as humanity has heretofore manufactured. It will be this oil world without oil in it—lovely in its continued, sanctioned blindness toward excesses unconsidered. It remains a question if even a 10,000-watt being can dissipate in lively, desirous, flagrant uselessness 250,000 times the energy it takes to make itself whole.

Notes

1 An earlier version of this paper "The Immaterialization of Power: The Case of Electricity" was presented at Center for Energy and Environmental Research in the Human Sciences (CENHS) Cultures of Energy conference, Rice University, Houston Texas, April 16–18, 2015. Many thanks to all involved for their enthusiasm, wit, and comments. Thanks also to Benjamin Johnson

for help at the end with the physics and for doubting Bataille every step of the way.

2 This quote is from the ninth episode of deGrasse Tyson's popular science show, *Cosmos: A Spacetime Odyssey.* Emphasis in original meme, which can be found here: https://me.me/i/mediamatters-org-we-are-dumping-carbon-dioxide-into-the-atmosphere-at-4397331/ accessed Feb. 18 2019.

3 The remaining volumes were reconstructed from notes posthumously.

4 Wrapped up in this adverb "naturally" is great debate, as the question for humans is not how much sun hits the earth but how much of it we can channel to our own uses with processes like industrial food production or solar electricity production. See esp. Stoekl 2007:38–42.

5 Slavoj Žižek would call this (or something similar to it) the parallax view. His interest is less in material disjunctures and more in the space between a thing and itself (Žižek 2006). What I like about Burke's approach, however, is the place for play, absurdity and humor (My sister, the king?) and its reliance on a grammatical form which is both commonplace and comfortable.

6 This « we » is given precise definition right around Image 5, of the current chapter.

7 Bataille, George. 1988 [1949]. *The Accursed Share*, 28.

8 Neoliberalism as an ethical as well as an economic system would have been a blindingly obvious example of this for Bataille.

9 It could well be argued that we don't have excess as a planet so much as a society. There are pockets of excess (in Europe, for example, during the twentieth century). Therefore, distribution across societies, as a form of gifting, could be a solution as much as more bellicose modes of dissipation. This only works, however, following a Bataillian logic, if what is given is *not* destined to be channeled into increased productivity elsewhere. Development programs that shuttle money from rich to poor nations are not thus modes for dissipating excess but rather for spreading modes of capitalist increase.

10 In 1949, four years after nuclear bombs had been dropped on Hiroshima and Nagasaki in the final days of World War II, the proliferation of such weapons seemed to spell a likely end to human life on earth. Today global warming is the weapon we turn upon ourselves. Despite the fact that the means have been updated, the story remains very much the same.

11 It is worth noting following Mintz (1986) that the factory system was also remarkable for its capacity to strip energy from persons and plants, and following Li (2014) that it was also a perfect machine for the production and increase of inequality. See also Freeman, Joshua. 2018. *Behemoth: A History of the Factory and the Making of the Modern World*, New York: W.W. Norton & Co.

12 Stoekl points out that Bataille too makes this mistake of thinking the sun by means of the energetics of oil (2007: 39), but he (Stoekl) is writing at a time before solar power technology became a viable means of making electric power, so his critique of Bataille's ignorance is bolstered by his own placement in time and the energetic truths then available.

13 All the NOs (N_2O, NO and NO_2) actually contribute to global warming, such that the term NO_x has entered circulation. Useful in many ways, none I wager, are quiet so charming as the potential of "NO to NO_x" as an addition to the lexicon of protest banners.

14 A gasoline powered lawn mower emits about 48 kilograms (106 lbs) of greenhouse gas in one season. Gas-powered lawn mowers are very inefficient,

which means that despite their small size they produce a lot of air pollution. In fact, running an older gasoline-powered lawn mower for one hour can produce as much air pollution as driving a new car 550 kilometers. Source: Ministry of the Environment-Canada

"A gasoline-powered lawn mower run for an hour puts out about the same amount of smog-forming emissions as 40 new automobiles run for an hour." Source: California Environmental Protection Agency, Air Resources Board. May 20, 1999. From http://www.cleanairyardcare.ca/sustainability/environmental-facts/ accessed Aug. 31 2016.

15 "Scientists have long known that permafrost contains vast quantities of carbon in dead plants and other organic material, about twice as much as the entire atmosphere. Now, that permafrost is melting more quickly as the Arctic warms up faster than anywhere else on Earth. The melt often takes place in Arctic lakes where water thaws long-frozen soil. The material released is digested by tiny bugs and turned into carbon dioxide and methane . . . The team captured some of those gases and subjected them to radiocarbon dating. They found the gases had been generated from carbon stored for anywhere between 10,000 and 30,000 years" (Weber 2016).

16 "Better and Better: The Myth of Inevitable Progress" by James Surowiecki in Foreign Affairs July/August 2007 (accessed 3/2012); It is a review essay of Indur Goklany's book *The Improving State of the World,* p.1; See also Maddison, Angus *Contours of the World Economy 1-2030 AD: Essays in Macro-Economic History, Oxford: Oxford University Press, 2007.*

17 Quote from U.S. Dept of Energy, *Annual Energy Review 1998*. 1999. Washington, D.C.: U.S. Department of Energy (Energy Information Administration): xviii.

18 For a longer more detailed discussion of this process, see Bakke 2016.

19 To begin with a point of comparison, on average oil produces almost 21 megajoules, or 5.8 kilowatt-hours, of energy per pound. Burning wood produces about six megajoules per pound, or 1.6 kilowatt-hours. Coal gives between 7 and 16 megajoules per pound depending upon its quality. A joule is defined as the work required to produce one watt of power for one second (one watt-second). A kilowatt-hour is thus about 3.6 megajoules. An average American household uses 1000 kilowatt-hours per month or 3,600 megajoules.

20 In NYC in 1920, there were only 150 home refrigerators (Nye 2010: 228).

21 Madrigal (2008) U.S. population in 1940 was 132 million people x 50 slaves = 6.6 billion people. In a way, the mainstreaming of electricity or electric power proved Malthus wrong, 6 million more workers, but no more mouths to be fed.

22 Fisker is now, curiously, an early retirement activist; still a student of "work," if differently.

23 Some say 130 watts (see Brown et al. 2015).

24 It is actually 66.67 times greater than we need biologically [100/1.5 = 66.6667]. For context, the most basic model of the new Tesla power wall battery system is 7.5 kilowatts or five times a hardworking human. This is not quite Marx's labor-power but it is a simple means of quantification. A $3,500 battery could in 2016 supply a house with the equivalent wattage of five working men. We might also say, to update the metaphor, that it supplies the power of a single muscular man with the tonnage and wattage of a small male giraffe.

25 Blue whales are 3x this size, but the water enables their bones to support their weight.

26 For purposes of conversation 1 BTU (or British Thermal Unit) is the rough equivalent of one kilojoule [1 BTU = 1055 joules]; 1000 BTUs is thus roughly a megajoule [947.82 BTUs = 1 megajoule]

27 A minimal investigation of oil fields will reveal that it is not quite so easy as Ziser claims to get that oil out of the ground, these spaces reverberate with sound of generators and screws pumps, as fossil fuels are mobilized to raise other fossil fuels from the earth. They are loud enough that the birds have changed their songs to carry over the clamor of industry (Tabuchi 2018). Anthropologist David Hughes makes a similar claim in "Ordinary Oil: Energy, Climate Change, and the Silence of Complicity" (a manuscript still in process) in which he argues convincingly that the notion of oil coming naturally to the surface *as if* mobilized by a sort of anthropomorphic antigravitional "desire" is a part of oil's mythic rather than physical structure.

28 Most nuclear reactors produce in the area of 1000 MW.

29 I have intentionally omitted the labor-power and material costs of transporting this oil to market and running the business end of things as related to this transport and sale. While necessary to produce an economy dependent on oil, it is not necessary for the quantification of the "free gift."

References

Air Resources Board. 1999. *Mow Down Pollution with Electric Mower Rebate*. Sacramento: California Environmental Protection Agency. www.arb.ca.gov/newsrel/nr052099.htm

Asimov, Isaac. 1972. *Electricity and Man*. Washington, D.C.: U.S. Atomic Energy Commission (Office of Information Services).

Bakke, Gretchen. 2016. *The Grid: The Fraying Wires Between America and Our Energy Future*. New York: Bloomsbury.

Bataille, George. 1988 [1949]. *The Accursed Share*. Cambridge, MA: MIT Press.

Broadberry, S., Campbell, B. M., Klein, A., Overton, M., & Van Leeuwen, B. 2015. *British economic growth, 1270–1870*. Cambridge University Press.

Brown, James H. and the New México Human Macroecology Group. 2013. "Gasoline and Fertility: We Consume Unlike any Other." *Nautilus*. Accessed April 4, 2015. http://nautil.us/issue/1/what-makes-you-so-special/gasoline-and-fertility

Brown, James H., William R. Burnside, Ana D. Davidson, John P. DeLong, William C. Dunn, Marcus J. Hamilton, Norman Mercado-Silva, et al. 2011. "Energetic Limits to Economic Growth." *Biosciences* 61 (1): 19–26.

Burke, Kenneth. 1984. *Permanence and Change: An Anatomy of Purpose*. Third ed. Berkeley: University of California Press.

———. 1968. *Counter-Statement*. Berkeley: University of California Press.

Energy Information Administration. 1999. *Annual Energy Review 1998*. Washington, D.C.: U.S. Department of Energy.

"Environmental Facts". *Clean Air, Yard Care*. Accessed August 31, 2016. www.cleanairyardcare.ca/sustainability/environmental-facts/

Fisker, Jacob. 2005. "The Laws of Energy" in *The Final Energy Crises*, eds. A. McKillop and S. Newman, London: Pluto: 74–86.

Freeman, Joshua. 2018. *Behemoth: A History of the Factory and the Making of the Modern World*, New York: W.W. Norton & Co.

Government of Canada. 2003. *Your Guide to the One-Tonne Challenge*. Government of Canada, 2003. http://publications.gc.ca/collections/Collection/M144-27-2003E.pdf

Long, Mark C. "Tending to the Imagination: Perspective and Incongruity in William Carlos Williams and Kenneth Burke." Paper presented at the Modern Language Association Conference, Toronto, December 1997.

Maddison, Angus. *Contours of the World Economy 1–2030 AD: Essays in Macro-Economic History*, Oxford: Oxford University Press, 2007.

Madrigal, Alexis. 2008. "Measuring the History of Electricity." *Wired*, September 14. Accessed September 15, 2011. www.wired.com/science/discoveries/multimedia/2008/08/gallery_electrical_meter?slide=5&slideView=4

Marx, Karl. 1993. "Part VI: Transformation of Surplus-Profit into Ground-Rent." In *Capital: A Critique of Political Economy (Volume III: The Process of Capitalist Production as a Whole)*. Translated by David Fernbach. London: Penguin Classics.

Mintz, Sydney. 1986. *Sweetness and Power: The Place of Sugar in Modern History*. New York: Penguin Books.

Murray Li, Tania. 2014. *Land's End: Capitalist Relations on an Indigenous Frontier*. Durham, NC: Duke University Press.

Nye, David E. 2010. *When the Lights Went Out: A History of Blackouts in America*. Cambridge, MA: The MIT Press.

Schmidt-Nielsen, Knut. 1984. *Scaling: Why is Animal Size so Important?* Cambridge: Cambridge University Press.

Smith, Adam. 2000 [1723–1790]. *The Wealth of Nations*, New York: Modern Library.

Stoekl, Allan. 2007. *Bataille's Peak: Energy, Religion, and Postsustainability*, Minneapolis: University of Minnesota Press.

Surowiecki, James. 2007. "Better and Better: The Myth of Inevitable Progress." *Foreign Affairs*, July/August. Accessed March 1, 2012. www.foreignaffairs.com/reviews/review-essay/2007-07-01/better-and-better-myth-inevitable-progress

Tabuchi, Hiroko. 2018. "Near Noisy Oil Fields, Lovesick Birds Change Their Tunes." *The New York Times*, March 13. Accessed March 13, 2018. www.nytimes.com/2018/03/13/climate/oil-field-birds-change-songs.html

Weber, Bob. 2016. "Melting Arctic permafrost releasing ancient carbon, study confirms." *The Globe and Mail*, August 24. Accessed August 31, 2016. www.theglobeandmail.com/technology/science/melting-arctic-permafrost-releasing-ancient-carbon-study-confirms/article31542434/

Yaeger, Patricia, Shannon Laurie, Vin Nardizzi, Ken Hiltner, Saree Makdisi, Michael Ziser, and Imre Szeman. 2011. "Editor's Column: Literature in the Ages of Wood, Tallow, Coal, Whale Oil, Gasoline, Atomic Power, and Other Energy Sources." *PMLA* 126 (2): 305–326.

Ziser, Michael. 2011. "Oil Spills" in "Editor's Column: Literature in the Ages of Wood, Tallow, Coal, Whale Oil, Gasoline, Atomic Power, and Other Energy Sources." *PMLA* 126 (2): 321–323.

Žižek, Slavoj. 2006. *The Parallax View*, Cambridge, MA: MIT Press.

4 Rhetorics of Toxicity, Racism, and Religion on the Gulf Coast

Oil and Environmental Justice in BP Spill Documentary Films

Juliette Lapeyrouse-Cherry

The British Petroleum Deepwater Horizon explosion and oil spill that began on April 20, 2010 and unfolded in the months that followed was the most devastating disruption of human, animal, and ecosystem health to occur in the Gulf Coast region in recent memory. Consequences included the immediate impacts of oil and the dispersant Corexit, along with harmful repercussions for the fisheries, petrochemical industry, and the wider Gulf coast economy. Yet the spill was just the latest catastrophe perpetrated by an industry with a decades-long history of negative impacts along the U.S. Gulf Coast, particularly south Louisiana. From refinery pollution in areas like Cancer Alley, the concentrated area of racially and socioeconomically disproportionate negative health impacts that surrounds petrochemical plants along the Mississippi River, to the slicing up of vital wetlands for industrial canals that accelerate coastal land loss, the industry's harmful effects are increasingly hard for environmental justice activists to ignore. Furthermore, climate change induced sea-level rise and extreme weather events are expected to compound the negative impacts of the petroleum industry on the Gulf Coast. Yet the reality of climate change, not to mention its causal ties to the oil and gas industry, is widely ignored or doubted in the region, thanks in large part to the efforts of major corporations (and major employers) like BP, Chevron, ExxonMobil, and Shell to fund and legitimize climate change denialism. Despite these increasingly visible injustices, the industry's grip on local cultures and economies remains pervasive; nearly everyone from southern Louisiana has friends or family members who work in some sector of the petroleum industry, or in a related industry like sugarcane farming, which depends on petrochemical fertilizers for higher yields.

In this chapter, I examine how documentaries on the BP oil spill have captured the ways that oil, a substance that many petroculture scholars have observed remains largely invisible in everyday life, becomes visible on human and nonhuman bodies, and contextualized the spill within cultural conditions that enable and perpetuate oil's spectrality.

Following the spill, several documentary films captured the complex and interlinked consequences of the catastrophe in the region. In this essay, I rhetorically analyze three of these documentaries: *The Big Fix* (2011), *Vanishing Pearls* (2014), and *The Great Invisible* (2014). These films were chosen because they were widely viewed at film festivals and received press coverage for their treatment of the spill. The films vary in scope, perspective, and focus, but they all were released within four years of the spill. Significantly, all three films were directed by Gulf Coast natives and illustrate how people deeply rooted in the place narrativize the spill. Together, these films construct the spill as the subject of a cover-up in the context of a corrupt political and economic system, show its impacts on marginalized and disappearing communities, and highlight individual unseen impacts and untold stories within the context of Gulf Coast oil culture. The documentaries I examine, which are intended for popular audiences, capture a variety of effects, ranging from

- the immediate impact on the Deepwater Horizon rig workers who died or have ongoing physical and mental health problems resulting from their traumatic experience;
- to struggling fishermen and seafood industry workers forced to take jobs with BP to make money;
- to coastal residents, animals, and ecosystems sickened by the immediate impact of the spilled oil and subsequent use of toxic dispersant;
- to the broader Gulf Coast population affected by the economic impacts of the disruption of the fisheries and offshore drilling moratorium following the spill.

They capture the magnitude of the spill, making present the often-invisible material substance of oil, and showing how Corexit, a toxic dispersant intended to render spilled oil invisible, reveals its toxic actions through sick humans and dead animal bodies. They also contextualize the spill, to varying degrees, in the cultural, racial, and religious milieu of the Gulf South.

The focuses of these three films vary, but taken together they capture the constellation of negative impacts on the Gulf Coast, and particularly Louisiana, following the spill. They construct and make visible petroleum's impacts on multiple scales both socially and materially, situating the spill in multiple scalar and temporal contexts. I look to the driving concerns and tensions of environmental justice, a movement defined from the beginning by its tension with the modern environmental movement, industrial impacts on health, and spatial environmental injustice, as a starting point for examining the spill and its effects, seeing it as a useful frame for examining how oil moves physically and figuratively through bodies and discourse. Taken together, and understood in light of environmental justice concerns, some recurring thematic patterns emerge across the films when they are placed in conversation. However, my analysis also reveals the films' cursory engagements with racism and religion, and I argue that these subterranean themes merit deeper consideration in light of oil culture in the Gulf Coast.

Reading these films rhetorically for oil's visibility and invisibility, I argue that they show some hints of influence of modern environmentalist wilderness concerns in their depictions of oiled wildlife. However, human health and toxicity are foregrounded, as all three films audiovisually construct, sometimes through the invocation of other senses, petroleum's social-material impacts on the Gulf Coast through representations of sickness and toxicity, in alignment with environmental justice concerns. I also argue that the films have varying degrees of engagement with racial justice, another central concern of environmental justice, though more could be done to highlight the impact of the spill, and the oil industry in general, on minority communities. Finally, I show that religious belief is a subterranean theme across the films, one that merits deeper consideration in light of the environmental justice movements' deeply rooted spiritual impetus.

About the Movies

The Big Fix

Film credits and production: The Big Fix was directed by Josh Tickell, a Louisiana native, and his wife, Rebecca Harrell Tickell. This film has the highest budget and production value of the three, with appearances by celebrities like Peter Fonda and Amy Smart; the credits list the popular singer-songwriter Jason Mraz as a co-producer, and Mraz's song "Collapsible Plans" plays as the end credits roll.

Film narrative: The film chronicles the filmmakers' experiences as they visit Gulf Coast communities affected by the BP oil spill and places the spill in the context of the long history of questionable business practices by British Petroleum around the world, and particularly in Louisiana. The film focuses on BP's use of the petrochemical Corexit to disperse (and thus hide) spilled oil, the effects of which are underscored in the film when Rebecca becomes sick after being exposed to Corexit on a beach. Alongside depictions of locals sickened by Corexit, the film documents her bodily experience of the dispersant's toxic effects, including respiratory and dermatological ailments.

Film Technique and Purpose: The Big Fix is the only film narrated in first person, as Josh Tickell explicitly highlights his familial roots in Louisiana in the film's opening minutes. The Tickells contextualize the spill in Louisiana's long history of political corruption, linking it to the revolving door of government and industry in Washington, D.C. The filmmakers understand their project as a kind of journalistic exposé, the narrator repeatedly stating he will reveal the "truth" about the spill. He places the film alongside social movements like civil rights and women's rights, calling the viewer to action.

Vanishing Pearls

Film credits and production: Like *The Big Fix*, *Vanishing Pearls* was directed by a Louisiana native, Nailah Jefferson.

Film narrative: The film focuses on the spill's impact on oyster fishermen in Pointe à la Hache, Louisiana, a small town south of New Orleans. Jefferson captures the struggle of these fishermen to receive compensation from BP for their financial losses resulting from the spill and also makes the case that the spill has devastated both the area's economy and its culture. In addition, *Vanishing Pearls* illustrates the physical and material impacts of the oil spill and its aftermath on animals, showing these impacts on their living and dead bodies.

Film Technique and Purpose: Unlike *The Big Fix*, *Vanishing Pearls* narrative is driven by on-screen text rather than first-person narration, though Jefferson is quietly heard asking questions of interviewees in a few scenes. With its focus on this predominantly black community of fishermen who have been working in the area for generations, the film offers an illuminating historical perspective on the long history of racist institutional, legislative, and business practices in one of the areas most affected by the spill and contextualizes the spill in the community's fight against these practices over the years.

The Great Invisible

Film credits and production: The director of *The Great Invisible*, Margaret Brown, is a native of the Gulf Coast like Tickell and Jefferson, but is from Alabama, not Louisiana.

Film narrative: The Great Invisible focuses on the experiences of Deepwater Horizon rig explosion survivors, as well as the communities across the Gulf Coast affected by the spill. Like *The Big Fix*, this film has a wide geographical scope, featuring interviewees from spill-affected areas across the Gulf Coast. The film explores the lasting effects of the rig explosion on the physical and mental wellbeing of two of the men who escaped and their struggle for fair compensation from the companies responsible. Brown also captures the impact of the spill on the fishing town of Bayou La Batre, Alabama, especially the economic impact of the spill's destruction of the fisheries. In addition, she visits Morgan City, LA, to highlight the complex range of reactions to the spill. She documents the frustration of local residents of this major center of the offshore drilling industry in south Louisiana, whose economic livelihoods depend on the petroleum industry, with President Obama's moratorium on offshore drilling following the spill. She also goes to Houston, where she shows oil executives smoking cigars and calling the Gulf of México a "frontier."

Film Technique and Purpose: Brown humanizes the range of diverse communities affected by the spill while also showing tensions between these communities' reactions to the spill and its aftermath.

Environmental Justice and Rhetorical Studies

To critically evaluate the rhetoric of these films, I approach them through the lens of the environmental justice movement's health, racial, and ethical concerns. The movement was founded on the claim "that certain minority populations are forced, through their lack of access to decision-making and policy-making processes, to live with a disproportionate share of environmental 'bads' – and suffer the related public health problems and quality of life burdens" (Agyeman, Bullard, and Evans 2003, 6). Environmental justice activists and scholars critique the environmental movement for its allegedly elitist interests in conserving pristine nature while ignoring the needs of minorities and the poor.[1] Furthermore, many environmental justice activists have spiritual motivations for their work, as evidenced by the frequency of prayers prior to meetings, as well as by the use of testimonials, a genre with roots in black Christian churches (Kaalund 2004). When placed within an environmental justice framework, the material and spiritual impacts of the spill, and of oil more broadly, on the Gulf coast region become apparent, articulated through tensions between the oil industry and the fisheries that are less present in official and technical documentation of the spill, but visible in some popular treatments of the event and its aftermath. In bringing environmental justice together with rhetorical criticism, I bring a novel lens to the evaluation of these documentaries.

In rhetorical studies,[2] research on the spill has come primarily from Technical and Professional Communication scholars studying textual artifacts, such as press releases and blogs. For example, Frost (2013) examines international, national, and local rhetorics across professional and nonprofessional genres including corporate, governmental, business, and educational documents to draw conclusions about transcultural risk communication, and she highlights the struggle to balance economic livelihoods and environmental concerns underscored by the spill, a conflict that reverberates with the long-standing tensions between industrial interests, mainstream environmentalism, and social justice advocates that animate the environmental justice movement. Wickman (2014) conducts a genre-based analysis of BP's rhetorical framing strategies in press releases as the company attempts to control the dominant narrative of the spill.

While these studies do offer important insights into BP spill discourse, neither Frost nor Wickman read the spill from an environmental justice perspective, neither devoting attention to the lived bodily experiences of those impacted by the spill. However, these issues must be engaged to conduct the systemic critique required to fully understand the spill. For example, neither scholar considers the effects of dispersants on humans and nonhumans. Frost emphasizes that fishermen are back to work and the tourism industry is recovering at the site of her study in Dauphin Island, Alabama, but she does not discuss the widespread illnesses that followed the use of dispersant recorded by the documentaries in my analysis. Frost gestures at ecocritical approaches in her analysis, but further engagement between rhetorical approaches and ecocriticism, especially in light of environmental justice concerns, are warranted in studies of the BP spill.

In extending rhetorical studies into environmental justice work on the BP spill, I examine how environmental rhetoric scholars have contributed to environmental communication, an emergent field that sees environmental justice concerns as central to its aims. Phaedra Pezzullo has led the way in rhetorical work on environmental justice since the 2000s, most notably in *Toxic Tourism* (2007), where she examines the rhetoric of the environmental justice movement's use of toxic tours. Recently, Pezzullo has called for "intersectional" research: "to interpellate more rhetorical critics into recognizing and valuing the contributions of environmental rhetorical criticism in alliance with queer, decolonial, racial/ethnic, feminist, disability, and working-class scholarship" (2016, 27). To respond to Pezzullo's call for intersectional work and to extend Frost's gesture toward ecocriticism, I also incorporate perspectives from the environmental humanities, an emerging interdisciplinary field, which emphasizes environmental justice concerns, and site of scholarship on the BP spill. This rhetorical analysis is informed by interdisciplinary visual environmental rhetoric, particularly the site of interaction between rhetoric studies and other humanities scholars interested in environmental communication. In "Ecosee and Just Sustainability," Salma Monani (2011) calls for research that brings together visual rhetorical methods and concerns for just sustainability. I also draw on Jennifer Peeples's (2013) work on the visual representation of toxins to consider how oil and Corexit are visible or invisible in these films, approaching them in my analysis as visual narratives that, when read together, share overlapping themes.

Oiled Animals and Human Senses

In the weeks following the BP spill, images of oiled animals, especially oiled pelicans, were ubiquitous in both mainstream and environmentally oriented media, such as *National Geographic* and *Orion Magazine*. Such images establish a narrative of the spill as a particular kind of environmental disaster, one that impacts wild places, with human costs given minimal attention. In some ways, these films align with this animal-centric narrative. For instance, in the opening of *Vanishing Pearls*, Byron Encalade covers a tabletop on his boat with dead oysters pulled from his usual fishing grounds. Later, a crab in a net and swimming dolphins are shown covered in the sheen of oil, and a dolphin is shown on a beach (either suffering or dead). A whale covered in thick oil is shown being handled by multiple men in masks. Cynthia Sarthou of the Gulf Restoration Network informs viewers that Gulf sperm whales have been shown to be the most polluted in the world, implicitly, though not visually, linking the immediate impacts of the spill and the long-term impacts of pollution in the Gulf. Here the whale is swimming freely in the water, not covered in oil; the film depicts the invisibility of toxicity: without Sarthou's explanation, viewers would not understand that anything is wrong with the whale in the scene.

Though *The Big Fix* gives less direct attention to the plight of animals, it does feature a scene in which dolphins are coughing, pointed out for viewers by the Tickells. In this case, the film goes beyond the shocking imagery of an animal covered in oil, evoking sympathy by showing an animal suffering in a way recognizable to humans. Dolphins and whales, widely understood as intelligent and social creatures, have long been what Dobrin and Morey (2009) call ecotypes, or archetypal animals that are emblematic of certain causes, concepts, or movements; they offer the example of the panda as instantly associated with the World Wildlife Fund. In the context of the Gulf Oil Spill, the oiled pelican has become an ecotype, a widely recognized image that shows the consequences of what LeMenager, following Klare, calls "tough oil," that is, oil that is "tough not just because it is hard to get, but because of the devastating scale of its externalities" (2014, 3). Although the three films depict animals, they ultimately focus on conjuring empathy for humans rather than oiled or dead animals.

The films also highlight how, in the absence of visible manifestations of toxins, humans draw on alternate senses. While animal victims of the BP spill could not avoid being oiled or ingesting Corexit, these films show humans seemingly drawn to touch the oil. Scenes of people physically touching oil are more prominently featured in *The Big Fix*, although similar images appear in all three films. For example, early in the film Tickell sticks his hand in oil on a beach and shows it to the camera. Later, he sits on a porch near the coast with marine toxicologist, Riki Ott, who wipes a white paper towel on the table and shows Tickell and the camera the black film blown in by the wind. Similarly, Latham Smith, a tugboat captain impacted by oil industry decline after the spill featured in *The Great Invisible*, spoons sticky oil he has collected from a plastic jug to show the camera. In *Vanishing Pearls*, Byron Encalade walks along the beach, grabs a tarball, and states, "You can smell the petrol." In *The Big Fix*, viewers learn that part of the process for determining whether fish affected by the spill were safe to eat was through a smell test; Tickell shows this officially sanctioned practice. Later, Robin Young, a resident of Orange Beach, describes planes spraying what she believes to be Corexit near the beach, and the smell that would follow the spraying. Similarly, Deepwater Horizon explosion survivor, Doug Brown, one of the main figures in *The Great Invisible*, recalls the night of the explosion as he smells the suit he was wearing. This evocation of senses other than sight echoes Peeples' (2013) narratives of Agent Orange: impacted individuals describe its taste and smell. These examples illustrate how, in the absence of a toxin's visibility, people rely on other senses to tell their stories.

Toxic Seafood, Sick Humans, and the Porosity of Bodies

Of the three films, *The Big Fix* features animals most prominently, but its focus differs from that discussed above. Rather than picturing living fish and turtles, it features animal bodies dead or explicitly understood as food. In one early scene, a flesh sample is taken from a large fish for testing, including smell testing, an officially sanctioned practice in the wake of the spill. The film then cuts to prepared restaurant food and talks about all the restaurants serving Gulf seafood. Soon after, Tickell finds dead crabs floating off a pier, then pulls one out and notes the black oil in its gills. A later scene shows an oil-blackened shrimp being peeled, followed by shots of oiled, dead fish and dead birds washed ashore. I argue that these films, in showing the penetrability of bodies by oil and Corexit, visually depict Alaimo's concept of trans-corporeality, "in which the human is always intermeshed with the more-than-human world, [and which] underlies the extent to which the substance of the human is ultimately inseparable from 'the environment.'" (2010, 2). Although Alaimo explains this concept in terms of human corporeality, it easily extends to all creatures. The films convey this concept with varying degrees of success, which hinges upon their use of imagery to depict toxic action.

The Great Invisible treats toxicity subtly and portrays animal bodies mainly in the context of their preparation for or during consumption. Although this portrayal may limit how the audience values animal life, it does implicitly convey trans-corporeality and links oil, ingestion, and toxicity: "Perhaps the most palpable trans-corporeal experience is food, since eating transforms plants and animals into human flesh" (Alaimo 2010, 12). This film features Frances Johnson, who works as an oyster shucker, and workers peeling crabs at Junior Barbour's Seafood, and in both cases, workers lament the decreased yields caused by the spill, which hinders their ability to prepare seafood for market and make a living. Soon after, Bryan St. Amant, a shrimper, pulls a shrimp from a freshly frozen bag, emphasizing the "black oily look." He then expresses concern about the use of dispersants and asks, "Why is this Gulf open?" In another scene, Latham Smith, an oil industry tugboat captain, and a group of people are peeling and eating boiled crawfish. As he eats, Smith reflects on contemporary desires for unrestrained mobility and use of lights and air-conditioning, all enabled by oil, and states, "The idea that civilization can last three hours without oil is ridiculous." Though crawfish are freshwater crustaceans that would not be directly impacted by the spill or Corexit aside from possible water column contamination, the act of eating accompanied by discussion of oil, in the context of the film's larger narrative in general and St. Amant's testimony in particular, offers an enthymematic argument about the entanglement of oil, the fisheries, ingestion, and ecosystems.

In their eco-rhetorical analysis of oil drilling films *Louisiana Story* and *Thunder Bay*, Robin L. Murray and Joseph K. Heumann describe,

> [The] interdependent relationship between the fishing and the oil industries that has taken center stage in media discussions after the Gulf of México Deepwater oil rig explosion and spill in April 2010, in spite of the 1989 *Exxon Valdez* disaster, which seemed to demonstrate that oil and wild nature don't mix. From a contemporary perspective the conflict between these two industries seems new, a product of the oil rig explosion and its aftermath. In fact, the conflict began with the first oil well in and around the Gulf in the second decade of the twentieth century, culminating with Kerr-McGee's successful well in 1947. Any conflict between the two industries however, has been whitewashed by media representations of their relationship, building toward [Vermont Public Radio host Debbie] Elliot's conclusion that they have learned to live together because oil brought money and jobs to the region. (2014, 161)

All three films point to this long history of the coexistence of the oil industry and the fisheries. Early in *The Big Fix*, Joel Waltzer, an environmental attorney, asserts that oil and fisheries are Louisiana culture. In both *The Great Invisible* and *Vanishing Pearls*, these two aspects of the culture are captured with shots of Morgan City, Louisiana's water tower (which features a shrimp wrapped around an offshore oil rig) beside oil infrastructure, and a view of oil infrastructure from a fishing boat, respectively. *Vanishing Pearls* conceptualizes marine animal bodies as seafood more as a symbol of a rich food culture that could be lost than in terms of their toxicity and potential toxic risks for humans. In this way, it differs from *The Big Fix* and aligns more with *The Great Invisible*. Early in *Vanishing Pearls*, Encalade is shown boiling crabs and describing the way in which, near the bayou, the "salt air gets in your food." The trans-corporeal movement of salt into the bodies of oysters is thus shown as crucial to Encalade's identification with place. The centrality of seafood to Louisiana culture is reiterated later as shots of the New Orleans oyster festival flicker on the screen, followed by an interview with

Leah Chase, the executive chef of the famous New Orleans restaurant Dooky Chase, who talks about New Orleans's unique access to fresh seafood.

The Big Fix emphasizes the dangers to eating and drinking after the spill. In one scene, Kindra Arnesen, a resident of deeply affected Venice, Louisiana, asks Ray Mabus, the Secretary of the Navy leading a public meeting, if he would feed his grandchildren shrimp from the Gulf; the question renders Mabus speechless. More visually persuasive perhaps is the scene discussed earlier in which fish is smell tested for oil and Corexit. As these tests are discussed, the image jumps to scenes of prepared Gulf seafood in New Orleans restaurants; this juxtaposition argues for the dangers of consuming contaminated seafood. This film uses a similar strategy to highlight how dispersants endanger the water column: as a graphic illustrates how Corexit breaks oil into tiny packets that living organisms can more easily absorb or consume, a person is shown drinking a glass of water.

The Big Fix explains explicitly how dispersants break apart oil, leaving small droplets that biological tissue more easily absorbs. The film also explains that dispersant was used directly at the wellhead, resulting in clouds of dispersed oil deep in the Gulf. Viewers learn that combining Corexit and oil is ultimately more toxic than oil alone, because Corexit breaks down cell walls and transports oil into organisms in a way that is otherwise impossible. Filmmakers use a cartoon to illustrate this invisible toxic action. *Vanishing Pearls* similarly uses animated graphics to show how the spill affected oyster beds. Encalade explains that freshwater was flushed into the Gulf to wash away the oil, but the mixture of fresh and saltwater led to widespread oyster death. An animated cartoon shows how oysters require a particular balance of salt and fresh water; when they take in too much freshwater, they swell and die. The point is made later that in such cases the oyster population generally rebounds and even flourishes, so the ongoing low harvests are attributable to Corexit rather than freshwater flushing. These animated representations successfully convey the trans-corporeal movement of oil and Corexit because they illustrate this movement on temporal and scalar levels otherwise inaccessible through the camera lens; that is, animated graphics detail toxic actions and the porosity of bodies in ways we can understand but cannot otherwise directly observe. In this sense, film is especially effective at communicating these invisible toxic harms and nefarious trans-corporeal agents.

Corexit's toxicity is a primary topic in *The Big Fix*. The film conveys this toxicity clearly through arguments involving human bodies. For example, it shows a clip of President Barack Obama visiting the Gulf Coast and swimming with his daughters. This gesture on President Obama's part is meant to argue through their bodily submergence in the water that things are fine in the Gulf: it is safe for swimming and, by extension, eating—although viewers ultimately learn that Obama and his daughters have swum in an unaffected bay. In contrast, Kindra Arnesen calls the spill and the subsequent use of Corexit, the "biggest toxic waste cover up in America's history," highlighting efforts to obscure the spilled oil's visibility using Corexit and adding to the exposé. In fact, the film explicitly links Corexit to Agent Orange, the defoliant used during the Vietnam War that compromised the health of both Vietnamese people and American soldiers. This comparison is especially apt; viewers learn in *The Great Invisible* that Kenneth Feinberg, the lawyer in charge of distributing settlements to victims of the BP spill, similarly dispersed claims to soldiers harmed by Agent Orange. My study resonates with Peeples's (2013) study of Agent Orange. She concludes that toxic imagery is embedded in cultural and national contexts and that these images acquire their meanings through narrative, findings that map onto my analysis.

The most vivid illustrations of trans-corporeality in these films occurs when they document sick human bodies. *The Big Fix*, in particular, reveals the dangers of exposure to spilled oil and Corexit. Early in the film, the Tickells ride on a boat in the oiled water, and the fisherman driving the boat chooses not to wear a mask, believing it too late for the mask to have any preventative effect. Later, in rapid succession, the viewer sees sores from Corexit exposure on arms, a torso, and legs. The film continues to make the case for the dangers of exposure when Rebecca Harrell Tickell, one of the filmmakers becomes sick with headaches, blisters, and rashes; the link between these symptoms and exposure to oil and Corexit are confirmed by a doctor, who has also experienced similar symptoms. As Peeples has argued, images of people affected by toxins allow for a certain kind of testimonial: "Especially important for environmental poisoning, images can give an opportunity for people to be involved in the social construction of a toxin, who might otherwise be excluded due to language, translation, marginalization, and/or reduced capacity" (2013, 206). Although Peeples specifically means photography, I believe her argument can be extended to documentary film. In the case of these BP spill documentaries, toxic images of victims, who are not necessarily limited by language but are marginalized and excluded by narratives of spectacle forwarded by media and cleanup forwarded by BP, can contribute to an alternative social construction of the spill as a specifically toxic event.

All three documentaries portray the illnesses caused by the spill. As noted, *The Big Fix* portrays the filmmaker's exposure-based illness, while both *The Great Invisible* and *Vanishing Pearls* foreground more the long-term mental trauma. In *The Great Invisible*, the viewer learns about rig explosion survivor, Stephen Stone's post-traumatic stress disorder, and Stone describes becoming frustrated about something one day, then realizing he is mindlessly cutting his own arm with scissors. The film also shows Brown, the other survivor featured in the film, taking numerous prescription drugs as a result of the explosion. The viewer learns in *Vanishing Pearls* that Stanley Encalade, Byron's brother, began taking sleeping pills because of the stress of the spill, and a prescription antidepressant is shown on his nightstand. Although these corporeal experiences are markedly different from those poisoned by Corexit, they do ultimately also show how an invisible illness spurred by oil, albeit in a somewhat different sense, makes itself visible.

These documentaries illustrate how oil and Corexit adhere to bodies, cross the porous boundaries of bodies, mark them, and cause sickness. Based on these examples, I argue that the toxic effects of spilled oil and dispersants on the bodies of humans and nonhumans documented in these films illustrate Alaimo's concept of trans-corporeality, with *The Big Fix* being most successful in this respect. I believe film is an especially useful medium to convey toxic action and trans-corporeality; as Jennifer Peeples has argued, toxicity often evades visual capture because it is fraught with uncertainty, and it often requires a collection of images to establish a narrative: "Single images are ill equipped to make the causal arguments necessary to establish contamination" (2013, 206). These films, I believe, succeed where documentary photography fails in establishing causal narratives, especially in their use of sick and oiled bodies. The interactions with oil described earlier could easily be captured in a photograph, but they cannot convey the trans-corporeal movement of toxins that film more easily visualizes, and, as I have shown, especially through animation. These affordances of the medium allow the filmmaker to convey time and show actions on large and small scales that are impossible through more static media.

Representing Race

Of the three films, only *Vanishing Pearls* deals directly with race, which is noteworthy, given the long history of racial tensions in the region. Early in the film, fishermen and locals explain that when the struggles after the spill of the Pointe à la Hache community were brought to the attention of the public, many people were shocked that black fishermen exist. The viewer then learns about the history of black fishermen in the area. Attorney and historian, Bill Quigley explains, "Historically [black fishermen] were like sharecroppers"; in other words, they were employed by white boat owners who demanded a percentage of their profits. Eventually, however, when the public fishing grounds opened, black fishermen could finally work independently. However, the white supremacist actions of those in power in the area continued to hinder their independence. Father and son, Leander and Chalin Perez held elected office in Plaquemines parish from 1920 to 1967 and 1967 to 1987, respectively, and both held racist views. In the film, the elder Perez states, "I know negroes [. . .] Fundamentally they are [sic] unmoral." It is in this context that voters in the area outlawed hand dredges (used predominantly by black fishermen), arguing that they harm the environment.

Where *Vanishing Pearls* explicitly highlights the history of race relations in the area, *The Great Invisible* treats race more subtly. Early in the film, white beachgoers are shown while predominantly black workers clean up in the background, although these shots are not narrated. Later, Roosevelt Harris, a volunteer for a church in Bayou La Batre, Alabama, who is black, is shown attempting to drop off food to a house with a large Confederate flag hanging over the porch. Harris elects to leave because he is afraid of the dog on the porch but later returns and speaks to the white resident about attending a BP claims meeting. In this second scene, the flag, though still visible, is tied up and less obvious. *The Great Invisible* also draws attention to the large population of Asian immigrants working in the seafood industry on the Gulf Coast, many of whom the viewer learns do not speak English and would have difficulty finding other work. In contrast, in *The Big Fix*, the racial dynamics of South Louisiana and the Gulf Coast are essentially erased. Though Louisiana is called an oil colony early in the film, and its long history of exploitation by the oil industry is examined, race is never mentioned, and all interviewees are white.

In the preface to an essay collection on Hurricane Katrina published shortly after the Deepwater Horizon disaster, Cedric Johnson contrasts the two disasters, stating that "Most of the workers who lost their lives were white, Republican, family men, and so were the many fishermen, bait shop owners, tour guides, hoteliers, and restaurateurs whose livelihoods were threatened by the disaster" (2011, vii). The relative invisibility of nonwhite Gulf Coast residents in *The Big Fix* seems to support Johnson's point; however, the Tickells' identification of their project with the Civil Rights movement at the end of the film is ironic in this light. While the spill did substantially impact the white population in Louisiana, which is significant when comparing it to Hurricane Katrina in the context of the dominant white culture of Louisiana and the south at large, Johnson's shortsighted comment is a result of the relative inattention given to the spill by scholars like Bullard, whose studies typically focus on black communities. However, such emphases in work about the spill ultimately minimize the experiences of affected nonwhite communities. However, the spill's impact on minority populations along the Gulf Coast is are represented, as indicated, in *Vanishing Pearls* and, to a lesser extent, in *The Great Invisible*.

Yet race is ultimately under examined across the three films; this fact becomes especially clear when the films are read from an environmental justice perspective. The environmental justice movement has been critiqued for assuming a static concept of race (Moore, Kosek, and Pandian 2003), but *Vanishing Pearls* successfully complicates this narrative by blurring racial categories and showing the mixed populations and culture in Pointe à la Hache. Early in the film, Byron Encalade, who identifies himself as black, speaks French in greeting other men in another boat as they cross paths. Later, we see that Encalade's father is white, although this is not discussed in the film's extended narrative on race in southern Louisiana. Future studies of the BP spill's impact on Gulf Coast communities should explore the complexities of race and its interaction with oil culture in the region by contextualizing the disaster in the region's history of environmental injustice from European colonialism to the current extractive petroleum-based economy.

Oil and Belief

Another subterranean theme across the films is the way in which the region's heavily Christian population interacts with petroculture. That religion and oil culture are entangled is particularly observable in *The Great Invisible*. Early in the film, an oil historian giving a tour of a rig to children in Morgan City states:

> One of the theories is that oil comes from fossils. [. . .] But is it a fossil fuel? You don't believe so? No, 'cause it's just a theory. I'll give you the theory I live by. God created the Earth to sustain life, so he gives us wind, he gives us solar, thermal, nuclear, coal, oil, gas, all of these things are created by God.

Religious belief is also present in the story of Roosevelt Harris, who does charity work through his Alabama church delivering food to those negatively impacted by the spill. Given Louisiana's historically Catholic culture, scenes linking Catholicism and oil are especially interesting. In one scene, a sign outside of a Catholic church is shown on screen, with a sign reading, "Running low on faith? Stop in here for a fill up." The metaphor is not discussed, but it is striking and suggests the centrality of oil in daily life for people in the region. Another intriguing scene captures the Shrimp and Petroleum festival mass, at which the people of Morgan City give thanks for the blessings of both the oil industry and the fisheries. This religious theme is far less explored in the other two films. *Vanishing Pearls* captures a prayer gathering led by a priest to mark the one-year anniversary of the spill, while *The Big Fix* only hints at religious belief by showing a sign reading "God Help Us" in the aftermath of the spill.

In the environmental justice movement, the importance of spirituality is notable. In a book on women leaders of the environmental movement in Louisiana, an entire section focuses on environmental health activism inspired by religious conviction (Frankland and Tucker, 2013).

Furthermore, as African American Studies scholar Valerie Ann Kaalund points out, "The spiritual dimension of the EJ movement can be seen in part in the ways meetings, roundtables, and summits usually open with prayer" (2004, 79–80). Clearly, then, the role of spirituality is important for a fully developed environmental justice analytical lens, although it is essentially absent in critical environmental justice scholarship. Future studies might explore the ways in which oil cultures conceptualize oil in a spiritual sense, for instance as a gift from God. Such understandings of oil render it an inert substance that is then easily removed from its causal links to health problems and climate change.

Conclusion

Rhetorical studies of the BP spill have been limited to textual analyses that fail to account for the full range of the spill's effects. I have argued that studies of the spill by rhetorical scholars would benefit from adopting an environmental justice lens for reading the spill and have applied such a lens to popular documentaries on the spill that capture this range of effects. Environmental justice thus illuminates the rhetoric of oil in the wake of the BP spill, bringing to light the ways in which oil impacts health, interacts with racial inequality, and informs religious belief. However, these latter two themes merit further examination in light of the spill and with respect to oil culture more generally. Future studies might extend to oil's impact on native populations like the residents of Isle de Jean Charles, Louisiana, who have been designated the first United States climate refugees and have been impacted by rapid erosion due to oil industry dredging (Davenport and Robertson 2016). In addition, greater study is warranted into the relationship between oil cultures and religious belief. Increased attention to environmental issues by Pope Francis may have some impact on the heavily Catholic culture of south Louisiana, and perhaps a closer look at religious discourse on climate can help us imagine new ways of conceptualizing oil that will allow for the cultural shifts necessary if we are to stop rapidly approaching the boundaries of a livable world.

Notes

1 In *Dumping in Dixie*, a foundational text of the movement first published in 1990, Robert Bullard points to the intertwined origins of the modern environmental, civil rights, and anti-war movements and highlights these movements' current conflicting values; forwards criticism of the environmental movement's inattention to justice issues; and points out that both environmentalists and industry had tension with social justice movements (Bullard 2000).

2 Rhetorical studies is here broadly understood as the allied scholars of English, Communication, Scientific and Technical Communication, Writing Studies, etc. with an interest in rhetoric.

References

Agyeman, Julian, Robert D. Bullard, and Bob Evans, eds. 2003. *Just Sustainabilities: Development in an Unequal World*. Cambridge: MIT Press.

Alaimo, Stacy. 2010. *Bodily Natures: Science, Environment, and the Material Self*. Bloomington: Indiana University Press.

Brown, Margaret. 2014. *The Great Invisible*. Brooklyn: Motto Pictures.

Bullard, Robert D. 2000. *Dumping in Dixie: Race, Class, and Environmental Quality*. 3rd ed. Boulder: Westview Press.

Davenport, Coral, and Campbell Robertson. 2016. "Resettling the First American 'Climate Refugees.'" *The New York Times*, May 3, 2016. www.nytimes.com/2016/05/03/us/resettling-the-first-american-climate-refugees.html.

Dobrin, Sidney I., and Sean Morey. 2009. *Ecosee: Image, Rhetoric, Nature*. Albany: SUNY Press.

Frankland, Peggy, and Susan Tucker. 2013. *Women Pioneers of the Louisiana Environmental Movement*. Jackson: University Press of Mississippi.

Frost, Erin A. 2013. "Transcultural Risk Communication on Dauphin Island: An Analysis of Ironically Located Responses to the Deepwater Horizon Disaster." *Technical Communication Quarterly* 22 (1): 50–66. doi:10.1080/10572252.2013.726483.

Jefferson, Nailah. 2014. *Vanishing Pearls*. Los Angeles: African-American Film Festival Releasing Movement.

Johnson, Cedric. 2011. "Preface: 'Obama's Katrina'." In *The Neoliberal Deluge: Hurricane Katrina, Late Capitalism, and the Remaking of New Orleans*, edited by Cedric Johnson, vii–xv. Minneapolis: University of Minnesota Press.

Kaalund, Valerie Ann. 2004. "Witness to Truth: Black Women Heeding the Call for Environmental Justice." In *New Perspectives on Environmental Justice: Gender, Sexuality, and Activism*, edited by Rachel Stein. New Brunswick: Rutgers University Press.

LeMenager, Stephanie. 2014. *Living Oil: Petroleum Culture in the American Century*. New York: Oxford University Press.

Monani, Salma. 2011. "At the Intersections of Ecosee and Just Sustainability: New Directions for Communication Theory and Practice." *Environmental Communication* 5 (2): 141–145. doi:10.1080/17524032.2011.562651.

Moore, Donald S., Jake Kosek, and Anand Pandian, eds. 2003. *Race, Nature, and the Politics of Difference*. Durham: Duke University Press.

Murray, Robin L., and Joseph K. Heumann. 2014. *Film & Everyday Eco-Disasters*. Lincoln: University of Nebraska Press.

Peeples, Jennifer. 2013. "Imaging Toxins." *Environmental Communication* 7 (2): 191–210. doi:10.1080/17524032.2013.775172.

Pezzullo, Phaedra C. 2007. *Toxic Tourism: Rhetorics of Pollution, Travel, and Environmental Justice*. Tuscaloosa: University of Alabama Press.

Pezzullo, Phaedra C. 2016. "Unearthing the Marvelous: Environmental Imprints on Rhetorical Criticism." *Review of Communication* 16 (1): 25–42. doi:10.1080/15358593.2016.1183874.

Tickell, Joshua, and Rebecca Harrell Tickell. 2011. *The Big Fix*. Bigstar.TV.

Wickman, Chad. 2014. "Rhetorical Framing in Corporate Press Releases: The Case of British Petroleum and the Gulf Oil Spill." *Environmental Communication* 8 (1): 3–20. doi:10.1080/17524032.2013.816329.

5 When Water Meets Oil

Rupturing Rhetoric and Reality in Energy Policy and Climate Science

Josh Wodak

To explore physical and symbolic ruptures emanating from oil, I trace the journey of this spectral substance from its unearthing in the Gulf of México, back to the dawn of the Space Program, into outer space, to crash back into the sea as military-industrial detritus that is then used to form Artificial Reefs. This spatial trajectory is mapped to the temporal trajectory of climate science and energy policy over Obama's presidential tenure, given the stark policy contrast between his first and second terms. Through recourse to key speeches, events, campaigns, and policy documents about climate change, climate science, and energy policy, I examine how ruptures challenge energy policy that simultaneously facilitates and decimates the existence of marine ecosystems in the Gulf.

Punctuated Equilibrium

> Oil, we learned in cooking class, does not mix well with water. The fish, sea animals and plants had already learned this lesson. The massive outpour of gas and oil destroyed the harmony of life in the water. (Landau, 2010)

The journalist Saul Landau's high school recollection that water and oil do not "mix well" appears to be an uncontestable reality. After all, you can perform the addition of one to the other before your own eyes. Mix and repeat; it will execute the same result, time and again. Meanwhile each execution begets two options for the comingled detritus: disposal, by pouring down the drain, or reuse, by boiling or freezing to disaggregate water from oil. Disposal transfers the detritus into a larger body of water (to an ocean, via the drain). Reuse requires additional energy intensive resources powered by fossil fuels as mainstay or catalyst (to source, produce, and maintain "renewable" energy).

The conflict created when water meets oil, and how to remedy their meeting, is a microcosm of contestations between rhetoric and reality that pertain equally to energy policy and climate science. In the discourse of energy policy and climate science, rhetoric is commonly posited as being discourse that is adversarial to "reality"—or what proponents advocate as commonsense human experience. In *Scientists as Prophets: A Rhetorical Genealogy*, Lynda Walsh (2013) traces the role of rhetoric in contestations between what reality (read: science) *is* versus what *ought to* be done about it (read: policy). Tracing the historical trajectory through to contemporary climate science, Walsh argues that contestations around what constitutes "reality" depend largely on whether an actor frames rhetoric as being opposed to reality. Consequently, interrogating these muddied waters requires greater fidelity to how the different actors in the drama use rhetoric.

Articulating what this fidelity would require in "The Visual Rhetoric of Climate Change," Walsh defines rhetoric as "the art of communicating in order to build and maintain just polities (communities that must reason together to stay together)." This art of persuasive argumentation in contestations between energy policy and climate science is central to how rhetoric "thus forms a bridge between the ideals of philosophy and the realities of politics." In the specific context of climate science, Walsh (2015, 61) argues for increased understanding of how politicians, scientists, policy analysts use rhetoric since "someone's values must always be attached to data before policy can be made."

Landau, a senior scholar at the Institute for Policy Studies, represents the compartmentalization of reality and rhetoric. His recollection above is from his op-ed response three months after the 2010 Deepwater Horizon spill in the Gulf of México. *The Rhetoric-Reality Gulf* byline reads: "Network media mavens evoke disaster about the Gulf's fate, while the gulf between reality and rhetoric grows accordingly." Here "gulf" is both the specific place of the Gulf of México and a trope for the divergence between the "rhetoric" of Obama's pro-oil policy and the biophysical "reality" in which "the massive outpour of gas and oil destroyed the harmony of life in the water" of the Gulf.

However, Landau's reality of ecosystem degradation and a commensurate energy policy contradicts contending notions of "reality" and energy policy so derived. Writing one week after the 2013 pipeline rupture and oil spill in Mayflower, Arkansas, Brigham McCown, a former U.S. energy transportation safety chief, argued in favor of the Obama administration's oil pipeline safety record, on the basis that the "development of Keystone XL will actually help to reduce the likelihood of spills in the future" (2013). This line of reasoning was pivotal for his *Forbes* op-ed *Pipeline Infrastructure: Rhetoric v. Reality*, in response to "last week's incident in Mayflower, Ark." McCown admonished "arguments against the construction of Keystone XL" which he decried as depending "almost completely on ideological rhetoric that has been consistently addressed and disproven by both historical operating statistics and forward-looking analyses by bodies ranging from the State Department to the Department of Energy."

Even though Landau and McCown are both responding to U.S. oil spills, the diametrically opposed responses highlight the entrenchment of contestations as to what is the 'reality' of U.S. oil production and distribution, and which actors are 'misusing' rhetoric to advocate for opposing energy policy. The schism reveals the ongoing disconnection between facts/values and is/ought in David Hume's Guillotine dilemmas. In Landau's three sentences above, he proceeds that human understanding of the adverse relationship between water and oil is achieved through scientific experimentation; that the more-than-human world "already" innately understood this; and that the human failure to keep incompatible entities separate (gas into the atmosphere, oil into the oceans) has detrimentally affected the more-than-human world. Yet for Walsh, a surfeit of data affirming any of these three claims, let alone any causal relationship between them, would require analysis of relevant actors' values before we could determine what policy would be commensurate with the data itself.

Does this then mean "philosophically" upholding the necessity of an ideal—whether ensuring water and oil do not meet, or energy policy is commensurate with climate science—which does not hold up in practice? How then do different actors—politicians, scientists, policy analysts—use rhetoric to bridge this ideal-real schism in relation to oil in the United States? Oil provides an apposite means by which to probe these questions because its physical and symbolic properties bring "ideals of philosophy and the realities of politics" (Walsh, 2015, 61) into sharp relief. For instance, during the eight years of his Presidency, Obama extolled the expansion of domestic oil production, which increased 70% over this time frame. During this time frame, he both maintained the necessity of mitigating climate change while simultaneously advocating for increased domestic oil production.

The cognitive dissonance of Obama's policy becomes most apparent when ruptures of oil and its associated infrastructure present facts and an evidential *is*. Ruptures of such magnitude as Deepwater Horizon may then also affect the less apparent *is* surrounding climate change, being largely out of sight, out of mind in causal relation to energy policy and hence the subject of much more entranced contestations. Ruptures of oil infrastructure may call into question the less apparent biophysical consequences of combusting oil itself, wherein the carbonic acid formed when atmospheric carbon dioxide meets water alters the chemistry of the atmosphere and oceans. Then, the full extent to which oil "does not mix well with water" becomes readily apparent for Landau's proxies of "fish, sea animals and plants." As Ruth Salvaggio (2014, 386) argues, "oil itself remains a spectral substance – until something ruptures and it all comes pouring out," such as Landau's offshore rig or McCown's onshore pipeline.

By affecting values and the *ought*, ruptures also bring the apparent impasse between energy policy and climate science into sharp relief. For Timothy Morton (2012), rupturing is central to the notion of what is and is not, 'reality.' He posits that "the current ecological disaster [of climate change], which we only know about because of very sophisticated interdisciplinary science, has torn a giant hole in the fabric of our understanding" (14). Consequently, the extent of the ecological disaster made known by climate science has produced a "tear in the real" (14). Morton maintains that such symbolic ruptures concern not only facts and *is* but also values. These ruptures create Landau's "gulf" between energy policy and climate science. For even without physical ruptures of oil rigs or pipelines, invisible atmospheric and oceanic changes in chemistry as a result of oil combustion have revealed the extent of another gulf—between energy policy and the science behind climate change.

This chapter explores the potential for the act of rupturing—both physical and symbolic—to interrupt the impasse between climate science and energy policy, that is, between facts/values and is/ought. My intention allies with Philip Wander and Dennis Jaehne (2000, 211) in *Prospects for 'A Rhetoric of Science,'* where they join "a debate which is pregnant with the future not of a field of study but of life on the planet." I argue that a symbolic rupture has been created, a "giant hole in the fabric of our understanding," through the context of Landau's "Gulf" as specific place and "gulf" as a trope representing the divergence between rhetoric/discourse and biophysical reality.

Rupturing by way of Morton's "tear in the real" is also relevant to the global anthropogenic perturbation of the more-than-human world. No apparent remedy exists to 'unmix' water from oil when we consider the actual size of drain needed for disposal or the energy required to recycle these quantities. So, too, have the historical legacies of energy and climate policies created an unwieldy concoction that resists any restorative *ought* for anthromes. In fact, Landau's notion that the "massive outpour of gas and oil destroyed the harmony of life in the water" actually contradicts the way in which water and oil have come to be mixed in the Gulf. Instead the Gulf's marine ecosystems have come to depend overwhelmingly on oil rigs and pipelines. So, while in the main "fish, sea animals and plants [may have] already learned" that water and oil do not "mix well," those in the Gulf have learned to thrive on the artificial life support structures of oil rigs and pipelines.

To explore physical and symbolic ruptures emanating from oil, I trace the journey of this spectral substance from its unearthing in the Gulf of México, back to the dawn of the Space Program, into outer space, to crash back into the sea as military-industrial detritus that is then used to form artificial reefs. This spatial trajectory is mapped to the temporal trajectory of climate science and energy policy over Obama's presidential tenure, given the stark contrast in policy between his first and second terms. Using speeches, filmed events, and policy documents related to climate change, climate science, and energy policy, I analyze how physical and symbolic ruptures challenge energy policy to simultaneously facilitate and decimate marine ecosystems in the Gulf. Physical ruptures, such as infrastructure for extracting oil on the Gulf floor, facilitate first unintentionally and now intentionally by serving as artificial reef habitats. They also decimate these ecosystems as oil combustion increases ocean warming and acidification at orders of magnitude faster than that to which marine organisms can adapt. The fact that these physical ruptures simultaneously facilitate and hinder marine ecosystems creates symbolic ruptures.

I examine how Obama's strategy of promoting oil as innocuous and necessary despite incontrovertible evidence of climate change was undermined by the increasing frequency and intensity of 'natural' and human-caused disasters. These disasters physically ruptured U.S. oil production and infrastructure and symbolically undermined policy that extolled oil production. I connect physical and symbolic ruptures through the fact that greenhouse gas emissions are increasingly influencing the frequency, severity, and distribution of extreme weather events. As Connie Hedegaard (2012), former European Commissioner for Climate Action, intoned one month before Hurricane Sandy: "Get used to 'extreme' weather, it's the new normal." Both Hedegaard's notion of "normal" weather and Landau's notion of "harmony of life in the water" have been punctuated. To explain how these punctuations constitute physical and symbolic ruptures, I examine how scientific framing formulates energy policy as commensurate with climate science by invoking rhetoric (read: policy) as adversarial to reality (read: climate science).

Climate Science: The Art of the Impossible

It is November 6, 2012 at the University of Bristol. The Cabot Institute, the University's cross-disciplinary research institute for twenty-first century environmental challenges, is holding its annual lecture as part of the University's Festival of Social Sciences and Law. The auditorium is filled to capacity, there to hear from Professor Kevin Anderson, one of the world's leading climate scientists. Anderson's career trajectory has shifted from industry, including over a decade on oil rigs in petrochemical engineering, to academia, having been Director of the UK's Tyndall Centre for Climate Change Research, one of the foremost climate change research institutes in the world, of which he is presently Deputy Director. He has also purposefully strayed outside of climate science and into the relationship between climate change and the politics and policy of energy, as Professor of Energy and Climate Change in the School of Mechanical, Aeronautical and Civil Engineering at the University of

Manchester. His straying outside of domains and disciplines extends beyond the normative role played by scientists and academics and into working in and against UK government commissions around climate and energy policy. This level of eclecticism appears to have fueled the capacity interest in his lecture.

The lecture title indicates the tenor and tone of Anderson's firebrand rhetorical style: "Real Clothes for the Emperor: Facing the Challenges of Climate Change." He walks into the room, and opens with a provocation:

> I think the Emperor's streaking in front of us naked while most of us are saying "aren't they beautifully attired", including many scientists. I think actually if you stand up and say that the Climate Change Emperor is naked most people will shut you down. They do not want to hear that, however obvious it may be.

Over the following hour, Anderson repeatedly invokes Hans Christian Andersen's fable (1837), *The Emperor's New Clothes*, to argue that an extensive gulf exists between the speed of anthropogenically induced biophysical change and the mitigation modeling and targets promoted by such climate science organizations as the Intergovernmental Panel on Climate Change (IPCC). For Anderson, reality and rhetoric are adversaries. Yet his umbrage is not with sceptics, but rather with mainstream modeling and the energy policy that is mapped to it. He posits such orthodoxy as constituting rhetoric in the pejorative sense, with slides titled "Stern vs. Reality" that position the foremost modeling of the economic impacts of climate change as being opposed to reality. Using a tone that is both conversational and confrontational, he critiques the many graphs of past, present, and projected warming rates per emission rates, pointing out perceived discrepancies, for example, "That's what we have to do for 2° Celsius and that's the void between. Here we have rhetoric; here's some reality."

Anderson critiques not only IPCC climate science but also its counterpart, policy forming organizations including the UN Framework Convention on Climate Change (UNFCCC). He maintains that these organizations' claims that human action can successfully limit anthropogenic climate change to 2° mean surface temperature increase above pre-industrial levels by 2100 resemble the consensual delusion of the Naked Emperor's subjects in the fairy tale. Anderson and his similarly outspoken colleagues Alice Bows-Larkin (Anderson and Bows, 2011) and James Hansen (2013) contend that even a 2° increase carries catastrophic consequences and that temperatures will probably increase orders of magnitude higher than 2°. Through a variety of media, Anderson emphasizes that the IPCC and UNFCCC are significantly downplaying forecasts that set the trajectory toward a 6° increase by 2100 (Anderson and Bows, 2011).

For Anderson, Bows-Larkin, and Hansen, rhetoric and reality are as easily distinguished as clear water is from opaque oil. Landau's "gulf" is Anderson's "void"; the latter maintains that "a prerequisite of responding to the climate challenge is exposing the void between the rhetoric and the reality around efforts to reduce emissions (mitigation)" (Anderson and Bows, 2011, 18). Anderson called for a collective 'ah ha!' that acknowledges that the Emperor has been naked all along, that is, a rupture sufficient to expose this void. He argues against the international energy policy "delusion that climate change can be addressed adequately through rhetoric, financial fine-tuning and piecemeal incrementalism" (2012).

Anderson concluded his "Real Clothes" lecture with a quote by Brazilian philosopher and politician, Roberto Mangabeira Unger (cited in Anderson, 2012): "At every level the greatest obstacle to transforming the world is that we lack the clarity and imagination to conceive that it could be different." After a flurry of questions for Anderson, the lecture ended with everyone filing out into the unseasonably warm winter night at 10°, exactly 2° above the Bristol average for that time of year (Bristol Airport, 2012). Interestingly, while Anderson was on stage quoting a Brazilian politician to conclude, the U.S. was choosing between two other politicians, Barack Obama and Mitt Romney, for the presidency.

Political Rhetoric: The Art of the Possible

A distinguishing property of the U.S. 2012 election was the fact that the Democrat and Republican campaigns were the first in a generation to not mention "climate change" or "global warming" in any campaign or presidential debate. This starkly contrasted earlier presidents who prominently included the topic, for example, Bill Clinton (1994, 469) declaring on Earth Day 1993 that "unless we act now, we face a future in which the sun may scorch us, not warm us; where the change of season may take on a dreadful new meaning." However, presidential candidates who pledged to adhere to energy-climate limits have historically fared badly with American voters. In *Voting for American Energy: Elections, Oil, and US Culture*, Georgiana Banita (2015, 101) recounts Jimmy Carter's failure, as a result, to win a second term in 1980.

Nevertheless, its absence in the 2012 campaign was frequently discussed in news reports outside of the United States at the time (see Broder, 2012; Walsh, 2012; Week, 2012), with one headline in *The Guardian* characterizing the silence as *US election 2012: Romney and Obama avoid the climate change elephant* (Hickman, 2012). Then Hurricane Sandy hit the U.S. Atlantic coast a week before the election, prompting U.S. news media to finally acknowledge "the elephant" in the room. Three days before the election, CNN, for example, mentioned the gap in campaign discussion: *Sandy reminds us of climate change and other forgotten campaign issues* (Merica, 2012). Neither of the presidential candidates, however, acknowledged climate change as a viable discussion topic, despite Sandy's physical rupture of the campaign.

At the same time, Hurricane Sandy still constituted a symbolic rupture with sufficient potential to bring into stark relief the gulf between U.S. energy policy and climate science. Although the hurricane has been characterized as "natural," research since the disaster suggests anthropogenic influences may have exacerbated the storm's severity. Historically, the Northern Polar Jet Stream sees phenomena such as a Polar Vortext confined to Arctic regions. However, anthropogenic climate change has destabilized global climate systems (Cohen et al., 2014), including shifting the northern polar jet stream south into the narrow longitudinal range between 40° and 50° North—that is, Europe and the United States (Francis and Vavrus, 2012, 2015), bringing "Arctic" weather with it. In the case of Sandy, Greene et al. (2013) have argued that anthropogenically influenced perturbations in the Northern Polar Jet Stream were responsible for the intensity and distribution of Sandy along the Atlantic coastline of North America.

The Sky Is the Limit: "All-of-the-Above Energy Strategy"

In addition to remaining silent on climate change, Obama chose a slogan that, while alluding to renewable energy, ultimately emphasized oil and its associated infrastructure. On March 22, 2012, exactly seven months before Sandy, Obama gave a re-election speech in Oklahoma, the second most tornado prone state in the United States, entitled "Remarks by the President on American-Made Energy." Obama's presentation outlined what he called his "all-of-the-above energy strategy," the adjective "above" suggesting renewable energy sources such as wind, solar, and hydroelectric, which are *above* ground. However, he delivered this speech against the backdrop of *above*-ground oil pipelines. And while renewable energy might seem to fall within the "all," Obama's speech revealed that he was referring chiefly to fossil-fueled energy (reinforced by the visible pipeline behind him). A slogan that aligned with his actual energy policy would be "mostly-from-the-below-and-a-little-bit-from-the-above energy strategy."

Once fossil fuels have been extracted, they are processed above ground, similar to the already above- ground renewable energy. Obama's podium was theatrically framed by this below-to-above ground metamorphosis. The rhetorical context and arrangement of the above-ground pipelines running behind and dwarfing his podium were not just for effect (McCabe, 2012). Cushing Pipe Yard in Cushing, Oklahoma, is one of the world's largest crude oil storage facilities. So much so that it proclaims itself to be the "Pipeline Crossroads of the World." While Cushing's global crossroad credentials are more symbolic than actual, "if the American oil industry has a spiritual capital, Cushing is it" (Walsh, 2012); it is the physical crossroad for domestic oil pipelines, holding between 5% and 10% of domestic oil per day. Obama used this occasion to declare he would "cut through the red tape" and "break through the bureaucratic hurdles" to expedite construction of the Keystone Pipeline System between Cushing and the Gulf of México at Port Arthur, 550 km west of the Deepwater Horizon spill site two years earlier. Obama (2012) extolled his administration's oil-centric policy by celebrating having "quadrupled the number of operating rigs to a record high" such that "we've added enough new oil and gas pipeline to encircle the earth and then some."

Two years earlier, on March 31, 2010, Obama had framed his pro-oil policy for an altogether different demographic. For the Andrews Air Force Base audience, he framed energy around security. The energy policy he announced would end a long-standing moratorium on new offshore oil and gas exploration in Alaska and the Gulf of México, which would now be open for substantially increased exploration and production. The rationale for so doing encapsulates the energy policy "delusion" that Anderson critiques, where "the bottom line" for Obama is that

> given our energy needs, in order to sustain economic growth and produce jobs and keep our businesses competitive, we're going to need to harness traditional sources of fuel even as we ramp up production of new sources of renewable, homegrown energy. (CNN Wire Staff, 2010)

Such pro-oil expansion occurred despite a significant increase in 'natural' and human-caused ruptures in oil infrastructure. Three weeks later, on April 20, 2010, the Deepwater spill ruptured the invisibility of oil once again, similar to how Sandy ruptured the innocuousness of climate change in the 2012 election campaign. In response, new and expansion of existing Gulf of México production was suspended until 2017.

Despite postponing oil policy expansion in response to Deepwater, the "natural" disasters of hurricanes such as Katrina, Ike, and Ivan rendered visible damage to existing oil infrastructure at the periphery of U.S. ocean borders. If a tree falls in the woods, the question arises as to whether it makes a sound. If 4,500 oil rigs in the Gulf of México are increasingly at risk of rupturing due to hurricanes, the question raised will reverberate across the U.S. mainland. That question is still largely in the abstract, due to policies that preemptively shut down production before storms reach the rigs. In fact, human-caused oil ruptures have already reverberated across the mainland. Three months after the Deepwater Horizon spill, a pipeline rupture on the Kalamazoo River, Michigan, in July 2010 created the largest land spill in U.S. history.

Event Horizon: "That's What We're Going to be Shooting For"

After winning his second presidential term in 2012, Obama foregrounded climate change and renewable energy as central to his administration. The extent of the difference in climate change and energy policy between his first and second terms was exemplified three years to the day since the 2012 U.S. election, in rejecting the Keystone XL pipeline extension. Keystone XL would have opened up the Alberta tar sands, one of the largest remaining, and dirtiest, fossil fuel reserves in the world, to the world, by connecting it to Cushing, the "Pipeline Crossroads of the World." Yet Obama's substantially revised rhetoric about his oil policy was more poignantly communicated through two seemingly unrelated domains: anecdotes about his professed love of coral reefs and analogies with the U.S. Space Program as it relates to climate and energy policy.

These two anecdotes and analogies were presented in an interview of Sir David Attenborough conducted by Obama (Attenborough and Obama, 2015), three months before he announced his rejection of Keystone XL. Their exchange at the White House on May 8, 2015, Attenborough's 89th birthday, was for a BBC interview about "the future of the planet, their passion for nature and what can be done to protect it." Here Attenborough takes on an air of the elder statesman, resigned to the fact that the natural world he has devoted his life to has become configured by whether the geopolitics of international energy policy, such as between the United States and China, will tip the scales from fossil fueled to renewable energy:

ATTENBOROUGH: What concerns me is that when we're sitting in Europe, we see what you did by saying, "We're going to put a man on the moon in 10 years." Supposing you said in 10 years the United States will organize the world, and energize the world to find a solution, to find a way of producing energy with no problems. That is to say, exploiting sunshine to a degree and finding ways of storing electricity. Because if you did that, so much would be, some problems would be solved.

OBAMA: Right, well that's what we're going to be shooting for. I mean we've made enormous investments. We doubled our investment in clean energy here in the United States. I just last year [2014] came back from China with an agreement from the Chinese to work with us on reducing emissions, but we're not moving as fast as we need to and part of what I know from watching your programs and all the great work you've done, is that you know these ecosystems are all inter-connected and that if just one country is doing the right thing but other countries are not, then we're not going to solve the problem. We're going to have to have a global solution to this. (Attenborough, 2015)

On the way to the White House Attenborough makes a telephone call that is filmed for the documentary of the interview. While the viewer only hears Attenborough's side of the conversation, it is possible to read between the lines to infer how he has an altogether different strategy for bringing U.S. energy policy in line with climate science. Attenborough's side of the telephone call reads almost like a script for a *Dr. Strangelove*-esque black comedy:

> SIR DAVID ATTENBOROUGH: [on mobile phone] Hello Martin. I'm in Washington and although this may sound rather fanciful, I'm just about to be interviewed by the President of the United States about conservation. I rang to ask whether in fact it was possible for me to use material from the report? Yeah, very good. Then I will . . . but I just didn't want to do it without referring to you or to Richard. Oh really? You are in the Vatican? And what did the Pope say about world population? Oh really . . . oh well that's something. . . indeed. (Attenborough, 2015)

The Martin and Richard referred to are Lord Martin Rees, former President of the UK Royal Society, and Lord Richard Layard, an economist at the London School of Economics. The report referred to, *A Global Apollo Programme to Combat Climate Change*, was launched four weeks later. In his interview with Obama, Attenborough alludes to the broad remit of the report, which was not public knowledge at the time.

Attenborough draws the analogy between the Space Race and energy policy, in reference to the argument of the *Global Apollo Programme*. The report proposes that the aspiration, collegiality, duration, and level of funding that the United States committed to the Space Race could can be applied to energy policy. The report authors, David et al. (2015) are exemplary economists and scientists, many of whose previous expertise did not pertain to energy policy or climate science. Though, like Anderson, such scholars have increasingly turned their work toward the *ought* (energy policy) commensurate with the *is* (climate science). Converting the 10-year budget of the Apollo program to contemporary figures, they argue that $150 billion of publicly funded research over the course of a decade would make renewable energy cheaper in its entirety than fossil-fueled energy. The advocacy is for a structured rupturing of the prevailing mentality surrounding energy policy, for instance, by establishing policy for a 10-year goal, irrespective of the vicissitudes of electoral cycles throughout.

Thirty-six-year-old Attenborough partook of the Europe-wide adulation when the then-president John F. Kennedy outlined his 10-year vision to put a person on the moon in his "We choose to go to the moon" speech on September 12, 1962. Fifty-three years later, Attenborough compares that adulation he felt with Europe then and now being a spectator, watching and waiting for a vision of equivalent grandeur from the current U.S. president to "energize the world." Attenborough here presents his own vision of Unger's adage that it is the lack of "clarity and imagination to conceive" the world to be different that is "the greatest obstacle to transforming the world" (cited in Anderson, 2012). However, he goes further, using Obama as a metonym for the presidents responsible for the space race: Kennedy (1961–1963), and his successor, Lyndon Johnson (1963–1969). In response to Attenborough's compliment that "we see what you did by saying, 'We're going to put a man on the moon in 10 years'" (Attenborough and Obama, 2015), Obama counters, "Well, that's what we're going to be shooting for," despite having been one year of age when Kennedy gave his "We choose to go to the moon" speech. Here Obama employs an additional metaphor, from the phrase "shoot for the stars," where the moon metonymically stands for "stellar success." Rather than celebrate the volume of oil pipe production that could encircle the earth, as he had done in 2012, here Obama, at Attenborough's suggestion, frames climate change in the grand narrative of the spatial, temporal, and financial scale of the U.S. Space Program.

Deepwater Horizon: Down to (underwater) Earth

The extent of what Anderson (2012) terms the "scale of the challenge that we now face" brought Obama and Attenborough together for their 2015 interview. The effect of fossil-fueled energy combustion on marine ecosystems was a major catalyst for their shared advocacy about redirecting our gaze from the sky to the underwater realm, given the ocean is absorbing 93% of the heat generated from fossil-fueled energy production, with only 2% being absorbed by the atmosphere (Intergovernmental Panel on Climate Change, 2013). Recalling how Anderson's "Real Clothes" lecture drew on a children's fairy tale and its associations with one's childhood, Obama also drew from his own childhood experiences in his interview with Attenborough, in his case of exploring tropical reefs around his Hawaiian home. He recounts how, "since I grew up in Hawaii . . . I have a natural affinity for the outdoors and an appreciation" for underwater swimming in coral reefs. Following an exchange where Attenborough recounts that his favorite experience and place in the world is diving on the Great Barrier Reef, the two ruminate on the conservation strategies for mitigating marine ecosystem degradation:

ATTENBOROUGH: The real problem on the reef is the global one which is what is happening with the increase in acidification and the rise in the ocean temperature and the Australians have done research on coral now and they know for sure it will kill [Great Barrier Reef] coral.

OBAMA: Right.

ATTENBOROUGH: It will kill the species of coral and what they're concerned about now, is I mean that seems almost inevitable. What it seems now is can they, can they find the right species to maintain the reef's population?

OBAMA: Right, so really there's a mitigation strategy that they're trying to come up with but what we're seeing is global trends that depend on the entire world working together. (Attenborough and Obama, 2015)

Obama's "mitigation strategy," or what Attenborough euphemistically terms finding "the right species to maintain the reef's population," entails the use of "assisted evolution" (Oppen et al., 2015) and synthetic biology to increase corals' tolerance thresholds relative to the rapidity of biophysical changes. Obama and Attenborough here reveal a further cognitive dissonance: between professed biophilia for "nature" while seeking to design "nature" that can tolerate the inhospitable biophysical conditions occasioned through fossil fuel combustion. In the same sentence, Obama frames this "mitigation strategy" in the context of energy policy produced by the "the entire world working together." The "global trends" Obama refers to concern how initiatives the United States previously dominated, including the Space Race and the artificial reef program, are now emerging across the globe as endeavors to go into space and mine underwater are rapidly taken up by new public and private programs.

Rockets to Reefs: When Oil Meets Water

NASA booster rockets fired into space from Cape Canaveral come back down to Earth in the so-called Space Coast off Florida. The return of spaceship components is a poignant reminder that what goes up must come down, whether an oil rig or space debris. The vast majority of such components are reused, by being recovered from where they fall into the Space Coast. One of the few exceptions to this came in 1996, when a solid rocket booster was deliberately sunk 35 km off the Space Coast, to create an artificial reef. It forms one of more than 600 artificial reefs in Florida alone, with half of these created since 1990.

The Space Race, including key infrastructure, is extensively entwined with oil production in the Gulf of México and the National Artificial Reef Program. The former relationship stems from the sheer energy intensity used in space exploration, given booster rockets are repositories for petroleum, including that extracted from the Gulf of México. The latter relationship stems from the increasing conversion of Apollo Space Program infrastructure into artificial reefs. This began with an oil rig that was repurposed in 1958 to be used as a space launch tower. In 1984, the tower was declared a National Historic Landmark. Two years later, it was in such disrepair that the Patrick Air Force Base responsible for the tower proposed to sell it to a private group who would convert it into an artificial reef next to Cape Canaveral (Rasche, 1986). In the same cape in 1989, a series of rocket-launching structures were converted into another artificial reef, followed by sections from *Titan II* being converted in 1999 and rocket launch towers in 2012. Following cessation of the U.S. manned Space Program in 2011, it appeared that U.S. space endeavors were now largely symbolic, culminating in the proposed sale of three massive mobile launch platforms in 2013. NASA stated they were interested in proposals that would repurpose the structures in ways that would "benefit the general public, the environment, or entities not associated with the space industry (e.g., museum exhibit(s), artificial reef(s), oil rig structure, etc.)" (Gray, 2013). The intended repurposing of platforms indicates the increasing relationship between Space Program equipment, oil infrastructure, and artificial reefs. In mirror image to the 1958 repurposing of an oil rig to become a space launch tower, in 2013 NASA indicated an intention to repurpose Space Program equipment into "artificial reef(s), oil rig structure"—with minimal distinction between rocket, reef, and rig.

Despite the first artificial reef, created in Florida in 1979, being a converted oil rig, only three reefs from rigs have since been constructed in Florida. The vast majority have been made in the Gulf of México, which holds the largest number and biggest network of rigs in the world. There, water meets oil *en masse* in artificial reefs. This meeting takes place through decommissioned oil rigs that are refashioned as catalysts for artificial reefs through the U.S. Government Rigs to Reefs program, initiated in 1985, the premise being that rigs provide a by-product of artificial reefs during their active life span, and that the above-ground metallic structure may expand upon the existing 'unintentional' artificial reef, by being cut up and strategically placed underwater. In the Gulf of México, an extensive marine ecosystem now relies on a network of 4,500 oil production platforms, 500 of which have been decommissioned and converted into intentional artificial reefs, collectively constituting what the U.S. Department of the Interior declares is "the world's largest artificial reef complex" (Dauterive, 2000).

Obama's energy policy further entwined water with oil in the Gulf of México, expanding intentional artificial reefs by encouraging increased conversion of decommissioned rigs into reefs. Ruptures, such as the Deepwater Horizon spill, prefigured the expansion of the artificial reef network, wherein his administration introduced an Idle Iron regulation in 2010 that required all nonproducing rigs to be removed or converted into artificial reefs. This policy reform effectively encouraged rig conversion over removal, by making conversion significantly less expensive for rig owners/operators. In 2013, the Bureau of Safety and Environmental Enforcement changed the removal and construction policy for decommissioned rigs. Their suite of measures made rig conversion even more amenable to rig owners/operators, as per the high proportion of decades old rigs ceasing production, having exhausted their supply of extractable oil and/or exceeded their operational life span.

With an increasing proportion of redundant rigs, the global dominance of the Gulf has also been replaced by massive increases in offshore production around the world. Since 2008, the Gulf has less than 20% of all active offshore rigs across the globe, compared to almost 50% in 2000 (Yen, 2015). In the Gulf, this combination of factors is precipitating the largest scale transformation of existing oil infrastructure on earth. As the network of pipes and rigs are increasingly decommissioned, that infrastructure will be converted into a mausoleum or the largest artificial ecosystem on earth, depending on the direction of U.S. offshore energy policy.

Similarly, U.S. dominance on determining international climate and energy policy has shifted from near unilateral to multilateral over the period of Obama's presidency, as signified by rapid increases in collective international influence of countervailing forces such as the BRICS bloc. In a parallel vein and over the same period, U.S. dominance of space has lessened considerably, signified by the end of the U.S. manned space program in 2011. This downscaling has occurred against the rapid increase of private U.S. and other state programs. As the U.S. space program is progressively dismantled and downscaled, the physical infrastructure and its symbolic loading will become increasingly entwined with artificial reefs and rigs in the Gulf.

From the sea surface to the first 400 meters, the Gulf has almost no natural substrate for reefs to begin to form, due to the floor of loose sediment. There is only one natural reef in the Gulf proper and one at the periphery. Ironically, the substrate provided by oil infrastructure has been framed, even by marine biologists, within the existential predicament of decimated natural reefs all around the world. In this vein, marine biologists Paul Sammarco, Amy Atchison, and Gregory Boland (2004, 70) argue that "once a rig is moved in any way, an entire ecosystem is gone." By this rationale, they maintain that since "we've created these ecosystems, now it's up to us to keep them alive. Removing old oil rigs is 'pulling the plug' on many of the Gulf of México's rare and important marine species." Following this line of argument, the unintentional reliance by marine ecosystems on oil infrastructure has created a responsibility to scale up rigs to reef conversion in general.

The mixing of water and oil in the Space Race and National Artificial Reef programs brings the apparently irresolvable tension between energy policy and climate science into sharp relief. As private and state space programs and offshore oil drilling ramps up around the world, it will be prudent to refer back to U.S. oil, space, and artificial reef programs. The expansion of the Rigs to Reefs program to Brunei since 1988 and proposed new programs for California, Malaysia, and the North Sea, indicate that intentional and unintentional artificial ecosystems will continue to increase, with the boundary between them mediated by the rhetoric of oil and its associated infrastructure.

Nevertheless, space programs, offshore drilling, and artificial reefs the world over will be impacted by ruptures from increasingly intense weather systems as the halcyon days of the Holocene climate are progressively destabilized in the Anthropocene. And as those weather systems increasingly confront lofty ambitions toward the sky above us and fond reminisces of the underwater realm beneath us, the stark transition in Obama's energy policy between his first and second administrations will become ever more applicable in understanding how on earth oil will continue to operate with spectral invisibility. As the art of persuasive argumentation in contestations between energy policy and climate science, rhetoric will thus continue to be central to forming "a bridge between the ideals of philosophy and the realities of politics." In turn, navigating between the contradictory states of oil will heavily influence whether the current U.S. "Climate Change Emperor" continues to uphold the prevailing "delusion that climate change can be addressed adequately through rhetoric, financial fine-tuning and piecemeal incrementalism" (Anderson, 2012).

References

Anderson, K. 2012. "Real Clothes for the Emperor: Facing the Challenges of Climate Change." Paper presented at The Cabot Institute, University of Bristol, November 6, 2012, Retrieved December 13, 2015, from http://www.bristol.ac.uk/cabot/events/2012/194.html.

Anderson, K., & Bows, A. 2011. "Beyond 'Dangerous' Climate Change: Emission Scenarios for a New World." *Philosophical Transactions of the Royal Society A: Mathematical, Physical and Engineering Sciences*, *369*(1934), 20–44.

Attenborough, D., & Obama, B. June 30, 2015 *When Attenborough Met Obama*, London: British Broadcasting Corporation.

Banita, G. 2015. "Voting for American Energy: Elections, Oil, and US Culture." In Georgiana Banita, and Sascha Pohlmann (eds.), *Electoral Cultures*. Heidelberg: Universitätsverlag Winter, 101.

Bristol Airport, day and night temperature records for November 6, 2012, Retrieved June 10, 2016, from http://www.wunderground.com/history/airport/EGGD/2012/11/6/DailyHistory.html?req_city=Bristol&req_state=&req_statename=United+Kingdom&reqdb.zip=00000&reqdb.magic=3&reqdb.wmo=03724

Broder, J.M. October 25, 2012. "Nearly Absent in the Campaign: Climate Change." *The New York Times*. Retrieved from http://www.nytimes.com/2012/10/26/us/politics/climate-change-nearly-absent-in-the-campaign.html

CNN Wire Staff. April 1, 2010. "Obama Energy Plan Would Open Atlantic and Gulf Drilling." *CNN*. Retrieved from http://edition.cnn.com/2010/POLITICS/03/31/obama.energy/index.html

Clinton, W. 1994. *Public Papers of the Presidents of the United States: William J. Clinton, 1993*. Washington: United States Office of the Federal Register.

Cohen, J., Screen, J.A., Furtado, J.C., Barlow, M., Whittleston, D., Coumou, D., ... Jones, J. 2014. "Recent Arctic Amplification and Extreme Mid-Latitude Weather." *Nature Geosci*, *7*(9), 627–637.

Dauterive, L. 2000. "Rigs-To-Reefs Policy, Progress, and Perspective." In *OCS Report*. Washington: United States Department of the Interior.

Francis, J.A., & Vavrus, S.J. 2012. "Evidence Linking Arctic Amplification to Extreme Weather in Mid-Latitudes." *Geophysical Research Letters*, *39*(6), 1–6.

Francis, J.A., & Vavrus, S.J. 2015. "Evidence for a Wavier Jet Stream in Response to Rapid Arctic Warming." *Environmental Research Letters*, *10*(1), 014005.

Gray, R. August 22, 2013. "For Sale: 4,100 Ton Nasa Shuttle Launch Platforms – Buyer Must Collect." *The Telegraph*. Retrieved from http://www.telegraph.co.uk/news/science/space/10259432/For-sale-4100-ton-Nasa-Shuttle-launch-platforms-buyer-must-collect.html

Greene, C., Francis, J., & Monger, B. (2013). Superstorm Sandy: A Series of Unfortunate Events? *Oceanography*, *26*(1), 8–9.

Hansen, J. 2013. "Climate Urgency." *Simulation & Gaming*, *44*(2–3), 232–243.

Hedegaard, C. September 19, 2012. "Get Used to 'Extreme' Weather, it's the New Normal," *The Guardian*, Retrieved June 10, 2016, from http://www.theguardian.com/environment/2012/sep/19/extreme-weather-new-normal-climate-change.

Hickman, L. August 24, 2012. "US Election 2012: Romney and Obama Avoid the Climate Change Elephant." *The Guardian*. Retrieved from http://www.theguardian.com/environment/blog/2012/aug/24/us-election-2012-romney-obama-climate

Intergovernmental Panel on Climate Change. 2013. "Chapter 3 Observations: Ocean." In *Climate Change 2013: The Physical Science Basis*. New York: Cambridge University Press, 255–316. Retrieved from https://www.cambridge.org/core/books/climate-change-2013-the-physical-science-basis/observations-ocean-pages/C838D9254F698BAEC672D6575CFDB20C#

King, D., Browne, J., Layard, R., O'Donnell, G., Rees, M., Stern, N., & Turner, A. 2015. "A Global Apollo Programme to Combat Climate Change." *London School of Economics*, London. Retrieved from http://cep.lse.ac.uk/pubs/download/special/Global_Apollo_Programme_Report.pdf

Landau, S. July 16, 2010. "The Rhetoric-Reality Gulf [Institute for Policy Studies]". Retrieved from http://www.ips-dc.org/the_rhetoric-reality_gulf/

McCabe, K. 2012. "Climate-Change Rhetoric: A Study of the Persuasive Techniques of President Barack Obama and Prime Minister Julia Gillard." *Australian Journal of Communication*, *39*(2), 35.

McCown, B.A. April 5, 2013. "Pipeline Infrastructure: Rhetoric v. Reality." Retrieved April 17, 2017, from http://www.forbes.com/sites/brighammccown/2013/04/05/us-pipeline-infrastructure-rhetoric-v-reality/

Merica, D. October 30, 2012. "Sandy Reminds us of Climate Change and Other Forgotten Campaign Issues - CNNPolitics.com." Retrieved December 20, 2015, from http://www.cnn.com/2012/10/30/politics/forgotten-campaign-issues/index.html

Morton, T. 2012. *The Ecological Thought*. Cambridge, MA: Harvard University Press.

Obama, B. March 22, 2012. "Remarks by the President on American-Made Energy." *The White House*. Retrieved June 10, 2016, from https://www.whitehouse.gov/the-press-office/2012/03/22/remarks-president-american-made-energy.

van Oppen, M.J.H., Oliver, J.K., Putnam, H.M., & Gates, R.D. 2015. "Building Coral Reef Resilience through Assisted Evolution." *Proceedings of the National Academy of Sciences*, *112*(8), 2307–2313.

Rasche, R. February 12, 1986. "Space Pioneer Stands Up For Tower." *Orlando Sentinel*. Retrieved from http://articles.orlandosentinel.com/1986-02-12/news/0200070187_1_air-force-tower-launch-complex

Salvaggio, Ruth. 2014. "Imagining Angels on the Gulf." In Ross Barrett and Daniel Worden (editors), *Oil Culture*. Minneapolis: University of Minnesota Press, 384–404.

Sammarco, P., Atchison, A., & Boland, G. 2004. "Expansion of Coral Communities within the Northern Gulf of México via Offshore Oil and Gas Platforms." *Marine Ecology Progress Series*, *280*, 129–143.

Walsh, B. October 23, 2012. "Why Climate Change Has Become the Missing Issue in the Presidential Campaign." *Time*. Retrieved from http://science.time.com/2012/10/23/why-climate-change-has-become-the-missing-issue-in-the-presidential-campaign/

Walsh, L. 2013. *Scientists as Prophets: A Rhetorical Genealogy*. Oxford and New York: Oxford University Press.

Walsh, L. 2015. "The Visual Rhetoric of Climate Change." *Wiley Interdisciplinary Reviews: Climate Change*, 6(4), 361–368.

Wander, P.C., & Jaehne, D. 2000. "Prospects for 'a Rhetoric of Science'." *Social Epistemology*, *14*(2–3), 211–233.

Week, A. November 2, 2012. "How Obama Softened on Climate Change." Retrieved December 20, 2015, from http://abcnews.go.com/blogs/politics/2012/11/barack-obamas-evolution-on-climate-change-a-brief-history/

Yen, T. September 22, 2015. "U.S. Gulf of México Share of Global Active Offshore Rigs Declines since 2000." *Today in Energy - U.S. Energy Information Administration*. Retrieved September 23, 2016, from http://www.eia.gov/todayinenergy/detail.cfm?id=23032

6 The Flaming Faucet as Fracking's Ideographic Synecdoche

Tracking its Emergence in the Rhetorics of *Gasland* and the U.S. Natural Gas Industry

Ross Singer

In 2011, Mark Brownstein, Vice President of the Climate and Energy Program at the Environmental Defense Fund, wrote: "The iconic image of shale gas development is the flaming faucet featured in Josh Fox's recent movie, *Gasland*. Inquiring minds want to know: 'how does methane get into a water faucet, and is hydraulic fracturing of shale to blame?'" (Brownstein, 2011). The HBO documentary, which prompted worldwide viral circulation of images of flaming faucets and narratives about them, made the flaming faucet a unifying symbol for an emerging movement against natural gas "fracking." The film intervened in a rapidly growing national trend toward unconventional gas extraction methods, especially horizontal hydraulic fracturing from deep earth shale (Shonkoff, 2015). Recent empirical studies correlate *Gasland*'s release in the United States with a significant increase in national attention to the issue (Mazur, 2016). The documentary bolstered online searches about fracking, generated social media chatter, and heightened mass media coverage. Local screenings prompted anti-fracking mobilizations, which, in turn, led to local fracking moratoria in states where drilling had been planned (Vasi et al., 2015). The film also motivated residents in fracking hot spots to post their own flaming faucet videos online. Summarizing this impact, Vasi et al. (2015) observe that in the United States, "Similar to how pictures of the burning Cuyahoga River energized the 1960s environmental movement, powerful images of burning water from *Gasland* energized activists." These activists charge that fracking has devastating effects on environmental health, particularly in areas adjacent to well drilling sites.

Gasland's immediate public impact earned it an Academy Award nomination, leading the U.S. natural gas industry to aggressively discredit the film ("Sparks Fly," 2011). In response, the industry created guidelines and standards for voluntary environmental stewardship practices during gas well construction, and allied with the Ground Water Protection Council to create a chemical registry that purportedly discloses all fracking fluid chemicals used to drill natural gas wells (For the environmental stewardship guidelines, see Appalachian Shale Recommended Practices Group, 2012. For the national fracking chemical registry, see http://fracfocus.org/). Studying this formative exchange, with emphasis on key rhetorical practices that constituted it, promises to grow our understanding of how public perceptions and political policies about fracking emerge at the meeting grounds of science, corporate power, and democracy. This investigation extends the relatively scant environmental rhetoric literature on fracking—particularly that on anti-fracking resistance and industry-activist argumentation at the national level (Cope, 2013; Guignard, 2013; Matz and Renfrew, 2015; Rich, 2016). Below, setting the stage for the case study that follows, I situate *Gasland* and industry responses to it in a broader context.

Surveying Rhetorics of Fracking in the U.S.

Gasland introduced and in other cases supported and publicized many of the currently circulating charges against the U.S. fracking industry. Grievances regarding water alone are numerous, and emerging scientific research on fracking's potential environmental and public health effects tentatively validates most of them. According to Paulson and Tinney (2015), concerns include groundwater contamination from well-casing failure, migration into aquifers through ground fractures, unknown drilling chemicals (and their quantities) found in fracking fluid used to drill wells, and known fracking fluid volatiles and carcinogens. Critics also cite hazards from leaks or spills of fracking fluid stored on-site and toxins in nearby containment pond wastewater (Paulson and Tinney, 2015). They refer to scientific findings that injecting fracking wastewater into the ground can increase seismic activity (Keranen et al., 2014; Shonkoff, 2015). Beyond citing the quantity of water used to drill and redrill gas wells, critics point to federal environmental policy loopholes that shield the industry (Shonkoff, 2015). Paulson and Tinney (2015) note that others target air pollution in forms including methane and carbon dioxide emissions produced by drilling, ventilation, and diesel truck transportation. Ground-level ozone production and gas well releases of benzene, xylene, and toluene are additional air pollution concerns. Various hazards raised paint a troubling environmental health picture (e.g., cancer, birth defects, lung disease, well explosions) (Paulson and Tinney, 2015). In contrast, fracking proponents focus on the smaller set of positive effects, including the ability to tap previously difficult to reach deep-earth gas reserves, resulting positive economic impacts such as job creation, and the value of inexpensive, abundant, and non-imported energy (energy independence and security) for national prosperity (Hassett and Mathur, 2013). Proponents also stress that natural gas is the cleanest burning fossil fuel, making it a vital part of a multifaceted solution to climate change (Shell Global, 2017).

Surveying contemporary fracking discourses, Finewood and Stroup (2012, 74) comment that, "Inherent in these arguments is an effort to heavily influence the discursive meaning of water with the intention of dominating the discourse around the value of fracking to local communities." The discord between *Gasland* and the industry manifests the rhetorical origins of this focus on water and must be understood within a context in which local communities and industry use discourses with contrasting geographical orientations to make their competing cases (Guignard, 2013). Guignard (2013, 16) writes that the U.S. natural gas industry often uses a "nationalized, displacing rhetoric that abstracts the region," while local communities invoke an "emplacing rhetoric that seeks to preserve a way of life." This case study supports Guignard's contention that industry and local communities vary significantly in the types of discourse they often focus upon, and it adds that these contrasting discourses may emerge from competing sides' reliance on the same key rhetorical devices.

These shared rhetorical devices indicate in part *Gasland*'s shaping of not only the content of subsequent industry public relations but also how industry spun this content rhetorically. The industry's rebuttal renders the local residents' flaming tap water faucets, in specific, as defining sites of discursive contestation. Both sides attached contrasting meanings to residents' flaming faucets, resulting in what Moore (1993) conceptualizes as clashing ideographic synecdoches. In other words, the flaming faucet functioned as a "part" representative of the "whole" of each side's ideological position and as it became emblematic of the entire dispute, took the form of a synecdoche (Burke, 1969, 508).

As a synecdoche, the flaming faucet became a key site for engaging pivotal questions such as how the public should understand fracking and why. *Gasland* associated the flaming faucet with the ideographic term "life" (<life> in the tradition of ideographic criticism) and specifically a threat to <life>. Industry agreed that the flaming faucet represents its conflict with Fox, but only because its theatricality and hysterical environmentalist appeal epitomize *Gasland*'s rhetorical threat to <science>. The ideographic articulations of tap water on fire are oppositional not only in the sense of favoring different parties' respective ideological motives, but also in their placement of significantly different degrees of emphasis upon scientific and narrative grounds. Whereas *Gasland* prioritizes local (lay) narrative, industry heavily stresses expert knowledge. Before presenting my analysis of this clashing of knowledge forms, I summarize the theoretical orientation informing my analysis.

Ideographs: Verbal, Visual, Representational

McGee (1980, 7) defines ideographs as widely accepted "one-sum terms" (e.g., <democracy>, <justice>) and commonplace phrases (e.g., <freedom of speech>) linking rhetoric and ideology, and capturing ill-defined collective ideals. By referencing widely accepted but ambiguous ideas and arguments, ideographs are potentially powerful devices for generating social control or stirring resistance. For example, U.S. public discourse on alternative energy sources currently deploys the ideographs of <American jobs>, <economic growth>, and <energy independence>.

In some instances, an ideographic concept becomes synonymous with a corresponding symbol (e.g., <fight climate change> and the polar bear). Extending McGee's theorizing, Moore's studies of controversies defined by a struggle to define and claim a single verbal and potentially visual symbol (e.g., owl, salmon, cigarette) show how multiple sides may deploy the same ideographic synecdoche against each other (1994, 2003, 1996, 2009). Such symbols refer audiences back to the ideographic term or expression as well as the ideological meaning given to it, and the symbol then represents the side's broader discourse and the dispute (Moore, 1993, 258–260). Moore (1993) theorizes the ideographic synecdoche as a symbol that itself becomes a topic of dispute as one or more parties attempt to use it to promote their social reality. Synecdoche, then, is a part that represents the broader complexity of the whole, or the whole is understood as representative of smaller parts comprising it (Burke, 1969). Ideographic synecdoches such as the flaming faucet provide rhetors with a shorthand political symbol to condense or refute broader ideological discourses and slogans (Moore, 1993). Moore showed how the timber industry and environmentalists used the spotted owl as a political symbol in the form of oppositional synecdoches in the 1990s discord over old-growth forest logging. For the industry, the owl represented a broader threat to commercial and individual <liberty>, and for environmentalists, the owl symbolized a broader threat to the forest—to <life> (Moore, 1993, 259–260). Moore argued that such symbols parallel the experiential patterns of competing groups and provide an "indicator" of their wider mental pictures (1993, 259).

Several other studies argue that, given ideographs' complex discursive associations and contextual interdependence, they may be verbal, visual, or both (Edwards and Winkler, 1997; Hayden, 2009). Cloud (2004, 288) contends that images may make concrete and "index, or point to" terms and verbal slogans that encapsulate guiding social principles. Often combined with words, key images "invoke identification with key social commitments; they are key vehicles by which an ideology becomes rhetorically effective." In the context of the verbal and visual politics of fracking, Neville and Weinthal (2016) attest to the power of a defining image to signify complex arguments. In their study of activists in Canada's Yukon region, Neville and Weinthal show how the image of the backup electrical generator became a defining visual emblem in protests in the community of Whitehorse and "a symbol in the wider fight against fracking" (570). The generator became "a specific emblem of what is otherwise an abstract and remote debate over energy developments" (583). Moreover, it helped "redefine and strategically deploy 'local' concerns, to advance territorial, national, and even global campaigns" (570). My case study extends these insights.

Next, I turn briefly to the texts analyzed including *Gasland* and a collection of online industry responses, in print and video, posted on industry association, natural gas company, and other industry-sponsored websites. To avoid speculating about whether the film implicitly prompted particular industry responses, I draw only upon texts that explicitly address *Gasland*. These overt responses include a campaign by the Independent Petroleum Association of America (IPAA) (national trade association representing 85% of natural gas produced domestically) called Energy in Depth (EID), which released several statements online.[1] EID and IPAA also funded and produced the half-hour film rebuttal, "Truthland: Dispatches from the Real Gasland" (2012)—included in the analysis. Lastly, I also engage the American National Gas Association (ANGA) and Colorado Oil and Gas Association's (COGA) responses, as well as statements from individual natural gas companies and industry executives.

Gasland's Anti-Fracking Discourse: The Contested Imagery of Water

Beyond the simplicity of *Gasland*'s provocative subtitle, "*Can You Light Your Water on Fire?*" the meanings and functions of the film's visual images and narratives of flaming faucets are precarious, multifaceted, and carefully crafted. However, it would be reductive to characterize *Gasland* as a film about flammable residential tap water faucets. Instead, the flaming faucet is one recurring and highly memorable piece of evidence contributing to the documentary's overarching structure of what Schwarze (2003) describes as juxtaposition. A rhetorical device used by agitators in past environmental health controversies, juxtaposition consists of placing conflicting forms of knowledge and evidence regarding the situation alongside each other to create the appearance of incongruities, alter dynamics of certainty and uncertainty, highlight moral issues, encourage audiences to take a side in outrage, and pressure the opposition to respond.

The documentary's opening scenes vividly set the stage for Fox's dramatic juxtaposition of the clashing ideological worldviews of the natural gas industry and the affected citizens residing near the drilling fields. Video footage features several natural gas industry panelists testifying before a congressional committee. One industry panelist states that, "In fact North America's natural gas supply is so plentiful it has been described recently by some experts as a virtual ocean of natural gas." The panelist adds that natural gas has "enormous" potential for "our nation, our economy, and our environment." Another industry representative adds that there have been "press reports and websites alleging that six states have documented over one thousand incidents of groundwater contamination resulting from the practice of hydraulic fracturing. Such reports are not accurate." He elaborates that, "studies and surveys by GWPC [Groundwater Protection Council], EPA [U.S. Environmental Protection Agency], and IOGCC [Interstate Oil and Gas Compact Commission] over the last eleven years have found no real credible threat to underground drinking water." *Gasland* shows clips of industry promotional ads shortly thereafter, including one where an executive, too, uses the phrase "ocean of natural gas." As *Gasland*'s critique develops, it invites suspicion about the stark difference between grim grassroots accounts and the industry's triumphant tone and romantic vision.

Much of the film focuses on exploring this incongruity between the industry's claim to be using safe and environmentally friendly <science>, and local residents' narrative contention that fracking is <life>-threatening. Fox introduces himself and, as video footage of his property appears on the screen, describes his home in the woods of rural New York where he grew up and now lives. Fox's voice-over explains, "There's a stream that runs down the property and connects to the Delaware River." The scene later shows Fox walking along the stream as his voice-over describes his own intimate connection with it: "This is a place I've known. It's a place that runs through my mind, and it's always there. It feels to me like it's the source of all <life>. And it is. You need water for <life>." Fox rhetorically associates his own existence and anti-fracking position with the place-based native's defense of the purity and innocence of <life>-giving water.

Setting up a moral dualism consistent with the film's juxtapositional structure, Fox then identifies a threat to everything he knows and cherishes: natural gas fracking. He explains that in 2009 he received a letter from a natural gas company informing him that his property is on the Marcellus Shale, a rich reservoir of natural gas, and that he could lease his acreage to the company for nearly $100,000. Viewers quickly learn that due to his deep concern for environmental health, Fox will not take the money. Fox explains that, as a result of the 2005 Energy Bill, the oil and natural gas industries are exempt from a dozen or more regulations including the Safe Drinking Water Act, the Clean Air Act, and the Clean Water Act. These exemptions have enabled the use of fracking technology to launch the most extensive gas drilling campaign in history. Compelled by his letter and by a widely publicized dispute over alleged tap water contamination in nearby Dimock, Pennsylvania, Fox sets out on a twenty-four-state tour to further explore whether Dimock is an exception or part of a troubling pattern.

These opening scenes are crucial to understanding the film's articulation of <life> and its use of the flaming faucet as a key device within what HuangFu and Singer (2012) call an American eco-populist moral frame. This frame champions a victimized, virtuous, and "ordinary" people, as well as their local ecosystems against elite, morally corrupt institutional threats to the nation's founding principles of democracy and freedom. Moreover, the way by which Fox rhetorically associates himself with <life> and dissociates himself from its potential destruction in this opening sequence reflects the anti-fracking strategy described by Neville and Weinthal (2016, 583) as "claiming insider status." These scenes imply that Fox's status as property owner and someone who lives close to nature affords him a greater claim on the water and the land than outsiders. Here he appeals to a place-based eco-populist ethos that defines the whole film. This emphasis on local narrative knowledge, not scientific generalization, helped make the film's flaming faucets emblematic of the anti-fracking cause.

Visually Exploding the Institutional Narrative

DeLuca (1999, 1) theorizes that some images used to promote environmental awareness function as "mind bombs" (a term borrowed from former Greenpeace director Robert Hunter): they generate media spectacles that explode into the public consciousness and reconstitute previous understandings of an issue. Within *Gasland*'s first forty minutes, flaming faucet images and narratives about fracking's toxic effects cast doubt on the institutional discourse of fracking companies and regulatory officials. During several stops early in Fox's tour, residents living near natural gas wells across Colorado describe the consequences of nearby fracking on their lives. To demonstrate anecdotes about their tap water becoming contaminated following nearby natural gas well drilling, several residents light their tap water on fire. In one scene (that Fox referred to in a later film as "the shot seen around the world in *Gasland*"), Colorado resident, Mike Markham, lights his faucet on fire and remarks, "That's the best I've done. I smell hair!" (Fox, 2012). Fox then asks if he can try it. Before allowing Fox to do so, Markham sets a fire extinguisher near the sink. Above the sink, a sign reads, "Do not drink this water." Almost immediately after Fox places his cigarette lighter under the running faucet, the water bursts into flames. Shaking his head amid very brief shock-induced laughter in the room, Fox exhorts, "It's really upsetting, actually." Then, from a faucet outside of his home, Markham fills and holds up a glass of water and observes, "That doesn't look very delicious, does it?" He then tests the water with an electronic device that beeps rapidly upon detecting contamination.

The Markham scene is the first image of a flaming faucet in the film and the most visually spectacular of any shown in *Gasland*. Through its repeat visual performances of two different people lighting a residential tap water faucet on fire, the scene not only strongly validates Markham's narrative knowledge claims, but more importantly, it functions as a visual and affective mind bomb that promises to rhetorically explode viewers' previous conceptions about fracking. The film's flaming faucet scenes invite viewers to replace the industry's constructed reality of fracking as <science>-based safety with a local narrative reality defined by fracking's threat to <life>. The concrete on-camera evidence invites deep emotion about local residents' grievances and roots previously abstract and seemingly naïve anti-fracking skepticism in embodied and place-based experiences of material hardship. In the Markham scene and others featuring flaming faucets, *Gasland* features local residents in different regions telling similar stories, thus reflecting an emergent formation of grassroots knowledge about fracking as a threat to <life>. Like the emblem of the electrical generator in Neville and Weinthal's study (2016), the flaming faucet functions as a unifying symbol, crucial to the film's amplifying, connecting, and coordinating of otherwise scattered local voices and communities. The flaming faucet also serves as a means of overcoming abstraction and the perceived remoteness of affected contexts. To borrow from Pezzullo (2007), when distant audiences can share viscerally in the sensory experience of otherwise invisible toxic symptoms and bodily ailments, local arguments have a better chance of securing a memorable psychological presence.

Gasland builds on these local experiential rhetorics by incorporating previous local television news coverage of the flaming faucets and corresponding stories of residents such as Jesse and Amee Ellsworth, and Renee McClure of Fort Lupton, Colorado. It appropriates the dramatic framing used in the news coverage: a local news co-anchor announces, "New information tonight on a story that you almost have to see to believe," with the other co-anchor adding, "That's right, flames shooting from faucets inside a home in Fort Lupton." Amee Ellsworth then states that she is "terrified" and that "shock is one word for it. Terror is probably more effective." Another reporter then invokes a fear appeal, alerting viewers that fracking is potentially <life>-threatening: "That's because Amee is living in a home that could explode, and now we've learned she isn't the only one with water contaminated by natural gas." The reporter continues, "Renee McClure discovered that her water is flammable after watching our story last night. Renee is worried that her family has been drinking the contaminated water for years." Fox then speaks with both women, who describe worsening health problems and fears about the future. Fox learns that Noble Energy, the company fracking wells nearby, provides Amee and Jesse with an alternative water source while denying responsibility for their contaminated water. Another resident in the same Colorado community explains that she speaks for some affected residents because they are silenced by nondisclosure agreements or completed settlements with natural gas companies. These testimonies suggest that at least behind closed doors, the industry has acknowledged responsibility for fracking's toxic threat to water and <life>.

In addition, some residents tell Fox that they previously lit their water on fire but had since closed their wells due to the threat that the flammable water posed to their lives. One family refuses to demonstrate the flammability of their tap water, noting, "If we turn it on, it's possible that it could explode or catch our house on fire." These residents juxtapose their own accounts with statements and reports from industry and government officials. In several cases, officials agreed that the water was contaminated but would not provide assistance or place responsibility with the companies. Other residents' narratives describe gas well workers personally assuring them that the water is safe to drink, only to decline a glass of it when offered to them. Some residents show Fox test reports indicating the presence of harmful fracking chemicals in their water.

Gasland supplements local knowledge with interview accounts from scientific and regulatory authorities, including renowned chemist and environmental consultant, Wilma Subra, and EPA employee, environmental engineer and whistleblower, Weston Wilson. Fox interviews Wilson about a letter he wrote to Congress arguing that conflicts of interest had led a 2004 panel to cease further EPA investigation into what the agency had identified as cases of fracking-related groundwater contamination. Subra affirms that fracking has clearly led to relatively widespread regional groundwater contamination in places such as southern Louisiana, where one third of all of the natural gas produced in the United States passes through an area known as the Henry Hub. She states that in "this whole area, the groundwater is contaminated from the production, from the drilling, from the old pits. . . with a lot of the heavy metals like barium, which is the weighing agent in drilling fluids." Arsenic, cadmium, chromium, and lead are also present. Testimonies from these scientists and officials corroborate the film's discourse on locals' experiences and scientifically validate allegations of industry causality.

The film's placement of the flaming faucet among a collection of striking images and narratives regarding fracking's consequences reinforces the idea of natural gas development as an explosive threat to water and therefore all <life>. A Wyoming resident, Louis Meeks, tells Fox that after nearby fracking contaminated his well water, he installed a second well and methane gas exploded from it for several days. A court-ordered moratorium forced the drilling company, Encana, to cement and cap the flow, and provide him with a replacement water source. *Gasland* then shows video footage of natural gas exploding from Meeks' water well, while Fox explains, "Natural gas exploded out of Louis Meeks' water well for three days. The Department of Homeland Security reported that over three million cubic feet of natural gas escaped into the atmosphere." The scene emphasizes that fracking's threat to <life> is not only explosive and irreparable but has proven impossible to contain. This anti-fracking charge reappears throughout the film. One resident shows Fox corpses of wildlife found near a stream by her home. Another resident, from Pennsylvania, describes her cat and horse losing their hair after drinking the tap water. Other locals give Fox jars of murky water from their taps and show him the water filtration and storage tank systems purchased and installed by natural gas companies.

As Fox's tour ends, he takes the jars of contaminated tap water back to Pennsylvania, where the tour began. There, Fox interviews Pennsylvania Department of Environmental Protection Secretary, John Hanger. When Hanger states that there was no evidence of chemical contamination across thirty-nine homes tested near natural gas wells in Dimock, Fox responds by showing Hanger that he has several jars of tap water taken from several spots near gas wells across the country, including Dimock. He states, "This is tap water. . . and I'm wondering if you're interested in drinking some of this." Fox's offer insinuates evidence of fracking as a toxic threat to <life> that officials are literally not willing to digest. As noted in the next section, the industry's response both affirmed and disaffirmed that these scenes regarding water contamination—especially those featuring flaming faucets, are the film's most significant.

Industry Response: *Gasland* Contaminates <Science>

Following the agenda for deliberation that *Gasland* sets forth, the U.S. fracking industry's response focuses relatively little on economic benefits and national strength, and almost exclusively on fracking's purported water-related environmental health harms. Mounting an image defense campaign heavily invested in reclaiming the mantle of scientific authority, the industry develops its reply around issues such as fracking fluid chemicals, whether fracking may cause groundwater contamination, the sufficiency of governmental environmental regulation, and the industry's own commitment to the truth. As the industry addresses these issues, its in-depth response implicitly grants Fox the status of a formidable critic. The content and key rhetorical devices found in the response attempt to reconfigure Fox's eco-populist insider moral frame and his local accounts of flaming faucets to work against him.

The fracking industry's reconfigured moral frame rests on its self-legitimizing appeals to moral commitments of applied <science> including accuracy, honesty, safety, and environmental stewardship. The frame simultaneously positions Fox and his film as using emotional speculation to identify villainous violation of these values. As such, the industry's competing moral juxtaposition of knowledge claims that emerges invokes what Killingsworth and Palmer (1995, 2) identify as the well-established institutional defense strategy of rejecting charges of wrongdoing by labeling them irrational "environmentalist hysteria." The charge of activist hysteria, of only an "aberrant imagination" as capable of finding trouble brewing in this project of Western progress (Killingsworth and

Palmer, 1995, 2), comes as the industry adopts *Gasland*'s topical agenda for deliberation but attempts to break free from what the film accepts as legitimate evidence. According to industry discourse, residents' firsthand accounts of bodily symptoms of environmental toxicity should be understood as manifestations of a kind of inorganic hysteria. In this discourse, residents' speculative narrative evidence is characterized as out-of-the-ordinary bodily symptoms and firsthand observations in contrast to a sound mind using scientific reason (On the psychoanalytic language of this charge, see Killingsworth and Palmer, 1995, 3–6).

By using this discourse of scientific rationality supplemented with local narrative, the industry redefines what counts as legitimate evidence and constructs an oppositional flaming faucet synecdoche. To reclaim its rhetorical association with science, regulatory compliance, and eco-friendliness, and to dissociate from the idea that it, too, may have an ideological agenda, the industry regularly appeals to its own dedication to "the facts." Guided by its campaign slogan "just the facts," EID charges that *Gasland* suffers from hysterical misrepresentation, which violates the public expectation of <scientific> accuracy and honesty:

> With larger audiences and greater fanfare comes the expectation of a few basic things: accuracy, attention to detail, and original reporting among them. Unfortunately, in the case of this film, accuracy is too often pushed aside for simplicity, evidence too often sacrificed for exaggeration, and the same old cast of characters and anecdotes – previously debunked.

In an apparent attempt to associate itself with a dominant, mainstream sensibility, EID points out that not only has Fox's previous work been recognized by New York City's Fringe Festival, but that as Fox's first foray into the mainstream, *Gasland* can be characterized as "politics at its worst, art at its most contrived, and contradictions of fact found around every bend of the river" (2016). EID director Lee Fuller's response to the documentary's Academy Award nomination uses cynicism to dissociate the industry's basis in <science> from the film's unfounded antics: "[T]his nomination is fitting, as the Oscars are aimed at praising pure entertainment. . . the Academy of Motion Picture Arts and Sciences nominated Gasland for its work in the field of art, not <science>" (Tucker, 2011). EID's Tom Shepstone (2011) also writes about Fox and his film using ridicule and cynicism: "Environmental hysteria is apparently very profitable and absurdity pays." Shepstone adds, "It allows its purveyors to make huge salaries" while claiming a "selfless" hero image. Fox reaps "new found respect, tons of free publicity and a chance to hob-nob with the rich and famous" (For another example of how industry has deployed the term "hysteria," see LeVine, 2012).

Labeling Fox as self-promotional and *Gasland* as activist hysteria, fringe art, and self-promotional sensationalism therefore provides a foundation from which the industry is able to equate its own supposed neutrality (its apolitical realism) with morality. The resulting moral persona is clearheaded and backed by <science>. However, this does not mean industry rhetors merely dismiss Fox and move on. In most instances, industry rhetors engage in counter-argumentation using counter-evidence, and the resulting discourse invites a conclusion of scientific doubt regarding fracking as a clear and causal threat to <life>. Although the industry responds to various environmental health charges, industry counterarguments tend to target Fox's flaming faucets. Counterarguments use two tactics to propose an alternate meaning for the flaming faucet ideograph. The first tactic frames chemicals in tap water as potentially naturally occurring. The second frames fracking chemicals as nontoxic, even commonplace in everyday life. These strategies enable the industry to re-appropriate juxtaposition as a rhetorical device to expose gaps and contradictions in anti-frackers' evidence, thus recontextualizing knowledge forms and altering dynamics of certainty and uncertainty (Schwarze, 2003). Through these tactics, industry deems *Gasland* and opponents of fracking as threats to <science> because they failed to prove a causal relation between fracking and contaminated water. As discussed in the next section, industry responses refute that fracking and fracking-related chemicals add any substances to water, people, and the environment that, from a scientific perspective, were not already there.

Chemicals in Tap Water May Be Naturally Occurring

The industry primarily invokes appeals to scientific authority to undermine the flaming faucet as a symbol of tap water contamination. These appeals refute Fox's causality claim by framing methane gas as naturally occurring. For example, Anadarko Petroleum (2013) cites scientific grounds for its refutation: "[H]istorical U.S. Geological Survey studies documented the presence of naturally occurring methane in Pennsylvania aquifers long before development of the Marcellus shale. Lohman, S.W., 1937 (reprinted 1957)." Anadarko then tempers these scientific grounds with reference to local narratives: "[O]ccurrence of methane gas in drinking-water wells and in rivers and streams in many areas of the U.S. is not a recent phenomenon as anecdotes from long-time residents have confirmed http://www.cabotog.com/pdfs/Tab1.pdf."

"Truthland," the short online documentary, takes a bolder stance, using narrative to raise doubt about *Gasland*'s charges of fracking-related environmental health consequences. This documentary frames methane gas as naturally occurring and goes even further by proposing that the flammable water phenomenon is also quite ordinary. "Truthland" begins with narrative testimony from Shelly, a teacher and family farmer, surrounded by the picturesque setting of her family farm. After being offered a land lease contract and viewing *Gasland*, Shelly investigates fracking's effects for herself. Her fact-finding tour begins with

Gasland's flaming faucets—what she calls "the burning water business" that scared her kids when they viewed the film. Shelly first offers narrative evidence, "Everyone around here knows that [flammable water]'s a natural thing. It's been going on for generations." The camera pictures Shelly walking on a rural farmstead with Patricia, from Brackney, Pennsylvania, who agrees, "Yeah, I remember years ago, taking a match, lighting it, and throwing it on one of my dad's ponds, and it would light, and that was long before fracking." Shelly's voice-over then interjects, "Somebody told me that even across the road at Salt Springs, they could capture and light the methane that bubbles up naturally. So I thought I'd give it a try." Shelly picks up a plastic bottle (with bottom cut off) from the stream, lights the water underneath it on fire and concludes, "Hmm, looks like the flaming faucet that Josh [Fox] showed might be a bit misleading." While the conclusion that water is supposed to catch fire or that this is normal may strike many viewers as absurd, if it puzzles at least some viewers and promotes uncertainty among them, it is to the industry's advantage. The narrative and the visual demonstration invite dissonance regarding industry causality, and Shelly's implicitly positive view of fracking suggests that *Gasland*'s narrative of disgruntled local residents is incomplete.

"Truthland" then elaborates on this bias in Fox's film by linking its own local narrative of flaming faucets with <science>. It juxtaposes Patricia and Shelly's narrative accounts with those of the residents featured in *Gasland* and then turns to expert testimony to resolve the matter. The explanation by Terry Engelder, a geoscience professor, rhetorically re-positions the flaming faucet as a synecdoche for *Gasland* posing a threat to <science>:

> [T]here is a tremendous amount of innuendo in [*Gasland*]. . . that all of the problems. . . are a direct result of. . . hydraulic fracturing. . . The most famous scene, of course, is. . . where this guy in northeastern Colorado lights his faucet, and the Colorado Department of Environmental Conservation has stated over and over again that this is biogenic [naturally occurring] methane.

Shelly and Patricia are shown to deny Fox the narrative ethos of an eco-populist insider, and Engelder serves to deny Fox the ethos of <science>. Shelly subsequently states her conclusion: "<Scientific> credentials. I believe him [Engelder] more than I believe some New York filmmaker."

Even as the industry itself uses a cadre of selected scientists and local residents to marshal its viewpoint as truth, Engelder's statements are part of a repeatedly stated industry rebuttal: *Gasland* relies on "the same old cast of characters" (Energy in Depth, 2010). Industry responses especially emphasize the Markham scene's synecdochic symbolism, describing it, for example, as "the film's signature moment" and "most memorable scene" (America's Natural Gas Alliance, 2011). EID juxtaposes conflicting claims, noting first that, "Fox blames a flammable faucet in Fort Lupton, Colo. on natural gas development" and then counters that this claim is "not true according to the Colorado Oil & Gas Conservation Commission (COGCC)." The commission states that, "Dissolved methane in well water **appears to be biogenic in origin. . .** There are no indications of oil & gas related impacts to water well (complaint resolved 9/30/08, signed by John Axelson of COGCC) (Energy in Depth, 2010)". This industry discourse affirms the flaming faucet as representational ideograph but redefines it with oppositional meaning.

Fracking Chemicals in Tap Water Are Not Necessarily Toxic

The industry uses a second tactic: it rhetorically normalizes methane contamination of tap water by framing the gas as not necessarily toxic. This discourse is crucial because it focuses on methane, the chemical blamed for residents' flaming faucets. This tactic invites uncertainty regarding residents' claims that their water is making them ill. The message is that even if fracking has affected the water, it may not be the cause of residents' illnesses because the chemical toxins are at levels not <scientifically> proven to be threatening to human health.

The framing of methane as a normal and safe part of tap water is pivotal to the industry's attempt to appropriate the voice of <science> to undermine *Gasland*'s overall thesis that fracking is a threat to <life>. Citing independent sources, EID (2010) claims that even if methane gas appears in residents' water, "Drinking water with methane, the largest component of natural gas, isn't necessarily harmful. The gas itself isn't toxic – the Environmental Protection Agency doesn't even regulate it." On the topic of regulation, EID adds that rather than being a sinister result of relatively recent political loopholes, as suggested in *Gasland*, "The process of hydraulic fracturing. . . has never in its 60-year history been regulated under the Safe Drinking Water Act." EID claims that objective authorities of <science> and regulation have deemed methane gas safe, even as the industry has been "regulated ably and aggressively by the states, which have compiled an impressive record of enforcement and oversight." Similarly, ANGA appeals to the objective process of <scientific> improvement and successful history of safe fracking technology:

> Hydraulic fracturing is a proven technology that has been refined over 60 years. It has allowed companies to safely produce natural gas from more than 1 million U.S. wells. The Environmental Protection Agency, Ground Water Protection Council, Interstate Oil and Gas Compact Commission and others have all examined the process and found it to be safe. (America's Natural Gas Alliance, 2011)

This statement, which appeals to the reliability of <science> in the form of technology, is also found verbatim in COGA's response. However, most industry rhetors responding to *Gasland*, including COGA and Anadarko Petroleum, also explicitly acknowledge that tap water contamination due to fracking is not only possible, but has occurred in the past. COGA (2011) states that, "The essential factor with respect to the safety of hydraulic fracturing is proper well construction, including casing and cementing to isolate the production formations being stimulated from shallow groundwater aquifers." Anadarko Petroleum (2013) offers a related disclaimer: "Like any activity, even with the implementation of controlling measures, there is a chance of accidents. . . but the American Water Works Association has stated that properly maintained and regulated wells are 'unlikely to directly cause groundwater contamination'" (2). The conclusion is that fracking is not an uncontainable and deadly threat to <life>, but instead <science> has shown that fracking contamination is rare, not necessarily toxic, and safely contained.

In addition to appealing to regulatory authority and the safety of fracking technology historically, the industry also associates fracking chemicals with popular consumer product chemicals that are part of ordinary everyday <life>. Here, the industry attempts to demonstrate that small quantities are not necessarily toxic. COGA (2011) states, "The truth is, the fracturing process uses a mixture comprised almost entirely (99.5%) of water and sand. The remaining materials, used to condition the water, are typically found and used around the house" (2). Of the methane gas that ignites flaming faucets, EID (2010) claims that it is not regulated and "escapes from water quickly, like bubbles in a soda." In these characterizations, fracking-related chemicals and water work in mutual harmony.

Similar practices of rhetorically associating natural gas and fracking with safe, ordinary everyday <life> are also present in Breitling Energy CEO Chris Faulkner's (2014) response to *Gasland.* Faulkner compares fracking chemicals to soft drinks: "Even where you have benzene, you have less than you drink in a can of Coke, and yet it sounds bad." What Fox describes as a concealed list of hundreds of fracking chemicals includes the same chemicals already familiar to most people as "common household cleaners." Not only are chemicals in fracking fluids "familiar," but some of them are actually essential to our existence: "One of the chemicals used in highest concentration is hydrochloric acid, naturally occurring as stomach acid" (Breitling Energy, 2014). These normalizing analogies constitute the applied chemical <science> of fracking as the ultimate authority for resolving the controversy. Industry discourse redefines *Gasland*'s flaming faucets as ideographic synecdoches while normalizing and naturalizing the presence of fracking-related chemicals in tap water and the environment more broadly. This framing deploys <science> to ease fears about potential environmental and health risks, and to cast uncertainty, confusion, and doubt on *Gasland*'s allegation of fracking as an explosive threat to <life>.

Summary and Implications

This study offers further evidence of the formative role that *Gasland* and its flaming faucet imagery played in the emergence and development of the debate over nature gas fracking in the United States. The film's flaming faucet imagery served as more than an attention-getter; it became an ideographic synecdoche, or political and normative value symbol, leveraged by activists *and* industry to encapsulate their broader arguments. The industry reframed *Gasland*'s flaming faucet synecdoche, which characterized fracking as a threat to <life>, as instead representing an "hysterical" environmentalist threat to <science>. This attempt to redefine the flaming faucet's meaning and the industry's continuous attention to water reflect *Gasland*'s success with setting an agenda for discussion about corporate-state accountability for environmental health risks and threats. As the industry directly engaged the documentary's charges, it invited uncertainty and confusion, but it also made the flaming faucet more prominent in the public sphere and elevated Josh Fox as a legitimate image threat.

Josh Fox's film also shaped the content and several supporting rhetorical devices that the industry used to respond to the film's charges. Replicating *Gasland*'s rhetorical structure, the industry juxtaposed competing forms of evidence to recontextualize them, reveal contradictions, invite uncertainty, and end discussion. The industry also contested *Gasland*'s insider ethos and eco-populist moral frame of innocent ordinary people victimized by greedy, sinister institutions. To this end, industry leveraged expert testimony to discredit the film's "same old cast of characters" and presenting its own local narratives to highlight the film's bias. Overall, the industry counter-argument relied largely on a rhetoric of <science> supplemented by local narrative. Conversely, *Gasland* prioritized residents' local narratives supported by scientific experts to corroborate residents' claims and contextualize their concerns. The parties involved prioritized different geographical orientations to discourse and knowledge to make their competing cases (Guignard, 2013). *Gasland* uses what Guignard calls "emplacing rhetoric," while the industry response is more "abstract" and "nationalizing" (16). The industry's "Truthland" represents some effort to characterize itself as a local community partner; however, the broader industry response takes a ridiculing and cynical tone toward residents that undermines its minimal expressions of sympathy.

It must be noted, however, that this investigation adds to existing literature about conflicting ideographic synecdoches by highlighting a case in which the goal is not the dominance of one over the other. Instead, both sides in this controversy recognize that <life> and <science> are mutually interdependent—not subject to potential trade-off or compromise. The dispute is not a matter of one versus the other at the level of normative values and goals, but rather about competing voices on how to preserve both <science> and <life> in relative harmony, and who may rightfully claim both for their side. Another scholarly contribution lies in adding to existing knowledge of how the oil and gas industries use discourses of uncertain causality to minimize the seriousness of methane-contaminated tap water. First, the industry used both science and narrative discourses to frame the methane responsible for the flammable water as naturally occurring (and therefore not introduced by fracking). Second, it used chemistry-based analogies to argue that methane in tap water is not necessarily toxic. Earlier research in environmental rhetoric has documented how the oil and gas industry has used analogy and metaphor to associate fracking fluid with banal household products (Guignard, 2013; Matz and Renfrew, 2015), making them seem benign. I have shown how the industry response to *Gasland* also used analogies and metaphor not only to normalize toxins (Cozen, 2010), but also to defend the industry's public image against charges of corporate irresponsibility regarding environmental health. Furthermore, a constitutive metaphor of industry as expert defines the industry response (Guignard, 2013). This metaphor has become standard in contemporary extractive energy industry rhetoric. The constructed case study further highlights the role that metaphor and analogy play in "abstracting and simplifying the process" of fracking and in helping industry downplay affected residents' concerns (Guignard, 2013, 20). These devices emerged as a reaction to *Gasland*'s imagery, which is vivid but must still leave abstract the purported underground cause and occurrence of contamination.

This precariousness of the ideographic synecdoches that the industry (<science>) and *Gasland* articulate (<life>) deserves a closer look. The gas and oil industry's synecdoche is limited beyond its partiality for invoking <science>. When coupled with the industry's speculation about Josh Fox's economic and celebrity-seeking motivations, the synecdoche of <science> omits the profit dimension of industry ideology and instead promotes an image of fairness-driven altruism. If, as Burke (1969) theorizes, effective synecdoches must be simultaneously simple and complex, then the industry's synecdoche falls short once it moves beyond its partiality for scientific discourse over narrative. *Gasland*'s synecdoche of <life> privileges local narrative knowledge, supporting Moore's (1996) observation that when a controversy becomes gridlocked by conflicting scientific knowledge, narrative may provide a way forward. *Gasland*'s narrative and visual discourse were particularly instrumental for generating meaningful, sustained critical publicity; the film prompted industry to respond in words and in action, and the controversy spurred significant non-industry sponsored scientific inquiry into fracking's environmental health risks.

Despite *Gasland*'s argument being hindered by uncertainty in the scientific community, the industry's synecdoche continues to be scrutinized. Although fracking continues to spread across the United States, three statewide moratoria, a host of counties, cities, and local communities around the country have made it illegal (Keep Tap Water Safe, 2017). The proliferation of anti-fracking movement groups, Josh Fox's release of subsequent anti-fracking films, and the fact that the controversy has waged on without scientific closure are also negative trends for the industry. Currently, the U.S. public continues to be uncertain about whether fracking is safe. Recent survey research, however, suggests that as the U.S. residents learn more about fracking's multiple facets beyond its potential economic benefits, approval decreases (Boudet et al., 2016). The rapidly growing science literature on fracking's risks may only increase public discontent in the future. In 2017, the EPA released the most comprehensive study to date assessing the relationship between fracking and drinking water contamination (U.S. Environmental Protection Agency, 2017). Due to "significant data gaps and uncertainties in the available data," the report is cautious about estimating the frequency and severity of fracking-related water contamination (U.S. Environmental Protection Agency, 2017, 2). However, the government agency concludes that fracking "can impact drinking water resources" and lists potential toxic groundwater contamination risks at almost every point in the fracking process (U.S. Environmental Protection Agency, 2017, 1). Today, fracking, like gas and oil generally, continues to be outside of the jurisdiction of most U.S. federal environmental statutes, including the Safe Drinking Water Act, the Clean Water Act, the National Environmental Policy Act, and the Resource Conservation and Recovery Act (SourceWatch, 2015). Whether or not these exemptions will continue amidst emerging research and public resistance remains to be seen.

Note

1 For these statistics and others, see "About IPAA," *Independent Petroleum Association of America*, accessed 21 June 2016, http://www.ipaa.org/about/

References

America's Natural Gas Alliance. January 24, 2011. "The Truth about Gasland." http://www.anga.us/media/blog/CE755EC1-CA09-3D03-F4A8C4BAF834C248/files/theF4A8C4BAF834C248/files/the%20truth%20about%20gasland.pdf

Anadarko Petroleum Corporation. December 2013. "Facts on Natural Gas from Shales: Protecting Groundwater." https://www.anadarko.com/content/documents/apc/news/APC-ShaleGasGroundwaterFAQs.pdf

Appalachian Shale Recommended Practices Group. April 30, 2012. "Recommended Standards and Practices." http://www.ourenergypolicy.org/wp-content/

uploads/2012/05/44703_ASRPGStandardsandPracticesDocumentApril 302012.3pdf

Boudet, Hilary, Dylan Bugden, Chad Zanocco, and Edward Maibach. 2016. "The Effect of Industry Activities on Public Support for Fracking." *Environmental Politics* 25(4), 593–612.

Breitling Energy. November 7, 2014. "Fracking Mythbusters." http://www.breitlingenergy.com /fracking-mythbusters-thenewamerican-com/

Brownstein, Mark, ed. May 10, 2011. *Environmental Defense Fund* (blog). http://blogs.edf.org/energyexchange/2011/05/10/poor-well-construction-is-the-culprit/

Burke, Kenneth. 1969. *A Grammar of Motives*. Berkeley, CA: University of California Press.

Cloud, Dana L. 2004. "'The Veil of the Threat of Terror': Afghan Women and the 'Clash of Civilizations' in the Imagery of the U.S. War on Terrorism." *Quarterly Journal of Speech* 90(3), 285–306.

Colorado Oil and Gas Association. June 17, 2011. "The Truth about GasLand Whitepaper." http://www.coga.org/wp-content/uploads/2015/09/The-Truth-About-GasLand-Whitepaper.pdf

Cope, Brian. 2013. "Eco-Seeing a Tradition of Colonization: Revealing Shadow Realities of Marcellus Drilling." In *Environmental Rhetoric and Ecologies of Place*, edited by Peter N. Goggin, 28–41. New York, NY: Routledge.

Cozen, Brian. 2010. "This Pear is a Rhetorical Tool: Food Imagery in Energy Company Advertising." *Environmental Communication* 4(3), 355–370.

DeLuca, Kevin Michael. 1999. *Image Politics: The New Rhetoric of Environmental Activism*. New York, NY: The Guilford Press.

Edwards, Janis L., and Carol K. Winkler. 1997. "Representative Form and the Visual Ideograph: The Iwo Jima Image in Editorial Cartoons." *Quarterly Journal of Speech* 83(3), 289–310.

Energy in Depth. June 5, 2010. "Debunking GasLand." http://energyindepth.org/wp-content/uploads/2010/06/Debunking-GasLand.pdf

———. January 24, 2011. "Just the Facts." http://energyindepth.org/just-the-facts/

Finewood, Michael H., and Laura J. Stroup. 2012. "Fracking and the Neoliberalization of the Hydro-Social Cycle in Pennsylvania's Marcellus Shale." *Journal of Contemporary Water Research & Education* 147(1), 72–79.

Fox, Josh. June 20, 2012. "The Sky is Pink." Produced and directed by Josh Fox. *Vimeo*. Video, 18:23. https://vimeo.com/44367635

Guignard, James. 2013. "A Certain Uncertainty: Drilling into the Rhetoric of the Marcellus Shale Natural Gas Development." In *Environmental Rhetoric and Ecologies of Place*, edited by Peter N. Goggin, 15–27. New York, NY: Routledge.

Hassett, Kevin A., and Aparna Mathur. 2013. "Benefits of Hydraulic Fracking." *Oxford Energy Forum* 91(1), 11–13.

Hayden, Sara. 2009. "Revitalizing the Debate between <Life> and <Choice>: The 2004 March for Women's Lives." *Communication and Critical/Cultural Studies* 6(2), 111–131.

HuangFu, JiangBo, and Ross Singer. 2012. "The Populist Argumentative Frame in the Environmental Vision of Van Jones." In *Across Borders and Environments: Proceedings of the 11th Biennial Conference on Communication and the Environment*, edited by Stacey Sowards. Cincinnati, OH: International Environmental Communication Association, 23–37.

Independent Petroleum Association of America. June 21, 2016. "About IPAA." http://www.ipaa.org/about/

Keep Tap Water Safe. October 16, 2017. "List of Bans Worldwide." https://keeptapwatersafe.org/global-bans-on-fracking/

Keranen, Katie M., Matthew Weingarten, Geoffrey A. Abers, Barbara A. Bekins, and Shemin Ge. 2014. "Sharp Increase in Central Oklahoma Seismicity since 2008 Induced by Massive Wastewater Injection." *Science* 345(6195), 448–451.

Killingsworth, Jimmie M., and Jacqueline S. Palmer. 1995. "The Discourse of 'Environmentalist Hysteria.'" *Quarterly Journal of Speech* 81(1), 1–19.

LeVine, Steve. May 4, 2012. "'Hysteria' over Hydraulic Fracturing is 'Scientifically Misplaced' -- Anadarko CEO." *EnergyWire*. Last modified. http://www.eenews.net/stories/1059963906.

Matz, Jacob, and Daniel Renfrew. 2015. "Selling 'Fracking': Energy in Depth and the Marcellus Shale." *Environmental Communication* 9(1), 288–306.

Mazur, Allan. 2016. "How Did the Fracking Controversy Emerge in the Period 2010–2012?" *Public Understanding of Science* 25(2), 207–222.

McGee, Michael Calvin. 1980. "The 'Ideograph': A Link between Rhetoric and Ideology." *Quarterly Journal of Speech* 66(1), 1–16.

Moore, Mark P. 1993. "Constructing Irreconcilable Conflict: The Function of Synecdoche in the Spotted Owl Controversy." *Communication Monographs* 60(3), 258–274.

———. 1994. "Life, Liberty, and the Handgun: The Function of Synecdoche in the Brady Bill Debate." *Communication Quarterly* 42(4), 434–447.

———. 1996. "The Cigarette as Representational Ideograph in the Debate over Environmental Tobacco Smoke." *Communication Monographs* 64(1), 47–64.

———. 2003. "Making Sense of Salmon: Synecdoche and Irony in a Natural Resource Crisis." *Western Journal of Communication* 67(1), 74–96.

———. 2009. "The Union of Concerned Scientists on the Uncertainty of Climate Change: A Study of Synecdochic Form." *Environmental Communication* 3(2), 191–205.

Neville, Kate J., and Erika Weinthal. 2016. "Scaling Up Site Disputes: Strategies to Redefine Local in the Fight Against Fracking." *Environmental Politics* 25(4), 569–592.

Paulson, Jerome A., and Veronica Tinney. 2015. "Potential and Known Health Impacts Associated with Unconventional Natural Gas Extraction." In *The Human and Environmental Impact of Fracking: How Fracturing Shale for Gas Affects Us and Our World*, edited by Madelon F. Finkel. Santa Barbara, CA: Praeger, 1–21.

Pezzullo, Phaedra. 2007. *Toxic Tourism: Rhetorics of Pollution, Travel, and Environmental Justice*. Tuscaloosa: University of Alabama Press.

Rich, Jessica L. 2016. "Drilling is Just the Beginning: Romanticizing Rust Belt Identities in the Campaign for Shale Gas." *Environmental Communication* 10(3), 292–304.

Schwarze, Steve. 2003. "Juxtaposition in Environmental Health Rhetoric: Exposing Asbestos Contamination in Libby, Montana." *Rhetoric & Public Affairs* 6(2), 313–336.

Shell Global. October 20, 2017. "Natural Gas and Its Advantages." http://www.shell.com/energy-and-innovation/natural-gas/natural-gas-and-its-advantages.html

Shepstone, Tom. November 8, 2011. "The Fox Theater of the Absurd." Energy in Depth Marcellus. http://energyindepth.org/marcellus/fox-the-charlatan/

Shonkoff, Seth B.C. 2015. "Foreword." In *The Human and Environmental Impact of Fracking: How Fracturing Shale for Gas Affects Us and Our World*, edited by Madelon L. Finkel. Santa Barbara, CA: Praeger, ix–x.

SourceWatch. March 26, 2015. "Fracking Regulations." https://www.sourcewatch.org/index.php/Fracking_regulations

"Sparks Fly Over 'Gasland' Drilling Documentary." February 24, 2011. *NPR*. http://www.npr.org/2011/02/24/134031183/Gasland-Takes-On-Natural-Gas-Drilling-Industry

"Truthland: Dispatches from the Real Gasland." June 12, 2012. Produced by Energy in Depth and the Independent Petroleum Association of America. Video 34:28. http://www.truthlandmovie.com/

Tucker, Chris. January 25, 2011. "EID Statement on GasLand Academy Award Nod: 'This Nomination is Fitting, as the Oscars are Aimed at Praising Pure Entertainment.'" *Energy in Depth*. http://energyindepth.org/national/EID-statement-on-gasland-academy-award-nod-this-nomination-is-fitting-as-the-oscars-are-aimed-at-praising-pure-entertainment/

U.S. Environmental Protection Agency. 2016. *Hydraulic Fracturing for Oil and Gas: Impacts from the Hydraulic Fracturing Water Cycle on Drinking Water Resources in the United States: Executive Summary.* Washington, DC: Office of Research and Development.https://cfpub.epa.gov/ncea/hfstudy/recordisplay.cfm?deid=332990

Vasi, Ian Bogdan, Edward T. Walker, John S. Johnson, and Hui Fen Tan. 2015. "'No Fracking Way!' Documentary Film, Discursive Opportunity, and Local Opposition against Hydraulic Fracturing in the United States, 2010–2013." *American Sociological Review* 80(5), 934–959.

Section II

Case Studies in the Global South

7 The Birth of a Myth

The Latin American Modern Oil Nation

Manuel Silva-Ferrer

According to the classic essay by Homi Bhabha, "Narrating the Nation," "nations, like narratives, lose their origins in the myths of time and only fully realize their horizons in the mind's eye." Thus, such an image of the nation, linked to traditions of political thought and literary language, far from being "romantic and excessively metaphorical," lies at the very base of the nation "that emerges as a powerful historical idea in the west" (1990, 1). What Bhabha intends to contend is that beyond this deep-rooted idea of the nation as a hermetic category, linked to the *Volk*'s self-generative concept, a nation is mostly a symbolic force; we could say, a construction determined by a "cultural temporality" that evokes the idea of a specific moment of a social space (1990–1–2).[1]

In this sense, during the Marcos Pérez Jiménez dictatorship (1952–1958), we can see some of the elements that paved the way for the narrations disseminated during the second half of the twentieth century regarding Venezuela as a "modern oil nation." In the global geopolitical context of its time, the Pérez Jiménez dictatorship allowed this narrative of the construction of the nation to position itself as an exceptionality in the Latin American scenario, and in turn, to project itself on a global scale.

Pérez Jiménez's dictatorship endorsed some of the guidelines of the *American New Deal* to undertake an ambitious plan of public works financed with abundant resources from the growing oil industry (Castillo 1990). The constant reference to the notions of "modernity" and "progress" that accompanied the program, based on a principle of "rational transformation of the physical environment," made it possible, as Venezuelan anthropologist and historian Fernando Coronil states, for the Venezuelan nation to become a "visible construct, a concrete appearance" (1997, 173), that spread the image of a country visible only to the political, military, and economic elite that revolved around the business of the oil enclave.

These narrations and imaginaries of progress, boosted on a global scale by oil-generated power, expanded rapidly because of the rearrangements that occurred in Latin America with the new geopolitics of power that emerged after the World War II; the intense transnational exchange that boosted the oil industry; and the original flows of mass media and the entertainment culture that early on were installed as technology in the country, as happened in the rest of Latin America.

At least four pillars supported the articulation of the discursive device that favored the dictatorship and helped consolidate the narratives of Venezuela as a modern oil nation. First, the dictatorship's need to articulate a program and a discourse to legitimize its existence in the Venezuelan and international political scene; second: the priority granted by the United States to consolidating the *status quo* in the continent, *vis-à-vis* the communist threat in the aftermath of the second postwar period (this circumstance allowed dictatorial regimes of different types to exist in Latin America as allies of Washington and the other western powers); third: the political and financial aid granted the dictatorship by transnational oil companies, interested as they were in intensifying their activities in Venezuela, a country that at the time had become one of the most important oil producers in the world. And lastly, the popular imaginary woven by an original mass culture that extended gradually through the press, literature, radio, and cinema, mediators who spread globally the narratives of progress set in the Latin American landscape.

In what follows, I demonstrate what I consider to be the way in which these discourses were organized. First, I tackle the propagandistic strategy deployed by the dictatorship, and the narratives about what was called "the rational transformation of the physical environment," in the frame of the so-called Cold War. Next, I describe how this transformation was translated in the capital city of Caracas. I later offer clues about the role of the international oil industry in this scenario. Lastly, I examine some examples of the so-called petrofictions, as diffusers of the imaginaries that favored the myth of progress associated with oil in Venezuela.

"The Rational Transformation of the Physical Environment" as Legitimizing Discourse of the Dictatorship

From the start the dictatorship of Marcos Pérez Jiménez had two crucial objectives: first, to establish a new political order that would annihilate all dissidence and allow unlimited control over the considerable resources of the petrostate. The second objective was to promote a program of public works as part of its political project baptized *El Nuevo Ideal Nacional*, copied from the American New Deal, according to which the State's aggressive intervention could help overcome the inequalities of Venezuelan society:

> Hence, it's not a simple matter of modifications in particulars, such as the ones achieved by opening up roads, repairing populated centers, and the implementation of sanitation in specific areas, but rather it was something much more ambitious and grandiose: to obtain a gradual reconditioning of the entire territory in all its physical

> aspects in order to make it more tailored to contemporary civilization. (In: Venezuela bajo El Nuevo Ideal Nacional en 1954. Caracas. 1954, 16). (My own translation from the Spanish)

El Nuevo Ideal Nacional was formulated as the sum of pragmatisms and the modernization theories of Walt Whitman Rostow popular during that time, and within the context that imposed the prompt development of a perceptible work that would justify the dictatorship's existence. *El Nuevo Ideal Nacional* became, then, not only a government program but also a philosophy, a slogan and the template of a publicity campaign repeated incessantly at each official act, in the newspapers, radio and in television; this slogan granted sense and arguments to the authoritarian regime (Castillo 1990, 61–93).

Implementing a huge program of infrastructure works generated an unprecedented public expenditure, one that on the one hand began in a significant occult indebtedness in growth figures aided by high oil prices, and on the other hand in an indirect transfer of the vast income provided by the expanding oil industry that would end up in the hands of the elite military in control of the petrostate and the industrial sector, ally of the dictatorship (González Abreu 1997, 78–81). Both the oil-fostered economic growth and the successful execution of a bountiful public works program fed the myth of Venezuela as a modern oil country.

By forcefully suppressing the political muscle of the parties, the men who held power after the *coup d'état* in 1948, and more so, after 1952, focused mainly on the execution—and ample media dissemination—of the visible physical work. Thereby, the military government pretended to modernize Venezuela through what it called a "rational transformation of the physical environment," while suppressing all individual freedom and limiting the political and social reforms initiated following the dictatorship of Juan Vicente Gómez (1908–1935).

This pursuit of modernity and progress then focused on constructing its most opulent visible symbols, not on modernity itself. Hence, luxury hotels, health resorts, highways, power plants, and other public works became not only symbols but also the conquerors of progress. By transplanting them "from metropolitan centers to the backward local soil, these fetishes of modernity were believed to carry the power to bring progress to Venezuela." In this sense, the dictatorship's vision was expressed not in a programmatic but in a pragmatic way (Coronil 1997, 173), expressed through narratives and advertising. Thus, the construction of these external icons of modernity was accompanied by massive national and international media representation that supported the creation of a myth that Venezuela was a very rich country on its way to achieving development. This discourse hid the reality of a country that continued to be very poor, while the State, by a geological twist of fate, had suddenly become a millionaire after discovering itself owner of enormous riches contained in the subsoil of the national territory, and at once it became administrator of the revenue that they produced.

Thus, the foundations of the "modern oil nation" became visible in a spectacular set of works carried out by the dictatorship, not in an organic program that supported a profound transformation of the structural causes that made Venezuela a mostly poor and backward country. Hence the insincerity of the typical cinematographic phrases of the newscasts of the day: "*booming republic,*" "*boomtown of South America,*" "the country of progress," etc. As Coronil states, "without a clear program for economic development, but having abundant monetary resources, Pérez Jiménez's government set out to purchase economic progress" (1997, 177). In this manner, although modernity was not reached, the myth of its proximity to it was born.

Boomtown of South America

In this way, Caracas was transformed from an uncomplicated and insignificant city within the Latin American context to an international tourist and architectural center that served as "palpable proof" of the discourse disseminated by the media that Venezuela was a modern oil nation. Although the oil-driven expansion had begun twenty years earlier, the fifties are seen as the beginning of a radical spatial transformation of the Venezuelan capital. As of that moment, the once tranquil Caracas was invaded by new and attractive buildings, avenues, and highways with peculiar names (La Araña—The Spider; El Pulpo—The Octopus; El Ciempiés—The Centipede) that modified its physiognomy and granted it a new and vibrant metropolitan dimension. But above all, it was overrun by a colossal migration from all corners of the country of people looking for opportunities not found in backward and rural Venezuela. Likewise, it was occupied by numerous Latin Americans, Europeans, and Asians who sought safe haven in that new "modern oil nation," attracted by the siren calls of unlimited prosperity, well-being, and progress fed by the new oil *gold rush.* Thus, Caracas experienced a relentless cycle of expansion, where vertiginous changes and cultural and human intersections were the most visible symbols of the modernity myth, constructed by the power of oil in a backward Caribbean country. Soon the valley of Caracas was overwhelmed by its inhabitants, and a desperate battle began to populate the surrounding hills. Rich and poor alike thus colonized the upper areas where the vistas and cliffs were distributed to the rhythm of socioeconomic inequalities.

Oil, it's well known, produces miracles. Thus, commissioned by the government, the architect Tomás Sanabria (1956) placed on top of El Avila, the mountain that crowns the city and separates it from the Caribbean, 2,140 meters above sea level, a cylinder-shaped, lavish hotel with a 360-degree view, which could only be reached via a cable car, built especially for it. The place instantly became incorporated into the capital's dazzling social life, which lasted throughout the fifties because of the immense oil wealth.

In this context, businessman Armando Planchart and his wife Anala set out to seduce Gio Ponti, one of the most important architects of the time, to design their house in Lomas del Mirador. He created the villa "El Cerrito" (1957), which included not only the house, but also the dishes, tables, curtains and bathroom facilities, which can be seen today in this house-museum, an icon of twentieth-century architecture. Spurred by the euphoria of this boomtown, Ponti celebrated the "modern spirit" that made Caracas a "city of the future" (Ponti 1961).

Amidst social clashes and overwhelming *nouveau riche* behavior, over the eastern hills of Petare, Italian Athos Albertoni (1958) designed for René Borges Villegas a mansion that today crowns Petare, the largest and poorest barrio in the country; some years later, Richard Neutra (1962) completed, within El Ávila national park itself, a spectacular house for the banker, José Joaquín González Gorrondona.

In the San Bernardino neighborhood, the office of Harrison & Abramovitz produced for Nelson Rockefeller, the *Hotel Avila* (1942). Well into the Pérez Jiménez dictatorship, Cipriano Domínguez completed the *Torres del Centro Simón Bolívar* (1952) which immediately became the tallest buildings in the city, iconic of the new urban scenery and the ideology that fed the progress myth. Soon after, Brazilian Roberto Burle Marx designed the gardens for the enormous complex *Hipódromo La Rinconada* (1959), a work designed by the firm Froehlich & Associates from Beverly Hills, and later, those of the *Parque del Este* (1961). In 1950, Fruto Vivas, a creative Venezuelan architect, designed *Club Táchira* (1950) in Colinas de Bello Monte. In the midst of the oil boom that boosted American interests in Venezuela, Donald Hatch designed the new headquarters for the United States Embassy (1957), in whose north façade an enormous metal mural by another American designer, Harry Bertoia, was installed. From these fragments was constructed the utopian narrative of a modern world among extreme wealth and the most abject poverty in Caracas.

Construction in the fifties of *Paseo Los Próceres* offered the city a monumental space it didn't have before. But the summit of this golden cycle of intense spatial transformation that served as one pillar of the myth of Venezuela as a modern oil nation is the construction of the *Ciudad Universitaria de Caracas* (1954). A work of Venezuelan architect, Carlos Raúl Villanueva, who proposed "a synthesis of the arts"—a sort of system of creation of a new architectural-sculptural organism—reached its finest realization in the *Plaza del Rectorado* with its auditoriums and library. There Villanueva saw his ideas realized in an exceptional complex, combining the buildings with elements proposed by some of the most creative exponents of geometric Latin American abstractionism, together with the work of another group of international artists. Above all, the Aula Magna, with its acoustic clouds (the famous "flying saucers" by Alexander Calder), the lobby of the *Biblioteca Central*, with a stained-glass work by Calder himself, as well as the small plaza that houses Jean Arp's "Pastor de Nubes," are a sample of the dynamism and yearning for experimentation and transcendence of the avant-garde of the times which, in turn, fed the discourses of a miraculous progress boosted by oil in Latin American soil.

"People and Petroleum": Oil Companies and the Myth of Progress

The irruption in the early twentieth century of diverse nationalistic movements around the world (that nationalized oil in México in 1938 and in Iran in 1951), and the pressure of international public opinion, which observed with displeasure the aggressive actions of the oil industry trusts, made the oil consortiums rethink how they were addressing the business, especially the relations with governments such as those that, like Venezuela, were absolute owners of the mineral wealth deposited in the subsoil of their respective nations. The new context offered by the geopolitical reconfiguration in the West that materialized from the second postwar period (more favorable to democratic regimes and those not-so-democratic but committed to the fight against communism), forced international oil capital to modify its methods of force that had been so effective.

As of that moment, and without abandoning altogether the old methods, a new persuasive strategy began that used intense publicity campaigns and public relations supported by the new mass media. It aimed to associate the political class and public opinion in general with the industry's interests and its role as "a motor for progress and a source of prosperity for all." Therefore, it incorporated the oil industries' values into Venezuela's political, social, and cultural structure, thus avoiding by way of all media the conflicts that in México, Iran, and other regions of the world had challenged their interests (Tinker Salas 2009, 191–199).

From this strategy emerged in Venezuela some of the most important communications media in service of the progress program. Modern advertising began in the country as affiliates of the larger publicity agencies, such as McCann Erickson, were installed in Caracas. Simultaneously, Venezuela's own mass communication media was installed and financed directly or indirectly by British and American oil companies (Pasquali 1972). This contribution by the private sector thus allowed the myth of modernity and progress to be inserted into the values and beliefs that the State was promoting, as part of this newly imagined community molded by oil.

Reporter Esso was essential in this strategy; it was a radio newscast created by the Eastern States Standard Oil (Esso), produced between

1942 and 1975, with material from the United Press and the United States Information Program. Even more important was the first Venezuelan TV newscast, *El Observador Creole*, produced by the same Standard Oil, Creole's parent company. The program was transmitted in prime time without interruption, first by Radio Caracas Televisión (1953–1972), and subsequently by Cadena Venezolana de Televisión (1972–1976). As Venezuelan television had been installed in 1952 according to the commercial American model, for almost two decades *El Observador Creole* was the main news broadcaster in Venezuelan television. It set the agenda for the country's public opinion on the oil industry's issues and perspective. Together with the newscasts, a collection of documentaries, advertising, and entertainment programs dominated the mass media in a strategy that Tinker Salas noted was the result of a communications policy formulated at the highest strata of the industry (2009, 194).

As part of its powerful PR program, Creole and Shell also actively supported directly or indirectly many activities in science, education, and culture. The magazines, *El Farol* and *Revista Shell*, are the best examples of corporate culture integrated into the local arts and intelligentsia sectors. The Shell Film Unit also had an essential role internationally; created in England under John Grierson's influence, it produced some noteworthy documentaries in Venezuela. The films directed by Lionel Cole clearly illustrate their role in promoting the myth of progress: *Harvest Tomorrow – Venezuela (1951)* and *Venezuela looks ahead (1952).*

At a time when few Venezuelan cultural institutions existed and the Instituto Nacional de la Cultura (INCIBA)—the first leading cultural institution in Venezuela—had not yet been created, the activity and financial muscle of Creole and Shell (certified later with the creation of the Fundación Creole (1956) and Fundación Shell (1959)) turned them into powerful patrons of science and the arts.

This cultural production supported mainly educational, artistic, and scientific activities, but other activities were more straightforward publicity material, such as the documentary *People and Petroleum: The Story of Creole in Venezuela*, produced by the Creole Petroleum Corporation to pave the way for its activities in the country. The documentary's introductory text summarizes precisely how the industry's advertising strategy is committed to the myth of progress:

> Stretching along the eastern shore of Lake Maracaibo in Venezuela, is one of the industrial wonders of modern times, the oil-producing complex of the Bolívar coastal field with more than 2.000 oil wells reaching almost to the horizon. One of the largest known oil deposits in the world, these resources brought a new light to the people of Venezuela. The oil beneath these waters belongs to those people, but the stupendous task of bringing it to the surface, refining it, and marketing it has been the work of private foreign capital and

> engineering genius. . . much of it is North American. Much of this work has been done by one company: the Creole Petroleum Corporation. Creole is an American company, an affiliate of the Standard Oil Company of New Jersey that operates exclusively in Venezuela, with headquarters in Caracas, a sparkling modern city whose progress is rooted in oil. At its Caracas offices, this company manages the business interests of Venezuelans, as well as of its own stockholders. This is the story of an American business firm which has become an integral part of the nation's social and economic progress. . . (*People and Petroleum: The Story of Creole in Venezuela*. Caracas: Creole Petroleum Corporation. circa 1954)

As Tinker Salas rightly noted, "increasingly Creole sought to associate itself with the very existence of the nation. The nation depended on Creole, and Creole depended on the goodwill of the nation" (2009, 196).

The oil companies bolstered their role in society and Venezuelan public opinion, while endorsing the dictatorship with their discourses as well as their actions; in turn, the dictatorship reciprocated. Hence, Pérez Jiménez, while avoiding conflict that challenged his government's stability, not only kept the syndicates outlawed, as well as the right to strike, he also avoided creating a national oil or gas company, relinquishing to the transnational companies the monopoly of extraction, refinement, and marketing of Venezuelan oil, within and without the country. The dictatorship, which never garnered popular legitimacy, but—at least in its beginnings—was supported by the military, a strategic alliance with the church, and the backing of economic national and international elites, was never interested in benefiting from increasing taxes for oil exploitation. This relationship was not always an easy one, but in the midst of high prices for commodities the government compliantly granted benefits to the corporate and financial sectors. This approach enriched the military leadership and helped create an international image of the modern and stable oil paradise (Castillo 1990, 183–201).

Thus, the material core generated by oil consolidated a lasting relationship among the international oil capital, society, and Venezuelan culture, a crucial link for understanding not only the inseparable evolution between society and oil in Venezuela, but also the manner in which throughout the last century—and also at the beginning of the twenty-first century—the positive image of different dictatorial and democratic regimes was spread, associated with the myth of progress fueled by oil wealth.

Petrofictions: The Discourses of Literature and Film in the Modern Oil Nation

Mark C. Carnes (1996) notes that the creation of myths only requires the suppression of history, and that history never stops reconstructing itself from the moment the myths are created. History has also shown that film and literature have played central roles in constructing specific narratives that, heightened on a massive scale by mass media, tend to become collective imaginaries (Ferro 2003). Sometimes these narratives result from premeditated maneuvers, whose goal is to legitimize those who deliver them. At other times, however, they emerge spontaneously. In both operations, consciously or otherwise, the masses tend to accept them as true.

Today it is clear that the expansion of narratives about Venezuela as a "modern oil nation" wasn't only the result of a premeditated structure, but also as a consequence of text production in the cultural field that intensified its permanence over time.[2] Literary and cultural studies have shown that although the debates regarding the so-called "black gold" lasted throughout the twentieth century, dominated by social sciences, it was in the field of literature where the first attempts occurred at contextualizing the complex problem that its exploitation produced in Venezuela.[3] These stories, anxious to fictionalize history, often combined the authors' experiences and memories in the heat of the prevailing conflicts in the first oil fields. Their testimonial nature marks many of the narratives of the first half-century in Latin American oil literature. This positioning reflects the original character of the industry and its methods and the need of those involved to describe the harsh conflicts revealed by the antagonism between modernity and tradition, translated here in the debate between civilization and barbarism.

Generally speaking, this first literature describes the economic, political, and social transformations (the ominous change, sudden wealth, ambition, corruption, internal complicity, plundering, murky deals, discrimination, the oil madness, the exodus of peasants, the superpower of the company, invasion of lands, anti-imperialism), and the characters, (the peasant, the foreign company, the magnate, the local intermediary, the engineer, the technician, the gringos, the State, the President, the graduate, the judge, the official, the prostitutes) that delineate some of the key issues that the oil novel will develop in later decades, as identified by Gustavo L. Carrera (1972).

To explore the narrations of oil associated with the myth of modernity and progress, I now turn briefly to three works of literary fiction that are mostly unknown to readers unfamiliar with Venezuelan literature: Ramón Díaz Sánchez's *Mene* (1936), Mario Briceño Iragorry's, *Los Riberas* (1957), and Miguel Otero Silva's *Oficina N° 1* (1960). I must underscore, in discussing these works, that the literary discourse, despite harshly criticizing the negative consequences created by applying the progress program in different fields in Latin America, managed simultaneously to abet the myth of the modern, oil-rich nation. This process resulted from the relatively widespread dissemination of these novels in their time as compelling records of how social expectations changed as oil arrived in Venezuelan society.

Thus, the projection of the myth via literature worked almost involuntarily, initiated by the desire of literature to organize an idea of life possible to achieve only through imagination. This was also due to the value bestowed on the narrative as a form of representation of reality (White 1981, 23).

Thus, German Carrera Damas, Venezuelan historiographer, saw in the tale of Alfonso Ribera in *Los Riberas,* from his origin as a small, rural businessman to his pinnacle as a banker, heir to the lucrative actions his father had successfully carried out between the State and the transnational oil companies, "an outline (. . .) for the study of the creation of Venezuelan bourgeoisie during the first half of the Twentieth Century." Carrera Damas appreciates the manner in which "the influx of the gigantic and murky oil business (. . .) carried out in the shadows of public power (. . .) would become the fastest method for accumulating capital: graft" (1961, 13–14). Thus, he illuminates elements that formed the fragile foundation for the programs for development and progress, both distinguishing traits of the Pérez Jimenez dictatorship, as much as they had been earlier during the dictatorships of Juan Vicente Gómez and later of Hugo Chávez and Nicolás Maduro.

From that moment, the complicity with foreign capital, the enjoyment of prerogatives cosseted by the State, and the blatant looting of public funds were the secret formula for accumulating enormous wealth that fueled the fables of the modern El Dorado in Latin America. Thus, when Don Vicente Ribera arrives at the capital from the province, he says to his son:

> My income comes from the participation in two or three sales of *aguardiente* (sugarcane liquor), with the help of the General, and my past part in the Lottery. Besides, you know about the part I've played in the agreements of the hydrocarbon sector with the English. At present, the Standard Oil Company is also doing business with the Government for obtaining rich concessions, and I'll get a nice slice from it. We'll talk about this in detail later, because with two or three things I'll get a hold of for you with the General, you'll be really rich in no time. (Briceño Iragorry 1957, 212)[4]

Beyond the political and economic transformations and the leap towards a miraculous cosmogony enhanced by oil, Briceño Iragorry focuses on the change in mentality created by the transformation from an agrarian community of large estate owners to a modern oil nation. This transition is described in the novel's first two parts, "A Man" and "Another Man":

> Just as yesterday cocoa symbolized the economic power of the colonial oligarchy—to the point of giving it its name—the new fly-by-night oligarchy could be called tomorrow the oil oligarchy. Black,

> foul-smelling crude oil would be in reality, the terrible symbol for the new era of the republic. (Briceño Iragorry 1957, 423)

Los Riberas describes how the myth of progress is tied to oil and how it sinks its roots into Latin America as a type of embezzlement: the violent, vertiginous accumulation of capital by the companies working with the new local elite, whose political influences assist in accomplishing the essential goal—to get close to the considerable resources and businesses offered by the rich petrostate.

However, if *Los Riberas* documents the emergence of the rich bourgeoisie associated with oil, *Mene* and *Oficina N° 1* show the simultaneous process through which marginalized classes and the proletariat emerge—the dark side of the myth of modernity and progress. From the birth of an oil town (El Tigre), Miguel Otero Silva (1960) in *Oficina N° 1* describes the peasants' exodus in search of progress, their creation of settlements out of the prosperity of the period, and their subsequent perishment at the same speed with which they emerged, as a metaphor for the "decadence of the large-estate farming system and small commercial entity (. . .) and the embedment and violent emergence of a different model, whose dynamic element is oil" (Araujo 1972, 137).

A sequel to *Casas Muertas* (1955), *Oficina N° 1* recounts the transformation of an oil well into an oil settlement. It narrates the rural world's abrupt modification and the implications for local and global space created by the exchanges that occurred. Thereon, a humble worker from Margarita, relocated to the oil fields of El Tigre, asks the American foreman with whom he lives:

> What's the use of this steel tower and this 6,184-foot pipeline and that platform endlessly turning? What's the use of this field bloated with oil? What are all of us who have searched and found oil like hound dogs good for? (. . .)
>
> -Everything serves the same end, little Robinson. An encrypted cable will arrive tonight at Pittsburgh, and tomorrow the price of the Company's shares will go up. What is the Company? Who is the Company? What are the shareholders of the Company doing at this moment? You and I, with our blistered hands and weary back are drinking warm beer in an immense treeless, womanless field. As for Taylor, he's dying in a hospital. Don't you understand? (Otero Silva 1960, 65)

Thus, Otero Silva's novel reflects not only the changes in the economic and social fields, but it also explores the structural changes in the field of everyday culture that resulted from the complex processes that emerge from the abrupt transition from an agrarian, semifeudal economy to modern capitalism based on oil. As Venezuelan writer, Juan Liscano, observed, the entire population, without being prepared for it, entered a vertiginous spiral of transformations similar to the geographic modification of the territory itself and the spatial repositioning of the population but also created a new system of social behavior, valuations, work, exchange rates, prices and value of things, habits, games, diversion and even language and speech (Liscano 1981, 17). These radical changes into a completely different society are typical of the incorporation of western modernity into Venezuelan and Latin American culture. As Jean Franco states in his analysis of the text, it's about "a violent and ruthless place that represents (. . .) the beginning of a new future;" he further notes that although oil wealth didn't unravel the social conflicts produced by the acute structural inequalities, Otero Silva did describe the creation of the "essential foundations for a modern State" (Franco 1971, 268).

In contrast, in *Mene,* Ramon Díaz Sánchez (1936) uses his own experience as a local judge of the city of Cabimas, on the Western Coast of Maracaibo Lake in western Venezuela, to describe the new modern poverty emerging around the oil fields, dragging with it large migratory groups attracted by the new myth of progress. Written at the beginning of the 1930s, *Mene* is thus a pioneer work, considered not only an important predecessor of the literature of oil in Latin America but also of special interest in the configuration of the Venezuelan modern narrative itself. In this novel, Díaz Sánchez proposes tensions between poetry and prose, writing and orality, history and fiction, in which the description of the new technological elements of the industrial world itself shapes a mythical version where oil becomes the engine of experiences and imaginaries hitherto unknown. The book is a fabulous narration that incorporates itself as cultural memory of those who live around the modern oil settlement (Bohórquez 2005, 108–114). It is also a history of wild progress, where modern machines and effortless wealth constitute a new scenario not only of landscape destruction, but also of a violent transculturation, a mix and hybridization of traditions and symbolic universes of those that, from now on, will be known as the oil community.

The novel is constructed as a chorale ensemble, in which a multitude of figures and scenarios alternate and where the importance is determined not by the development of particular characters' conflicts but by a geological fact: the power of the subsoil that turns the so-called black gold into the new cohesive element of nature and the men that inhabit in it:

> The squads grew endlessly, organized under a steely discipline like that of the machines. Now it wasn't only fair-haired people and Indians on the wounded soil. Every morning more boats arrived filled with strange men, with strange languages, with strange colors. Babel embodied its myth on this portion of a feverish land. They all brought with them the same fervor, the same yearnings.

> Dark towns –Cabimas, Lagunillas, Mene– were incorporated into the frenzy of the world. Footpaths became streets, clusters of thorn trees became houses: makeshift houses, made from cardboard from the machines, and covered with zinc sheets. The madness of a dream stolen from the oniric borders. (Díaz Sánchez [1936] 1958, 30)

Thus, the silence of the jungle and the lake swamps was suddenly confronted by the sound of machines, the modern wonders: steamboats, the Buicks, Fords, airplanes, the refrigerator, electricity, electric stoves—suddenly the paradigm that ruled becomes another one: everything can be electric—and the uproar of entire towns transformed into oil fields:

> (. . .) each drill has a pumpjack that sucks (. . .), each pumpjack has a palpitating motor (. . .), each motor has a boiler that regurgitates like a grotesque torn artery. Besides this, at the place of "El Hijo de la Noche" there were a thousand mouths screaming and laughing, two thousand feet pounding, a derelict band screeching desperately, destroying a *paso-doble*, and a thousand fists pounding on the table tops and on the iron chairs. From the street came the roar of the automobiles and the wounded cry of the gramophones. (Díaz Sánchez [1936] 1958, 54)

In *Mene,* as in *Oficina N°1,* are found some of the discursive pillars that fueled the myth of oil-driven progress, seeking to reconstruct through fiction the contradictory transcultural processes of mixtures and copresence which impose "the atmosphere in which modern sensibility is born" (Berman 1982, 5). It is sudden wealth pouring out. Combat, in the midst of the twentieth century, between troops commanded by oil engineers opening up jungle roads and the indigenous people defending themselves with bows and arrows, symbolizing the progress that's dragging everything in its path; faith in the future and the ideals of an era pretending to be modern; the struggles between foreign bosses and the emerging working class that discovers the value of unions and strikes. The improvised swarming streets with the hawking ice-cream man where one can hear spoken Chinese, English, Italian, Arab, and German. The cardboard and tin huts, or the shacks where the *chinchorros* hang, together with acclimatized, hermetic bungalows create a new urban landscape. Geologists and workers mingle with robbers and prostitutes; cockfights, dice, lottery and dominos share space with the club, tennis, baseball, billiard, and the casino: "Play seven, you win, play eleven, I win." Stews, canned food, and Corn Flakes. Rum, bottles of sugar cane liquor laced with spices and fruit, mingled with martinis, whisky, ginger ale, and colored soda drinks. The bar and dancing, the rock-cola, the phonograph, the radio and the cinematograph, the itinerant library, the school, and the theater.

Le salaire de la peur

Despite the extensive local dissemination of this literature, it was not until the film, *Le salaire de la peur (The Wages of Fear)* by French author, Henri-George Clouzot (1953), that the petrofictions set in the Latin American context reached global perceptibility, and with it also, a part of the narrations that exacerbated the idea of modernity associated with oil in Venezuela.

Le salaire de la peur is the adaptation of a novel of the same name, successfully published in France in 1950 by Georges Arnaud, a journalist, writer, and adventurer who had lived in Venezuela two years earlier. Consequently, with firsthand knowledge of life in the oil field, he was easily able to question in his story the myth of progress associated with oil.

The narration unfolds in a miserable, unnamed oil town in Latin America, where a group of lowlife men, expelled from Europe during the second postwar period, remains trapped without a future. Without money or employment, their life transpires while they wait for a stroke of luck that will allow them to change their destiny. What happens when the North American oil company that dominates the town's economy offers them an escape from their boring nightmare, in exchange for driving two trucks loaded with nitroglycerin, destined to stifle the fire in an oil well located 400 kilometers away?

What follows is a worthy representation of the "modern tragedy" heightened by oil exploitation, a drama in which, with great sensibility, Clouzot draws the narrative of poverty and the destruction of natural landscapes that Arnaud, like his Latin American colleagues, had managed to convey in literature:

> –Yesterday there was a catastrophe. This is not correct, this is not fair. . . once again we have to bear all the consequences. We always have to die. But *los gringos* never die. They kill your parents, your brothers. . . then they give you a handful of money and it's over (. . .) The mountain is burning, from Los Santos Angeles you can see the flames. . . (Clouzot, 1953)

However, despite connections with the literary corpus of oil, *Le salaire* transcends the tendency to denunciate that characterized many of these narratives that emerged in the early twentieth century. These stories simplify the enormously complex cultural universe inside the oil landscapes, turning them into a series of binary dualisms: the good man of the land confronts the evil vices summarized in "the gringo" and the foreign companies. This formula reproduced itself many times in the narratives that Venezuelan writer, Miguel "Angel" Campos (2005), characterized as the "social (thesis) novel." In such texts, the chronicle materialized the desire to fix a testimony, a tool for recording a vanishing time, where fiction served as a pedagogical discourse.

As in *Mene* and *Oficina N° 1*, *Le salaire de la peur* stands out as a meticulous attempt to reconstruct the contradictions under which the new industry developed. It is the novelty of the miraculous oil settlement, the myth of El Dorado come true amongst indigenous people and unprivileged peasants, settlers of lands of miseries that float above a subsoil that contains an energy capable of moving the world. Despite Arnaud offering a less local view of the elements that belong to everyday life and articulate the particular constellation of the oil fields, this perspective allows him to develop other dimensions beyond the class struggle or the foreign penetration to focus on an essentially human drama: risk as a condition of physical survival and the need to overcome fear to be worthy of receiving a living wage—in other words, the condition of the wage earner in the modern world, as Spanish writer, Manuel Vásquez Montalbán suggests in his prologue to the Spanish translation. In *Le salaire*, a political discourse about capitalist exploitation and economic colonialism becomes clear: the modern tragedy in the third world, but beyond the denunciation, "it matters more 'the message' about the human condition and a fully existentialist idea of destiny" (Vázquez Montalbán 1990, 4).

Clouzot translates this work about the human condition into a film with enormous realism. The staging conjures the details of a chaotic space that emerges from nowhere in the burning semi-desert savannah, where the first oil settlement materializes almost spontaneously. These descriptions dominate the film's first half, where the exoticism of an impoverished landscape introduces a polyphonic world of different languages and cultures.

The second part, however, takes an unexpected turn as landscape recedes to focus on the conflicts within the characters. Mario (Yves Montand), Jo (Charles Vanel), Bimba (Peter van Eyck), and Luigi (Folco Lulli) abandon their archetypal roles as foreign workers to become central to a powerful tragedy, one led by four hungry subjects fleeing the European postwar drama of poverty, unemployment, and a sort of destiny marked in a lost town in Latin America:

> "That no one looks in this book for that geographical exactitude that is nothing more than a trick: Guatemala, for instance, does not exist. I know it, I have lived there": the introductory epigraph to Arnaud's book is a paradox that synthesizes this contradiction that defines myths as powerful narrative instruments, the blurring boundary between reality and fiction, myth and history. Where does mythology end and history begin?, Claude Lévi-Strauss wonders (2012, 69)

The reference to this "geographical exactitude" that someone could look for in the town of Las Piedras, where *Le salaire* takes place, is not, then, impossible, despite being about a deliberate act of literary and cinematographic creation. And this is because Las Piedras is not only an imaginary place, but also the reconstruction of a part of Arnaud's own experiences as an adventurer in Latin America. Therefore, although there is no geographical exactitude, we can find an experiential base that supports fiction and carries with it the imaginary construction of a myth. That is why, even when Arnaud claims that Guatemala does not exist, it is the fact of having been there that allows him to assure the audience that that territory is mere artifice, just like Otero Silva's El Tigre, the fields in Díaz Sánchez' *Mene*, or Marcos Pérez Jiménez' Venezuela.

The enormous success of *Le salaire de la peur* served to project straightaway the oil narratives in Latin American soil to the arts circuits and global entertainment.[5] Hence, without setting out to do so, the widespread dissemination obtained by the novel and the film converged with the international propaganda in circulation as part of the publicity apparatus of the Pérez Jiménez dictatorship and the oil trusts.

Thus, out of the juncture of the tales inspired by this "modern tragedy" and the official discourses of progress promulgated by the oil companies and the propaganda apparatus of Pérez Jiménez' dictatorship emerged a good part of the myth of the "modern oil nation." This myth was a fabricated, immensely attractive space for the cultural industry that thereafter focused on presenting an entire literary and cinematographic production whose goals were focused not on the problematization of the complex reality of the oil landscapes, nor on the Pérez Jiménez's dictatorship, nor on a direct political propaganda, but rather on making the cultural novelty of a phenomenon commercially profitable. It was an enterprise that simultaneously—and unwillingly—helped to disseminate worldwide the narratives that for decades had fed the myth of "Venezuela as a modern Latin American oil nation".

The production of these narratives of the oil theme set in Latin America sprang thus in countless examples of pocket literature and B movies, merchandise in which oil, unconstrained by now of all context, became a simple footing for making cultural productions without much attempt at authorship, much more interested in exploiting the oil landscapes as scenarios than in understanding the local complex hardships.

Beginning with those texts, the expansion of the notion of Venezuela related with the oil imaginary has been ever present in countless documentaries and fiction films that have built a narration of the nation as a system of cultural significations in the same manner that the oil enclave was built: as a limited and exceptional space, isolated from the complex national and global reality.

Concluding Remarks

On January 23 1958, a movement led by an alliance of political parties and military sectors managed to overthrow the Pérez Jiménez dictatorship. As of that moment, a vehement activity of reconstruction of the memory commenced in different scenarios in the country. The new democracy attempted to retrieve what had been made invisible: torture, abductions, disappearances, exile.

Thus, a radical change in international communications policies took place, a communications policy that had been an essential footing for the Pérez Jiménez dictatorship, and now the same international newscasts that months before had celebrated the efficiency of the government talked about the ill-gotten fortune of the ex-dictator.

But the cart loaded with the narrations of an era of progress had been set in motion. Hence, echoes of the memory encouraged by its most visible founding icons continued to exert a silent task that fed from a distance the nostalgia of an allegedly modern nation.

However, the most recent developments in Venezuelan history have shown that the much-desired progress, the modernity that inspired all types of democratic and dictatorial governments throughout the twentieth century, was only a temporary illusion, a barely sustained, costly, "cultural representation"—in the sense proposed by Bhabha (1990)—or, as the Venezuelan writer, Arturo Uslar Pietri, pointed out, a part of our history's panorama defined by the most important and decisive event: "the geological fact that oil had formed in immense quantities in its subsoil" (1955, 223).

Notes

1 During the congress of the Asociación de Historiadores Latinoamericanistas Europeos, held in Berlin on September 2014, a Mexican historian asked me with regard to the paper I presented there: what is so attractive to historians and cultural scientists about the period of the military dictatorship of Marcos Pérez Jiménez in Venezuela, within the context of Latin American history? The following pages are an attempt to elaborate further on my answer. As such, this essay contains fragments of a paper presented by me at the *Congreso de Historiadores Latinoamericanistas Europeos* – AHILA, held in 2014 in Berlin, between September 9 and 13. Some notes were also published in my blog of the Hispanic American Historical Review, HAHR-Online.

2 Notwithstanding, I emphasize that during Marcos Pérez Jiménez's political domination, literature was also useful propaganda favorable to the dictatorship's project, although it didn't produce works identified as petrofictions. In the essay *Historia de un encargo: "La Catira" de Camilo José Cela*, Gustavo Guerrero (2008) addresses the relationship between the young Spanish writer, who had not yet been awarded the Nobel prize, and the dictatorship's need to spread its propaganda program to other international areas.

3 Discussions of the literary phenomenon in Venezuela can be found in Campos (1994, 2005) as well as Carrera (1972). Discussions of other regions of Latin America can be found in Negrín (1995, 1997), Rapp (1957), Schneider (1989, 1997). These narratives produced by literature very early on, rather than intensifying the myth of progress, focused more on formulating acrid critiques, while denouncing the social and ecological consequences produced as a result of the violence with which the exploration and implantation of

the industry was being carried out. These works also revealed "the darker side of modernity" (in Walter Mignolo's formulation) associated with oil in Latin American soil. Hence, *Mancha de aceite* by César Uribe Piedrahita (1935), *Guachimanes* by Gabriel Bracho Montiel (1954), *Los Riberas* by Mario Briceño Iragorry (1957), *Mene* by Ramón Díaz Sánchez (1958), or *Oficina N° 1* by Miguel Otero Silva (1960), are but a few novels of a long genealogy that begins some two decades back; these manage to accomplish a reconstruction, early on, of the radical changes in mentalities, experience schemes and social expectations, that as a result of the oil exploitation and the arrival of a new phase of globalization, was happening in Venezuela at the same time as in other Latin American, North American, Nordic, Arab, and African societies.

4 Since no English translations exist of the texts quoted, the author has translated these paragraphs from the Spanish.

5 The film, *Le salaire de la peur,* obtained the Cannes Film Festival Palme d'Or Award in 1953, and the Silver Bear Award in the Berlin Film Festival; in 1954, it received an award by the Film Critics Syndicate of France, and in 1955, England's BAFTA Prize for best film.

References

Araujo, Orlando. 1972. *Narrativa venezolana contemporánea.* Caracas: Editorial Nuevo Tiempo.

Arnaud, Georges. 1950. *Le salaire de la peur.* Paris: Julliard.

Berman, Marshall. 1982. *All That is Solid Melts into the Air: The Experience of Modernity.* New York: Penguin Books.

Bhabha, Homi (ed.). 1990. "Narrating the Nation." In *Nation and Narration,* 1–7. London/New York: Routledge.

Bohórquez, Douglas. 2005. "Mene: vanguardia y petróleo." *Revista de Literatura Hispanoamericana,* 50: 101–121.

Bracho Montiel, Gabriel. 1954 [2010]. *Guachimanes: doce aguafuertes para ilustrar la novela del petróleo.* Caracas: El perro y la rana.

Briceño Iragorry, Mario. 1957. *Los Riberas.* Caracas/Madrid: Ediciones Independencia.

Campos, Miguel Angel. 1994. *Las novedades del petróleo.* Caracas: FUNDARTE/ Alcaldía de Caracas.

———. 2005. *Desagravio del mal.* Caracas: Fundación Bigott.

Carnes, Mark C. (ed.). 1996. *Past Imperfect: History According to the Movies.* New York: Holt.

Carrera, Gustavo Luis. 1972. *La novela del petróleo en Venezuela.* Caracas: Servicios venezolanos de publicidad.

Carrera Damas, Germán. 1961. "Proceso a la formación de la burguesía venezolana. A propósito de "Los Riberas" de Mario Briceño Iragorry." *Crítica Contemporánea,* 5: 11–22.

Castillo D'Imperio, Ocarina. 1990. *Los años del bulldozer. Ideología y Política (1948–1958).* Caracas: Fondo Editorial Tropycos, Asociación de Profesores UCV, CENDES.

Clouzot, Henri-George. 1953. Le Salaire de la peur. (Film). Francia/Italia: Compagnie Industrielle et Commerciale Cinématographique (CICC), Filmsonor, Vera Films.

Coronil, Fernando. 1997. *The Magical State. Nature, Money and Modernity in Venezuela*. Chicago: The University of Chicago Press.

Díaz Sánchez, Ramón. 1936 [1958]. *Mene*. Caracas: Reproducciones Gráficas.

Ferro, Marc. 2003. *Le Cinéma, une vision de l'histoire*. Paris: Le Chêne.

Fotografía Urbana Venezolana 1850–2009. 2009. Caracas: Fundación para la Cultura Urbana.

Franco, Jean. 1971. *La cultura moderna en América Latina*. México: Joaquín Mortiz.

González Abreu, Manuel. 1997. *Auge y caída del perezjimenismo: el papel del empresariado*. Caracas: Universidad Central de Venezuela – Consejo de Desarrollo Científico y Humanístico.

Guerrero, Gustavo. 2008. *Historia de un encargo: "La catira" de Camilo José Cela*. Barcelona: Anagrama

Lévi-Strauss, Claude. 2012. *Myth and Meaning*. London: Routledge.

Liscano, Juan. 1981. "La industria petrolera como factor de transculturación." *Geosur*, 27: 12–25.

Negrín, Edith.1995. "La estridencia y el petróleo." *Literatura Mexicana*, 6 (1): 153–186.

———. 1997. "En los inicios de la novela mexicana del petróleo: La hermana impura de José Manuel Casauranc". In *Varia lingüística y literaria: 50 años del Centro de Estudios Lingüísticos y Literarios*, edited by Yvette Jiménez de Báez, 409–426. México: El Colegio de México.

Otero Silva, Miguel. 1960 [1961]. *Oficina N° 1*. Buenos Aires: Editorial Losada.

Pasquali, Antonio. 1972. *Comunicación y cultura de masas*. Caracas: Monte Avila Editores.

People and Petroleum: The Story of Creole in Venezuela. circa 1954. Caracas: Creole Petroleum Corporation.

Ponti, Gio. 1961. "Villa Planchart, Caracas 1953–1957." *Domus* No. 375. http://www.domusweb.it/it/dall-archivio/2011/02/02/villa-planchart-caracas-1953-57.html

Rapp, Helen Louise. 1957. "La novela del petróleo en México." Thesis for Master degree in Spanish Literature, Universidad Autónoma de México.

Schneider, Luis Mario. 1989. "La literatura del petróleo en México." In *México: a cincuenta años de la expropiación petrolera*, edited by Agustín Reyes y Lorea San Martín Tejedo, Lorea San Martín, 295–308. México: UNAM.

———. 1997. *La novela mexicana entre el petróleo, la homosexualidad y la política*. México: Nueva Imagen.

Tinker Salas, Miguel. 2009. *The Enduring Legacy: Oil, Culture and Society in Venezuela*. Durham: Duke University Press.

Uribe Piedrahita, César. 1935. *Mancha de aceite*. Bogotá. Edited by the author.

Uslar Pietri, Arturo. 1955. "El petróleo en Venezuela". In *Nuevo mundo, mundo nuevo*, 223–241. Caracas: Biblioteca Ayacucho.

Vázquez Montalbán, Manuel. 1990. "Introduction to the Spanish edition of *Le salaire de la peur*." Madrid: Editorial Debate.

Venezuela bajo el Nuevo Ideal Nacional (1952–1954). Caracas: Servicio Informativo Venezolano. 1954.

White, Hayden. 1981. "The Value of Narrativity in the Representation of Reality." In *On Narrative*, edited by W.J.T. Mitchell, 7–23. Chicago: The University of Chicago Press.

8 Untangling the Myth of Culture as Renewable Oil

A Barthesian Exploration of PDVSA La Estancia's Visual Campaign *Transformamos el petróleo en un recurso renovable para ti*[1]

Penélope Plaza

A historical narrative in Venezuela has regarded the arts, and by extension culture, as a resource analogous to oil. This was most eloquently stated by Venezuelan artist and playwright César Rengifo in an interview with newspaper *El Nacional* in 1973:

> We are like oil: a reserve; but in Venezuela we have yet to be put in motion[2]. (Rengifo 1973, 12) (translation by the author)

By saying that artists are like oil, Rengifo asserts his value and repositions himself as a natural resource suggesting that the Petrostate would invest in artists like him, and culture in general, only if they are viewed like a reserve of crude oil. In the midst of the oil bonanza of The Great Venezuela[3], his statement reveals the clout oil carries in shaping the relationship between the Petrostate and culture in Venezuela. This chapter reveals how the twenty-first century Petro-socialist national oil industry privileges a particular understanding of culture.

In the first of four parts in this chapter, I review George Yúdice's proposition that culture's expediency as a resource enables its use for economic, social, and political purposes. In part two, I describe the context for PDVSA La Estancia's[4] advertising campaign, especially the visual and textual elements of the adverts. In part three, I apply Barthes' theory of Mythical speech to the advertisements' visual and verbal elements to elucidate the intended meanings behind the slogan, 'We Transform oil into a renewable resource for you,' to identify the notion of culture mobilized when the city is represented as an oil field. Finally, I draw on George Yúdice to investigate the discursive construction of oil as a renewable resource to examine how the adverts construe the notion of Culture as Renewable Oil (Plaza 2018). Culture, I argue, becomes inextricable from land, akin to a mineral deposit, and justifiably, then, tightly controlled by the Petrostate. The inclusion of giant oil workers and their interactions with the urban spaces depicted in the adverts point to a re-signification of the city as an oil field, an explicit attempt to naturalize a direct mechanistic relationship between oil, culture, and the city.

The Expediency of Culture as a Mineral Resource

The analysis of the visual and verbal elements in the adverts draws on George Yúdice's expediency of culture as a resource to argue that PDVSA La Estancia, the social and cultural arm of the Venezuelan state-owned oil company PDVSA, discursively renders oil and culture as equivalent by construing what I define as the notion of Culture as Renewable Oil, as if culture could be extracted and processed like crude oil. In *The Expediency of Culture: Uses of Culture in the Global Era*, Yúdice (2003) explains how the notion of culture as a resource may be used as an instrument to aid social and economic development. He argues that culture has acquired status similar to a natural resource as a result of globalization, which has accelerated the transformation of all realms of modern life into a resource. He argues that, nonetheless, the idea of culture as a resource is not a perversion or a reduction of its symbolic dimension. On the contrary, the expediency of culture as a resource is a feature of contemporary life. It has been transformed into a performative force—a style of social relations—generated by diverse organized relationships between state institutions and society such as schools, universities, mass media, and markets (Yúdice 2003, 47, 60–61). Yúdice characterizes performativity "as an act that 'produces [that] which it names,'" revealing the power of discourse to produce realities through repetition (Yúdice 2003, 47, 58) and the particular institutional preconditions and processes by which culture and its effects are produced.

Whilst the term expediency refers to the merely political with regard to self-interest, Yúdice's performative understanding of the expediency of culture "focuses on the strategies implied in any invocation of culture, any invention of tradition, in relation to some purpose or goal," that feature that makes it possible to invoke culture as a resource "for determining the value of an action" (Yúdice 2003, 38). The expedience, or convenience, of culture as a resource is what allows its use for economic, social, and political purposes. For Yúdice (2003, 279), the expediency of culture as a resource has become, in practice, the only surviving definition, becoming impossible not to turn to culture as a resource as it is congruent to the way we now understand nature, affecting the way culture is viewed and produced. Similarly, I argue that it would be close to impossible for the national oil company not to turn to culture as a mineral resource.

Yúdice's discussion frames my approach to the work of PDVSA La Estancia. PDVSA La Estancia has the privilege of direct access to the oil rent, making it a founder of culture. Given its organizational and legal autonomy, PDVSA La Estancia need not negotiate with the government or follow any other agenda than its own. Finally, PDVSA La Estancia can even surpass in financial and political power the jurisdictions of the state and other public institutions whose functions overlap with their work over the city. For PDVSA La Estancia, culture has acquired the same status as natural resources.

Profile of the Campaign "We Transform Oil Into a Renewable Resource for You"

PDVSA La Estancia launched the campaign *Transformamos el petróleo en un recurso renovable para ti* in early 2013, the year of Hugo Chávez' unexpected death, right at the start of what would have been his fourth term in office. Chávez had outlined an ambitious presidential program for the 2012 elections that aimed to transform Venezuela into a world power of oil energy by expanding extraction of its vast crude oil reserves (Chávez 2012, 7, 27; Terán Mantovani 2014, 161). Nonetheless, the majority of the public art and public spaces restored by PDVSA La Estancia between 2005 and 2014 depicted in the adverts predate Chávez's arrival to the presidency in 1998; they are symbols of the modern oil nation, built and erected during the era of what Chávez renamed the Fourth Republic — 1959–1998[5] — vilified by his Bolivarian Revolution.

In July 2014, I interviewed the General Manager of PDVSA La Estancia at their headquarters in Caracas. At the end of the interview, the Department of Public Relations handed me a CD with photographs of every public artwork and public space it had restored to that point including Alejandro Otero's Abra Solar, Jesus Soto's Esfera Caracas, and Sabana Grande Boulevard.

Those photographs formed the campaign's basis. Just adding PDVSA La Estancia's logo to the photographs would not have sufficed to evidence its direct involvement in restoring these locations. To show its authorship, visual and linguistic strategies were devised, such as including giant oil workers and verbal text to differentiate it from other institutions that had traditionally carried out such works: municipalities or the National Heritage Institute.

The campaign consisted of twenty-three posters of the city spaces and public art that had been restored by PDVSA La Estancia between 2005 and 2012.[6] The adverts were displayed on most PDV petrol stations, on PDVSA La Estancia's main headquarters in Caracas, as well as on an album in their Facebook page (PDVSA La Estancia 2013). Each poster features a giant oil worker, captured as if in the middle of work.

Each advert is composed of a photograph of public art or an architectural structure and a digitally added giant oil worker, accompanied by the words "we transform oil into a renewable resource for you." The majority of the adverts feature public art; they show not only the regeneration, but they also associate the public art aesthetically and artistically with the oil company. Nineteen of the adverts are located in Caracas, highlighting that PDVSA La Estancia's investment in urban regeneration has taken place predominantly in the capital. The public art works are identified by name, the name of the artist, and their location, listed below in alphabetical order:

Abra Solar, Alejandro Otero, Caracas-Venezuela
Esfera Caracas, Jesús Soto, Caracas-Venezuela
Fisicromía, Carlos Cruz-Diez, Caracas-Venezuela
Fuente Plaza Venezuela, Santos Michelena, Caracas-Venezuela
Gazebo del Calvario, Parque "Ezequiel Zamora", Caracas-Venezuela
Los Cerritos, Alejandro Otero, Mercedes Pardo, Caracas-Venezuela
Pariata 1957, Omar Carreño, Caracas-Venezuela
Uracoa, Mateo Manaure, Caracas-Venezuela
Venezuela Ocho Estrellas, Ender Cepeda, Edo. Zulia, Venezuela

The labels do not indicate their date of creation; the adverts don't differentiate between the Abra Solar, created in 1982[7], and the restored structure of the Gazebo of El Calvario, which dates back to the late nineteenth century. No locations are given for playgrounds or sports fields. Sports fields are simply labeled *canchas* (courts), while playgrounds are labeled *Parques La Alquitrana* (Tar Parks), implying that PDVSA La Estancia has built them across the country. *La Alquitrana* is a feminized Spanish term for tar; PDVSA La Estancia's website explains that the circuit of La Alquitrana parks is named after Venezuela's first oil well that spurted crude oil in 1878, located in the Andean region of Táchira (PDVSA La Estancia 2016). Overall, the adverts depict material spaces of leisure and cultural recreation: playgrounds (childhood), sports grounds (youth), public art and parks (families)—all made possible by PDVSA La Estancia (oil). But these material spaces are miniaturized by the focus of the campaign: the giant oil worker. The next section uses Barthes' visual-rhetorical analysis of Myth to illuminate the visual semiotics of the adverts.

Giant Oil Workers and the Myth of "Renewable Oil"

Next, I examine the advertisements' composition: photographic images and the verbal text. The image depicts a giant oil worker interacting with the material space of the city while the verbal text solidifies the message. The advert combines urban space, giant oil worker, and verbal text. Barthes pioneered the semiotic study of images, especially in photography in *The Photographic Message* (1961) and *The Rhetoric of the*

Image (1964). However, here I draw on *Mythologies* (1957), an earlier influential work focusing on advertisements.

For Barthes, Myth is a type of speech, "a system of communication, that it is a message;" it is not a concept or an idea: it is a concrete entity, a form, a "mode of signification defined not by its literal sense but by its intention" (Barthes 1993, 109, 124). In his sense, myth is a type of speech "chosen by history: it cannot possibly evolve from the 'nature' of things" (Barthes 1993, 110). For Barthes, everything can be a myth as long as "it is conveyed by a discourse," but it is not confined to the written or oral word; all visual medias including cinema, photography, reporting, and advertising can be a vehicle for mythical speech:

> we are no longer dealing here with a theoretical mode of representation: we are dealing with this particular image, which is given for this particular signification. Mythical speech is made of a material which has already been worked on so as to make it suitable for communication: it is because all the materials of myth (whether pictorial or written) presuppose a signifying consciousness that one can reason about them whilst discounting their substance. (Barthes 1993, 110)

Myth does not hide or lie: "its function is to distort, not to make disappear" (Barthes 1993, 121). Myth is an inflexion of the concept, and through this inflexion rather than revealing or dissolving it, naturalizes it: "we reach the very principle of myth: it transforms history into nature" (Barthes 1993, 129). Therefore, myth is read as a reason, never a motive; it aims to cause an immediate impression, "experienced as innocent speech not because its intentions are hidden – if they were hidden they would not be efficacious - but because they are naturalized" as factual (Barthes 1993, 130–131). This factualness characterizes myth as "depoliticized speech" (political understood in its deeper meaning as the power humans have in making their own world); by transforming history into nature, contingency appears eternal as things lose their historical quality and memory: "things lose the memory that they once were made" (Barthes 1993, 142). Based on this discussion, I posit that PDVSA La Estancia propagates the myth of Culture as Renewable Oil within the advertising campaign, communicated through two modes of discourse: the visual component and the verbal text. As noted, the photograph depicts the interaction of a giant oil worker and the material space of the city. The verbal text fuses the visual interaction between the worker and the city and enriches the meaning.

The public art and spaces depicted in the photographs from PDVSA La Estancia's Department of Public Relations were photographed mainly at dusk under dark blue skies, the lights blurring the motorized traffic and people at rush hour. Most of the art and spaces restored by

PDVSA La Estancia predate Hugo Chávez's presidency. As preexisting structures, the subjects of the photographs alone would not evidence PDVSA La Estancia's direct involvement in restoring them, after years of disrepair and vandalism, to their original state. PDVSA La Estancia intervenes in the photographs of actual, identifiable material spaces of the city, enhancing them with digital images of the giant oil worker but the advertisements' focal point is not the restored structures but the giant oil workers themselves, who direct viewer attention. The giant oil worker connects both to the human-scale worker (since actual giant oil workers do not exist) and the existential relationship with the oil industry, including the extraction of crude oil. They wear red working gear (the color that identifies the Bolivarian revolution and the new revolutionary PDVSA[8])—hard hats, coveralls, boots, and gloves manipulating the public art or architectural structures as if they were heavy machinery in a oil refinery—the natural environment of an oil worker—and not in the midst of the city. Of an unnatural monumental size, the gargantuan oil workers are portrayed collectively as benevolent giants beautifying the city, as a naturalized and ubiquitous presence in a city miniaturized by their monumental scale. These spaces, although already completed, are shown unfinished in the adverts, in the midst of the active process of being either manipulated or recently repaired. In the posters of Sabana Grande Boulevard, the giant oil workers install a sculptural canopy but they appear to be screwing a piece of a giant oil drill into the ground. The artwork loses its monumental scale through the interaction with the giant oil worker: for.

The giant oil workers also function as visual-cultural ambassadors of PDVSA La Estancia, the *obrero petrolero* (oil worker), who gets down and dirty to perform the extraction of crude oil from the subsoil. If the giant oil workers are the oil industry's visual-cultural ambassadors, their inclusion and interaction with the spaces depicted point to a repossession of the city visually reconstructed as an oil field in a clear attempt at naturalizing a direct and mechanistic relationship between oil and urban space. The giant oil worker functions as a visual metaphor that transfers the extractive activity of the oil field to the city, mediated by public space and public art. As an artificially constructed image, the giant oil worker directly connects the oil company and the viewer and, within the advert, the oil worker and city dwellers, subverting the historical social division between oil workers and the rest of the population:

> Many directly employed or indirectly benefiting from the oil industry subsequently assumed key positions in Venezuelan society, government, commerce and industry. Their views reflected a series of self-sustaining myths about the oil industry and its importance to the nation and society. Paramount among these was the notion

> that for Venezuela the oil industry was the means to achieve modernity in all its forms. For those employed by the industry, these new modern traditions accentuated certain traits and behavior patterns – discipline, efficiency, work ethic, meritocracy, and in some cases even bilingualism - that helped define the "collective consciousness" of the oil industry and distinguished those working in it from the rest of society. (Tinker Salas 2009, 5)

But the colossal scale of the giant oil workers contradicts this symbolic break with social hierarchy that used to distinguish those working for the oil industry from the rest of Venezuelan society. The low-angle shot emphasizes their monumental scale and superiority. They do not gaze directly at the viewer; instead they focus on their duty or engage in a cordial manner with the miniaturized city inhabitants below them. The giant oil workers do not address or acknowledge the viewer, and their gaze does not demand anything from viewers (Kress and van Leeuwen 2006, 121–122); rather, their scale incites deference. The campaign also romanticizes the dirtiness of work in the oil fields by offering a sanitized version of oil workers in the midst of the city. Oil is presented as the source of prosperity and the producer of culture through the labor of a "workers elite." The giant oil workers are a symbol of PDVSA's benevolence and power while the adverts are a sign of the city appropriated by the state-owned oil company; PDVSA is presented as the provider of beauty and prosperity through the actions of PDVSA La Estancia materialized in beautifully restored urban spaces and public art.

Please note: Caracas is not, and has never been, a site of oil extraction or refining; no crude oil lies in its subsoil. However, the actions of the giant oil workers as a collective of images represent a cause-effect relationship regarding the impact of the work by PDVSA La Estancia on the city, a relationship impossible to convey by pairing the company logo with a photograph of the restored space; these adverts need to tell the story, to make evident to the viewer the institution that is behind the restoration: PDVSA.

The adverts present two types of cause-effect relationships: one natural and one artificial. The natural is that those spaces were, in fact, restored by PDVSA La Estancia. However, the use of the giant oil workers obscures the bureaucratic mechanisms and institutional structures needed to accomplish this scale of restoration, and only the authorship of the oil company is acknowledged. In reality, public works are only possible after completing a sophisticated and complex set of decisions and institutional arrangements; the visual emphasis on giant oil workers depoliticizes the process. In a country currently submerged in deep political polarization, the use of *petroleros* (oil workers) as an identity is not controversial and divisive in a nation whose identity is unified by oil (Coronil 1997). This choice confirms the campaign as mythical depoliticized speech in Barthes' terms. The adverts locate all public art, sports fields, and public spaces, in the same present temporality, the same quality of newness, placing them in a history-less setting, in an attempt to dissolve the historical memory that they "once were made" (Barthes 1993, 142). They abolish history and appropriate public art, spaces, and heritage for the Bolivarian revolution. The absence in the labels of dates when the artwork and spaces were built emphasizes this appropriation. In these adverts, Abra Solar, Esfera Caracas, Fisicromía, Pariata 1957, Los Cerritos, Gazebo del Calvario, Sabana Grande Boulevard, and Plaza Venezuela are all stripped of their political and cultural history. The artificial cause-effect relationship is created through the claim that through their actions the giant oil workers are transforming oil into a "renewable resource." It also provides the images with volition; it expresses the idea of possibility latent in the advert, condensed by the verbal text.

We now turn to the verbal text to identify mythical speech. Barthes' analytical framework helps to decipher the reality that the advertisements' language aims to create and the notion of culture construed by PDVSA La Estancia. The verbal text of the advert, *Transformamos el petróleo en un recurso renovable para ti* (We transform oil into a renewable source for you), expresses eloquently the campaign's purpose. This expressed purpose reveals the verbal text as the construction of myth in Barthes' terms, completed by the interaction between the verbal text and the visuals of the campaign.

The campaign presents as a fact that PDVSA La Estancia is transforming oil into a "renewable resource," but it does not clarify what this renewable resource is. Instead it is suggested through the images of the oil workers manipulating the city's public art and architectural structures. The coloring and layout of the typography emphasize the myth; the words in the slogan are colored either white and red or black and red. In every poster, the same three words are red and bold:

Tranformamos el PETRÓLEO
en un recurso RENOVABLE PARA TI
We transform OIL
into a resource RENEWABLE FOR **YOU**

The implied *nosotros* (we) in the plural of *Transformamos* (we transform) in the verbal text is the voice of the institution represented by the collective voice of the giant oil workers, the visual-cultural ambassadors of PDVSA La Estancia. The "we" excludes viewers. Added to the giant oil workers' monumental scale, this "we" hales viewers as the beneficiaries of PDVSA's philanthropy, setting them as one-down to the company. Next, *Petróleo* (oil) is emphasized through highlighting and a larger font size. In the layout, the left half of the text appears in lowercase letters while the right half dominates in all capital letters and bold red typeface. Kress and van Leeuwen (1996) propose that elements on the left are presented as Given, while those on the right are presented as New:

> For something to be Given means that it is presented as something the viewer already knows. . . . For something to be New means that it is presented as something which is not yet known . . . hence as something to which the viewer must pay special attention. (Kress and van Leeuwen 1996, 187)

The key message here is presented on the right: OIL RENEWABLE FOR YOU. The position of *Petróleo* (oil) and *renovable* (renewable) in the layout puts *Petróleo* above *renovable*, visually suggests they should be read together as *Petróleo renovable* (renewable oil). The paired meaning is incongruent: oil is finite, a nonrenewable natural resource. But the paradox implied here is metaphorical. The paired words suggest that PDVSA La Estancia is claiming that an endless supply of oil is possible as PDVSA "magically" transforms it into a renewable resource: oil becomes metaphorically renewable when the oil rent is invested in culture. Hence, if oil can be renewed by investing in culture, then culture is like renewable oil. Oil, culture, and the city are conflated into one entity: Culture as Renewable Oil.

The next red word identifies the campaign's intended audience: *TI* (you). Oil/culture is made renewable "for you." This direct address of viewers aims to create a sense of closeness between them and the institution. The audience—the "you"—is potential users of the refurbished spaces, the city dwellers where these structures are located, but given the national scope of PDVSA La Estancia, it also implies Venezuela's larger population—every citizen of the Petrostate shares the national identity of oil.

The adverts as a set are the material form of the sign. Barthes' concept can take a variety of forms because it only re-presents itself, and this multiplication allows us to decipher the myth through the repetition, in this case, of the idea of transforming oil into a "renewable resource." The concept relies on understanding culture as crude oil, as an expedient natural resource that accumulates in the subsoil that upon extraction yields political and social benefits but that, unlike oil, can be renewed. Oil then becomes a double-sided cultural entity; it is invoked as a singular force capable of producing palpable cultural effects: a producer of culture and a cultural product in itself. If culture is like a mineral deposit extracted from the subsoil of the nation, then culture and the discursive and political wealth produced by Culture as Renewable Oil is, like the subsoil, the exclusive property of the Petrostate.

Culture as Renewable Oil: Culture and Oil as Analogous Natural Resources

The advertisements present the myth that oil is made renewable by investing in culture; therefore, culture becomes renewable oil. Culture, oil, and the city coalesce into one entity through this myth. The myth of "renewable oil" becomes real through the performative force of PDVSA's giant oil workers and rests on the certainty that Venezuela possesses the world's largest crude oil reserves, certified by OPEC in 2011. In the manner of the demiurgic exercise of power of the Magical State defined by Coronil (1997), PDVSA La Estancia becomes the sorcerer that makes possible the impossible by transforming oil into *the* renewable resource: culture. Oil and culture become equivalent when culture turns into crude oil, as if culture were a physical material that could be industrially extracted, measured, exploited, processed, and commercialized. Moreover, "renewable oil" attaches to culture conflicting notions of resource: resource as nature and resource as deposits extracted from the subsoil that yield wealth.

In this context, the notion of Culture a Renewable Oil is more than a discursive construction. It implies that by tying culture to the land, culture is constructed as a material entity that accumulates in the subsoil of the nation, ready to be extracted and processed under tight control by the Petrostate. Therefore, modern and abstract manifestations of culture such as the ones depicted in the adverts can only be quantified as valuable if they are transformed into oil machinery, rather than as symbols of modernization and progress. However, for culture to fit this rhetoric, it has to be defined more narrowly and made the exclusive property of the Petrostate. To paraphrase Yúdice, the state-owned oil company cannot view culture as anything other than a reserve of crude oil. Therefore, PDVSA La Estancia's discursive construction of culture can be defined as the instrumentalization of Culture as Renewable Oil which is not oriented towards the conventional model of development discussed by Yúdice, rather it is instrumentalized for political aims. Culture is not required to provide financial returns, as the Petrostate's distributive expenditure policies do not require financial accountability or representative bargains. Culture as Renewable Oil condenses the materiality lost by oil when it was reduced to the fetish of rent money (Pérez Schael 1993, 94), becoming inextricable from land. The advertising campaign renders oil and culture as equivalent, as if culture could be extracted, exploited, and processed like crude oil. In the notion of Culture as Renewable Oil, culture is discursively bound to the subsoil, so that it is the exclusive property of the state and belongs to the realm of PDVSA. But unlike oil, culture can be renewed, reconverted, and transformed.

Conclusion

The advertising campaign is a symbol of PDVSA's discursive power. The space of the city is envisioned as an oil field, where giant oil workers are seen repairing or installing architectural or sculptural structures. They give a face—or rather a collective face—to oil in the campaign as their colossal figures subliminally communicate that the urban spaces, and the city at large, exist within the state-owned oil industry's realm.

PDVSA La Estancia devised the visual strategy of the giant oil workers to establish their ownership over the city. The giant oil worker functions as a sign of PDVSA, their inclusion and interaction with the spaces depicted in the adverts visually reframes them as oil fields in a clear attempt at naturalizing a direct and mechanistic relationship between oil and culture. The labor of the giant oil workers transforms oil into a renewable resource as an illusion congruent with how PDVSA La Estancia conceptualizes Culture as Renewable Oil to discursively render oil and culture equivalent as if culture could be extracted, exploited, and processed like crude oil. This rendering provides a new illusion, a novel dramaturgical act: Culture as Renewable Oil is tied back to the land and thus inextricable from the land of the nation and its subsoil; if culture is extracted from the soil, then the Venezuelan Petrostate can claim complete ownership and tight control over culture as a renewable resource within the remit of the Law of Hydrocarbons.

This is the context of the naturalization of the giant oil workers metaphorically transforming oil into culture, acting outside of their natural environment—the refinery and oil fields—and stripped of the dirtiness of handling crude oil. Their colossal scale provides them with a mythical aura, while simultaneously performing the material quality that oil lost by being reduced to rent money. Culture as Renewable Oil is grounded on the land of the world's largest crude oil reserves, essential for the survival of the Bolivarian revolution. In the specific context of this campaign, the verbal text suggests that oil is being transformed into culture, inferring that culture is the quintessential renewable resource, naturalizing as truth that PDVSA La Estancia was making possible an utopia of inexhaustible oil.

Notes

1 This text is a condensed version of the book chapter titled "Giant Oil Workers and the Expediency of Culture as Renewable Oil", (pp. 121–137) included in my monograph *Culture as Renewable Oil. How Territory, Bureaucratic Power and Culture Coalesce in the Venezuelan Petrostate* published in 2018 by Routledge.

2 Original in Spanish: "Somos como el petróleo: una reserva; pero en Venezuela aún no se nos ha puesto en marcha."

3 In 1973 the outbreak of another Arab-Israeli war and the oil embargo enacted by Arab oil-producing countries generated a rapid increase in oil prices. For oil exporting countries like Venezuela, it produced an unprecedented windfall in oil revenues. The oil bonanza prompted the recently elected president

Carlos Andrés Pérez to launch the ambitious national development plan The Great Venezuela (1973–1979) promising to transform Venezuela into a developed country in just a few years. However, the decades that followed the Great Venezuela were of gradual economic and political decline with the plunge in oil prices in the 1980–1990s, leading to the election of Hugo Chávez in 1998. See: Straka, T. (ed.). 2016. *La Nación Petrolera: Venezuela, 1914–2014*. Caracas, Venezuela: Universidad Metropolitana.

4 Petróleos de Venezuela Sociedad Anónima (PDVSA) is the Venezuelan state-owned oil company created by decree in 1975 by president Carlos Andrés Pérez, followed by the nationalisation of the oil industry in 1976. PDVSA La Estancia takes its name from its main building in Caracas, the eighteenth-century colonial house of Hacienda Estancia La Floresta, a former coffee and sugarcane plantation. The hacienda house and gardens were purchased by PDVSA in the 1980s. In 1990 La Estancia was declared a National Historic Monument; PDVSA took on the restoration and refurbishment of the hacienda house and gardens to adapt its use as private venue for corporate events and accommodation for V.I.P. guests. The Centro de Arte La Estancia (La Estancia Art Centre), opened in 1993. After the events of 2002–2003 (failed coup d'état and national oil strike/lockout), Hugo Chávez announced the rise of a 'new PDVSA' ideologically aligned with the Bolivarian revolution. Coinciding with the launch of the Sowing Oil Plan 2005–2030, PDVSA's Centro de Arte La Estancia, regarded as an elitist institution by the revolution, reopened its doors in 2005 as PDVSA La Estancia, the social and cultural arm of the new PDVSA. See: Plaza, P. 2018. *Culture as Renewable Oil*. p. 97.

5 The majority of the public art was erected between the 1960s and 1980s, the historical period of 40 years of the Pact of Puntofijo representative democracy, from the end of Marcos Pérez Jiménez' dictatorship in 1958 ending with the Constituent Assembly set up in 1999 by Hugo Chávez on his first presidential period to draft a new constitution. This inaugurated what Chávez defined as the Fifth Republic, to differentiate it from the Fourth Republic which saw the decline of the Pact of Puntofijo between the traditional political parties Democratic Action (AD) and the Social Christian Party (COPEI) that had dominated Venezuelan politics.

6 PDVSA La Estancia would not give the author permission to reproduce any of these advertisements.

7 Visual Artist Alejandro Otero represented Venezuela at the XL Venice Biennale held in 1982; his work on display of a wide array of mediums and formats included two large scale structures, the Abra Solar and the Aguja Solar, installed at the entrances of the Biennale and Lido, respectively. In 1983 the Abra Solar was installed in Plaza Venezuela, Caracas, and the Aguja Solar in Ciudad Guayana.

8 On May 1, 2007, Hugo Chávez announced during a national television broadcast that his Bolivarian Revolution was seizing control of the Orinoco Oil Belt from multinationals, as dictated by the new Law of Hydrocarbons. The Minister of Energy and President of PDVSA greeted the 4,000 oil workers who would be transferred from the multinationals to PDVSA by saying "Welcome to the new PDVSA!" as the workers, in a symbolic act, traded their traditional blue hard hats for red ones. The broadcast ended with Chávez celebrating a "new, red, red PDVSA."
Sources:http://www.noticias24.com/actualidad/noticia/4490/cascos-de-color-rojo-como-simbolo-de-la-toma/ http://www.pdvsa.com/index.php?tpl=interface.sp/design/readmenu.tpl.html&newsid_obj_id=3910&newsid_temas=130 http://news.bbc.co.uk/hi/spanish/business/newsid_6614000/6614063.stm

References

Barthes, Roland. 1993. *Mythologies*. London: Vintage.

Chávez, Hugo. 2012. "Propuesta Del Candidato de La Patria Comandante Hugo Chávez Para La Gestión Bolivariana Socialista 2013–2019." *www.mppeuct.gob.ve*. Caracas, Venezuela: Comando Campaña Carabobo. http://www.mppeuct.gob.ve/el-ministerio/politicas/leyes-y-planes/propuesta-del-candidato-de-la-patria-comandante-hugo-chavez.

Coronil, Fernando. 1997. *The Magical State: Nature, Money, and Modernity in Venezuela*. Chicago: University of Chicago Press.

Kress, Gunther, and Theo van Leeuwen. 1996. *Reading Images: The Grammar of Visual Design*. New York: Routledge.

———. 2006. *Reading Images: The Grammar of Visual Design*. First. New York: Routledge.

PDVSA La Estancia. 2013. "Facebook." *Transformamos El Petróleo En Un Recurso Renovable Para Ti*. https://www.facebook.com/media/set/?set=a.296539377135848.64316.130175993772188&type=3.

———. 2016. "Zonas de Injerencia." Accessed April 14. http://www.pdvsalaestancia.com/?page_id=574.

Pérez Schael, María Sol. 1993. *Petróleo, Cultura Y Poder En Venezuela*. Caracas: El Nacional.

Plaza, Penélope. 2018. *Culture as Renewable Oil. How Territory, Bureaucratic Power and Culture Coalesce in the Venezuelan Petrostate*. London: Routledge.

Rengifo, César. 1973. "Los Artistas En Venezuela Somos Como El Petróleo: Una Reserva." *El Nacional*, sección C, p. 12.

Ricardo, David. 1817. *On the Principles of Political Economy and Taxation*, 3rd ed., 2.2. London: Empiricus Books.

Terán Mantovani, Emiliano. 2014. "El Fantasma de La Gran Venezuela: Un Estudio Del Mito Del Desarrollo Y Los Dilemas Del Petro-Estado En La Revolución Bolivariana." *CLACSO*. Caracas, Venezuela: Fundación CELARG. http://www.clacso.org.ar/libreria-latinoamericana/libro_detalle.php?id_libro=1092&pageNum_rs_libros=0&totalRows_rs_libros=1057.

Tinker Salas, Miguel. 2009. *The Enduring Legacy: Oil, Culture, and Society in Venezuela*. Durham: Duke University Press.

Yúdice, George. 2003. *The Expediency of Culture: Uses of Culture in the Global Era*. Durham: Duke University Press.

9 Against All Odds

Oil Culture and the Commodity Consensus in Argentina's Patagonia

Natalia Barrionuevo and Stefan Peters

Towards a Situated Analysis of the Oil Culture

While oil-based products are omnipresent in our daily life, the locations where oil is extracted attract less public interest, and their social configurations are often largely unknown. The general public usually hears about the extractive zones only in times of political turmoil. Academic work, too, focuses on crises, conflicts, and catastrophes related to natural resources and especially oil extraction. The terms that are used in the debates about oil and development are telling: Michael Watts (2011) analyzes conflicts in the Niger Delta in Nigeria using the term, "Blood Oil;" Philippe Le Billon (2005) studies (not exclusively focusing on oil) "Resource Wars;" Kristin Reed (2009, 44–69) looks at "Petro-Violence" in Angola; Roberto Briceño León ([1990] 2015) highlights the "Perverse Effects of Petroleum" in Venezuela. In general, scholars have referred to commodity dependent countries in terms of a "resource curse" (Auty 1993)[1] or, in the case of Michael Ross (2012), even as an "oil curse."

Generally speaking, the majority of ongoing academic and journalistic work agrees that raw material extraction, and especially oil, entails negative economic, social, and political consequences in resource-dependent societies of the Global South. As noted, scholars highlight poor economic and social performance, weak institutions, socio-environmental damage, and increasing danger of authoritarianism and/or violent conflicts; in the 1980s these effects were dubbed the 'resource curse' thesis.

Developmental studies seized the idea that "more of a good thing might be bad for development" (Brunnschweiler and Bulte 2009, 670), and the idea continues to dominate approaches in this area. Consequently, scholarship enumerates why oil-based societies should mistrust commodity-led development and reject extractivism. However, many extractive societies instead evince a "commodity consensus" (Svampa 2015). Svampa defines "commodity consensus" as a mode of economic, social, and political regulation, but we argue that this consensus is deeply rooted in social relations and collective imaginaries in many oil-based rentiers societies (Peters 2015).

In this chapter, we discuss the puzzle of the surprisingly harmonious coexistence between the series of quiet yet perceivable negative effects of the extractive industry daily and the equally perceptible support for oil-based local development in an oil-centered society. We present a case study of the oil city, Comodoro Rivadavia, located in the Patagonian province of Chubut in Southern Argentina. Comodoro Rivadavia is a poster child for an oil city with its economy, society, and politics intimately linked to the industry. The importance of oil for the city and the province generates a broad social consensus on oil that permeates the whole local society, and this consensus even strengthens during crises. We argue that this broad support for the oil industry arises out of a combination of material issues (e.g., rent distribution, employment, and economic dependency) and the construction and resignification of historical social imaginaries and collective identities.[2] However, we argue that both the material issues and social imaginaries are linked to social inequalities, thereby producing different configurations of support for oil extraction.

This chapter relies on qualitative data (interviews, newspaper, observations, etc.) from extensive fieldwork in Comodoro Rivadavia and Chubut. First, we briefly review current international scholarship on oil and development; then we introduce Comodoro Rivadavia and Chubut as rentier societies with ambivalent development outcomes. Based on arguments from theory and our empirical evidence, we then identify the problems of framing oil-led development in terms of curse or blessing and propose reorienting to study oil culture as a crucial factor for understanding why the oil industry enjoys support *despite* its adverse consequences. This argument unfolds in two steps: first, we detail oil's negative aspects on the local level (i.e., environmental damages, social problems, and socioeconomic inequalities), and second, we discuss the (unequal) material benefits as well as the deep-rooted social imaginaries and local identifications that facilitate construction and (re-)production of broad support for the oil industry in Comodoro Rivadavia.

Beyond Curse vs. Blessing in Oil-led Development: Bringing Society and Culture Back In

The once widely accepted notion of natural resources fueling development changed in the 1980s with the emergence of the resource curse thesis. Despite Latin American structuralism and dependency theory having already highlighted the developmental dead ends of resource-based development models in the Global South (Kay 1989), the resource curse thesis propelled this position into the mainstream of development studies. This thesis contrasts dependency theory by focusing on endogenous development obstacles related to resource-dependency. It argues that economic development in resource-dependent countries is crisis-prone, shows volatile and modest growth rates, and hinders economic diversification. Apart from the volatility of commodity prices, three additional factors explain natural resource-dependent countries' poor economic performance: (i) 'Dutch Disease' effects; (ii) the creation of extractivist enclaves; and (iii) poor institutions.

The *Dutch Disease* thesis argues that a booming resource sector causes a shift in production factors towards the extractive sector and an appreciation of the currency, which hinders the development of agriculture and industry because of increased export costs and cheap imports (Sachs and Warner 2001).[3] Low economic diversification is reinforced by the *enclave character of extractivist industries*. Large-scale mining and the hydrocarbon sector create little employment for the domestic population and few forward and backward linkages to the rest of the economy; therefore, they create structural heterogeneity in a country's economy. Finally, natural resource extraction has been argued to weaken *institutions* (Mehlum, Moene, and Torvik 2006; Gilberthorpe and Papyrakis 2015, 384). According to this argument, natural resource rents encourage rent-seeking behavior, corruption, nepotism, and clientelism. Weakened economic and political institutions distort markets and discourage investment in sectors beyond the extractive industries.

Although mainly discussed in economic terms, the resource curse thesis further states that resource-dependent societies are also characterized by high poverty rates, relatively low human development scores, and huge social inequity (Karl 2004). Pro-cyclical spending may aggravate the effects of boom and bust cycles and generally contributes to converting the economic crisis into a social crisis. But even in times of plenty, riches from both the natural resource sector and the socio-environmental impact of extraction are often distributed unequally, creating 'growth without development' (Kappel 2011, 144) and excluding many people from extraction's benefits.

Regarding the political consequences of resource-dependency, proponents of the rentier state theory argue that the massive influx of rent income weakens institutions and encourages rent-seeking behavior, corruption, nepotism, and clientelism. It also states that rent income helps stabilize authoritarian regimes due to a weak fiscal contract and the quieting of opposition through generous rent distribution and repression (Beblawi and Luciani, 1987). However, if rent income does not satisfy the state's class will for self-enrichment and the population's claims for rent distribution, resource-dependent (but not abundant) countries may be plagued by endemic violent conflicts (Le Billon 2005). Thus, the 'resource curse' theory concludes that structural reasons inhibit resource-dependent countries from obtaining positive development outcomes.[4]

The resource curse paradigm was widely accepted until the turn of new millennium. In the context of a new worldwide commodity super-cycle (Canuto 2014), accompanied by the expansion and intensification of primary goods extraction especially in the Global South, the resource curse thesis has been critically re-examined and even rejected altogether. Generally speaking, alternate perspectives have questioned the conclusion that structural problems are unavoidable, argued that sound resource governance measures can prevent negative outcomes from resource-based development models, and even stated that oil is a blessing rather than a curse. This theoretical re-examination allowed for new resource optimism in development studies (Brunnschweiler and Bulte 2008; Sinnott, Nash, and de la Torre 2010; Bárcena and Prado 2016, 176–183). Turning conventional wisdom of the resource curse argument upside down, Menaldo (2016, 3) states that "natural resources and especially oil, help improve the quality of political and economic institutions, strengthening the state, democracy, and the rule of law." Although authors following this line of argument agree that several cases exist that manifest the negative symptoms associated with the resource curse and rentier state perspectives, researchers emphasize numerous empirical cases that demonstrate that resource-dependency does not obligatorily result in those negative outcomes, thereby questioning the causal link between natural resource exploitation and development failures. However, when commodity prices fell in 2013/2014 and relatively low-price levels continued thereafter, a new context emerged, characterized by economic and social crisis and increasing political turmoil in resource-dependent countries. This current dynamic undermines the positive balance sheets of resource-led development. Moreover, growing concerns about ecological damage and increasing socio-environmental conflict further weaken the new resource optimism. Indeed, qualitative research especially has contributed numerous case studies to a growing body of evidence about the negative social and environmental consequences and the lack of sustainability of extractivist development models (Reed 2009; Watts 2011; Dietz et al. 2015; Burchardt et al. 2016).

What is too often ignored in academic work is the crucial question of why, in spite of these negative outcomes, the zones of extraction usually experience little resistance to oil exploitation. Of course, this is not to claim that no conflicts erupt due to oil extraction, but any conflicts focus on oil rent appropriation and/or distribution (Collier and Hoeffler 2004; Watts 2011). Oil extraction itself is generally not contested but rather welcomed by large parts of the society.[5] The strong support for oil extraction at the local level can be explained by the creation and reproduction of an oil culture in rentier societies. Rentier societies are defined as those where the economy, social structures, and politics depend for several generations on rent income.[6] In these social formations, oil rents permeate society and generate particular social structures and power relations, aspects generally omitted in the curse vs. blessing discussion (Peters 2017). Moreover, whereas a general consensus exists that oil-based societies create sociocultural particularities, relatively few investigators have empirically studied the characteristics of oil culture.[7] Our research aims to contribute to this research gap by highlighting how oil's socioeconomic and sociocultural imprint contributes to the reproduction of the commodity consensus in Comodoro Rivadavia.

Comodoro Rivadavia and the Province of Chubut as an Exemplary Case Study

Comodoro Rivadavia (colloquially called Comodoro) sits on the Atlantic coast of the province of Chubut in southern Argentina (Patagonia). Almost 1,800 kilometers away from Buenos Aires, it is one of the most important Patagonian cities. With officially 177,038 inhabitants, according to the last national census from 2010—various locals estimate 300,000 people living in the city—it is a commercial, transport, health, and education node. Almost since its founding in 1901,[8] its economic development and social dynamics have been linked to the oil industry, making the city a rentier society. In boom phases, Comodoro attracts migrants from Northern Argentina and other Latin American countries, searching for job opportunities and a better life. In times of declining activity in the oil industry, the whole city usually falls into crisis.

Comodoro earned the title "National Capital of Oil" when the resource was discovered in 1907. Its early years were marked by the presence of the state-owned oil company Yacimientos Petrolíferos Fiscales (YPF), founded in 1922, and the company towns of private European and American capital. YPF had developed an extensive network of institutions including providers of social benefits, symbols and values that bound their employees to the state oil company: "YPF was everyone's daddy" (Interview with a public servant from the tax authority of the Municipality of Comodoro Rivadavia, February 25, 2016, in Comodoro Rivadavia). This resulted in the formation of a strong "ypefiana identity" of its workers and their families, a legacy that continues (Torres 1995; Carrizo 2016).

However, low oil prices and the privatization of YPF in the early 1990s generated huge increases in unemployment, cut social cohesion bonds, dismantled the YPF family, and set a scenario marked by outsourcing by operating companies of much of the activity to smaller companies. The renationalization of YPF in 2012 (with the expropriation of 51% equity interest by the Argentine government) arguably did not change this panorama. Currently, for example, the Chinese-British company Pan American Energy holds the concession for Cerro Dragón,[9] the largest oil and gas field in Argentina. Located 70 kilometers from Comodoro Rivadavia, in 2012 it produced 17% of the country's oil.[10]

Oil continues to be the single most important activity in Chubut. Today, the oil industry employs around 25,000 people in and around

Comodoro and fuels the province's economy: in 2013, oil accounted for 26% of Chubut's fiscal income,[11] 40% of the province's GDP, and 40%–60% of its exports (MEFP 2015; Bellato 2016). This extreme oil dependency also makes the province vulnerable to oil market volatility and global capitalism (Laveglia 2004). Comodoro's and Chubut's strong and historic dependencies on oil classify them as rentier societies. However, Comodoro is not easily fit into the curse vs. blessing framework: quantitative data suggests that in Chubut and Comodoro oil stimulates economic and social development. In 2013, the province's per capita GDP reached 89.900 pesos argentinos,[12] i.e., 25% above the national average, whereas poverty, social inequality, and infant mortality were below the national average. As a consequence of high oil prices and the expansion of extraction activities, between 2003 and 2014 Comodoro witnessed a boom phase interrupted only by the global crisis of 2009. The oil boom resulted in economic growth, rising wages, provincial fiscal surplus, increasing commercial and construction activities, decreasing poverty rates, and strong population growth due to many migrants arriving in the town looking for work (Peters 2016). This picture of economic dynamism and relative social well-being arguably contradicts the bleak scenario presented by the resource curse literature. Quite the contrary, in fact: being an oil-rich province in a non-oil country seems to have eased Chubut's development success.

However, qualitative data tempers the numbers. This view suggests deepening marginalization and poverty in a city collapsed under the weight of its growth, with unmet demand for infrastructure and social services, growing insecurity, social disorder, a general lack of social capital,[13] and countless land occupations (Bachiller et al. 2015). Maristella Svampa and Enrique Viale describe Comodoro in a Dantesque way, emphasizing a problem with contamination that supersedes environmental issues to include also "the social, economic and cultural sphere." They call Comodoro "an emblem of bad development" (Svampa and Viale 2014, 126–127; see also Budiño 1971).[14]

These two descriptions might raise doubts about whether they refer to the same city. However, we stress that both perspectives represent a part of the empirical reality. And this contradictory picture explains why exactly, even in contexts with omnipresent adverse consequences, the local population welcomes oil exploitation. To explain this conundrum, researchers must reorient to analyze the sociocultural consequences of long-term resource dependency. We argue that studying the mechanisms that permit the emergence and the (re-)production of a generalized consensus on oil exploitation can help us to better understand the particularities of rentier societies. Therefore, we first analyze the main drawbacks of oil in Chubut to explain how socioeconomic and sociocultural factors contribute to a situation where local society—against all odds—overwhelmingly supports oil extraction.

The Detriments of Oil in Chubut

Although material benefits from oil extraction are present in Chubut, qualitative research highlights how the oil industry has brought detriments. These detriments include environmental damage, social problems, and socioeconomic inequalities. Chubut's socio-geographical characteristics and its socioeconomic structures entail that the detriments are especially present in the extractive zones in the southern part of the province. Not by accident did Svampa and Viale (2014) refer to Comodoro Rivadavia rather than to Chubut as a poster child of 'bad development.' Comodoro's negative image is reinforced in everyday conversation and comments. For example, regionally people caution against a possible "commodorization" in discussions about negative effects of installing other forms of mining (Baeza and Chanampa 2016). And pitying comments of Argentinean colleagues after telling them about an upcoming research trip to Comodoro give further anecdotal evidence about Comodoro's disreputability.

This negative perception of Comodoro is rooted in its characteristics as a typical oil city. Oil's presence in everyday life is not mere metaphor. The city was literally built on oil and today nearly all of life turns around the activity. Children grew up playing close to oil wells that marked the cityscape, and currently hundreds of sealed oil wells across the urban territory and various active drilling rigs within Comodoro demonstrate the intimate relationship between the city and its main industry (Baeza and Chanampa 2016). This presence entails serious socio-environmental problems. During the early years of oil exploitation, environmental concerns were absent, creating significant environmental damage, including soil degradation and water contamination (Interview with the Director of the Department for Environmental Control of Hydrocarbons of the Province Chubut, February 25, 2016, in Comodoro Rivadavia). Although today public entities, oil unions, and the industry alike highlight environmental concerns, oil extraction still entails significant pollution: for instance, oil leakages occur daily.[15] Despite massive environmental damage and related health problems, oil industry-caused contamination provokes isolated protest. A socio-environmental movement criticizing oil extraction itself is strikingly absent in Comodoro where we can instead observe oil extraction (Baeza and Chanampa 2016; Interview with an Activist from the Foro Social y Ambiental de la Patagonia, October 21, 2015 in Comodoro Rivadavia) becoming naturalized.[16] This lack of organization against extractivism in Comodoro is a first sign of the city's deep-rooted consensus on oil.

Comodoro also shows salient features of an 'oil culture.' The city's extended working hours in often hostile conditions are notorious far beyond Comodoro. These hardships are compensated by a consumption-oriented lifestyle and extended markets for (both legal and illegal) drugs, prostitution, gambling, etc. (Svampa and Viale 2014). Thus, the city possesses similar features of other oil or mining towns past and present around the world (Tinker Salas 2009; Obeng-Odoom 2014). For example, oil workers in Comodoro purchase illegal substances such as cocaine to escape from the unpleasant working conditions at the wells. Excessive consumption of illegal drugs has prompted concern by the workers' union, employers, and the government alike (Etchezar 2007; Ministry of Labor 2015, 26) and become widely discussed in local newspapers. Some voices state that illegal drugs have replaced alcohol in generalized use at the wells, whereas others highlight the increasing problem of drug trafficking and consumption all over the provincial territory (Interview with Public Servants from the Secretary of Social Policies of the Ministry of Social Development and Family of the Province Chubut, February 17, 2016, in Rawson).[17] Furthermore, prostitution is also a topic of concern in Comodoro. Sexual consumption appears historically linked to the oil camps and the booms of activity. Currently, so-called 'VIPs departments,' 'whiskerías,' and nightclubs proliferate. The growing demand for sexual consumption is often satisfied by migrant women from Paraguay and the Dominican Republic, often involving human trafficking (Baeza 2010).[18]

Finally, the city is marked by large inequalities that quantitative measurements like the Gini indicator do not necessarily reflect. Local society is shaped by a net of well-established hierarchies of prestige, (dis-)respectability, and (il-)legitimate claims. First, based on the figuration of established/outsiders introduced by Elias and Scotson (1965), a social frontier exists between the 'born and raised' (*nacidos y criados*, nyc) and the migrants in Comodoro. The "nyc" assume that they should enjoy privileges over the migrants and strongly question the latter's rights to access jobs, housing, health, and education. Regarding access to land, nycs enjoy institutionalized privileges over migrants (Baeza and Chanampa 2016). Moreover, migrants are scapegoated for stealing the nyc's jobs and increasing crime. This open discrimination against foreigners is based on the imaginary that migrants only come to the city to "make fast money," "keeping their suitcases behind the door" to leave the city in times of crisis. In contrast, the nyc perceive themselves as defenders of the city who persist in times of crisis (Fueyo 2010). Based on this reasoning, the nyc articulate quasi-naturalized claims,[19] that are manifested, for example, by former "ypefianos," who use roadblocks and hunger strikes to demand jobs for their children and grandchildren in the renationalized YPF, seeing it as a form of historical reparation for their suffering while toiling in the industry.[20] To obtain a desirable job in the oil industry, individuals generally need social capital, as understood by Bourdieu (1986), i.e., contacts or intermediaries who recommend the potential worker (family, friends, trade unionists, politicians). Especially following oil booms, being a nyc becomes nearly a *condition sine qua non* for being employed in the industry. Consequently, the numerous migrants, although striving for work in the hydrocarbon sector, are generally excluded from this type of job (Baeza 2010).

Yet the nyc is neither a homogenous group nor a well-defined signifier. Its meaning depends on the actor using it, and hierarchies of prestige and (dis-) respectability exist within the nyc. For instance, both the white-collar established middle class and the blue-collar oil workers often identify themselves as nyc. However, the former strongly stigmatize the blue-collar oil workers who, despite their high purchasing power, lack social respectability. In this case, income is not an appropriate indicator for analyzing social inequity. Rather, a combination of migrant origin, educational credentials, occupational status and habitus (Bourdieu 1986) confirms the local middle-class self-identification in opposition to those "black (as a class mark) with money" (Grimson and Baeza 2016) from the oil industry who might have consumption power but lack 'good taste' in choosing their goods.

In addition to class inequalities, oil work historically (re-)produces gender inequalities because of males' preferential treatment in the labor market. In the "ypefiana" era during the twentieth century, women were fixed to their roles as 'daughters/mothers/wives.' Even today, Comodoro, in general, and the oil industry, in particular, remain a man's world,[21] especially when it comes to hierarchies of prestige and (dis-) respectability. Here the gender border generally reinforces the class border (Barrionuevo 2016). Whereas both male blue-collar oil workers and their spouses are despised by the established middle-class, men's "annoying" behavior is often justified, pointing to them as victims of their partners. The oil workers' wives are objects of a strong rejection that often includes moral repudiation, and the male oil workers participate in stigmatizing their wives (Baeza 2010).

These examples illuminate the arguably negative ecological and sociocultural consequences as well as the deep-rooted social inequality and discrimination in the oil industry. Most of these problems are concentrated in the southern part of the province around Comodoro, where oil extraction takes place. However, these detriments do not challenge the 'commodity consensus' in the city. Arguing against extraction in the oil city of Comodoro—and probably in other oil cities around the world—would not be perceived as a valid objection. Opposition would be construed as a lack of solidarity with the city's material interests and development needs and a betrayal of Comodoro's history and identity.

"Everybody Lives On Oil...": The Material Foundation of the Oil Consensus

"Everybody lives on oil. [...] The whole province, the police, the hospitals, all you see in each of these cities live on this" (Interview with Jorge

Ávila, President of the Union of Private Oil Workers and Director of Petrominera S.E., February 15, 2016, in Comodoro Rivadavia). Jorge Ávila, the mighty boss of the oil workers' union and simultaneously the current director of *Petrominera S.E.*, a provincially owned oil-company, expresses what everybody knows: Chubut virtually lives on oil. Oil money permeates the whole society and creates material interests that explain, at least partly, people's broad support for extraction. However, whereas (nearly) all parts of the population receive direct or indirect material benefits from oil exploitation, these do not reach all social groups in the same manner. We now analyze the material foundation of the consensus on oil in Chubut, highlighting the socio-geographical and socioeconomical inequalities it produces.

Chubut manifests a clear north-south divide: the *Cuenca del Golfo San Jorge* around Comodoro in the South is the place of oil, business, and labor, whereas the North, including the province's capital, Rawson, and the commercial and administrative city, Trelew, is the home of politics (Barros and Carrizo 2012). However, both parts are united in depending on oil revenue. Article 124 of the Argentinean Constitution establishes that the provinces execute the "rights on natural resources present on their territory." Thus, in Argentina the royalties from oil extraction correspond to the provinces.[22] In Chubut, the royalties are unequally divided between the provincial government, municipalities with oil extraction and those without. While the division between the different public entities is highly contested (Interview with Ezequiel Cufré, then Minister of Hydrocarbons of the Province Chubut, October 21, 2015, in Comodoro Rivadavia), we emphasize that the whole province benefits from oil money.

However, the way in which oil money permeates society differs between Comodoro and the rest of the province. In areas without oil extraction, the provincial and municipal governments channel oil money by financing social services, hiring and employing civil servants, subsidizing the local economy to permit relatively low tax rates, and investing in infrastructure and public works. In Comodoro, oil rent and local society are directly connected. Of course, in Comodoro public spending is also a powerful tool to channel oil rent into the local economy. In addition, the oil industry's presence allows the municipal government to sponsor incomes above the provincial average although the "tax burden in Comodoro is one of the lowest [...] at the national level" (Interview with a public servant from the tax authority of the Municipality of Comodoro Rivadavia, February 25, 2016, in Comodoro Rivadavia). Due to the industries' investments, production cost spillovers, and oil workers' high salaries, oil money pervades daily life. Money turns Comodoro into a dynamic and prosperous city with impressive consumption capacity despite the high cost of living and overpriced goods and services. Consequently, in Comodoro the material benefits from oil extraction not only exceed those of the northern valley but are also more obvious. Whereas people in the valley may be less aware of their oil-dependence, in Comodoro everybody recognizes the intimate connection between the oil industry and the city's fate.

A second crucial aspect is that oil benefits are not distributed equally within society. Thus, distributing rent (re-)produces social inequality, especially in Comodoro. Although nearly everyone receives material benefits from oil, the amount varies significantly among different groups. Apart from the industry itself and oil-related local business (service, transportation, etc.), the oil industry's white- and blue-collar workers benefit most directly through high incomes. In 2014, the average salary in the mining and oil sector was 2.3 times higher than the average wage in Chubut (MEFP 2015, 6). This difference produces income inequalities between the oil industry and other economic activities. These inequalities are partially explained by the extended work hours, overtime, viands, long trips to the oil wells (drive-in drive-out system), etc. However, high wages also manifest the strength of the oil workers' trade unions, who use their collective bargaining power to appropriate a share of the oil rent. Oil workers' high wage-levels inflate the prices of goods, services, and rentals in the city. Thus, oil workers are usually blamed for price inflation (with the consequent wage devaluation) by non-oil groups.

However, these "non-oil groups" include regional traders, entrepreneurs, or landlords who actually benefit from the city's high wages that enable them to charge inflated prices. For example, house and apartment owners rent to oil companies' incoming employees or to local oil workers and their families. This practice of overpricing, criticized by some sectors as an "unfair attitude of many merchants and [...] also from different chambers such as the real estate chamber" (Interview with the Director of Public Relations of the Union of Hierarchic Staff in Oil and Gas of Southern Patagonia, October 22, 2015, in Comodoro Rivadavia), is common in rentier societies and represents an indirect mechanism for capturing rents: "They have a drugstore: To whom do they sell? To the oil workers. They charge for the medicine 40% more than elsewhere. Oil workers can pay it" (Interview with Jorge Ávila, President of the Union of Private Oil Workers and Director of Petrominera S.E., February 15, 2016, in Comodoro Rivadavia). Local business gets additional (indirect) benefits from the industry, especially in boom times. Typical for extractive societies, during the last boom (2003–2013) construction activity skyrocketed 280% (MEFP 2015, 9). Increasing oil revenue financed this construction boom through public investment in infrastructure. Despite rumors of irregularities and overbilling, these expenditures generated massive profits for local entrepreneurs (Interview with Public Servant of the Ministry of Territorial Development and Productive Sectors of the Province Chubut, February 18, 2016, in Rawson). Lastly, public oil revenues also benefit local business through subsidies and under-taxation (Interview with a public servant from the tax authority of the Municipality of Comodoro Rivadavia, February 25, 2016, in Comodoro Rivadavia).

The general population also benefits from public oil revenues through low taxation, increased public employment and welfare spending, and from the industries' spillovers into the local economy and society. Finally, although the elevated living costs devalue the relatively high nominal incomes of socially disadvantaged groups, they do benefit from social assistance programs, allowing them to benefit from the "fragmentation of the state" (Interview with Public Servants from the Secretary of Social Policies of the Ministry of Social Development and Family of the Province Chubut, February 17, 2016, in Rawson; Interview with a public servant from the tax authority of the Municipality of Comodoro Rivadavia, February 25, 2016, in Comodoro Rivadavia; Interview with Public Servant of the Subsecretary for Childhood, Youth and Family of the Municipality of Comodoro Rivadavia, February 24, 2016, in Comodoro Rivadavia). Although these programs focus on short-term improvements, often lack coordination and planning, and enable arbitrary granting (Interview with Public Servant of the Subsecretary for Childhood, Youth and Family of the Municipality of Comodoro Rivadavia, February 24, 2016, in Comodoro Rivadavia), they still function to distribute public oil revenue to disadvantaged social groups. And, while total amounts are relatively small, the oil companies also finance social projects via Corporate Social Responsibility measures such that oil money is visible in the daily lives of Comodoro's citizens.

Summing up, oil is the goose that lays the province's golden eggs. Except for during times of crisis, the whole Chubutean population receives benefits from oil extraction. Especially, in Comodoro people are well-aware that the foundation of these benefits is oil. However, this overview also confirms that the repartition of these benefits diverges widely and (re-)produces social inequalities. Distributing the oil rent produces winners and losers, causes both "progress and poverty" (Obeng-Odoom 2014, 187). The winners include established merchants, service providers, businessmen, or landlords realizing gains from extra profits due to inflating prices; the construction sector profiting from oil money channeled into infrastructure projects and housing projects; local business accessing subsidies and a low tax burden; and rent-seeking intermediaries benefiting from fees for easing contract conclusions. Thus, oil workers earning high salaries would be but one of many social groups with material interest to maintain oil extraction. Whereas the rest of the society might not be part of the winning coalition of the rent distribution, public servants receive their salaries in large part from oil money, and even poor people who manage to get social assistance from different public entities still have something to lose if the oil industries' leading role in Comodoro were to change.

Oil in Everyday Life: Social Imaginaries around Extractivism

We argue that the "commodity consensus" on oil in Chubut is also built on the constitution and redefinition of socio-historical imaginaries around extractivism. As common sense, these ideas pervade local society and help to explain why, even in times of crisis, no critical voices promote a categorical transformation of the local oil-based development model. We focus on three aspects: the construction of a history-based local oil identity; consumption and distinction patterns present in daily life; and the fear that the end of oil would initiate the death of Comodoro.

The history of Comodoro Rivadavia is the history of oil. Since its foundation the city's fate has been linked to the oil industry. The resource and its extraction are omnipresent in daily life. Numerous urban signifiers—museums, monuments, neighborhoods, public buildings like the airport—evoke the city's history connected to oil and, more specifically, to the YPF era and the historical leader of the national oil company, General Enrique Mosconi. Today the blue-collar oil workers characterize the cityscape, dominate local news, and assure fresh stories for local gossip (Barrionuevo 2016). The oil-related trade unions and the oil companies—due to community work, charity, CSR, and their political and economic power—also loom large in the city. That is, one cannot be in Comodoro and not talk about oil. Rodríguez (2013, 106) notes, "[T]he air in Comodoro [...] is dense, is potent, is oil." Both the historical relationship with oil and its pervasiveness in life make oil essential to the local 'commodorense' identity (Interview with Ezequiel Cufré, then Minister of Hydrocarbons of the Province Chubut, October 21, 2015, in Comodoro Rivadavia). For example, during the mid-twentieth century, local beauty contestants for 'Oil Queen' (*Reina del petróleo*), held in the local YPF stadium, carried a jar of oil blessed by the bishop. This ritual shows the importance of this sacred resource, perceived as key to guaranteeing local economic development and social well-being (Carrizo and Oviedo 2014) as well as establishing local identity. Today, oil remains a source of local identity and pride, expressed in local narratives of the sacrifice of working at wells in remote areas and the hardships of living in a hostile climate with few natural amenities, away from other regional towns and major national cities. Persistence under these adverse conditions becomes a source of local pride:

> I mean, constantly, by the media, you'll see, for example the Mayor saying [...] that we are the ones who generate wealth and other towns depend on us; that what we are doing is working for the progress of the country. (Interview with an Activist from the Foro Social y Ambiental de la Patagonia, 21st October 2015, in Comodoro Rivadavia)

In Comodoro, people stress that their labor enables Argentinians—especially people from Buenos Aires—to enjoy heating in wintertime.[23] The current crisis actualizes multiple senses of this local identity, including its historical opposition to the capital city of Buenos Aires. Politicians, highlighting that "Patagonia also exists" and complaining about oil extraction benefits "always going north," express the intention to foster local identity (Interview with Jorge Ávila, President of the Union of Private Oil Workers and Director of Petrominera S.E., February 15, 2016, in Comodoro Rivadavia). In this context, union representatives threaten to leave the country without gas and oil if job security is not guaranteed.

Furthermore, the intimate relationship between Comodoro and oil extraction also accounts for social imaginaries (Castoriadis 2003) about modernity and consumption. The relationship between oil and progress is represented by a widespread consumption-oriented lifestyle and the 4 × 4 off-road vehicle as a local oil-related status symbol. The relatively elevated earnings of oil workers support a high level of consumption. Although their consumer practices are strongly challenged by the middle class, who question the (irrational) forms of spending and the occupation of public-commercial space by oil workers and their families, the prospect of maintaining a consumption-oriented lifestyle or of being able to fulfill long-awaited consumption desires turns working in the oil industry into a desirable objective for youth who conceive of these jobs as a quick way to achieve personal progress, social promotion, and economic success. That is, working in the oil industry becomes an attractive prospect in a society that revolves simultaneously around consumerism and immediacy (Fueyo 2010), "an obsession" even for many young people and their families (Interview with a Teacher of the Colegio 707, October 23, 2015, in Comodoro Rivadavia) as a way to increase their social status. Our data also show that, while many young men finishing secondary education in the area dream of becoming oil workers, women want to "get one": oil work is a means of "saving" oneself and others.

Lastly, estimations about the future of oil are strongly contested in Comodoro. Even though social discourse argues that "oil is going to end" and is backed by studies evaluating the known reserves and current extraction rates that state that Comodoro will run out of oil in about twenty years (Hirschfeldt 2014, 19; Vásquez 2016, 11), different politicians and stakeholders from the oil industry estimate that the future of Comodoro, and therefore also of Chubut, will continue to rely on oil.[24] For example, during 2011–2015 Martín Buzzi's provincial government administration emphasized the potential of technological innovation. According to the Chubut Minister of Hydrocarbons at that time, it could ensure that "Chubut province live 100 years more in relationship with the oil industry" (Interview with Ezequiel Cufré, then Minister of Hydrocarbons of the Province Chubut, October 21, 2015, in Comodoro Rivadavia). However, both versions fear a future without oil, as represented in idiomatic expressions, such as "Comodoro was born and will die as an oil camp." Further, Jorge Ávila, union leader, forecasts that following the current crisis "the city will end with half of its current population" (Interview with Jorge Ávila, President of the Union of Private Oil Workers and Director of Petrominera S.E., February 15, 2016, in Comodoro Rivadavia). This concern about the city's future reflects the region's lack of economic diversification. Although ideas,[25] proposals, and initiatives toward diversification are discussed, projects are not consistently implemented. Those projects that do advance maintain the tradition of natural resource extraction such as shale gas or other mining activities.

Consequently, people perceive oil extraction as the means to escape from an impoverished past that also permits a life of oil work, high salaries, and economic security. However, this perception also fosters a culture of immediacy, where people, uncertain about the future, enjoy the fruits of their labor by consuming today (Fueyo 2010). The bemoaned lack of planning by both politicians and individuals must be interpreted against the background of an uncertain future for local development. Generally speaking, as fear prevails over a city that dies with the end of oil, neither local politics prioritizes planning for a future without oil, nor do people invest in long-term projects. This inaction perpetuates a self-fulfilling prophecy, as projects that might transcend the local extractive model are not implemented and consequently the social imaginary of the city's future continues its intimate link with oil. Combined with the frequent appeal to the myth of a resisting Patagonia, this context enhances the broad consensus on the extractive model and the marginalization of positions critical of oil activity (Interview with Brígida Baeza, Professor at the Universidad Nacional de la Patagonia San Juan de Bosco, February 25, 2016, in Comodoro Rivadavia). Consequently, even in the current industry crisis, alternative proposals are scarce and rarely go beyond suggesting changes within the extractive model.

Conclusion

The Argentine province of Chubut and, especially, Comodoro Rivadavia illuminate the configuration of a subnational oil-based rentier society in a non-oil country. Despite sharing many characteristics with classical cases of rentier economies, in this case international debates about oil dependence and development in Comodoro are strikingly absent. We argue that contemporary researchers focus on the macro-levels of nation states and ignore cases of subnational rentierism such as Comodoro because they do not fit the resource as curse or blessing framework. In fact, Comodoro highlights flaws in mainstream thinking on oil and development. It is a puzzle because, despite detrimental consequences from oil extraction for the local economy, society, and the environment, little opposition to it exists at the local level. While scholarship has focused on the social movements and local organizations that reject extractive projects (e.g., Bebbington and Bury 2013), Comodoro as a case invites us to reflect upon the reasons why broad support exists for extraction within the "zones of sacrifice" (di Risio et al. 2012), despite its visible negative consequences.

This puzzle can only be solved if we consider the material interests, social imaginaries and collective identities (Brubaker and Cooper 2000) constructed around oil extraction at the provincial, national, and local levels. The massive influx of oil money changes the political game at the provincial level. Although they receive different amounts of money from it, the rent distribution within Chubut prompts provincial and municipal authorities to continue support for oil extraction. At the social level, whereas most groups directly or indirectly benefit from oil extraction, these benefits differ significantly until it becomes questionable whether oil necessarily makes all groups better off. Oil extraction in Chubut produces winners and losers, so focusing only on a blessed or cursed society is misleading (Peters 2016). However, all social levels also fear losing something once oil extraction ends. In contrast, to understand oil and society's close relationship in Comodoro we must consider how the historical legacies of decades-long oil dependency have shaped the social imaginaries and the sociocultural imprint, or the society's "mental infrastructures" (Welzer 2011). Undoubtedly, history matters in the creation of an oil culture, but as this case study highlights, we must also consider culture and daily practices because (re-) producing and actualizing this oil culture require ongoing social and cultural confirmation. These dynamics happen daily, restricting the political space to question or resist extraction. These findings substantiate the need to study an oil culture's particularities and dynamics to allow better understanding of how support for extraction is created. Secondly, such analyses can contribute to insight into possible strategies to successfully question the 'commodity consensus' in oil-based social formations and/or encourage discussion about transitioning to a post-extractivist development model. Thirdly, we need a more comprehensive understanding of oil cultures. Additional case studies and small-N comparisons would allow us to identify an oil culture's case-specific expressions and commonly shared characteristics to permit development of empirically based theory about rentier societies' sociocultural imprint and even political strategies for overcoming rentierism.

Notes

1 In a recent publication Auty (2015) prefers to talk more precisely about a "rent curse."

2 Social imaginaries are a condition of the possible or the impossible, the true or the false, and the valid or the invalid in the field of values, beliefs and desires for a society at a historical moment (Castoriadis 2003). In the social

world these symbolic aspects overlap irreducibly with material aspects in co-construction processes. Since meaning schemes also involve processes of self-identification, collective identification, and distinction through categorical attributes, these processes intrinsic to social life suppose "the emotionally laden sense of belonging to a distinctive, bounded group, involving both a felt solidarity or oneness with fellow group members and a felt difference from or even antipathy to specified outsiders." (Brubaker and Cooper 2000, 19).

3 For a critical reexamination of this concept see di John (2009) as well as Saad-Filho and Weeks (2013).

4 For a review of the debates see Karl (2004), Peters (2015), and Papyrakis (2017).

5 Of course, this is not to neglect the existence of important social mobilizations against hydrocarbon extraction itself in many parts of the world. Perhaps the widespread critique and resistance against nonconventional extraction of shale gas (fracking) is the best example (for Argentina see: Savino 2016). When it comes to more traditional forms of oil exploitation, the (failed) resistance against oil extraction in the Ecuadorian Yasuní-ITT national park represents a well-known case of massive mobilization against oil extraction.

6 Rent can be defined as income generated by mere ownership, which derives neither from investments nor from labor (Sørensen 1996). As a consequence, rent does not share the constraints of requiring continuous reinvestment, as is the case in capitalist systems. On the contrary, rentiers (the recipients of economic rent) can dispose of their rent income freely.

7 Some exceptions include Hafez (2009), Tinker Salas (2009), Quinteros ([1972] 2014), Soares de Oliveira (2015), and Peters (2017).

8 Comodoro's foundation in 1901 was marked by the precept "to govern is to populate" under Julio A. Roca presidency, commander of the "Desert campaign" also known as "War against the Indigenous."

9 In 2007, the former governor of the province Mario Das Neves extended for thirty years the concession contract of the area. This renegotiation is now being investigated by the justice for alleged irregularities, including payment of bribes.

10 http://www.lanacion.com.ar/1485917-quienes-son-los-dragones-el-grupo-que-tiene-en-vilo-a-chubut

11 Revenues of the municipality of Comodoro Rivadavia depend, estimated by an official from the Department of Revenue, about 90% of the oil industry (Interview with a public servant from the tax authority of the Municipality of Comodoro Rivadavia, 25 February 2016 in Comodoro Rivadavia).

12 Based on data from the Dirección General de Estadísticas y Censos of Chubut.

13 We refer here to social capital as understood by Robert Putnam (2000).

14 These negative aspects of oil-led development will probably worsen in the context of the current crisis with comparatively low oil prices. Against this background, cutbacks of oil wells and forced retirements are recorded; while oil unions—together with the provincial and municipal governments—seek agreement programs with operators companies to avoid layoffs.

15 Please note that a basic insight from political ecology also applies to Comodoro: ecological problems do not affect the whole population similarly but (re)produce or even reinforce socio-environmental inequalities concerning the resilience against environmental damages and the capacity to adapt to them.

16 The lack of an environmental social movement in Comodoro is even more striking keeping in mind that one of the few successful popular resistances against mining in Argentina took place in the town of Esquel, Chubut.

17 See for instance: "En Comodoro la industria petrolera genera un aumento del consumo de drogas" (El Patagónico, 9 de mayo de 2012), "Ávila reconoció que entre los petroleros existe un elevado consumo de drogas" (El Patagónico, 7 de junio de 2013) y "Revelan datos sobre el consumo de drogas entre los petroleros" (El Patagónico, 13 de noviembre de 2014).

18 A report by the International Organization of Migration (2008) revealed that in Comodoro even government officials, some of whom were indicted, supported the spread of trafficking by receiving money for not registering irregularities, reporting controls in advance, and solving problems with open files.

19 For different forms of articulating quasi-naturalized rights in the Venezuelan oil-based societies, see Bautista Urbaneja (2013) and Peters (2017).

20 See: http://www.elpatagonico.com/ypf-realizara-una-seleccion-del-personal-presentado-la-agrupacion-mosconi-n663721.

21 Palermo (2015) finds a relationship between the construction of masculinity, company policies, and factory discipline, in a process that shapes a "factory-oil-male subject" according to production interests.

22 The National government appropriates part of the oil rent by levering export taxes (*rentenciones*) and by taxing extraordinary profits from the oil companies.

23 Based on this affirmation, in times of crisis, Comodoro demands assistance and solidarity not only from the rest of the country but also from the oil companies. See for example: http://www.diariojornada.com.ar/161811/politica/Legislatura_dara_apoyo_a_Das_Neves_para_exigir_a_Nacion_recupero_historico_por_45_mil_millones, http://www.poderlocal.net/leer_noticias.asp?ID=29595, http://www.diariojornada.com.ar/noticias/noticia.aspx?id=59714&s=politica&t=Di_Pierro_llega_a_Rawson_el_jueves_con_petroleros_y_vecinalistas_para_asistir_a_debate_del_marco_regulador

24 These estimations are based on a technological optimism regarding innovations in extraction techniques and high prices for oil on the world market.

25 These projects reach from building a logistical hub connecting the Atlantic and the Pacific, or hinting at the region's potential for generating wind energy, or the proposal to build an oil refinery in the region up to exploiting the natural resources from the Atlantic Ocean.

References

Auty, Richard M. 2015. "From Resource Curse to Rent Curse: A Theoretical Perspective." In *Natural Resources and Economic Growth: Learning from History*, edited by Badia-Miró, Marc, Vicente Pinilla, and Harry Willebald, 26–53. London: Routledge.

Auty, Richard M. 1993. *Sustaining Development in Mineral Economies: The Resource Curse Thesis*. London: Routledge.

Bachiller, Santiago, Brígida Baeza, Letizia Vázquez, Bianca Freddo, Natalia Usach, Sergio Kaminker, and Carolina Laztra. 2015. *Toma de tierras y dificultades de acceso al suelo urbano en la Patagonia central*. Buenos Aires: Miño y Dávila.

Barros, Santiago and Gabriel Carrizo. 2012. La política en otro lado: Los desafíos de analizar los orígenes del sistema político chubutense, historiapolitica.com http://historiapolitica.com/datos/biblioteca/territoriosaprovincias_barrosycarrizo.pdf

Baeza, Brígida. 2010. "Andá a tirar la cuña"... Desigualdades económicas y desigualdades simbólicas: el caso de los trabajadores petroleros en Comodoro Rivadavia, Chubut. 4° Jornadas de Historia de la Patagonia.

Baeza, Brígida and Magalí Chanampa. 2016. La naturalización de las problemáticas medioambientales en torno a la explotación petrolera en Comodoro Rivadavia. *Revista Identidades*, Dossier 3, Año 6, 7–31.

Bárcena, Alicia and Antonio Prado. 2016. *El imperativo de la igualdad: Por un desarrollo sostenible en América Latina y el Caribe*. Buenos Aires: Siglo XXI.

Barrionuevo, Natalia. 2016. "Trabajo petrolero y desigualdades de género en Comodoro Rivadavia: reactualizaciones históricas." *Revista Identidades*, 3 (6), 88–109.

Bautista Urbaneja, Diego. 2013. *La renta y el reclamo: Ensayo sobre petróleo y economía política en Venezuela*. Caracas: Alfa.

Bebbington, Anthony and Jeffrey Bury. 2013. *Subterranean Struggles: New Dynamics of Mining, Oil, and Gas in Latin America*. Austin: University of Texas Press.

Beblawi, Hazem and Giacomo Luciani. 1987. *The Rentier State*. London: Croom Helm.

Bellato, Roberto. 2016. "La crisis petrolera afecta a 25.000 trabajadores del sector." En: El Inversor Online, 30 de junio de 2016, http://elinversoronline.com/2016/06/la-crisis-petrolera-afecta-a-25-000-trabajadores-del-sector/

Bourdieu, Pierre. 1986. "The Forms of Capital." In *Handbook of Theory and Research for the Sociology of Education*, edited by John G. Richardson, 241–258. John G. New York: Greenwood.

Briceño León, Roberto. [1990] 2015. *Los efectos perversos del petróleo*. Caracas: El Nacional.

Brubaker, Rogers and Frederick Cooper. 2000. "Beyond 'Identity.'" *Theory and Society*, 29, 1–47.

Brunnschweiler, Christa N. and Erwin H. Bulte. 2009. "Natural Resources and Violent Conflict: Resource Abundance, Dependence and the Onset of Civil War." *Oxford Economic Papers*, 61, 651–674.

Brunnschweiler, Christa N. and Erwin H. Bulte. 2008. "The Resource Curse Revisited and Revised: A Tale of Paradoxes and Red Herrings." *Journal of Environmental Economics and Management*, 55, 248–264.

Budiño, Lino Marcos. 1971. *Comodoro Rivadavia, 'sociedad enferma'*. Buenos Aires: Gáramont.

Burchardt, Hans-Jürgen, Rafael Domínguez, Carlos Larrea, and Stefan Peters. 2016. *Nada dura para siempre: Neo-Extractivismo tras el boom de las materias primas*. Quito: Abya-Yala.

Canuto, Otaviano. 2014. "The Commodity Super-Cycle: Is this Time Different?" World Bank Economic Premise, http://siteresources.worldbank.org/EXTPREMNET/Resources/EP150.pdf

Carrizo, Gabriel. 2016. *Petróleo, peronismo y sindicalismo: La historia de los trabajadores de YPF en la Patagonia, 1944–1955*. Buenos Aires: Prometeo.

Carrizo, Gabriel and Guillermina Oviedo. 2014. "Cuando Comodoro era una fiesta. Ampliando el horizonte sobre el 40° Aniversario del Descubrimiento del Petróleo de 1947 en el período de la Gobernación Militar." *Pasado porvenir*, 8 (9), 1–21.

Castoriadis, Cornelius. 2003. *La institución imaginaria de la sociedad*. Buenos Aires: Tusquets.

Collier, Paul and Anke Hoeffler. 2004. "Greed and Grievance in Civil War." *Oxford Economic Papers*, 56, 563–595.

Di John, John. 2009. *From Windfall to Curse? Oil and Industrialization in Venezuela, 1920 to the Present*. University Park: Pennsylvania State University Press.

Di Risio, Diego, Marc Gavaldà, Diego Pérez Roig, and Hernán Scandizzo. 2012. *Zonas de sacrificio: Impactos de la industria hidrocarburífera en Salta y Norpatagonia*. Buenos Aires: América Libre.

Dietz, Kristina, Bettina Engels, Oliver Pye, and Achim Brunnengräber. 2015. *The Political Ecology of Agrofuels*. London: Routledge.

Elias, Norbert and John L. Scotson. 1965. *The Established and the Outsiders*. London: Sage.

Etchezar, Damián. 2007. "La vida en el pozo. Riqueza y pobreza de los petroleros." *El Extremo Sur de la Patagonia*, V.

Fueyo, María Lucía. 2010. Oro negro. Jóvenes petroleros, representaciones sociales en torno al consumo. Thesis, Licenciatura en Comunicación Social. Facultad de Periodismo y Comunicación Social, Universidad Nacional de La Plata.

Gilberthorpe, Emma and Elissaios Papyrakis. 2015. "The extractive industries and development: The resource curse at the micro, meso and macro levels." *The Extractive Industries and Society*, 2, 381–390.

Grimson, Alejandro and Brígida Baeza. 2016. "Desacoples entre nivel de ingreso y jerarquías simbólicas en Comodoro Rivadavia: Acerca de las legitimidades de la desigualdad social." *Revista Identidades*, 6 (10), 1–21.

Hafez, Ziad. 2009. "The Culture of Rent, Factionalism, and Corruption: A Political Economy of Rent in the Arab World." *Contemporary Arab Affairs*, 2 (3), 458–480.

Hirschfeldt, Marcelo. 2014. Análisis de Madurez de la Cuenca del Golfo de San Jorge: desafíos actuales y futuros para un desarrollo sostenible y sustentable, http://oilproduction.net/files/Jornadas_produccion_2014-v6.pdf

International Organisation of Migration. 2008. *La trata de personas en Argentina, Chile y Uruguay. Estudio exploratorio sobre la trata de personas con fines de explotación sexual en Argentina, Chile y Uruguay*. Rosario: Serapis.

Kappel, Robert. 2011. "Nigeria – Ressourcenreichtum und Wachstum ohne Entwicklung." In *Machtquelle Erdöl: Die Außen-, Innen- und Wirtschaftspolitik von Erdölstaaten*, edited by Matthias Basedau and Robert Kappel, 141–166. Baden-Baden: Nomos.

Karl, Terry Lynn. 2004. Oil-led Development: Social, Political, and Economic Consequences. In *Encyclopedia of Energy*, Vol. 4, edited by Cutler Cleveland, 661–672. Philadelphia: Elsevier.

Kay, Cristóbal. 1989. *Latin American Theories of Development and Underdevelopment*. London: Routledge.

Laveglia, Fernando. 2004. *Apuntes de la economía de Chubut: Una visión al comienzo del siglo*. Buenos Aires: Dunken.

Le Billon, Philippe. 2005. *Geopolitics of Resource Wars: Resource Dependence, Governance, and Violence*. London: Routledge.

MEFP. 2015. Chubut: Ficha Provincial, Octubre 2015. http://www.economia.gob.ar/peconomica/dnper/fichas_provinciales/Chubut.pdf

Mehlum, Halvor, Karl Moene, and Ragnar Torvik. 2006. "Institutions and the Resource Curse." *The Economic Journal*, 118 (508), 1–20.

Menaldo, Victor. 2016. *The Institutions Curse: Natural Resources, Politics, and Development*. Cambridge: Cambridge University Press.

Ministry of Labor. 2015. *Manual de buenas prácticas de la industria petrolera*. Capítulo 1: Transporte, montaje e inicio de perforación, http://www.srt.gob.ar/images%5cpdf%5cMBP.IndustriaPetrolera.pdf

Obeng-Odoom, Franklin. 2014. *Oiling the Urban Economy. Land, Labour, and the State in Sekondi-Takoradi, Ghana*. London: Routledge.

Palermo, Hernán M. 2015. "'Machos que se la bancan': Masculinidad y disciplina fabril en la industria petrolera argentina." *Desacatos*, 47, 100–115.

Papyrakis, Elissaios. 2017. "The Resource Curse – What Have we Learned from Two Decades of Intensive Research: Introduction to the Special Issue." *The Journal of Development Studies*, 53 (2), 175–185.

Peters, Stefan. 2017. "Beyond Curse and Blessing: Rentier Society in Venezuela." In *Contested Extractivism, Society and the State: Struggles over Mining and Land*, edited by Kristina Dietz and Bettina Engels, 45–68. New York: Palgrave Macmillan, 45–68.

Peters, Stefan. 2016. "Petróleo, política y sociedad en Chubut: Reflexiones teórico-conceptuales en torno al rentismo." *Revista Identidades*, 3 (6), 144–164.

Peters, Stefan. 2015. "Mit Erdöl zur Entwicklung? Rentengesellschaften im 21. Jahrhundert". In *Der Staat in globaler Perspektive. Zur Renaissance der Entwicklungsstaaten*, edited by Hans-Jürgen Burchardt and Stefan Peters, 149–174. Frankfurt (Main): Campus.

Putnam, Robert. 2000. *Bowling Alone: The Collapse and Revival of American Community*. New York: Simon & Schuster.

Quinteros, Rodolfo. [1972] 2014. *Antropología del petróleo*. Caracas: BCV.

Reed, Kristin. 2009. *Crude Existence: Environment and the Politics of Oil in Northern Angola*. Berkeley: University of California Press.

Rodríguez, María Graciela. 2013. "La ciudad visitada, la ciudad vivida", *Revista Identidades*, 5 (3), 106–111.

Ross, Michael L. 2012. *The Oil Curse. How Petroleum Wealth Shapes the Wealth of Nations*. Princeton: Princeton University Press.

Saad-Filho, Alfredo and John Weeks. 2013. "Curses, Diseases, and Other Resource Confusions." *Third World Quarterly*, 34 (1), 1–21.

Sachs, Jeffrey D. and Andrew M. Warner. 2001. "The Curse of Natural Resources." *European Economic Review*, 45 (4–6), 827–838.

Savino, Lucas. 2016. "Landscapes of Contrast: The Neo-Extractivist State and Indigenous Peoples in 'Post-neoliberal' Argentina." *The Extractive Industries and Society*, 3, 404–415.

Sinnott, Emily, John Nash, and Augustino de la Torre. 2010. *Natural Resources in Latin America and the Caribbean. Beyond Booms and Busts?* Washington, DC: World Bank.

Soares de Oliveira, Ricardo. 2015. *Magnificent and Beggar Land. Angola Since Civil War*. London: Hurst & Company.

Sørensen, Aare B. 1996. "The Structural Basis of Social Inequality." *The American Journal of Sociology*, 101 (5), 1333–1365.

Svampa, Maristella. 2015. "Commodities Consensus: Neoextractivism and Enclosure of the Commons in Latin America." *South Atlantic Quarterly*, 114 (1), 65–82.

Svampa, Maristella and Enrique Viale. 2014. *Maldesarrollo: La Argentina del extractivismo y despojo*. Buenos Aires: Katz.

Tinker Salas, Miguel. 2009. *The Enduring Legacy. Oil, Culture, and Society in Venezuela*. Durham: Duke University Press.

Torres, Susana. 1995. *Two Oil Company Towns in Patagonia: European Immigrants, Class and Ethnicity* (1907–1933). Dissertation, Graduate School-New Brunswick, Rutgers, The State University of New Jersey. Unpublished.

Vásquez, Patricia I. 2016. Argentina's Oil and Gas Sector: Coordinated Federalism and The Rule of Law, Wilson Center, Latin American Program. https://www.wilsoncenter.org/sites/default/files/argentinasoilgas.vasquez.pdf

Watts, Michael. 2011. "Blood Oil: The Anatomy of Petro-Insurgency in the Niger Delta." In *Crude Domination: An Anthropology of Oil*, edited by Andrea Behrends, Stephen Reyna, and Günther Schlee, 49–79. Oxford: Berghahn Books.

Welzer, Harald. 2011. *Mentale Infrastrukturen: Wie das Wachstum in die Welt und in die Seelen kam*. Berlin: Heinrich-Boell-Stiftung.

Section III

A Closer Look at the Oil Sands in Alberta

10 Still Ethical Oil

Framing the Alberta Oil Sands

Roberta Laurie

Ethical Oil: The Case for Canada's Oil Sands

Ezra Levant popularized the term "ethical oil" with the 2010 publication of his polemic, *Ethical Oil: The Case for Canada's Oil Sands*. Levant's book soon became a national bestseller, and the following year, it won the National Business Book Award.

Ezra Levant has long been known for embracing controversy. As publisher of the *Western Standard*, Levant was one of few in Canada who reprinted the notorious Danish Jyllands-Posten Mohammed cartoons in 2006. Later he joined Sun Media as a columnist, and for a short time, he also hosted their TV talk show, The Source, where he championed his passions: discussing radicalization in Canadian Mosques, Islamic State propaganda, Russian appeasement, and other provocative issues (TheRebel.media 2015). After the network failed, Levant launched his online platform, Rebel Media, where he has continued to champion right-wing causes: critiquing provincial NDP policies, denying climate change, condemning federal immigration policies, and advocating for the Alberta oil and gas industry. He has been called "the closest thing that Canada has to Glenn Beck or Rush Limbaugh" (*Gatehouse*, January 13, 2013), but despite—or perhaps because of—his controversial and often combative prose, he has been able to connect with a segment of right-wing Canadians on current and, more often than not, contentious issues.

In *Ethical Oil*, Levant (2010) claimed that the Alberta oil sands produce "the most ethical oil in the world" (234). While some believed the book "provided some desperately needed perspective" (Foster, September 21, 2010), Levant's thesis was not universally accepted. *The Petroleum Economist* (September 30, 2010) argued that the book contained "strange arguments that show little grasp of the global economy, or the way its most important commodity is traded." Jennifer Good (2013), Associate Professor of Communication, Popular Culture, and Film at Brock University, called the "ethical oil" frame a "have your cake and eat it too" message (10). The Pembina Institute also criticized Levant's premise, claiming that as a diversionary tactic: [It] "would have Canadians forget all about the serious and so far, unresolved native impacts of unrestrained development of the oil sands and ask ourselves instead whether Canada's system of government is better than Saudi Arabia's or Iran's" (Grant, January 7, 2011). If its critics were to be believed, Levant's book should not have gained an audience.

In spite of the initial criticism, Levant effectively promoted his book and its "ethical oil" frame. Excerpts appeared in Sun Media publications, and in 2011, it won the National Business Book Award (Bolin, May 12, 2011). Levant often debated environmentalists critical of his position: Mike Hudema, climate campaigner for Greenpeace Canada; Ben West, tar sands campaign director for ForestEthics; and Andrew Nikiforuk, journalist and author of *Tar Sands: Dirty Oil and the Future of a Continent*. By nearly any measure, Levant's book was a national success.

As book sales rose so did the term "ethical oil." Supporters of Alberta oil sands development soon picked up on the term. The Conservative government embraced the concept. The then-Environment Minister, Peter Kent explained, "There has been a demonizing of a legitimate resource. It is ethical oil. It is regulated oil. And it's secure oil in a world where many of the free world's oil sources are somewhat less secure" (Findlay 2012). Levant's ideas were also endorsed by Alberta Premier Ed Stelmach and Danielle Smith, then the leader of Alberta's Wildrose Alliance. Brian Jean, then a Fort McMurray MP, urged people to read Levant's polemic (Gutstein, January 26, 2011). Stephen Harper explained, "Canada is an ethical society and a very secure source of energy for the U.S. compared to other sources" (Kennedy, January 7, 2011). All this buzz suggested "ethical oil" was making its way into the Canadian lexicon.

After the book's publication, the "ethical oil" message was further promoted by the website EthicalOil.org. Initially created by Alykan Velshi—Velshi soon moved to the PMO to become a strategist for Stephen Harper—the website aimed to rebut "inaccurate and unfair criticisms of the oil sands" (2014) and encourage readers to "write letters to their local newspapers, call talk radio stations and suggest ideas for Access to Information requests to expose the network of anti-oil sands lobbyists who meet regularly with senior Environment Canada officials" (2014). The website garnered attention in the afterglow of Levant's publication, but it has not been updated since 2014.

In the last few years, Levant's message has lost its veneer of objectivity. His anti-Muslim attacks appear vindictive, and he seems to be in a state of perpetual litigation. In 2010, Levant was charged with defaming Canadian Human Rights Commission lawyer, Giacomo Vigna. In his decision, Justice Smith stated that Levant "spoke in reckless disregard of the truth" and ordered him to pay Vigna $25,000 (Brean, November 20, 2010). In 2014, Levant lost a libel case and was forced to pay $80,000 in damages for defaming Khurrum Awan after calling the lawyer an "illiberal Islamic fascist" (Brean, November 27, 2014). In her ruling, the judge condemned Levant's actions: "I find that the defendant's dominant motive in these blog posts was ill-will, and that his repeated failure to take even basic steps to check his facts showed a reckless disregard for the truth" (Houpt, November 27, 2014). The Supreme Court later refused to hear Levant's appeal (*The Canadian Press*, June 8, 2017). Levant has not disappeared from the public eye, but he is increasingly seen as a right-wing provocateur, lacking credibility within mainstream media. His advocacy for the oil and gas industry has lost its ethos—except with his most ardent supporters.

With a few notable exceptions, the term "ethical oil" is seldom used by politicians or mainstream journalists these days. King (April 28, 2016), blogging for the *HuffPost*, qualifies his commentary supporting Energy East pipeline, by explaining that he receives feedback from his readers, telling him that the term "ethical oil" has been "soured." He uses this qualifier as a means to segue to his belief that we "can't have a legitimate discussion about the topic of oil without considering the ethics underlying our oil supply." He writes that Energy East would allow us to "supply conflict-free Canadian oil to a Canadian ally" (the United States) while "taking money out the pockets of despots, tyrants and murderers." In this way, King argues for the "ethical oil" frame without directly using it himself.

In another clear example of this frame, on March 6, 2018, UCP leader Jason Kenney responded to Bill Nye's criticism of the oil sands on Twitter by tweeting: "Nye has no business attacking Alberta's ethical oil & gas industry." The tweet was accompanied by a meme that quotes Nye saying, "I have been to Fort McMurray, Alberta, it really is an amazing place in the most troubling way." The meme's footer encourages Kenney's Twitter followers to "Like and share if you think millionaire celebrity Bill Nye has no business slagging our ethical oil industry." Despite these exceptions, the term "ethical oil" has not stood the test of time. As Good (2013) writes, "Ethical oil fail[ed] to live up to its potential as a framing device" (11). But outside the term the frames that Levant constructed around "ethical oil" continue to thrive.

Frames and Framing

Cognitive linguist, George Lakoff (2004) explains that "frames are mental structures that shape the way we see the world" (xv). They are the mental connections that we make when we see an image or hear a word. They include "semantic roles, relations between roles, and relations to other frames" that are "physically realized in the neural circuits of the brain" (Lakoff, 2010, 3). As we acquire knowledge, we acquire frames; "every word is defined through the frames it neurally activates" (Lakoff, 2010, 3). Once established, this network of frames becomes part of our unconscious thought. Like air, we breathe them in without noticing.

They fuel our impressions, our understandings, and our actions, but for the most part they remain unremarked.

Language that activates frame networks associated with values, belief, identity, and ideology can be particularly powerful. The more often they are activated the stronger these networks become. Intentional framing can be used to persuade an audience or add salience to an issue. By focusing on some associations and avoiding others, we can emphasize some details and de-emphasize others.

Robert Entman (1993), the J.B. and M.C. Shapiro Professor of Media and Public Affairs and Professor of International Affairs at George Washington University, further attests to the potential persuasiveness of cognitive framing:

> To frame is to select some aspects of a perceived reality and make them more salient in a communicating text, in such a way as to promote a problem definition causal interpretation, moral evaluation and/or treatment recommendation for the item described. (52)

In this way, frames shape our perception of local, national, and international events, gently nudging us towards tolerance or intolerance for a particular demographic, acceptance or rejection of a new idea. They hint at the morality or immorality of supporting an industry, the benefit or disadvantage of adopting a proposed policy. By giving people the words to express their thoughts and beliefs, framing can inform ideology, discourse, and ultimately behavior. Therefore, through repeatedly engaging specific frames, public and private discourses can shift within a society—often without the public becoming aware.

The Framing of Ethical Oil

In his book, Levant (2010) uses framing to make the case that the development of the Alberta oil sands is ethical. Levant's thesis is exemplified in this passage:

> Canadian oil sands oil is the most ethical oil in the world, and the people who invest there, work there, and support the oil sands with their patronage and their encouragement should be proud. Whether they realize it or not, they are all, gradually, helping to make the world a more moral, humane, and better place. (234)

The "ethical oil" frame is—in a way—genius. It speaks to our need for moral authority while maintaining our self-interest. Let's look at its components more closely.

In Levant's framing, even the term "oil" is used purposefully. Until the 1960s, the "oil sands" were called the "tar sands," and for decades, the two terms were interchangeable. Only recently has "tar sands" become the sole domain of those opposed to the sands' development. However, neither term is technically correct. The substance extracted from the Alberta oil sands is actually bituminous sand: a mixture of sand, water, clay, and bitumen. Bitumen is a thick gelatinous form of petroleum that "contains a noxious combination of sulphur, nitrogen, salts, carcinogens, heavy metals and other toxins" (Gailus, 2012, 6). Jeff Gailus (2012), author of *Little Black Lies*, explains the dichotomy between the frames:

> "Oil sands," you see, conveys a certain usefulness, a natural resource that creates jobs, increases government revenues, enhances energy security and makes investors rich beyond measure. Tar, on the other hand, is dark and heavy, the kind of glop better suited to paving roads, or coating dangerous subversives before feathering and banishing them from society altogether. (11)

Therefore, the term "oil" communicates more positive frames than "tar." Unsurprisingly, the petrochemical industry has embraced "oil sands."

The term "ethical" is well-chosen too. "Ethical" denotes "conforming to a high standard of morality or virtue": it is synonymous with good, honest, honorable, and just ("ethical," 2016). As such, "ethical" is industrial-strength language, encased in frames that invoke our fundamental values.

By fusing "ethical" and "oil," Levant links the concepts. The associations embedded in the term "ethical"—goodness, honesty, honor, and justice—stick, and the Alberta oil sands assume these moral qualities. As Lakoff (2010) explains, "Ideological language repeated often enough can become 'normal language'" (72). Once normalized, it becomes part of the way we think.

Once we accept the "ethical oil" frame and accept that the Alberta oil sands are "ethical," it seems rational to believe that those who oppose development of the oil sands are somehow "unethical." Levant states this explicitly:

> It would be unethical to oppose an industry that brings so much benefit to so many if you are doing so for your own selfish interests, and that is certainly worth keeping in mind when we next hear these various anti-oil sands groups hectoring us about "morals" and "ethics." (233)

Levant doesn't just attack environmental groups such as Greenpeace; he calls them "unethical televangelists milking their congregants" (148). He ridicules the Beaver Lake Cree for opposing oil sands development and mocks the Pembina Institute's research methodology, calling it that of "Dr. Doolittle" (134). The "ethical oil" frame implies that Canadians objecting to oil sands development, for whatever reason, must be "unethical." Levant's framing divides the country into those who support the oil sands and those who do not, those who are "ethical" and those who are not.

We vs. They

Levant's "ethical oil" frame extends beyond the term "ethical oil," invoking a "we vs. they" frame. This frame suggests that other oil producers are unethical because they support terrorism, have barbaric human rights practices, and have a poor environmental record; therefore, the Alberta oil sands is ethical (Laurie, 2013). This argument relies on a false dichotomy, the "either/or fallacy," which presents a case imposing "a two-valued rather than a multi-valued system" (Corbett & Connors, 1999, 67). Such arguments specify two options: "We have not posed alternatives which take all the possible actions in the case into account" (Corbett & Connors, 1999, 67). The "we vs. they" frame is limiting; it precludes exploring other possibilities.

The "we vs. they" frame constructs a dichotomy: oil producers who are "torture loving" (234) and "medieval" (234) versus Canada, "an ethical superpower" (233). Levant summarizes his argument: "Every drop of oil from Alberta is one less drop from some fascist theocracy or some brutal warlord; one less cent into the treasuries of Russia's secret police and al-Qaeda's murderers" (234). Levant issues a moral imperative:

> There is only one choice: to pump as much oil as we possibly can out of Fort McMurray. Pump and steam and dig and drill and get that oil out of the sand in any and every way we can. (233)

According to the "we vs. they" frame, we must choose: support the "fascists" and "murderers" or dig every dollop of bitumen from the earth. Once established, this frame easily connects Canadians opposed to oil sands development with the "fascists" and "murderers." They can fit nowhere else because they reject the "ethical oil" narrative. Here the two frames interact, as I explore further in the next section.

The Rhetoric of Oil in Action

While at EthicalOil.org, Velshi created an advertising campaign that illustrates the "we vs. they" frame, a campaign that would, as a Calgary journalist explained, "knock some sense into the craniums of critics of the single greatest wealth and jobs generator in the country" (Corbella, July 29, 2011). The campaign comprised seven advertisements that share a consistent design. A green banner across the bottom of each ad declares in reverse text: "Ethical Oil. A choice we have to make." Each ad also contains two images. Above the image on the left a red banner reads, "Conflict Oil." Above the image on the right a green banner reads, "Ethical Oil." In one ad under the "Conflict Oil" banner we see a photo of a dark-skinned man walking across a desolate landscape and pointing to a raging inferno emitting a cloud of thick, oily smoke (EthicalOil.org, 2011). The scene's location is unclear, but we are encouraged to assume that it is some nameless African country. Superimposed on the image a red text box reads, "Degradation." The image conveys a sense of "otherness." The location is foreign and frightening.

Under the "Ethical Oil" banner, saplings emerge from the earth. Among them stands a worker wearing a hard hat and reflective vest and holding a clipboard. He appears to be studying the new trees' health. His dress implies responsibility, that he is caring for the forest. Across the peaceful scene a green text box reads, "Reforestation." The diffused light from the leaves is calming and complements the green banner. We are invited to recognize a successful reclamation project. Together, the panels unambiguously announce: degradation on the left is "bad" and reforestation on right is "good."

In another ad, the left-hand image shows dark-skinned soldiers patrolling a desert landscape. A skeleton lies in the foreground. The banner reads, "'Sudan's oil fields': indigenous peoples killed." This image contrasts the right-hand one, a young aboriginal woman in hard hat, safety goggles, and ear protectors beaming happily (EthicalOil.org, 2011). The text box reads, "Canada's oil sands: Aboriginals employed." The implied message: "Conflict oil" kills Indigenous people; "ethical oil" employs Indigenous people.

The meme in all these ads contains an element of truth: indigenous people are killed in countries such as Sudan, and indigenous people are employed in the Alberta oil sands. But the ad ignores the remaining story. In Canada, many First Nations communities in the Fort McMurray area and westward do oppose the proposed pipelines that would affect their land (Droitsch & Simieritsch, 2010; Associated Press, March 10, 2018). Rather than examine the complex relationships among all players, the ad simplifies our choice: would you rather support the oil-producing nation that employs happy Aboriginals or the one that brutalizes and murders its Indigenous people?

The images are chosen to generate unconscious responses in their audience. The images in the "Conflict Oil" panel attempt to evoke fear of the unknown, discomfort, and disgust. The images in the "Ethical Oil" panel evoke a sense of order, comfort, and safety. The latter images encourage viewers to reflect on their "ethical" superiority. The tropes are cliché: a woman stoned, a public hanging, an anonymous killing field contrasted with a smiling woman mayor, rainbow bracelets on a couple's clasped hands, and a smiling oil sands worker.

Implied messages also inhabit these ads, ranging from "Canada is morally superior to these backward countries" to "There is no alternative to oil." The ads argue, "It's either ethical oil or bloody, conflict oil," but they omit a possible alternative: "no oil" or "less oil." The ads deny the chance to discuss other options and invest in alternative sources of energy. Instead, they focus on Canada's moral authority, and put the "ethical oil" frame to work. "Ethical oil" connects to our dearest values as Canadians: valuing nature, creating jobs for minorities, keeping the peace, safeguarding democracy. The ads imply that two camps exist in the world: those who share our values (we), and those who embrace persecution, degradation, terrorism, dictatorship (they). The "ethical oil" frame becomes embedded within the "we vs. they" frame. If we wish to be "ethical," we must choose the "we" camp.

The "we vs. they" frame allows for a convenient but ultimately utopian representation of oil sands development. As Laurie (2013) writes:

> Levant's framing attempts to diminish the perception of the environmental damage done by oil sands extraction and justify the production of oil sands oil by way of a relativistic argument that proposes the ethical superiority of Canadian oil over that of other producers. (38)

The "we vs. they" frame focuses audience attention on a "red herring" and ignores the very real and troubling issues surrounding Alberta oil sands development: GHG emissions, tailings pond cleanup, Indigenous rights, and economic dependency.

Framing Energy East

In the years since Levant's book became a best seller, we've heard less of the term "ethical oil," but many of the associated frames remain. The "ethical oil" frame is bigger than a single term, and one of its major themes lives on in the "we vs. they" frame.

With the American presidential veto of the Keystone XL Pipeline project and the seemingly overwhelming opposition to Enbridge's Northern Gateway Pipeline, the Canadian government's and the public's focus shifted to the Energy East Pipeline proposal, but there was opposition to that proposal. Greenpeace publicly stated, "[Energy East] would fan the flames of climate change by increasing the production of high-carbon fuel sources" ("The Energy East Pipeline" 2016). National Program Director for the Sierra Club, Gretchen Fitzgerald (August 9, 2016) explained the organization's concerns about the project in a press release: "The pipeline is a huge investment in fossil fuel infrastructure when we need to be switching as quickly as possible to renewables and efficiency." Even so, for many it seemed a more palatable project: the pipeline would supply dilbit (diluted bitumen) to eastern upgraders, allow for expanded development of the Alberta oil sands, and reduce the use of railways for transporting bitumen. Even so, opposition to the project grew.

In early 2016, Montreal's mayor, Denis Coderre spoke on behalf of the Montreal Metropolitan Community, "We are against [Energy East] because it still represents significant environmental threats and too few economic benefits for greater Montreal" (as quoted by CBC, January, 21, 2016). He explained, "In a context where the Earth's nations are talking about even more restrictive measures to limit (greenhouse gas) emissions, we cannot justify the construction of a pipeline" (as quoted by Southwick, January 25, 2016). He also cited concerns for the region's drinking water and the potential for expensive oil spill cleanups. Coderre was immediately criticized by then Wildrose Party leader Brian Jean, Calgary Mayor Naheed Nenshi and other western Canadian leaders.

Along with the prairie province leaders, Ezra Levant also criticized Coderre's response. On Twitter, he posted: "@DenisCoderre prefers OPEC sharia oil than Canadian ethical oil" (January 22, 2016) and "When @DenisCoderre says no to ethical oil from Alberta, he says yes to sharia oil from OPEC countries." Levant even took his message to Montreal. When Outfront Media declined to run his ad, Levant arranged for it to be displayed on the side of a panel truck that was driven throughout the streets of Montreal (Montpetit, August 10, 2016). The billboard featured a photo of Saudi Arabia's sovereign, King Salmane Ben Abdelaziz al Saoud, and read:

> Lorsque Denis Coderre dit non au project d'Energie Est il dit oui au petrole de la charia exporte par l'OPEP [When Denis Coderre says no to the Energy East Project, he is saying yes to Sharia oil exports from OPEC]. (Levant, August 3, 2016)

Levant relied upon the audience's negative associations with the punishments of "sharia law." He invites viewers to believe that Denis Coderre and others are taking the side of foreign extremists. He implies that in challenging the Energy East Pipeline construction the mayors support an "unethical" religion and reject their own country's "ethical oil." However, because the "ethical oil" frame now contains the "we vs. they" frame, no explicit mention is necessary: the connection is implicit.

But the message relies upon a shallow understanding of the Middle East, a North American interpretation of a complex region and a multifaceted religion. It makes no mention of the mayor's concern for Quebec waterways, instead redirecting the conversation into an ad hominem attack on Saudi Arabia. It also implies that Quebec purchases oil from

Saudi Arabia, but that is not the case. According to Canadian Energy Systems Analysis Research, Quebec's two refineries import 0% of their crude from Saudi Arabia (Israel & Layzell, 2015).

Among the western leaders critical of Coderre's position was Saskatchewan Premier, Brad Wall. As a perennial proponent of oil and gas development, Wall was an outspoken champion of TransCanada's Energy East Pipeline. Charles Smith, assistant professor in the department of political science at St. Thomas More College, explains that Wall is the "unabashed voice of the oil industry—in terms of more extraction of oil, quicker extraction of oil—in fact going so far as to say that the public should clean up the mess left by oil companies" (Lanenegger, March 31, 2016). Wall's pro-development position and populist manner have made him popular with his constituents.

Regarding the Energy East Pipeline, Wall emphasizes the ethical superiority of Canadian energy policy and oil production: "Can you imagine Saudi Arabia releasing an energy strategy for the country and listing wind power ahead of their oil assets?" (Bell, July 16, 2015). Here Wall asks a rhetorical question to contrast the environmental policies of Canada and Saudi Arabia. He relies on our "knowledge" that we are ethically superior to Saudi Arabia.

Wall summarizes his view of the situation:

> I think we need to point out to the rest of Canada that we currently import oil. We have the third greatest oil reserves on Earth and yet we import oil from places like Saudi Arabia. That just doesn't make any sense. (as quoted by Bell, July 16, 2015)

Here he frames the issue as a dichotomy: Without the Energy East Pipeline we will continue to get our oil from Saudi Arabia; with the Energy East Pipeline, we will get our oil from Canada. Both of these premises are incorrect. Canada doesn't get all of its oil from Saudi Arabia (and countries like it), and if Energy East is constructed, Canada will not get all of its oil from within its borders. There is an element of truth to these statements, but once again Wall over simplifies. Wall cherry-picks the details he wishes to emphasize while ignoring others.

Proponents of Energy East often call it a "made-in-Canada solution" to Canada's energy needs ("Support Energy East," 2016), but a briefing memo to Natural Resources Minister Jim Carr states, "TransCanada's proposed Energy East project would provide access to new markets in Europe and India" (Fletcher, July 14, 2016). This statement confirms the pipeline's many critics' notion that "Energy East is an export pipeline, not a made-in-Canada solution" (DeRochie, August 9, 2016), but the "ethical oil" frame silences these dissenting voices.

In the Energy East debate, the "we vs. they" frame has been repeated often and by many: Peter Tertzakian, an energy analyst and economist with ARC Financial, explained that Canada has "some of the best oil in the world in terms of its responsible development and its cleanliness" (as quoted by Wherry, May 27, 2016). Former National Energy Board (NEB) chairman Gaetan Caron engaged the frame when he said somewhat sarcastically, "We are going to buy oil instead from these countries and we are going to fund these kinds of international behaviors ... and that's OK because we feel better in our conscience" (Cattaneo, February 9, 2016). The frame has become so established, that it no longer requires explanation.

The popular press has also employed the "ethical oil" frame. In her energy op-ed, *National Post* columnist Claudia Cattaneo (February 9, 2016) was harsh in her criticism of the federal government's attempt to curb greenhouse gas (GHG) emissions and rhetorically questioned Canada's loyalty to its oil and gas producers:

> Where is the political outrage over oil imports from rogue nations with inferior environmental records and deplorable behaviours toward women, dissidents and minorities? Where are the beefed up regulatory reviews of Saudi Arabia's climate change impacts, or their dumping practices?

The sarcasm is thick in an op-ed for the *Calgary Herald* by Chris Nelson (June 20, 2016): "Johnny and Jane Canuck are giving the House of Saud the old double thumbs up by importing more of their oil than ever before." These writings appear to select some details while deliberately omitting others. Absent from these claims of moral outrage is a call for the use of sustainable energy sources. Instead, the focus remains on the ethical shortcomings of others.

More recently after a protest broke up the NEB hearings in Montreal, the *Calgary Herald* printed an editorial denouncing the behavior of the protesters, saying, "Some people would like to continue relying on imported oil from countries such as Saudi Arabia, which have dodgy human rights records and less rigorous environmental standards, than use Canadian oil or see it exported" (Calgary Herald Editorial Board, August 30, 2016). Once again, the issue is placed within the "we vs. they" frame with no third option presented while the concerns of the various stakeholders are ignored or trivialized.

Framing KMX

The election of Donald J. Trump to the U.S. White House brought a change in administrative policy and a reversal of Obama's veto of the Keystone XL pipeline. Trump's Presidential Memoranda of January 24, 2017, states that the "cross-border pipeline project ... would 'serve the national interest.'" Suddenly the KXL pipeline was back on the table.

Not long after Keystone XL reemerged as a viable project, TransCanada abandoned Energy East. In a press release dated October 4, 2017, TransCanada Corporation made the following announcement: "We will no longer be proceeding with our Energy East and Eastern Mainline applications." These developments left Canada with the potential for expanding bitumen exports to the United States, but in terms of increasing bitumen exports out of the province east-west, that left Kinder Morgan's Trans Mountain Expansion (KMX).

The KMX promises to increase current capacity of the sixty-five-year-old pipeline by threefold, and as the company website (TransMountain, 2018, "Project Overview") tells us, "Canada's oil will fetch a better price if we give ourselves the option of shipping more of it via Trans Mountain's Pacific tidewater terminal in Burrard Inlet." But since the expansion's approval, the project has faced unprecedented opposition. The Cities of Burnaby and Vancouver both oppose the project as do numerous BC and Alberta First Nations, many environmental organizations, Green Party MLAs Elizabeth May and Kennedy Stewart, and BC's provincial NDP government. On the other side of the debate, Rachel Notley and the Alberta NDP (ANDP) fervently support the KMX as do Trudeau's governing federal Liberals.

Debate over the project heated up in early 2018 after the BC provincial government announced a proposal to restrict future increases in dilbit until "the behaviour of spilled bitumen can be better understood and there is certainty regarding the ability to adequately mitigate spills" (as quoted by Morgan, January 30, 2018). If the restrictions were adopted, they would curb the increased flow of dilbit that the KMX is meant to facilitate. This announcement was met with a forceful reaction from the ANDPs. Within days, Alberta's Premier Notley announced a boycott of all BC wines (Graney, February 6, 2018). The boycott was soon lifted, but this tit-for-tat exchange marked the beginning of intensified debate over the soon-to-be-constructed KMX.

With each pipeline debate, the "we vs. they" frame reignites as a rallying cry within public discourse. Not long after this interprovincial altercation, Tim McMillan (as reported by Meyer, February 26, 2018), president of the Canadian Association of Petroleum Producers (CAPP), spoke at a press conference on Parliament Hill. McMillan explained that "emerging economies" would require a supply of fossil fuel, and "as an environmentally responsible person, I want to see Canada stepping in to be that supplier, not Nigeria or Iran." Here McMillan invokes the "we vs. they" frame. He clearly equates environmental responsibility with promoting Canadian fossil fuels over fossil fuels produced by nations that his audience will associate with corrupt regimes or poor environmental practices or maybe just a sense of "otherness." McMillan's vision for the future is one where the world goes on with business as usual, but with Canada as a leader in fossil fuel production and—presumably—GHG emissions.

In an attempt to garner support for the KMX, Alberta Premier Notley (as quoted by Wood, September 30, 2017) uses a variation on the "ethical oil" frame. In an interview, Notley told reporter James Wood that "the world" needs oil in the "short to medium term" and that "what they're looking for is a product that is ethically developed, that is developed in an environmentally-responsible way." Notley doesn't fuse the terms "ethical" and "oil" like Levant, but she comes close. Perhaps with the renewed political urgency of fighting for the pipeline expansion, politicians are willing to flirt with the "ethical oil" frame.

Deron Bilous, MLA for the ANDP, not only supports the pipeline expansion, he also supports Notley's variation on the "ethical oil" frame. On December 11, 2017, he tweeted, "Our energy industry is the most ethical and responsible in the world" (December 11, 2017). Bilous was even quoted by UCP MLA Jason Nixon in a meme tweeted to Nixon's followers: "The world is moving toward more ethical, sustainable ways of extracting and producing our resources" (December 7, 2017). In this way, both Notley and Bilous engage the "ethical oil" frame without connecting it to Ezra Levant and his 2010 publication.

Canadian supporters of oil sands development also use this variation of the "ethical oil" frame. KMX supporters showed up at a Calgary rally on April 10, 2018, with signs reading "Alberta Oil Most Ethical in the World" (Cattaneo, April 11, 2018). At that same rally, UCP leader Jason Kenney (as quoted by Cattaneo) spoke to the audience. While he didn't use this new variation of the "ethical oil" frame, he did invoke the "we vs. they" frame:

> If enemies of our economic progress succeed, we will simply hand a monopoly over the growing global energy market to some of the world's worst regimes... This isn't just about our economy. This is about human rights, and the world is counting on Canada to win this fight.

Here the "we vs. they" frame and the newer "ethical oil" frame are reflected and amplified from protester to speaker and back again, each reinforcing the other's framing. But in Kenney's speech, there is a troubling extension of the frame. He is not only placing "the world's worst regimes" in the position of "they" or "the other." He is framing Canadians who are opposed to the KMX as "enemies." And since he states that "the world is counting on Canada to win this fight," one must assume he counts the Canadians who are opposed to the expansion—and remember this includes Indigenous nations, political leaders, environmental advocates, Burnaby and Vancouver residents, among others—as "enemies" of Canada and part of the "they" group.

Kenney was not the only politician to engage the "we vs. they" frame at the rally. Conservative MP Michelle Rempel (as quoted by Cattaneo) also engaged the "we vs. they" frame when she spoke:

> It's not fair to denigrate an industry that provides energy products in one of the most ethical and sustainable ways in the world. It's not fair to let vocal minority groups that don't run on fact to control the fate and prosperity of an entire country.

She may have trivialized the opinions of KMX opponents, but Rempel stopped short of calling them "enemies." She did, however, claim that it was not fair of "vocal minority groups" to express their opposition to the project. Does she mean that people living in a democratic society should not speak openly about a project that will affect their communities and their country? It seems so. In this way, she appears to echo Kenney's criticism.

In her speech, Rempel euphemizes the oil sands extraction industry, calling it "an industry that provides energy products." This designation conjures the image of a benevolent gifter of goods—a far cry from the reality of oil sands extraction. She is more delicate in her delivery than Kenney, but Remple also evokes the "we vs. they" frame. She does not call out "the world's worst regimes," but suggests a similar dichotomy when she says Alberta industry's practices are "ethical and sustainable" compared to others "in the world." Rempel's and Kenney's approaches may vary, but they both evoke the same frames.

Conclusion

Cognitive framing has power. It doesn't challenge; it maneuvers. It builds upon existing cultural understandings, personal beliefs, and national narratives to give salience to some ideas while reducing the importance of others. The "ethical oil" frame was not created in a cultural vacuum. It rises out of existing beliefs, desires, prejudice, and biases. "Ethical oil" and its associated frames connect with a population primed for its message.

The "ethical oil" frame is effective for another reason: it speaks to self-interest. It gives Canadians the solution to a daunting quandary: how do we make the choice between short-term economic prosperity and long-term environmental sustainability? "Ethical oil" supplies the answer. We pay cursory attention to long-term environmental dilemmas, and instead focus on Canadian ethics and values. William Freudenburg calls this the "social construction of quiescence or 'non-problemacity'" (2005). The "ethical oil" frame simplifies the issues, allowing us to avoid difficult discussions.

While the "ethical oil" frame focuses on the benefits of the Alberta oil sands and the ethical beliefs of the people who most profit from their development, it ignores and normalizes the disadvantages: "The illness and death of workers, Natives, and wildlife is both denied and shown to be compensated for by the benefits of developments" (Gordon, 2015, 34). We avoid acknowledgment of the inherent social and environmental shortcomings of oil sands development until they appear minimal. In this way a narrative myth is created, one in which the oil and gas industry is the protagonist and countries such as Saudi Arabia, Venezuela, Iran, and Nigeria are the villains. In this narrative, there is no middle ground.

Finding and implementing solutions to complex problems can seem daunting. Climate change requires that we reexamine our dependence upon fossil fuels, both as a resource and as a means of energy production. Coping with climate change will require honest discussion and a willingness to view change as an opportunity rather than a formidable trial. It will require that we reevaluate our priorities and our expectations and will lead to "a stark transformation in our understanding of fossil fuel availability" (McGlade & Ekins, 2015, 190).

"Ethical oil" offers a narrative that lets us maintain conventional norms: continuous economic growth, increased wealth, plentiful jobs, limitless energy, the established order. Good (2013) explains, "Just when we thought we might actually have to change our energy consumption habits, Levant makes a strong and appealing case for business as usual" (2). What a relief!

But we can't maintain "business as usual." The Alberta oil sands comes encumbered with a host of problems: water pollution, soil contamination, habitat destruction and disruption, and risks to First Nations' communities both near the oil sands and along the proposed pipeline routes. But climate change may just trump them all.

The science of climate change doesn't care about rhetoric or profits or public approval. Climate change is deaf to our wishes and our provincial feuding, but climate change does make a promise. It promises to shape the course of our lives in the decades to come. According to the Fifth Assessment Report delivered by the Intergovernmental Panel on Climate Change, "Recent climate changes have had widespread impacts on human and natural systems" (2014, 2). The report warns that "without mitigation efforts beyond those in place today ... warming by the end of the 21st century will lead to high to very high risk of severe, widespread and irreversible impacts globally" (18), so it calls for "substantial emissions reductions over the next few decades" (17). At a UN ceremony in 2016, Prime Minister Trudeau signed the Paris Climate Treaty, which commits Canada to a reduction of 30% from 2005 levels by 2030 (Cullen, April 24, 2016). And how does this affect Alberta oil sands development?

The Alberta oil sands is the largest unconventional oil reserve in the world, and as climatologist James Hansen explains, "We need to leave the unconventional fuel in the ground" (Carrington, May 19, 2013). Full development of the oil sands would be "game over" for the planet. In a report that lays out a plan for a global carbon budget, Christophe McGlade and Paul Ekins (2015) write, "Any increase in unconventional oil production [is] incommensurate with efforts to limit average global warming to 2 degrees Celsius" (187), a limit agreed upon by most governments and policy makers, a limit that Canada has agreed to by signing the Paris Climate Treaty.

All this nuanced discussion is lost in the "ethical oil" and the "we vs. they" frames. Instead of discussing alternative sources of energy, we are forced to decide where to source our oil. The environmental and social costs of the oil sands are never mentioned. They are silenced. Within the "we vs. they" dichotomy, there are villains, and there are heroes. Canada (and its allies) are the heroes while Saudi Arabia (and those other countries) as well as Canadians who oppose further oil sands development are the villains. Are you a hero or a villain? Make your choice!

References

Associated Press. March 10, 2018. "Indigenous and Environmental Leaders Protest Canada Pipeline." *New York Post*. Retrieved from https://nypost.com/2018/03/10/indigenous-and-environmental-leaders-protest-canada-pipeline/

Bell, R. July 16, 2015. "Alberta Premier Notley and Saskatchewan Premier Wall Scrap over Pipelines." *Calgary Sun*. Retrieved from http://edmontonsun.com/2015/07/16/alberta-premier-notley-and-saskatchewan-premier-wall-scrap-over-pipelines/wcm/ef823f19-c165-4570-8db6-8d231e542bcd

Bilous, D. December 11, 2017. *Twitter Post*. Retrieved from https://twitter.com/DeronBilous/status/940365818918969350

Bolin, C. May 12, 2011. "Ezra Levant Wins National Business Book Award." *The Globe and Mail*. Retrieved from http://www.theglobeandmail.com/arts/books-and-media/ezra-levant-wins-national-business-book-award/article579630/

Brean, J. November 20, 2010. "Judge Orders Ezra Levant to Pay $25,000." *National Post*. Retrieved from http://www.pressreader.com/canada/national-post-national-edition/20101120/283128540250218

Brean, J. November 27, 2014. "Ezra Levant Loses Libel Case, Must Pay $80,000 to Man he Defamed as 'Illiberal Islamic Fascist'." *National Post*. Retrieved from http://nationalpost.com/news/canada/ezra-levant-loses-hate-speech-case-must-pay-80000-to-man-he-defamed-as-illiberal-islamic-fascist

Calgary Herald Editorial Board. August 30, 2016. "Editorial: Energy East Protesters Go Too Far." *Calgary Herald*. Retrieved from http://calgaryherald.com/opinion/editorials/editorial-protesters-go-too-far

Carrington, D. May 19, 2013. "Tar Sands Exploitation Would Mean Game over for Climate, Warns Leading Scientist." *The Guardian*. Retrieved from https://www.theguardian.com/environment/2013/may/19/tar-sands-exploitation-climate-scientist

Cattaneo, C. February 9, 2016. "As Oilsands Punished, Tanker Loads of Cheap Saudi Oil Sail into Canadian Ports Daily." *National Post.* Retrieved from http://www.nationalpost.com/oilsands+punished+tanker+loads+cheap+saudi+sail+into+canadian+ports+daily/11708173/story.html

Cattaneo, C. April 11, 2018. "With Almost Nothing Left to Lose, Albertans Rise up against Ottawa's Empty Pipeline Promises." *Calgary Herald.* Retrieved from http://calgaryherald.com/commodities/energy/with-almost-nothing-left-to-lose-albertans-rise-against-ottawas-empty-pipeline-promises/wcm/fc5f36ec-6795-4f40-9aea-3eb59a10714a

CBC News. January 21, 2016. "Montreal Mayor Denis Coderre Says Energy East Pipeline Too Risky." Retrieved from http://www.cbc.ca/news/canada/montreal/montreal-mayor-denis-coderre-energy-east-opposition-1.3413117

Corbella, L. July 29, 2011. "Corbella: Ethical Oil Campaign Aims to Silence Critics." *Calgary Herald.* Retrieved from http://www.pressreader.com/canada/windsor-star/20110829/282428460891382

Corbett, E. & Connors, R. 1999. *Classical Rhetoric for the Modern Student,* 4th edition. New York, NY: Oxford University Press.

Cullen, C. April 22, 2016. "Justin Trudeau Signs Paris Climate Treaty at UN, Vows to Harness Renewable Energy." *CBC News.* Retrieved from http://www.cbc.ca/news/politics/paris-agreement-trudeau-sign-1.3547822

DeRochie, P. August 9, 2016. "Time for a Reminder: Energy East Would be an Export Pipeline." *Environmental Defence.* Retrieved from http://environmentaldefence.ca/2016/08/09/time-reminder-energy-east-export-pipeline/

Droitsch, D. & Simieritsch, T. September 2010. "The Pembina Institute Briefing Note. Canadian Aboriginal Concerns with Oil Sands." Retrieved from https://www.pembina.org/reports/briefingnoteosfntoursep10.pdf

Entman, R. M. 1993. "Framing: Toward Clarification of a Fractured Paradigm." *Journal of Communication,* 43(4), 51.

Ethical. 2016. *In Merriam-Webster Online Dictionary.* Retrieved from http://www.merriam-webster.com/thesaurus/ethical

EthicalOil.org. 2011. *Ad Campaign Images.* Retrieved from http://www.theglobeandmail.com/news/politics/ethical-oil-ad-campaign/article637242/

EthicalOil.org. 2014. Retrieved from http://www.ethicaloil.org/about/

Findlay, M. H. April 20, 2012. "Please Stop Calling It 'Ethical Oil.'" *The Globe and Mail.* Retrieved from https://www.theglobeandmail.com/news/politics/please-stop-calling-it-ethical-oil/article4101409/

Fletcher, R. July 14, 2016. "Energy East Memo Reveals Conflicting Government Views on Pipeline's Value." *CBC News.* Retrieved from http://www.cbc.ca/news/canada/calgary/energy-east-value-jim-carr-memo-pipeline-capacity-1.3677473

Foster, P. September 22, 2010. "Ethical Oil." *Financial Post.* Retrieved from http://business.financialpost.com/fp-comment/peter-foster-ethical-oil

Freudenburg, W. 2005. "Privileged Access, Privileged Accounts: Toward a Socially Structured Theory of Resources and Discourses." *Social Forces, 84*(1), 89–114.

Gailus, J. 2012. *Little Black Lies: Corporate & Political Spin in the Global War for Oil.* Victoria, BC: Rocky Mountain Books.

Gatehouse, J. January 12, 2013. "Ezra Levant: The Right-Wing Gadfly Who Loves to Offend." *Maclean's.* Retrieved from http://www.macleans.ca/news/canada/going-on-the-offensive/

Good, J. E. 2013. "The (Potential) Brilliance of 'Ethical Oil': Morally Relativistic Discourse and Business as Usual." Unpublished manuscript. Communication, Popular Culture and Film, Brock University.

Gordon, J. 2015. *Unsustainable Oil: Facts, Counterfacts and Fictions*. Edmonton: The University of Alberta.

Graney, E. February 6, 2018. "Rachel Notley Announces Boycott of BC Wine in Wake of Trans Mountain Pipeline Spat." *Edmonton Journal*. Retrieved from https://edmontonjournal.com/news/politics/alberta-mulls-breaking-trade-rules-over-b-c-trans-mountain-pipeline-spat

Grant, J. January 7, 2011. "'Ethical Oil' Argument Attempts to Camouflage Serious Problems in the Oilsands." *The Pembina Institute*. Retrieved from http://www.pembina.org/blog/ethical-oil-argument-attempts-to-camouflage-serious-problems-oilsands

Greenpeace Canada. 2016 "The Energy East Pipeline." Retrieved from http://www.greenpeace.org/canada/en/campaigns/Energy/tarsands/Learn-about/The-Energy-East-Pipeline/

Gutstein, D. January 26, 2011. "Ethical Oil and the Right-Wing Echo Chamber." *Rabble*. http://rabble.ca/news/2011/01/ethical-oil-and-rightwing-echo-chamber

Houpt, S. 2014. "Ezra Levant Ordered to Pay $80,000 in Libel Suit; Judge Cites 'Reckless Disregard for the Truth.'" November 27. Retrieved from https://www.theglobeandmail.com/arts/books-and-media/judge-orders-ezra-levant-to-pay-saskatchewan-lawyer-80000-in-defamation-suit/article21824295/

IPCC, 2014: *Climate Change 2014: Synthesis Report. Contribution of Working Groups I, II and III to the Fifth Assessment Report of the Intergovernmental Panel on Climate Change* [Core Writing Team, R.K. Pachauri and L.A. Meyer (eds.)]. Geneva, Switzerland: IPCC. Retrieved from http://ar5-syr.ipcc.ch/ipcc/ipcc/resources/pdf/IPCC_SynthesisReport.pdf

Israel, B. & Layzell, D. January 6, 2015. "The State of Energy in Quebec – 2015. Canadian Energy Systems Analysis Research." Retrieved from http://www.cesarnet.ca/blog/state-energy-quebec-2015

Kennedy, M. January 7, 2011. "Harper Defends Oilsands as 'Ethical.'" *Postmedia News*. http://www.canada.com/business/Harper+defends+oilsands+ethical/4077547/story.html

Kenney, J. November 2017. *Twitter Post*. Retrieved from https://twitter.com/jkenney/status/926580799129841664

King, B. April 28, 2016. "Let's Have an Honest Conversation about Pipelines and Ethical Oil." *HuffPost*. Retrieved from https://www.huffingtonpost.ca/blair-king/pipelines-ethical-oil_b_9789672.html

Lakoff, G. 2004. *Don't Think of an Elephant: Know Your Values and Frame the Debate*. White River Junction, VT: Chelsea Green Publishing Company.

Lakoff, G. 2010. "Why it Matters How We Frame the Environment." *Environmental Communication*, *4*(1), 70–81.

Lanenegger, S. March 31, 2016. "Saskatchewan's Brad Wall Will Continue to Speak 'Plainly' to Ottawa if Re-elected." *CBC News*. Retrieved from http://www.cbc.ca/news/canada/saskatchewan/sask-brad-wall-continue-speaking-out-nationally-1.3504626

Laurie, R. 2013. "Framing Ethical Oil: Shaping the Canadian Media's Response to the Alberta Oil Sands." Unpublished thesis, School of Environment and Sustainability, Royal Roads University, Victoria, Canada.

Levant, E. 2010. *Ethical Oil: The Case for Canada's Oil Sands*. Toronto, ON: McClelland & Stewart.

Levant, E. 2016. *Twitter Post*. Retrieved from https://twitter.com/ezralevant?ref_src=twsrc%5Egoogle%7Ctwcamp%5Eserp%7Ctwgr%5Eauthor

McGlade, C. & Ekins, P. 2015. "The Geographical Distribution of Fossil Fuels Unused when Limiting Global Warming to 2 °C." *Nature, 517*, 187–190. Doi:10.1038/nature14016

Meyer, C. February 26, 2018. "Canada's Top Oil Patch Lobbyist Says it's 'Irresponsible' to Plan for Oil-Free World." *National Observer*. Retrieved from https://www.nationalobserver.com/2018/02/26/news/canadas-top-oilpatch-lobbyist-says-its-irresponsible-plan-oil-free-world

Montpetit, G. August 10, 2016. "We've Heard Ezra Levant's Pipeline Rhetoric Before – From Trump." *Huffington Post*. Retrieved from http://www.huffingtonpost.ca/gerard-montpetit/ezra-levant-energy-east_b_11429574.html

Morgan, G. January 30, 2018. "B.C. Proposes New Rules to Restrict Oilsands Exports in Fresh Setback for Trans Mountain Pipeline." Retrieved from http://business.financialpost.com/commodities/energy/b-c-proposes-new-rules-to-restrict-oilsands-exports-in-fresh-setback-for-trans-mountain-pipeline.

Nelson, C. June 20, 2016. "Nelson: Protest Saudi Crude before Picking on Alberta Oil." *Calgary Herald*. Retrieved from http://calgaryherald.com/opinion/columnists/nelson-protest-saudi-crude-before-picking-on-alberta-oil

Nixon, J. December 7, 2017. *Twitter Post*. Retrieved from https://twitter.com/JasonNixonAB

Petroleum Economist. September 30, 2010. "Ethical Oil and OPEC." Retrieved from http://www.petroleum-economist.com/articles/markets/outlook/2010/ethical-oil-and-opec

"Politicians and Industry Defend Energy East in Light of Comments by Montreal's Mayor." January 21, 2016. *NewsTalk770*. Retrieved from http://www.newstalk770.com/2016/01/21/e/

Sierra Club Canada Foundation. August 9, 2016. "Energy East Hearings Start with Questions but Few Answers." Retrieved from http://www.sierraclub.ca/en/media/2016-08-09/energy-east-hearings-start-questions-few-answers

Southwick, R. January 25, 2016. "Opposition to Energy East Pipeline Might Have Backfired." *Calgary Sun*. Retrieved from http://www.calgarysun.com/2016/01/25/opposition-to-energy-east-pipeline-might-have-backfired-expert

Support Energy East Pledge. 2016. "Canada Action." Retrieved from http://www.canadaaction.ca/energy_east

The Canadian Press. June 8, 2017. "Ezra Levant's Libel Appeal Denied by Supreme Court." Retrieved from https://www.cbc.ca/news/canada/calgary/ezra-levant-supreme-court-denies-libel-appeal-1.4151925

TheRebel.media. 2015 Retrieved from http://www.ezralevant.com/category/the-source-sunnews/page/3/

TransCanada Corporation. October 5, 2017. News Release. Retrieved from https://www.transcanada.com/en/announcements/2017-10-05-transcanada-anounces-termination-of-energy-east-pipeline-and-eastern-mainline-projects/

TransMountain. 2018. "Project Overview." Retrieved from https://www.transmountain.com/project-overview

Trump, D. January 24, 2017. White House Presidential Memorandum. Retrieved from https://www.whitehouse.gov/presidential-actions/presidential-memorandum-regarding-construction-keystone-xl-pipeline/

Wherry, A. 2016. "Both Sides of Pipeline Debate Play out at Liberal Convention in Winnipeg." May 27. *CBC News*. Retrieved from http://www.cbc.ca/news/politics/wherry-liberals-convention-pipelines-1.3603276.

Wood, J. September 30, 2017. "Q&A: Notley on the Oilsands—'The World is Still Going to Need It.'" *Calgary Herald*. Retrieved from http://calgaryherald.com/business/energy/qa-notley-on-the-oilsands-the-world-is-still-going-to-need-it

11 From Pipeline to Plate

The Domestication of Oil Sands through Visual Food Analogies

Adam Thomlison

Introduction

In 2010, the environmental group Sierra Club of Canada complained to Advertising Standards Canada (ASC), a self-governing body of the advertising industry, that an oil-industry advertisement was misleading audiences by comparing oil sands tailings (the toxic by-product of oil extraction) to yogurt (Sierra Club of Canada, 2010). The Sierra Club argued that the ads would produce an inaccurate understanding of the by-product as being natural and nonthreatening, an argument which the ASC rejected (CBC News, 2010a), though the advertiser removed the yogurt reference afterwards anyway. That advertisement, produced by the Canadian Association of Petroleum Producers (CAPP), proved to be the precursor of a trend: comparisons to food have become a repeated theme in the promotional material produced by oil companies working in Alberta's oil sands region. The desired effect seems to be to *domesticate* (Aupers et al., 2012; Haddon, 2011; Rodino-Colocino, 2006) the oil sands products and by-products—that is, to reshape their popularly understood meaning and to render them less strange to audiences as commodities (see Moffat et al.'s chapter in this volume)—while the debate over the benefits of oil sands extraction continues.

Studies of domestication look at practices in the incorporation of new innovations into the lives of users, with the term referring to the idea that the outside innovations are being brought inside, into the domestic sphere (Haddon, 2011). Food is a site where the domestic sphere and nature intersect (Barthes, 1977). Can the presence of food imagery in the public relations and advertising campaigns of the petroleum industry in Alberta be explained by a strategy of domestication? And if so, how might such a strategy influence viewers' opinions about the extraction of this resource? In this chapter, I combine multimodal and semiotic analysis to develop an original framework, then apply that framework to the rhetoric of four advertisements promoting oil sands extraction to answer these questions.

Mining of Alberta's oil sands deposits—mixtures of sand, water, clay, and bitumen (a type of heavy oil) which cover 140,200 square kilometers in the province's northern regions (Government of Alberta, 2014)—has emerged as a high-profile and contentious national issue. Though the potential economic and other benefits of extraction are large, the oil is also more emissions- and resource-intensive to extract than drilled oil. Although the resource has been under industrial-scale development since the 1970s, the environmental and economic issues related to oil sands extraction only began receiving popular attention in 2008, when the death of 1,600 ducks in a tailings pond (that is, a reservoir of the toxic effluent left over from the extraction process) maintained by the oil company, Syncrude, became a national news story (Holden, 2013; Paskey et al., 2013;).

Paid advertising has been a particular site of controversy. Along with CAPP's ad comparing tailings to yogurt, other advertisements, produced by both the industry and by anti-extraction NGOs, have been accused of deception (CanOils, 2010; CBC News, 2010b; Linnitt, 2014). The industry ads are generally accused of greenwashing the activities of extraction and transportation companies—that is, trying to make them seem environmentally benign (Budinsky and Bryant, 2013; Greer and Bruno, 1997).

The content and delivery of pro-extraction messaging have already drawn some academic attention (e.g., Gismondi and Davidson, 2012; Kim, 2012; Paskey et al., 2013); however, food has emerged as a common visual theme in the corporate communications which has so far been overlooked by scholars. This study examines how food is used in such messaging and in so doing offers an empirical contribution to the sparse visual analysis of oil sands advertising.

The study offers a contribution to the field of visual environmental communication, pioneered by Anders Hansen (e.g., Hansen, 2006; Hansen and Machin, 2008; see Hansen and Machin, 2013, for an evaluation of the current state of the field), by proposing domestication as a technique within the field, and by proposing food as an eco-image category that can be used to commute (i.e., transfer) connotations of nature—in Hansen's words, "goodness, legitimacy, universal acceptability and a state of affairs beyond questioning" (2006, 829)—onto a signified element. The study also applies, and slightly modifies, the multimodal-analysis process developed by Lefsrud et al. (2015), and combines it with Parisian-semiotic concepts to build a critical apparatus for examining the rhetorical work of multimodal communication products.

Food, Environment, and Domestication: Literature Review and Theoretical Approach

Scholars have only recently begun unpacking the visual rhetoric of oil sands ads (Lefsrud et al., 2015; McCurdy and Thomlison, 2019). However, having identified food as a recurring theme in oil sands advertising,

I can incorporate previous studies addressing food imagery into my analysis. In so doing, I develop a critical apparatus to examine the rhetorical work being performed by the ads that could be of use in future visual environmental communication studies. Food is a domestic image and domestic images are comforting and nonthreatening (Barthes, 1977; Rodino-Colocino, 2006). This connection is predetermined, so the ads proceed from there to present food and oil sands together so that the sense of comfort is commuted from the former to the latter, thus domesticating the oil sands. Food is also a natural image and previous studies of greenwashing as a rhetorical strategy have found a similar phenomenon where natural images are deployed as metaphors to commute desirable associations onto a referent.

Relating food imagery to domestication calls on both the nutritional and social significance of food (as explored by Kass, 1994, and Rozin, 1998). It also assumes a link not only between food and home, but between food and comfort, since increasing audience comfort levels is the goal of domestication (Douglas and Isherwood, 1980; Haddon, 2011; McCracken, 1990). This term relates to the popular concept of "comfort food," defined by Wansink and Sangerman (2000) as "a specific food consumed under a specific situation to obtain psychological comfort" (66). Food evokes feelings of "safety, love, homecoming, appreciation, control, victory, empowerment" (67), and they argue that "because comfort foods are often based on apocryphal memories, tapping into these memories can tap into a deep well of emotions" (67). Activating such emotions is, in Aristotelian terms, a rhetorical appeal to pathos, and is a powerful way to share connotations among items presented together in an advertisement (Barthes, 1977).

The term 'domestication' is more commonly used today, and more literally, to refer to the act of incorporating a thing into the domestic sphere. However, domestication as a strategic communication technique traces its roots back to anthropology (Douglas and Isherwood, 1980) and consumption studies (McCracken, 1990), and to the broader concept of rendering something less strange as part of the process of incorporating its use into new contexts (Haddon, 2011). It is in this sense of the term that, for example, Aupers et al. (2012) argue that a series of contemporary commercials which present a new line of automobiles in natural settings are attempts to domesticate the unfamiliar cars by associating them with nature. The concept of domestication in relation to nature has traditionally been understood in terms of taming the wild. However, new articulations are being developed in modern (particularly advertising) discourse wherein nature is the familiar concept being related to unfamiliar technology (in their study, cars) to tame the "wild" concept. In making this argument, they also reinforce the connection I make between nature, domesticity, and comfort. No studies were found examining food imagery specifically as a tool of domestication;

however, one study looked at the marketing of a personal digital assistant (PDA) intended for women and found that the company framed it as a kitchen tool, in part by capitalizing on the construction of "the kitchen as the primary domestic production zone and establishing it as a family gathering place" (Rodino-Colocino, 2006, 384). The article cites a review of the PDA in *PC World* magazine at the time of its launch in 2000 which said, "[T]he decision to apply the familiar language of the kitchen and laundry room to e-mail and Web browsing is a well-considered one. Toasters hold few mysteries; computers hold many" (as cited in Rodino-Colocino, 2006, 383). Thus, references to the domestic sphere are deployed as a strategy for inducing comfort. Building from these uses, this study uses domestication to mean a discursive strategy employed to reshape the meaning of an object to make it seem to fit into the everyday lives of an audience. In this case, the object is oil sands bitumen, the discourse is discussion of the bitumen in popular media, and the audience is the viewers of those mediated messages.

Though there has been no previous application of domestication in the study of environmental discourse, studies of visual communication related to the environment have found examples of other strategies enacted by commercial actors to associate their products or services with nature and thus reshape meaning in their interest—that is, to greenwash their public images (Budinsky and Bryant, 2013; Greer and Bruno, 1997). Hansen has conducted reviews of previous visual environmental communication and identifies multiple examples (Hansen, 2006, 2011; Hansen and Machin, 2013). He finds that "nature" images are frequently deployed as metaphors to commute onto their referents a sense of being "good, authentic, genuine" (2002, 507), as well as connotations of "legitimacy, universal acceptability and a state of affairs beyond questioning" (Hansen, 2006, 829). In both cases, he is echoing Williams (1983), who argued that the concept of '"nature" is popularly understood "in the selective sense of goodness and innocence. Nature has meant "the countryside," the "unspoiled places," plants and creatures other than man" (1983, 223). Hansen also finds a preference for symbolic representations in lieu of actual ones in commercial uses of environmental imagery (Hansen and Machin, 2008).

By including food in Hansen's conceptualization of "nature images," this study aims to situate itself within the field of visual environmental communication. Hansen himself called for such an extension of the concept of "natural."

> If one wishes to understand how the media contribute to public understandings of environmental issues, one needs to look at media imagery and constructions of nature more generally, with 'nature' being a much broader and, more importantly, a historically and culturally much deeper, older and more significant concept than the relatively recent concept of 'the environment'. (Hansen, 2002, 500)

Williams (1983) supports such a broad and pervasive understanding of nature, saying it has been taken at times to mean the entire material world, either including or excluding humanity, though always retaining a fundamental connotation of goodness. He calls it "perhaps the most complex word in the language" (219). References to food are thus references to nature and when deployed to promote an environmentally controversial practice such as oil sands extraction, become attempts at greenwashing.

Methodology: A Multimodal Semiotic Approach

My methodology draws from, and expands upon, the multimodal-analysis process developed by Lefsrud et al. (2015) for examining the interplay between textual and visual elements of a piece of communication. The process involves four stages: (1) creating a corpus of texts; (2) selecting a sample from the corpus; (3a) analyzing the textual elements; (3b) analyzing the visual elements; (3c) combining those results to analyze the words and images together; and finally (4) comparing this analysis across texts to examine patterns and interactions (228). The result is an analysis that addresses the interplay between the multimodal elements in a piece of communication, and how these elements come to be received as a single message.

The corpus of texts for my study (Stage 1) is the Mediatoil database of more than 2,000 pieces of visual oil sands communication. The Mediatoil project has collected images from oil-industry companies, environmental and other interested nongovernmental organizations (NGOs), and the governments of Canada and Alberta. Oil-transportation companies (specifically pipeline operators) were included due to their economic interest in oil sands extraction. For example, images produced by Enbridge (one of whose ads is used in this study) were included in the Mediatoil database because it is attempting to build pipelines to transport oil out of the oil sands region. Furthermore, while the Enbridge ad used in this study does not refer specifically to its proposed pipelines out of the oil sands region, the ad ran in *Report on Business* magazine's special oil sands issue in November 2014; the context of the ad's placement is certainly an aspect in its reception.

The four ads were selected (Stage 2) because they are the clearest examples of the food-comparison theme, although other examples were found. The CAPP yogurt ad[1] is used here as the paradigm case because of the controversy it produced and the subsequent attention it received. The statements made for and against the ad were useful for understanding the positions and fears of stakeholders in the oil sands debate.

In this study, I am interested in the textual and visual reference to food in the ads and the use of oil and oil production-related images and text (or, as will be seen, lack thereof). The advertisements are analyzed qualitatively for how images and text representing these two conceptual categories (food and oil) are used to shape the viewer's understanding of and feelings about oil sands development.

Analytically (Stages 3 and 4), I employ a Parisian social semiotic approach to perform a multimodal rhetorical analysis of the ads in my sample. I explore the textual and visual elements of the advertisements as they interact to produce a desired interpretation—i.e., a single rhetorical message. It is "Parisian" in the sense that it is derived from Barthes (1977) and from the structural-linguistic approach to semiotics that is generally associated with the Parisian school (mainly Barthes and Saussure). It is "social" because it is informed by Kress and van Leeuwen's (2006) interest in reception.

A Parisian approach views images as a form of speech and applies linguistic rules (and the work of previous semioticians such as Saussure) to images. "Formal relations of elements" (Barthes, 1977, 49), or rhetorical figures, outlined previously in linguistics, can be used to understand how connotative meaning is shared between signifier and signified. Barthes singles out two such figures, metonymy and asyndeton, as being responsible for such connotative work. Metonymy is a process of direct comparison, whereby a signifier is linked directly to a signified via a shared attribute, so that one thing is allowed to "stand in" for another (Barthes considers metonymy to be a subcategory of metaphor). Asyndeton is a linguistic term referring to the omission of a conjunction between two parts of a sentence which implies a relationship. In visual communication, the juxtaposition of different scenes, images, or concepts similarly implies a relationship.

Kress and van Leeuwen (2006) build upon Barthes, restating these "formal relations of elements" as the "symbolic attributive structure" (110) of an image, wherein the symbolic attribute of one element is conferred onto another through co-presentation in the same image. Thus, the symbolic attributes of the signifier are shared with the signified via either metonymy or asyndeton, resulting in the symbolic-attributive structure of the image. (This process is similar to the concept of semantic prosody discussed in Chen's chapter in this volume.) This is the conceptual underpinning of this study: it is possible for one image to commute some of its meaning onto another image through co-presentation. These semiotic frameworks propose how this is done.

Barthes used a print advertisement as his case study because "in advertising the signification of the image is undoubtedly intentional" (1977, 33). Advertising is characterized by a high level of control over the final product/image (as compared to earned media, which bears the stamp of other actors such as editors). This is useful to note here because, in parsing out the connotations within the oil sands advertisements, I ascribe a good deal of intention to the producers.

Two Rhetorical Figures: How Text and Images Interact

The four sampled ads were chosen for the clarity and prominence of their deployment of food imagery. They exemplify the two rhetorical figures outlined by Barthes: metonymy and asyndeton. In the two television ads, both produced by CAPP, food serves as a metonym for oil—that is, the latter is directly compared to the former via a shared characteristic. Experts explain the nature of oil sands bitumen by comparing it to a commonly known type of food. In the two print ads, one produced by Cenovus and one by Enbridge, images of food and textual discussion of oil are presented next to each other, juxtaposed—that is to say they are related to each other via asyndeton. In this section, I will analyze the text and visuals of these ads independently, as per Stage 3a and 3b of Lefsrud et al.'s (2015) approach, and then engage in a multimodal analysis of the images together (Stage 3c).

The texts of the ads differ along figurational lines. The ads deploying metonymy refer to both oil and food in their texts (these being television ads, the texts are spoken, but nonetheless represent verbal rather than pictorial representation). In the ads deploying asyndeton, the juxtaposition depends on the multimodality of the communications: they deal strictly with oil in the text and food in the visuals.

Advertisements Deploying Metonymy

Both of the ads which deploy metonymy are taken from the same ad campaign by CAPP, in which employees of the association's member companies are presented as experts explaining oil sands operations. The ads were produced as thirty-second TV spots that were also adapted as outdoor poster advertisements.[2]

Ad 1: CAPP Yogurt TV Ad

In this ad, the speaker is identified early on, via superimposed text on screen, as Suncor executive, Shelley Powell. She discusses the company's extensive efforts to reclaim the tailings ponds that result from the extraction process: "It has a lot of fine particles in it and if left on its own would take decades to settle." She describes oil sands tailings as being "essentially like yogurt," and it is this textual detail which proved controversial. In 2010, the Sierra Club of Canada complained to the ASC about this ad, saying that its comparison of toxic tailings to yogurt "misleads the public by downplaying the toxicity of tailings ponds that contain numerous chemicals like arsenic, mercury and poly aromatic hydrocarbons produced by the tar sands operations" (Sierra Club of Canada, 2010). The ASC ruled on November 29, 2010 that the ad was not, in fact, misleading. In a letter released by the Sierra Club, ASC Vice President Janet Feasby explains: "Ms. Powell's reference to yogurt referred only to the apparent physical consistency of the tailings and did not humanize or soft pedal the more controversial aspects surrounding tailings" (as cited by Sierra Club of Canada, 2010). Regardless of this,

CAPP opted to remove the reference from the English version of the ad for subsequent airings (CBC News, 2010a). A French version, containing a similar reference to yogurt, continued to run unchanged.

Although the original version of the advertisement is no longer available, various accounts about the controversy said that the original statement's exact wording was: "It's essentially like yogurt." (CBC News, 2010a; Sierra Club of Canada, 2010; Vanderklippe, 2010). The French video uses the phrase "consistants comme du yogourt." Literally translated, that would be "consistent like yogurt," but English does not use the adjective "consistent" that way, so "with a consistency like yogurt" would be more accurate. CAPP Vice President of Communications Janet Annesley explained her company's position, and the lack of alteration to the French version, to the Globe and Mail: "The French translator clearly understood the consistency simile, Advertising Standards Canada clearly understands the consistency simile. If some members of the activist community believe we are suggesting tailings are good to eat, that is not our intent" (Vanderklippe, 2010). That is to say that the yogurt is present only to present a familiar substance through which viewers can understand a strange one.

Visually, the context of the video seems to be a Suncor work site. Powell is shown out of doors, clad in safety glasses, a hard hat, and an orange safety vest. All of this lends a sense of industry to the ad and a direct association with the extraction process. The reference to yogurt is made in a voice-over, paired with footage of a container of tailings being stirred with a stick. The stick is then pulled out so the bitumen can drip off to show its consistency, which does appear similar to that of yogurt, or another substance with similar thickness and viscosity.

Ad 2: CAPP Peanut Butter TV and Print Ad

In this ad, Eddie Lui, vice president of oil sands development and research for Imperial Oil, explains the process of diluting oil sands bitumen so that it is thin enough to be extracted from the ground. He explains in the video that, "Heavy oil is located underground. It is more like peanut butter than liquid." As mentioned earlier, the video ads were also adapted as poster ads and in this case the subtle difference in their texts is important. The poster ad (see Figure 11.1) states the food comparison more blatantly (in bold text and a larger font, no less): "Heavy oil is like peanut butter." This comparison was used elsewhere as well. Lui's employer, Imperial Oil, compares oil sands consistency to peanut butter on its Oil Sands 101 web page (Imperial Oil, 2015), suggesting there is no spontaneity in Lui's reference. It is also interesting that Lui's statement is made at the nine-second mark in the ad, the very same second as the yogurt statement in the other video. It should not be surprising to note that two ads in the same campaign follow similar scripts, but it again serves as evidence that there is nothing accidental or spontaneous about what occurs therein, including how and when the food comparison is made.

Like Powell, Lui is shown in a work environment, in this case a busy laboratory (for more on the significance of the industrial setting, see Laurie's chapter on *Ethical Oil* and frames in this volume). He is shown looking at diagrams, holding up a specimen jar of a similar black liquid substance, and inspecting other lab facilities. There is also footage of pipelines and outdoor pumping operations paired with his voice-overs. Again, the goal here seems to be to give a sense that this expert is on the ground, so to speak—that he is giving the viewer a tour of the real business of oil sands extraction. Also, as in the yogurt ad, this statement is paired with an image of the substance in question—in this case, it seems to be diluted oil being poured from one container into another. It would seem that the image of oil being poured is shown to demonstrate the desired, diluted consistency. However, in that case the image shown is not related to the food discussed—peanut butter cannot be poured. Thus, there is a break here between the visual imagery and the textual imagery, but regardless, the ad still succeeds in communicating the simile: unrefined bitumen is "like peanut butter." A metonymic relationship is produced between oil and food.

The metonymic relationships in these two CAPP ads (and the asyndetonic relationships in the ads to be examined next) are defined by the way the text and images interact. The metonymic comparison between oil product and food in the CAPP ads is located mostly, though not entirely, in the text. The ads refer to both the food and the oil product verbally, connecting them via simile ("like" yogurt/peanut butter). However, the statements are paired with visuals which drive this comparison home. The viewer is told that tailings are like yogurt while looking at a jar of them being stirred with a stick, and the viewer is told that heavy oil is like peanut butter while looking at an image of heavy oil being poured from one container into another. These visuals add veracity to the comparison, but they also emphasize it.

As a contrast, in the next two ads, produced by Cenovus and Enbridge, the comparison is made by asyndeton, which is achieved entirely by juxtaposition of text and image. The relationship is not stated explicitly; it is left implicit, suggested by the copresence of images of food and textual discussions of fossil fuels.

Advertisements Deploying Asyndeton

Ad 3: Cenovus Morning Coffee Print ad (Cenovus, 2014)

This print ad is part of Cenovus' Fuelling Our Lives multi-ad campaign launched in 2014. It is a split image, with a photo of a press-pot of coffee at the top and a photo of a container ship at the bottom, divided by a bar with the Cenovus logo and two lines of text. The text says:

> Oil keeps the economy on the move. With 92% of our transportation needs fuelled by oil, it moves people, and the goods and services that drive our economy and improve quality of life. Find out more at More2theStory.com. (Cenovus, 2014)

There are two notable absences here, one textual and one visual. It is most striking that oil is visually absent from the advertisement; the viewer is instead shown images of what it affords us. But note also that coffee, pictured at the top, is absent from this explanatory paragraph. The only instance in which the food element of this ad is mentioned in text is in the words "morning coffee," which are superimposed at the bottom left of the coffee photograph. Still being in the press pot, the coffee is black; it stands next to two white coffee cups on a red-and-white gingham napkin, all of which are atop a white wooden serving tray. The photo at the bottom of the ad, which lacks superimposed text, depicts a container ship at sea, in calm waters on a clear, sunny day. The ship is stacked high with shipping containers—so high they extend out of the frame.

Ad 4: Enbridge Guilty Pleasures Print ad (Enbridge, 2014)

This ad, part of the company's Life Takes Energy campaign also launched in 2014, shows a single photo of a number of chocolate cupcakes sitting on a countertop—a scene of baking in progress. A large "E =" is superimposed over the scene, in the same yellow as Enbridge's logo, which is set off in a box at the bottom left, below a paragraph of text:

> Guilty pleasures. We didn't crack the eggs. Or splurge on the Belgian chocolate. But we did heat the oven to bake the gourmet cupcakes that'll be eaten before they've had the chance to cool. When the energy you invest in life meets the energy we fuel it with, sweet things happen.

Unlike in the coffee ad, the text addresses both the food and oil element of this ad. It should be noted that the oil is presented in terms of "energy," and the energy powering an oven is more likely to be natural gas. However, given that this ad ran on Pages 2 and 3 of the special oil sands issue of Report on Business, and given that Enbridge is the company that was pushing for the controversial Northern Gateway pipeline to move oil sands bitumen west, and recently reversed its preexisting Line 9 pipeline to move it through Ontario east to Quebec, oil from the oil sands is a large part of what is being sold here.

In the photo, some of the cupcakes are uniced and on a cooling rack, some are iced with chocolate icing and arranged carefully on a plate, next to a bowl of raspberries and a smaller bowl of what appears to be icing sugar. Some of the icing sugar dusts three of the iced cupcakes in a haphazard manner, adding to the sense that the baking is still in progress. Both ads use asyndeton; although they lack a direct comparison between the material characteristics of oil and the material characteristics of food, they do use foods that are nonetheless visually similar to oil. Enbridge's cupcakes are very dark chocolate, the uniced ones displaying an almost black hue. Similarly, Cenovus' coffee is black, not pale brown from the milk or cream that most Canadians take in their coffee (Coffee Association of Canada, 2013). Indeed, Cenovus' coffee is still in the press pot, yet to be poured—to be extracted, one could say. In the Cenovus ad, coffee is not even mentioned, so people are left to draw their own conclusions about the relation between it and oil—returning to linguistic/semiotic terms, the preposition which relates the two concepts is omitted. Yet nonetheless, thanks to the fact that they are both part of the same advertisement, one which is explicitly about oil, coffee serves as a signifier for oil. The connection between the text and the photo of the container ship is direct—it is a mode of transportation powered by oil, as laid out in the text. The connection with coffee is not laid out in the text, but its selection must be considered significant, given that it was chosen from the enormous range of potential signifiers covered by the words "people, goods and services," provided in the text. The coffee could be replaced by anything else that travels by shipping container and the ad would still make logical sense; the coffee, then, presumably has been chosen as a signifier because of the particular value and associations the communicator expects the audience to attach to it. As with CAPP's defense of the yogurt reference, this can be seen as an attempt at domestication, in which the image of coffee is deployed here to confer associations of comfort and home (Wansink and Sangerman, 2000) to the concept being discussed—i.e., oil sands.

By comparison, with the mention of the cupcakes and their ingredients in the Enbridge ad, the relationship between the food and a petroleum product is more explicit, but again we are presented with an ad that juxtaposes an image of food with a discussion of petroleum—an oil industry ad that chooses not to show us oil (again, though the ad only talks in general terms about "energy," given that the ad's placement and given Enbridge's involvement in building pipelines to the oil sands, it can be said that this is an ad about oil). The food signifies the oil, but not because of an explicit relationship laid out in the text—that is to say, the cupcakes are not being compared to the oil. Rather, the signification is a result of their co-presentation, because the viewer is asked to think about cupcakes while reading about oil. Performing a similar thought exercise to the one applied to the coffee ad, if one were to not read the text of this ad, it could be promoting any of the myriad substances and processes involved in the production of cupcakes, or even an ad for cupcakes. Thus, in both these ads there is no attempt to visually represent the oil industry in any way.

Parodies: Exposing the Meaning-Making Framework

Opposition groups have attempted to highlight these techniques through parody ads, amplifying to the level of absurdity the oil companies' attempts at re- or mis-direction away from the realities of extraction. Indeed, the poster version of the second ad examined in this study, the CAPP ad comparing heavy oil to peanut butter, was chosen for a direct kind of mockery in which the group changed the first line (see Figure 11.1) to "Heavy oil is like toxic peanut butter. We have to make it thinner so it can kill." Much like the original ad, the parody crops the comparison there, going on to discuss the environmental damage of oil sands extraction and the industry's attempts to "greenwash" its activities through these ads. Only the text of the ad is changed—the photographic backdrop, of Imperial Oil executive Eddie Lui with arms crossed and wearing safety glasses, remains.

Another parody ad, released by Greenpeace, provides an original image, but is designed to mimic the style of the CAPP poster ads, a waist-up photo of a person in front of a backdrop photo, with superimposed text which is their testimony about the value of oil sands extraction. This parody ad, which is not food related, shows the then Canadian Prime Minister Stephen Harper holding a kitten in front of a backdrop of what we must assume is an oil sands extraction site—similar images of torn-up landscapes speckled with large dump trucks and sprawling tailings ponds are frequently featured in Greenpeace's oil sands opposition campaigns (Greenpeace, 2019). The bolded text at the top of the ad, again a hallmark of the CAPP poster ads, addresses the mis-directive nature of CAPP's campaign: "Don't look at the destruction behind me, just look at this cute little kitten. Isn't he just so ADORABLE? I just want to squeeze him and squeeze him. Tar sands are great, just like kittens!" The implication is that these ads, in which oil-company experts discuss the positive aspects of their activities, are designed to draw attention away from the reality of oil sands extraction, and they do so by presenting an image which will comfort and please the viewer. Cuddling a kitten is a very pleasant domestic image. However, there is also an implication of violence, of a crime against nature, in his stated desire to "squeeze ... and squeeze" this kitten. The overall result is a suggestion that the industry's relationship with nature is not benign, and what it says about that relationship is not to be trusted. Finally, the choice of Stephen Harper as a spokesperson for the oil sands implies political support for, and perhaps collusion with, the oil sands industry.

Figure 11.1 The poster version of the CAPP peanut butter ad. Reproduced with permission from the Canadian Association of Petroleum Producers.

The rhetorical effect of this suggestion is that opponents—the target audience of the parody—are facing a daunting challenge, to which they must rise (Figures 11.2 and 11.3).

Clark (2016) argues that parody ads offer attempts to reverse the flow of meaning intended by the original advertisers—to recomplicate the images which advertisers attempt to simplify (by indicating a single

Figure 11.2 A parody of CAPP's peanut-butter ad. Reproduced with permission from Greenpeace.

intended meaning among many potential ones). Parodies "foreground these elements in ways that make them less effective forms of greenwashing" (188). The elements being foregrounded in these two parody ads are the rhetorical figures discussed in this chapter. The parodies derive their satirical humor from the absurdity of directly comparing two disparate things, one of which having negative connotations and the other positive.

Figure 11.3 A Greenpeace parody of CAPP's ad campaign. Reproduced with permission from Greenpeace.

The peanut-butter parody ad foregrounds the workings of metonymy by revealing the incongruity of the choice of referent: it says it is absurd to compare heavy oil to peanut butter because peanut butter is not dangerous, and because what is important about heavy oil is not its consistency. The kitten parody reveals the function of asyndeton by making a joke of the fact that the two images being compared have no direct connection. And though the kitten is not a food image, this parody is actually more useful in demonstrating the rhetorical workings of all four industry ads studied in this chapter. The kitten is an image of comfort and the image of comfort is displayed to add comforting connotations to the topic addressed in the text. Much like Stephen Harper with his kitten, the oil companies with their food comparisons are asking viewers not to look at the destruction being wrought by oil sands extraction. Instead, they are asking them to feel comforted by the familiar food images. Having felt that, viewers are expected to feel comfortable with the oil extracted from the oil sands, just like food.

Oil, Food, and a Social License for Extraction

The framework built in this chapter, through a combination of multimodal and semiotic analysis, revealed two rhetorical figures performing work in the sampled ads. Two ads deploy metonymy, a process of direct comparison, whereby a signifier is linked to a signified by direct comparison; the others use asyndeton, an indirect comparison achieved through juxtaposition.

In the CAPP ads (deploying metonymy), the viewer is told explicitly that oil products and by-products have similarities to food. In the Cenovus and Enbridge ads (which deploy asyndeton), images of food and textual discussions of oil are presented together and viewers are asked to make connections between the two because of their copresence. The difference between the rhetorical strategies in the CAPP campaign and the rhetorical strategies used by Cenovus and Enbridge can be understood as the difference between replacement and progression.

Metonyms share a common characteristic and suggest an act of replacement: the "like" used in both metonymy cases (tailings are "like yogurt," and heavy oil is "like peanut butter") is a preposition which explains the relationship between signifier and signified and suggests that one is, in terms of their shared characteristic at least, replaceable by the other. However, in the process of suggesting a replacement, connotation happens as well, through the choice of replacement (of signifier)—the qualities of the signifier are commuted directly onto the signified.

Asyndetons lack the element of the shared characteristic and lack a preposition or conjunction which explains the connection. Instead there is a progression: there is oil and then there is food. This is stated explicitly in the Enbridge ad—the text explains that the cupcakes were made possible by the earlier presence of oil. This progression is implicit in the Cenovus ad—the text refers to transportation and it is up to the viewer to make the connection between that and the presence of coffee. These progressive moments are juxtaposed in a single image, which provides the connotation. The qualities of the subsequent moment, i.e., of the signifier, are commuted on to the signified by this act of juxtaposition. In this way, these ads function as narratives—the companies are trying to communicate a story about their products. The story, which is told not in text, but in the interplay of text and photo, is that oil leads to food.

However, in all four cases, there is an attempt to mix concepts up in viewers' minds. The central commonality is that they enact a symbolic-attributive structure whereby the positive symbolic attributes of food are commuted to oil sands through two types of co-presentation. CAPP's own defense of its yogurt ad is that the description was only intended to give people a more familiar substance through which to understand the strange one, and that is the essence of domestication as a technique. It is the choice of what substances are used in this process which is of interest here and which suggests a specific meaning-shaping strategy at work. Just as Cenovus could have chosen any other item from the category "people, goods and services" to help deliver its message about oil's role in the transportation industry, so too could CAPP have chosen any substance of similar thickness and viscosity to describe tailings or undiluted bitumen.

Mud is an obvious choice for comparison to oil sands bitumen. It is as familiar a substance to most people as yogurt and is far more similar. Of course, there are negative connotations attached to mud (it is dirty, inconvenient, without value) that an advertiser would not want to attach to its product. Plaster or bricking mortar not only has a similar consistency but also the granularity of oil sands, and generally lack negative connotations. However, they do have connotations of male-centric and somewhat humdrum labor that makes them less than ideal as a signifier, and they are somewhat more obscure. This brief list shows that a food signifier was not the only option. Any choice would have some preexisting connotations; the corporations chose the connotations to improve their image and bolster the social license for their extraction activities. The context of these ads is the ongoing controversy about the oil sands project and its effects. This is explicit in the two CAPP ads, which attempt to explain how techniques being used by Suncor and Imperial Oil mitigate environmental risks posed by oil sands extraction. The Cenovus (coffee) and Enbridge (cupcake) ads do not mention the oil sands directly, but they are both active players in the oil sands, and both ads do attempt to justify their companies' energy-related activities (both arguing that things we as a society enjoy doing are dependent upon the energy their activities produce).

Referring to previous big debates in environmentalism, such as climate change and the ozone layer, Hansen (2011) said that "it appears that the battles over these issues are now as much to do with communication aimed at 'winning hearts and minds' as they are to do with communicating science-based or expert evidence" (8). The same could be said about these attempts to communicate the nature of oil sands: they have more to do with winning approval for oil sands—i.e., obtaining a social license for extraction—as they do with giving a sense of their consistency or of their role in our lives.

The difference in the context is significant. In the ads deploying asyndeton, an attempt is made to dissociate the discussion of oil from the context of its production. In an overt example of the domestication strategy in action, they display domestic scenes while discussing energy production: a kitchen in Enbridge's ad, and a serving tray with a press pot of coffee in Cenovus' (along with the words "morning coffee," making it clear that this coffee is not being enjoyed on-the-go). The viewer is thus placed at 'home' when being told of the virtues of energy production and its role in enabling the domestic scene. The provenance of the oil is not addressed. By contrast, in the metonymy examples, the technological and industrial context of extraction is very much in the foreground. The ads feature two oil-company executives, one at what we are led to believe is an outdoor Suncor work site, the other in a laboratory (though outdoor scenes are also presented). Both are wearing safety equipment, emphasizing the suggestion that they are at the front lines of oil production. However, this context is largely left unexplained, presented rather as a rapidly changing series of images, locations, and backgrounds. So, while the abundance of context perhaps makes these ads seem more forthright and sincerer (and make a classical-rhetorical appeal to ethos) through the use of company employees on location as spokespeople, it also serves to emphasize the complicated and technical nature of oil sands extraction and to highlight the value of a familiar point of reference through which to understand the issue.

All three companies chose to feature food in their carefully crafted messages. Food is a powerful source of imagery because of its connection to family and domestic life (Barthes, 1977; Rodino-Colocino, 2006). It can also be seen as the kind of natural image that holds connotations of goodness and authenticity (Hansen, 2002, 2006; Williams, 1983), which in these cases are then commuted onto the oil-related signified. The rhetorical effect, in semiotic terms, is connotation—the positive, domestic associations people have with food are commuted onto the referent (oil sands products). The effect in classical terms is an appeal to pathos—an attempt to trigger positive emotional associations that would not otherwise be associated with oil.

Aupers et al. (2012) found in their study of car commercials that they were attempts to erode the divide between technology and nature. That can be seen here as well: the oil sands extraction process is the technology being sold, so to speak, by the ads, while the food imagery being used represents nature. The rhetorical work performed by these ads is an attempt to erode the divide between these concepts. As the struggle to define meaning in the oil sands debate continues in the popular discourse, these companies chose, in separate but remarkably uniform ways, to use food as a central part of their meaning-making efforts. The presence of food imagery is a strategy of domestication. If successful, such a strategy would lead people to attach the comforting associations of food to the controversial, and thus potentially discomforting, products of oil sands development, thus positively influencing popular opinion about extraction.

A social license for extraction continues to be important to the companies working in the oil sands. Recent months and years have seen ongoing battles over the construction of pipelines to transport oil out of Alberta, including Enbridge's struggle to get its Line 3 replacement approved. While parts of these battles have played out in courtrooms, they have also played out in the court of popular opinion. Opposition by particular polities—e.g., in Quebec to the Energy East pipeline and in the city of Burnaby to the Trans Mountain pipeline—caused major problems for these companies. The pipeline cases are particularly clear examples, but in general the success of advertisements like the ones in this study, which attempt to gain social license, are critical for companies working in the oil sands.

The biggest question raised by this study, then, is: how successful were these advertisements? The vast differences in support for the oil sands in different regions of the country suggests these ads were not hypodermic needles injecting opinion into the national discourse. Yet the political activity that has been seen among both extraction opponents and supporters suggests they are being mobilized somehow.

Among the other questions raised by the results of this study are: how is domestication used elsewhere in communication related to energy, the environment, and climate change? Where else might domestication be employed? Having attempted to synthesize a working theory of food as a tool of domestication, this study could help with future research on food imagery in the domestication of other concepts and innovations. It also suggests the potential for other types of imagery to be used as domestication tools, and for the inclusion of other types of imagery to be included under the academic umbrella of visual environmental communication. Lastly, its analytical framework revealed two rhetorical figures at work in the interplay between image and text; could it be used to reveal others?

Notes

1 In the early stages of the study, the two CAPP television ads chosen for the sample were publicly available on the CAPP.ca website and its associated YouTube channel. However, in the winter of 2014/2015, shortly before

in-depth analysis of the videos began, CAPP revoked public access to the videos so that they could no longer be viewed. Fortunately, the actual pages on the CAPP.ca site that held the videos were still viewable, and they contain textual transcripts of the ads. Also fortunately, a YouTube user named motocross5 posted low-resolution versions of those CAPP ads (along with dozens of others) to his/her own YouTube channel. The audio of those videos matched the scripts on the CAPP.ca site, suggesting they were indeed the same ads. Those videos were paired with the scripts to perform the analysis in this study. However, between the analysis stage and publication, motocross5's YouTube was terminated for Terms of Service violations and CAPP has removed all reference to the videos from its site.

2 Televisual ads have a multimodal nature beyond text and image—they include sound and temporal action—and thus include elements that are not addressed in this analysis. However, since the ads in the campaign were designed to also be presented as poster advertisements, as seen in Figure 11.1, their texts and visuals can fruitfully be isolated and addressed without reference to these other elements.

References

Aupers, Stef, Dick Houtman, Peter Achterberg, Willemm de Koster, Peter Mascini, Jeroen van der Waal and Johan Roeland. 2012. "Beyond the Domestication of Nature? Restructuring the Relationship between Nature and Technology in Car Commercials." *European Journal of Cultural Studies* 15 (1): 3–18.

Barthes, Roland. 1977. "Rhetoric of the Image." In *Image–Music–Text.* (S. Heath, Trans.) New York: Hill and Wang.

Budinsky, Jennifer and Susan Bryant. (2013). "'It's Not Easy Being Green': The Greenwashing of Environmental Discourses in Advertising." *Canadian Journal of Communication* 38 (2).

CanOils. 2010. "Canadian Association of Petroleum Producers: Activist Oil Sands Ads Inaccurate; Canadians Want Truth, Balance–Not Propaganda." *CanOils*, July 10. www.canoils.com/Universal/View.aspx?type=Story&id=6909.

CBC News. 2010a. "Sierra Club, CAPP Both Claim Victory in Ad Ruling: Oil Firms Will Change Ad Saying Oilsands Ponds 'Like Yogurt.'" *CBC News,* November 30. www.cbc.ca/m/touch/news/story/1.964020.

CBC News. 2010b. "Anti-Oilsands Video Has 'Editing Error': U.S. Group Admits Mistake About Size of Area Affected." *CBC News,* July 16. www.cbc.ca/news/business/anti-oilsands-video-has-editing-error-1.872795.

Cenovus. 2014. "Fuelling Our Lives." *Cenovus Energy.* Accessed January 27, 2015. www.cenovus.com/images/content/news/morning-coffee.jpg.

Clark, Joseph. 2016. "Selling with Gaia: Advertising and the Natural World." In *Ecomedia: Key Issues*, edited by S. Rust, S. Monani and S. Cubitt, 176–195. London: Routledge.

Coffee Association of Canada. 2013. "Canadian Coffee Drinking Study 2013 Highlights–Infographic." *Coffee Association of Canada.* Accessed January 28, 2015. www.coffeeassoc.com/coffee-in-canada/canadian-coffee-drinking-study-2013-highlights-infographic.

Douglas, Mary & Baron Isherwood. (1980). *The World of Goods: Towards an Anthropology of Consumption.* London: Penguin.

Enbridge. 2014. "Life Takes Energy." *Enbridge Inc.* Accessed January 27, 2015. www.enbridge.com/lifetakesenergy.

Gismondi, Mike and Debra J. Davidson. "Imagining the Tar Sands: 1880–1967 and Beyond." *Imaginations: Journal of Cross Cultural Image Studies*, 3 (2).

Government of Alberta. 2014. "Alberta's Oil Sands: About the Resource." *Government of Alberta.* Accessed January 26, 2015. http://oilsands.alberta.ca/resource.html.

Greenpeace. 2019. "#Oil." *Greenpeace.* Accessed January 16, 2019. www.greenpeace.org/canada/en/tag/oil/.

Greer, Jed and Kenny Bruno. (1997). *Greenwash: The Reality Behind Corporate Environmentalism.* Lanham, Maryland: Rowman & Littlefield.

Haddon, Leslie. 2011. "Domestication Analysis, Objects of Study, and the Centrality of Technologies in Everyday Life." *Canadian Journal of Communication* 36: 311–323.

Hansen, Anders. 2002. "Discourses of Nature in Advertising." *Communications* 27: 499–511.

Hansen, Anders. 2006. "Tampering with Nature: 'Nature' and the 'Natural' in Media Coverage of Genetics and Biotechnology." *Media, Culture & Society* 28 (6): 811–834.

Hansen, Anders. 2011. "Communication, Media and the Environment: Towards Reconnecting Research on the Production, Content and Social Implications of Environmental Communication." *The International Communication Gazette* 73 (1–2): 7–25.

Hansen, Anders and David Machin. 2008. "Visually Branding the Environment: Climate Change as a Marketing Opportunity." *Discourse Studies* 10 (6): 777–794.

Hansen, Anders and David Machin. 2013. "Editors' Introduction: Researching Visual Environmental Communication." *Environmental Communication* 7 (2): 151–168.

Holden, Michael. 2013. "From Dead Ducks to Dutch Disease: The Vilification of Canada's Oil Sands in the Media." *Canada West Foundation*, January. Accessed January 26, 2015. http://cwf.ca/publications-1/from-dead-ducks-to-dutch-disease.

Imperial Oil. 2015. Oil Sands 101. *Imperial Oil.* Retrieved January 26, 2015, from www.imperialoil.ca/Canada-English/operations_sands_glance_101.aspx.

Kass, Leon. 1994. *The Hungry Soul.* New York: The Free Press.

Kim, Rebecca. 2012. "Refining Advertisements of the Canadian Tar Sands." *Seattle Journal for Social Justice* 10 (2): 845–885.

Kress, Gunther and Theo van Leeuwen. 2006. *Reading Images: The Grammar of Visual Design, Second Edition.* London: Routledge.

Lefsrud, Lianne M., Heather Graves, and Nelson Phillips. 2015. "Chapter 22: Analyzing Visual Rhetoric in Organizational Research." In *Handbook of Qualitative Organizational Research: Innovative Pathways and Methods,* edited by K.D. Elsbach and R.M. Kramer, 225–238. London: Routledge.

Linnitt, Carol. 2014. "PostMedia Gets Away with Running Unmarked Advertorials." *DeSmog Blog*, June 20. www.desmog.ca/2014/06/19/postmedia-gets-away-running-unmarked-oil-advertorials.

McCracken, Grant. (1990). *Culture and Consumption: New Approaches to the Symbolic Character of Consumer Goods and Activities.* Bloomington and Indianapolis: Indiana University Press.

McCurdy, Patrick and Adam Thomlison (2019). "Beyond Bitumen: How Advertising Sells the Myth of Canada's Oil/Tar Sands." In *Advertising, Consumer Culture, and Canadian Society: A Reader,* edited by K. Asquith. Toronto: Oxford University Press.

Paskey, Janice, Gillian Steward and Amanda Williams. 2013. "The Alberta Oil Sands Then and Now: An Investigation of the Economic, Environmental and Social Discourses across Four Decades." *Oil Sands Research and Information Network*. Edmonton, Alberta: OSRIN Report No. TR-38.

Rodino-Colocino, Michelle. 2006. "Selling Women on PDAs from 'Simply Palm' to 'Audrey': How Moore's Law Met Parkinson's Law in the Kitchen." *Critical Studies in Media Communication* 23 (5): 375–390.

Rozin, Paul. 1998. "Food is Fundamental, Fun, Frightening and Far-reaching." *Social Research* 66 (1): 9–30.

Sierra Club of Canada. 2010. "CAPP Withdraws Yogurt Ad in Response to Sierra Club Canada Complaint." *Sierra Club of Canada*, November 30. www.archive.sierraclub.ca/en/tar-sands/media/release/capp-withdraws-yogurt-ad-response-sierra-club-canada-complaint.

Vanderklippe, Nathan. 2010. "Oil Patch Yogurt Ad Not Misleading, Council Says." *The Globe and Mail*, November 30. www.theglobeandmail.com/globe-investor/oil-patch-yogurt-ad-not-misleading-council-says/article1316199/.

Wansink, Brian and Cynthia Sangerman. 2000. "The Taste of Comfort: Food for Thought on How Americans Eat to Feel Better." *American Demographics*, July 2000: 66–67.

Williams, Raymond. 1983. *Keywords: A Vocabulary of Culture and Society (Rev. ed.)*. New York: Oxford University Press.

12 Everything You Ever Wanted to Know about the Alberta Oil Sands (But Were Afraid to Ask Jacques Lacan)

T.R. Kover

Just the Facts?

The psychoanalytic theory of Jacques Lacan may not seem to have much to offer by way of insight into the current controversy over the Alberta oil sands. After all, the common stereotype of Albertans, frequently promoted by their political and economic elites, is that of a down-to-earth, hard-nosed, rough around the edges straight shooter who has little time for the verbal or intellectual sophistries often associated with French philosophy. The oil sands are also understood as an economic issue, strictly a rational matter of calculating profits, losses, and bottom-lines rather than the unconscious emotions, drives, and fantasies dealt with by psychoanalysis. It is seen to be a matter more of monetary than libidinal investments. This is the way the controversy over the Alberta oil sands has been framed by the Canadian energy establishment, where critics of the oil sands are routinely accused of relying on emotion, rather than reason.

In 2007, for instance, then Premier of Alberta Ed Stelmach warned Albertans against environmentalists "waging a mean and dirty PR campaign attacking Albertans" instead of engaging in "reasoned debate based on evidence (and) facts" (Quoted in Kowalsky & Hazula-Delay 2015, 84). As Jerry Bellika, a spokesperson for Stelmach's office, elaborated in an interview with the Canadian Broadcasting Corporation, "A lot of critics out there – people who want to shut down the oilsands– aren't constrained by the facts" (Quoted in Gailus 2012, 18). Nor was the Stelmach government alone in framing this controversy as one of emotional rhetoric versus fact-based rationality. As Canadian Minister of Natural Resources, Greg Rickford told an audience at the Canadian Association of Petroleum Producers conference, "Much of the debate over energy is characterized by myth or emotion," suggesting that scientists and environmental activists critical of the oil sands "were crowding out the facts" (quoted in the *Guardian* 2016). Similarly, in an opinion piece in the *Globe and Mail* entitled "Leaders must counter Bogus Oil Sands Spin," retired Encana C.E.O. Gwynne Morgan declared that "while the innuendo and deliberate distortions" of "environmental zealots" are "rarely questioned," the industry had to "inject some realities into this dreamscape" (Morgan 2010). To do so, Morgan called on the industry to counter the negative spin and coordinate with government to get the facts and their message out there to the general public or risk losing their social license.

With this end in mind, the Alberta Government launched its own extensive $14 million "Alberta – Tell it like it is" campaign in 2010. This endeavor was augmented by other PR campaigns by the Canadian Association of Petroleum Producers (CAPP), major corporate players such as Cenovus, Suncor, Enbridge and Total Oil, as well as citizen groups such as EthicalOil.org, each accompanied by a broad array of print, Internet and television ads, and all professing the need to combat negative PR by getting the facts out there.

Yet while advocates claimed to be motivated by the need to get information to the public and to promote reasoned debate, critics have noted that the ads seemed to be distinguished by the absence of argumentative debate or factual refutation of environmental criticism of the oil sands (Gailus 2012). Instead, in ad after ad, they observe, one is presented with tantalizing and glowing images of majestic forests, happy children, glowing, proud parents and heroic para-athletes, in which oil sands production (although frequently barely even mentioned) is linked to everything from the triumph of the human spirit and paternal love to environmental, democratic and social flourishing. Indeed, it seemed that far from wanting to "inject some reality into the dreamscape," these ads were intent on promoting a dreamscape of their own, and many were left with the impression that these campaigns were concerned less about correcting the facts than correcting the public image of oil and the oil sands, an impression many industry insiders candidly admit.

In the magazine *Oilweek: Canada's Oil and Gas Authority* ("Changing the Message: How Cenovus and Others are Helping Counter Anti-Oilsands Sentiments"), for instance, the journalist R.P. Stastny revealed that many of those responsible for crafting the pro-oil sands PR campaigns admitted that their strategy was to rely less on the marshalling of facts and figures and more on evoking powerful positive emotions. As Cenovus Energy's Vice President of Communications, Liz Hannah, confided, her company's ads explicitly made sure "that the kind of messaging we get out there is not overwhelming or *using facts and figures to get our point out,*" but instead reminds Canadians "of the value of oil, the value of energy and what role it plays in their lives" (Stastny 2013, 24, italics added). To do this, Esther Thorson, associate Dean for Graduate Studies and Research at the Missouri School of Journalism, explained to Stastny, pro-oil sands ads rely on positive affect advertising which pairs the product with "fundamental human values" as well as powerful positive emotions, experiences, and symbols (23). In other words, the appeal of such campaigns is not so much factual as emotive, in that they aim to dispel not the public's factual misconceptions about the oil sands but rather its negative perceptions about oil, by linking it to feel-good symbols and experiences.

From this perspective, one suspects criticisms of factual inaccuracy leveled at these ads by Jeff Gailus and other critics of oil sands development, however legitimate, are likely to fall wide of the mark and prove largely ineffective in countering their rhetorical appeal and effectiveness, for these campaigns, as with most PR and advertising campaigns, aim to persuade not through an appeal to the discursive reasoning of their audience but rather to their shared affective dispositions and emotively charged symbols. In short, they aim to capture not so much our minds, but our heart's desire.

In this light, Lacan has a great deal to tell us about the rhetorical strategies involved in the promotion of the oil sands. While Lacanian theory has been underutilized by rhetoricians, scholars such as Christian Lundberg, Gilbert D. Chaitin and Barbara A. Biesecker have championed this work as offering a conceptually rich account of the role that desire, affective attachments, and fantasy play in accounting for the effectiveness of rhetorical practices (Chaitin 1997, 2017; Biesecker 1998; Lundberg 2012). At the heart of Lacanian thought is the attempt to disclose and conceptually schematize the interplay between identity, desire, affect, and symbolic culture. Lacan argues that underlying all communicative action is an attempt to evoke desire by alluding to the jouissance or enjoyment hidden behind the symbolic order. According to Lacan, human subjectivity is characterized by an ontological division and lack at the core of its very being, and the human condition, he contends, consists of the endless quest for something or literally "the Thing" to fill this lack and make the subject ecstatically whole. Human societies, social bonds, and political projects, Lacan contends, are held together by the collective fantasy that behind the ideals or master-signifiers of the symbolic order of culture is the miraculous 'Thing,' the object cause of desire or *objet petit a*' which will heal all social and psychological divisions in subjects, by filling this lack and making them complete. Using a Lacanian framework to analyze print and multimedia examples from the pro-oil sands public relations campaign, this chapter argues that these campaigns present a fantasy in which oil is presented as the *objet petit a*' that will heal social and political divisions and environmental ills and bestow ecstatic personal and communal harmony. Before doing so, however, it is necessary to familiarize ourselves with the outlines of Lacan's thought as it pertains to rhetorical theory.

Lacan and the Subject of Rhetoric – Between Lack and *Jouissance*

While Lacan is not generally thought of as rhetorical theorist, he himself, as Christian Lundberg observes, had little difficulty in acknowledging the relevance of rhetorical theory to his thought. Indeed, this intimate linkage between his theory and rhetoric, as Gilbert Chaitin discerns, is readily apparent in Lacan's well-known dictum that "The unconscious is structured like a language" (Lacan 1993: 166–167) as well as his articulating the unconscious processes of displacement and condensation in terms of the rhetorical tropes of metaphor and metonymy (Chaitin 2017, 683). In fact, near the end of his life, Lacan not only asserted "that the universe itself is a flower of rhetoric" but also declared that "the psychoanalyst is a rhetor," suggesting that the psychoanalytic enterprise was in a sense a form of rhetoric in which the analyst uses language and speech in order to provoke the analysand (Quoted in Lundberg 2012, 1). Nor is this acknowledgment on Lacan's part surprising for those familiar with his thought, as the utter centrality of speech and language to the formation of the human subject and psychoanalytic enterprise itself is at the fundamental core of his teachings. From the start of his teaching until the very end, he insisted that subjectivity is constituted in and through the symbolic order or language. Yet, while Lacan always emphasized the fundamental importance of language and symbolic communication in the formation of the subject and all human affairs, it is clear what interested him in language and speech is less how it functions as a medium of totally transparent intersubjective communication (a complete impossibility, according to Lacan, as Lundberg points out, as the symbolical order or language is marred by a fundamental incompleteness) and more how it worked as a form of persuasion. The "function of language in speech" Lacan notes "is not to inform but evoke" (Lacan 2006, 247) – and what it evokes, he argued, is the desire of the other for the ineffable and ultimately unobtainable jouissance[1] or fullness of the Real or Thing that always escapes what is said. For the entire intersubjective discursive enterprise, according to Lacan, is founded on the attempt to mobilize subjects via an appeal to symbols that they have affectively invested in, which promise to fill the fundamental incompleteness at the heart of their being. Perhaps the most straightforward way to elucidate this dynamic is in terms of Lacan's understanding of the relationship between language and the subject of jouissance.

The subject, according to Lacan, is defined by a fundamental sense of incompleteness that haunts its core. Human life is characterized by unending desire to fill this lack by recapturing the lost sense of wholeness and full jouissance that the subject unconsciously believes that it experienced at birth and early infancy (Fink 1995; Stavrakakis 2007). This hope fuels the subject's acquisition of language and entrance into the symbolic order, or what Lacan refers to as the Big Other, as the subject believes that that their identification with the symbols and values or master signifiers of their sociolinguistic community will complete it and restore to it a sense of ecstatic wholeness or *jouissance*. Yet such a quest for the lost 'object' of desire or the full jouissance of the real,

Lacan maintains, is always an impossible and futile one, for just as the subject is marked by a fundamental lack or incompleteness, so too is the symbolic order or the Big Other. This fundamental incompleteness of the Big Other is more apparent if we examine Lacan's conceptualization of language or the symbolic order.

Lacan is perhaps most famous for his importing of structuralist linguistics into psychoanalytic theory. Drawing on Saussure's distinction between the signifier and signified as well as his understanding of language as structured according to a differential system between signifiers, Lacan prioritized the signifier over the signified and denied any essential link between the two. Meaning is generated not by any inherent relationship between signified and signifier but rather the position the signifier has in relation to other signifiers in the signifying chain. This raises the problem that because signifiers refer only to other signifiers and can be related to one another in an infinite myriad of ways, the chain of signification and reference would appear to be not only endless but groundless, with meaning sliding between signifiers (Fink 1995). Consequently, Lacan posited, with any discursive network or system of signs, there must be certain privileged signifiers which function to fix or anchor meaning and stop the endless sliding of the signifying chain, thereby rendering it intelligible. These privileged signifiers Lacan initially dubbed as nodal points or "points de capiton;" he would go on to refer to them as 'master-signifiers.' Master signifiers anchor the symbolic chain and provide the ultimate guarantors and bedrock of meaning and significance. They represent the most important terms and values of the symbolic chain. Instructive examples would be words like justice, goodness, nobility, decency, democracy, God, country, etc. The significance of these master-signifiers is not simply linguistic, but also affective. They represent "nodal points" of affect which the subject during their acculturation into the symbolic order passionately invests in and identifies with. They are the terms that anchor the subject's identity and the means by which we solicit the love of the Big Other by identifying[2] ourselves with signifiers which we think the other desires and thereby render us completely whole. Thus, these master-signifiers are, for Lacan, the very basis of our wider social bond as it is by means of these master-signifiers that the other will address us, appealing to these signifiers as an attempt to capture our desire and mobilize or curtail our actions. In other words, it is by means of these shared symbols and signifiers in which we have affectively invested that others have discursive purchase upon us as we have discursive purchase on them. Arguments appealing to these master-signifiers and enlisting chains of signification seek to capture the subject's desire by commissioning paths for affective investment, while simultaneously decommissioning or repressing others.

Yet, despite the centrality of these master-signifiers to the organization of the symbolic and libidinal economy, a fundamental aspect to them, Lacan claims, is that they are also "empty signifiers" or "signifiers without a signified." These master-signifiers have no concrete referent or fixed meaning and thus permit an endless succession of varying applications and extensions. This very emptiness or lack of any concrete reference also means that they can admit a plurality of chains of signification and can signify a great many things to a great many people, all of whom remain in some way identified with or against—what it is thought to signify. The master-signifier "freedom," for instance, can mean for one person guns, free-markets, and French fries, while for another socialized Medicare and gun-control.

Language, therefore, far from being a perfect medium of transparent communication, is always characterized by miscommunication or what Lundberg has termed a failed unicity. In the rhetorical situation, both speaker and auditor are speaking at cross purposes or past one another as there is no ultimate ground or absolute correspondence between signified and signifier that would anchor transindividual meaning. Nevertheless, although unicity may be impossible, it remains the background assumption underscoring all communicative action (Lundberg 2012). Moreover, and perhaps more importantly, the emptiness of these master-signifiers and lack of fixity between them and the Real means that the Big Other can never provide the promised full jouissance. Indeed, these signifiers are always inadequate in that some excessive remainder of the real or jouissance always escapes or is left out. Thus, language or the symbolic, according to Lacan, can merely evoke, not completely capture or manifest the full jouissance of the Real.

Despite the unconscious expectations that such symbolic identifications will fill the fundamental lack in the subject, therefore, such identifications always fail to realize the expected full jouissance of the real promised, and the subject always experiences a sense of something missing or not quite right: "'That's not it' is the very cry by which the jouissance obtained is distinguished from the jouissance expected" (Lacan 1998b, 111). For this acculturation (of the subject into the symbolic order) comes at a profound cost, as it is based upon the founding sacrifice (or castration) of full *jouissance*, enacted in the name of the Big Other. Thus, subjects, to the extent they become enculturated, are cut from the primal object of their desire—the maternal Real of *jouissance*—and instead are forced by social law to observe the strictures of the *master-signifiers* by respecting their society's linguistically mediated conventions to defer satisfaction.

To cope with the traumatic loss involved in this founding sacrifice as well as guard against the profoundly debilitating confrontation with the emptiness at the heart of the Big Other or symbolic order, Lacan contends that subjects stabilize their position by constructing a fantasy. In the fantasy, behind the master-signifiers of the symbolic order is the full jouissance of the maternal real held by the Big Other and manifested in what Lacan terms the *objet petit a'* and variously refers to the unobtainable object of desire or the remainder of the real. The fantasy, therefore, consoles the subject by positing that at one point they did enjoy access to full *jouissance* but that at castration, it was taken away by the Big Other. Because it was taken away, it can also be regained. It is this imaginary promise of recapturing our lost/impossible *jouissance*, Lacan argues, that provides the fantasy support that structures human relations and underwrites many of our social, theological, economic, and political projects and conventions. What sustains human social bonds, projects, and acts of identification at the affective level, Lacan claims, is this promise of fullness and that at some future date the lost *jouissance* of the maternal Thing can once again be regained. In this way, fantasy operates to stabilize and legitimate the prohibitions and sacrifices made upon the subject in the name of the collective good and ideals of its social and political regimes, by providing a means of orienting and co-ordinating desire with coordinates through which to identify a promise that if we just continue to strive to fulfil the symbolic mandates of the Big Other, this desire will eventually be fully realized if not in this world then the next. Moreover, if the promised jouissance and fullness fail to be realized, then a corollary of this fundamental fantasy is that this jouissance has been stolen from the Big Other by what Yannis Stavrakakis, informed by Lacan's teachings on paranoia, has dubbed the "'obscene other'" (2007, 218). This fantastic logic is evident in the corporate sponsored oil sands campaign.

"More than Just Fuel": Romancing Bitumen

In a presentation to employees of Cenovus Energy, one of the largest industrial developers of the oil sands, the company's vice president of Communications, Liz Hannah, unveiled the corporation's latest effort to fight the "many emotional accusations about oil" (Hannah 2016). It consisted of getting its employees to "voluntarily" wear a T-shirt with the slogan "I ♥ Oil" emblazoned on it in order to get the "conversation" started (ibid). Hannah noted that in the face of an emotional climate of "negativity," "fear and mistrust" in which oil is accused of everything from being "dirty" to "single handedly ruining the planet," people "have lost sight of its value" and "what oil gives us," and they needed to be reminded "that there is not much in this world that's as important as oil" (ibid). Proudly wearing the aforementioned T-shirt and passionately declaring her love for oil, Hannah observed "Wouldn't it be something if everyone felt (this) way, and felt comfortable about wearing a T-shirt like this! There'd likely be no cries to stop oil sands development and no issues about building new pipelines" (ibid).

The first thing that bears noting is that Hannah, far from trying to counter the "emotionally charged" and by implication "irrational" critiques of the oil sands through reasoned debate, ups the emotional volume further by calling on us to assume an emotional relationship to an inanimate object and claiming that all current difficulties facing oil sands production would be solved if oil just got a little more love. Leaving aside, however, the absurdity and anthropomorphism of Hannah's statements, perhaps a more intriguing question is, what does it mean to love oil?

For Lacan, all love relationships involve some form of transference or identification (akin to idealization or sublimation) with the love-object. Taking his cue from Freud, Lacan argues that, in the love relationship, the subject believes that the love-object possesses all the virtues and embodies all positive values (master-signifiers) which the subject holds dear. Moreover, the love-object is held to have a value far beyond if not extrinsic to its strictly utilitarian and instrumental uses. Indeed, its value is so great that it is deemed to be irreplaceable or unsubstitutable in that no other object will suffice or do, as it is possessed of a certain "je ne sais quoi" or hidden indescribable quality, or what Lacan refers to as the *objet petit a'*.[3] In *Seminar VII: The Ethics of Psychoanalysis*, Lacan observes that love as a form of sublimation involves "raising the object to the level of the Thing" or the pre-symbolic Real of the maternal Thing. He expands on this in *Seminar XI: Four Fundamental Concepts of Psychoanalysis*, noting that all love relationships implicitly involve the ascription to the love-object of being in possession of the *objet petit a'* or, as he expresses it, when I say I love you, it is "*because inexplicably I love in you something more than you* –objet petit a" (Lacan 1998a, 268). Lacan claims that love involves seeing in the love-object the existence of an elusive, ineffable, and indefinable surplus of *jouissance* capable of filling the lack in the subject. Hannah's avowals of her love for oil amount to a claim that she sees in oil something that is more than just oil, something that transcends any mere use-value it may have, and that all the master-signifiers she ascribes to it allude to the existence of the *objet petit a'*.

In Cenovus' "more than just fuel" campaign, this understanding of oil as the object cause of desire or *objet petit a'* is evident. In one of the ads, for instance, we are presented with an image brimming with familial bliss. A wholesome young couple gaze lovingly into each other's eyes as the man reverently holds a sonogram of an unborn child, with the caption, blazoned across the center, pronouncing "125 years ago it illuminated a room. Today, it illuminates a life." The image leaves no indication as to what this 'it' may be, leaving the viewer's mind to immediately race through a series of associations seeking what this source, so powerful as to illuminate life itself, could be: could it be love? The word of God? Democracy? The answer to this question is given in a smaller section of text at the bottom left hand of the ad, where we are informed that "Oil is more than just a source of fuel;" it is "an essential part of the material needed to develop cutting-edge technologies that make positive differences in our lives" (Cenovus 2016).

Other ads promote a similar message. One ad features an image of a lone para-athlete running down an idyllic country road with the tagline reading "90 years ago it ran a car. Today, it runs a marathon" (ibid), while yet another ad presents an image of what appears to be a young girl gazing down at a picture of the globe on a computer tablet with, superimposed over it, the words "100 years ago, it sparked an engine. Today, it sparks an imagination" (ibid). Again, in neither ad is any visual cue given as to what 'it' is.[4] The only clue we are given to its identity is once again the text in much smaller print on the bottom left hand side, where the campaign's slogan is repeated: "Oil is more than just a source of fuel."

The text of these ads is straightforward and uncontroversial, even a little banal. It is an incontrovertible matter of fact that oil is not just used as a source of fuel; it is also an important material element in the manufacture of thousands of products from detergent, glue, fertilizer, and ear plugs, to touch screen technology, ultrasound equipment, and artificial limbs. The visual rhetoric of these ads, however, makes a far more tenuous and ethereal link between oil and the somewhat more intangible, ineffable qualities of motherhood, imagination, courage, and even the human spirit, suggesting that oil is at the source of such qualities and enjoys a mysterious affective connection. In other words, oil is presented in these ads as the object cause of desire or *objet petit a'*. It is more than just fuel. In fact, oil is more than just oil. It possesses an indefinable, sublime joyous quality beyond the means of mere language to express it.

Oil is similarly presented as the elusive object of desire in EthicalOil.org's media campaign, although in this case oil is linked not to master-signifiers and ideals of parenthood and the human spirit but to social justice, human rights, democracy, and cultural tolerance.[5] In 2011, the newly created EthicalOil.org website and institute, inspired by Ezra Levant's book of the same name, started a media campaign, including billboards and television commercials. Drawing on Levant's argument that the oil from the oil sands is in fact ethical in that it is produced in a country with a far higher reputation for human rights, cultural tolerance and gender equality than those of other oil producing nations, the campaign reproduces Levant's binary division between 'ethical oil' and "conflict oil" in a series of billboard ads, in which ethical oil produced by Canada is paired with images of social inclusion, democracy, and justice, while 'conflict oil' from non-Western countries is paired with disturbing images of injustice, intolerance, violence, and social exclusion.

Neither the Ethical Oil campaign nor Levant's book seek to justify their ascription of the term 'ethical' to Canadian oil by way of any appeal to ethical theory. Nor do they provide any underlying sociopolitical and cultural context to the link between oil production and such disparate issues as political, economic, and gender inequality. Both are content to appeal to entrenched xenophobic stereotypes and prejudices operative in Canadian society, which link "Canada" to progressive ideals of social justice, democracy, gender equality, and multiculturalism while lumping together very different non-Western societies under the category of unenlightened savagery. What is significant, however, is the way this campaign links oil from the oil sands, suggesting an underlying mysterious and unexplained linkage between it and the propagation of democracy, multiculturalism, feminism, and social justice. By symbolically coupling the oil sands to images of gender equality, freedom, and social inclusivity, these ads promote the impression that oil is in some sense responsible for these qualities, and that production and consumption of oil from the oil sands somehow makes us as consumers and Canadians more ethical, more just, and more inclusive. These ads, therefore, employ a fantastic logic to suggest that there is a mysterious, elusive quality in oil from the oil sands, the *objet petit a'*, unlike oil produced elsewhere, whose possession will satiate our yearnings for social justice and inclusivity.

This logic is even employed to counter what is perhaps one of the biggest criticisms of the oil sands: its ecological destructiveness. For, if Levant and the Ethical Oil campaign rarely raise the issue of the environmental impact of the oil sands production, other ads from CAPP, Cenovus Energy, and Total Oil do, albeit in a very roundabout way, by almost entirely avoiding any direct mention of the negative environmental impact of the oil sands, while surreptitiously suggesting through means of visual and symbolic associations that oil sand production might actually be the key to achieving ecological harmony and improving the environment. Throughout many of these ads, for instance, we are presented with very little visual evidence of any environmental destruction whatsoever and only the slightest acknowledgment that there might be anything amiss: rather we are shown countless images of verdant forests and pastoral landscapes, inexplicably linking oil with the promise of a flourishing natural environment.

In one print ad produced by CAPP, for example, a headline over an image of a bucolic forest glade lit by a resplendent sunrise reads, "Energy the world needs. The approach Canadians expect." Given that the image contains no explicit visual cues to oil or oil production, one could easily be forgiven for assuming that the energy in question was solar. In fact, the only mention of either oil or the oil sands is in the URL for the campaign's website: OilSandsToday.ca. Moreover, while a smaller block of writing speaks of Canadians' expectation of a "constant effort to improve our environmental performance," there is little indication of any underlying environmental problem or issue that needs to be addressed or indeed that the oil sands itself might be responsible for any environmental damage. In fact, faced with an image of such dazzling natural splendor and bucolic harmony, there seems little to repair; the oil sands are actually part of the effort to improve this environment.

This link between environmental improvement and the oil sands is even more overtly made in another CAPP sponsored ad, where we are presented with the image of a clean cut, earnest-looking young man in the midst of a lush green evergreen forest with, superimposed upon it the headline, "I grew up on a farm. I know what it means to have the land restored" (Canadian Association of Petroleum Producers 2012).[6] From the image and the above lines, it almost appears that the oil sands are simply a gigantic tree farm operation or environmental restoration project. While great emphasis is placed on restoring the land, the ad is almost completely silent over why the land needed to be restored in the first place. In this sense, the identification of oil with environmental harmony and the refusal to make visible its actual environmental costs work as a form of discursive repression, masking or redirecting the viewer's attention away from potentially disturbing questions or associations. Thus, rather than see the oil sands as culpable in the environmental destruction, the oil sands are presented as part of the effort to improve nature.

Indeed, a print ad by Total Oil makes it appear that the oil sands are responsible for and the source of the natural environment. Under the banner reading "Commitment to the environment," we are presented with the image of a beautiful healthy evergreen forest mirrored below by the upside-down image of an oil refinery; the image thus presents the forest as literally growing out of or generated by oil production. Through the lens of the fundamental fantasy, therefore, what would seem to be one of the oil sand's biggest detractions, its environmental impact, is symbolically transformed into its biggest selling point, for by virtue of semantic and imagistic associations, the oil sands are transformed from "dirty oil" to, in the words of one of its promoters, "green oil" (Das 2009), the essential key to a clean, healthy environment.

This fantasy of oil, in which it is presented as the means by which to achieve indescribable personal fullness, and social, political, and ecological harmony, reaches its apotheosis and perhaps fullest expression in Suncor's "What Yes can Do?" television ad, where, over with the requisite montages of images of epic mountain ranges, verdant boreal forest, and dynamic high-tech cityscapes populated by upbeat people brimming with barely contained energy and enthusiasm, a voice assures us that:

> Ours is a world of opportunity, a world of challenges, along with the energy that makes lives easier; the energy that creates solutions. We need the energy to always ask is there a better way to get things done? Can we learn, teach and listen and hear everyone's points of view? Can we do the remarkable and yet still celebrate the everyday?

> Can we pioneer, innovate and renew? Can we put our energy into high-tech cities and still live as neighbors in all the places we call home? Are there ways to do more with less so that everyone can benefit? Can we hold onto the things we value in a world that is changing fast? Can the Canada we build today be a blueprint for tomorrow's world? These questions we ask every single day in playing our part in shaping the world we share. Our answer is yes! These things can be done, will be done, are being done right now. Together let's see what yes can do! (Suncor Energy 2016)

Here, the development of the oil sands, while not even overtly mentioned (the only hint that it might be directly involved is a few pictures of an oil refinery and a SAGD facility), is presented as the key to a golden world of social, political, and ecological prosperity, for according to the ad's fantasy all social discord and environmental damage will be healed and resolved thanks to the miraculous mediation of oil, and the social body, environment, and ourselves will be made whole and full. In this utopian future, we will have a world where everybody wins and is possessed with glowing vigor, and we will have high-tech energy-intensive cities without sacrificing pristine wildernesses or the health of the environment. A joyous world of total social and ecological harmony awaits: we just have to say "yes!" to oil. Indeed, faced with such overpowering and boundless optimism and a glowing, joyous picture of a future seemly devoid of any flaw or fault, it is hard to know why anybody would say no. Who could say "no" to a world in which all contradictions and conflicts were resolved and where we can have everything we could ever imagine with no downside? Within the logic of the fundamental fantasy, the obvious answer is the obscene other.

Green Grinches and the Obscene Other

Despite the beatified visions of wholeness promised by such fantasies, such projects never manage to provide the promised fullness. Frequently, this inability of the fetish to produce total enjoyment fuels a paranoid fantasy that postulates that this lack of promised fullness is due to the fact that it has been stolen by the obscene other. Explanations of social disorder and discontent, and failure to achieve the full jouissance promised by the fetish, are traced to the existence of what the Lacanian theorist Yannis Stravrakakis refers to as the obscene other, who is secretly scheming to steal or destroy the community's jouissance.

This frame is evident in the way proponents of oil sands development characterize their opponents, particularly environmentalists. For aside from the frequent accusations of irrationality leveled at environmentalists (a charge that seems to stem in large part from the fact that, as those advocating checks on the unhindered running of the market, how can they not be irrational?), a recurring theme among oil sands proponents is that environmentalists are kill-joys and attempting to steal or subvert Canadian prosperity and hence enjoyment or *jouissance*.

In the *Oilweek* March 2011 cover article on the environmental opposition to the oilsands, for instance, Oilweek's then chief editor Dale Lunan charged environmentalists with being not just simply "irrational," "mean-spirited" ecoterrorists but also "Green Grinches" (Lunan 2011, 22–23). A well-known character from children's fiction, the Grinch has become synonymous with an individual whose only pleasure is derived from destroying other people's merriment and happiness. In other words, Lunan is implying that environmentalists are motivated by little more than an intrinsic desire not only to steal but also to destroy the *jouissance* of oil. Similarly, Ezra Levant identifies environmentalists as one of a group of leftist organizations waging a "war on fun" (Levant 2005).

Conclusion

We have seen how the pro-oil sands PR campaign presents a fantasy in which oil is held up as the *objet petit a'* which will fill the constitutive lack in the subject and render both the social and natural world ecstatically whole, while critics are dismissed as malevolent kill-joys who threaten our collective joy. Numerous critics of oil sands development have accused these campaigns of being factually inaccurate and verging on blatant propaganda (Gailus 2012). Accurate though these criticisms may be, they fail to account for the level at which such rhetoric works and how it aims to persuade and enlist wider public support. For it is not enough to criticize these campaigns on factual grounds alone without acknowledging and investigating the deeper libidinal, affective, and symbolic levels upon which these ads draw. Lacan's understanding of rhetoric, in providing a conceptual account of the way in which identity, symbolism, and desire underscore discursive action and account for their persuasive power, does precisely this.

The question that remains, however, is what are we to do with such insights? Does Lacan's largely descriptive account of rhetorical persuasion merely amount to a form of highly intellectual but ultimately cynical acquiescence, implying that subjects are purely puppets helplessly under the lure of any clever marketing campaign, impassioned demagogue, or the hegemonic discourses of their culture, bereft of any ground or means of effectively confronting or challenging their powerful sway? Not at all! For we are never, according to Lacan, totally under the sway or dominance of any master-signifier or discourse, no matter how hegemonic, as the hold of even the most hegemonic of discourses upon the subject is never absolute or total. Behind the symbolic order or the Big Other, there is always a lack, and thus no discourse can provide full unicity or even the final word. It is upon this very recognition that the Lacanian theory, particularly in its therapeutic context, is based and which, I would argue, offers up the hope of possible effective rhetorical intervention.

One of the chief aims of Lacanian psychoanalysis is to challenge the hegemonic sway of these master narratives and linkages by getting the patient to realize that no symbol, no discourse, and no-thing will render them ecstatically whole and complete and that they must 'traverse the fantasy' by facing the fundamental incompleteness both at the heart of the symbolic order and their own lives. Yet this need not be a process of sullen resignation but rather of liberation. Part of this process consists in identifying the patient's master-signifiers and bringing to light how these master-signifiers function to subjugate the subject by repressing and eliding other alternatives. As Bruce Fink writes: "In the analytic situation a master-signifier presents itself as a dead–end, a stopping point ... (it is) a term, a word or phrase that puts an end to association, that grinds the patient's discourse to a halt" (1995, 135). Consequently, Lacanian analysis aims at freeing up the subject, clearing the blockages that freeze them in this discursive dead-end, challenging the dominance imposed by certain master-signifiers by bringing them into relation to other signifiers and repressed chains of meaning.

How then would this clinical approach work as a form of rhetorical intervention in respect to government and corporate sponsored rhetorical promotion of the oil sands? There is not the space here to offer anything other than a few tentative suggestions. We might begin, as is done in the clinical context, by taking their words at face value and repeating back to them their own speech, thereby calling them to work through the meaning of its enunciated content. We might ask Liz Hannah, for instance, "You said that you love oil. What did you mean by that exactly, or are you aware of what this seems to imply?" We might bring to light how the identification of certain master-signifiers with oil actually works to repress other less consoling and more painful patterns of meaning and signification, such as its incredible environmental costs. Finally, and perhaps most importantly, we could introduce new relationships between these master-signifiers and other signifying elements previously repressed or deemed unthinkable. We might, for instance, demonstrate how a master-signifier such as "Albertan" could also be linked to renewable energy. For, if in some sense these master-signifiers define us, it should not be forgotten that by the same token we define them.

Notes

1 *Jouissance*, a very crucial term in Lacan's thought, is uses in a number of ways. Though *jouissance* is often translated in English as "pleasure" or "enjoyment," this rather lukewarm term does not fully capture the "over the top" or "excessive" connotations that the word has in French. Indeed, in French *jouissance* connotes orgasm as well as pleasure and can be used to

indicate any sort of ecstatic experience where one feels the barriers between oneself and another are broken down or suspended. Certainly, it is this excessive sense that Lacan's usage frequently implies and in Seminar VII Lacan describes it not just as excessive pleasure but also "a superabundant vitality" (Lacan 1992, 298) or an excessive sense of fullness and complete absence of any lack. It is in this latter sense that the term will be used throughout this chapter.

2 Chaitin points out that for Lacan "the essence of metaphor is not, as tradition would have it, a matter of comparison or similarity but of identification" (Chaitin 2017, 687). Indeed, Lacan in Seminar VIII argues that all identificatory acts are in some sense a form of transference or a love relationship (Lacan 2015).

3 Lacan calls *objet petit a'* the small fragment of the real of jouissance, whose possession promises to provide the full enjoyment and wholeness lost to the subject. He also refers to it elsewhere as the object cause of desire or impossible object of desire (Lacan 1998).

4 This lack of any actual visual presentation of oil or bitumen is ubiquitous throughout the pro-oil sand media campaign. Indeed, I'm unaware of any example of pro-oil sands marketing in which either oil or the open pit bitumen mines are actually visually presented. This may be due to the fact that visually oil and bitumen are commonly perceived to be ugly and unattractive and thus actually visually presenting them would run the risk of puncturing the fantasy as it were. Moreover, not actually concretizing oil and referring to it simply by its name makes it easier for audience to conceive that perhaps behind such an abstract signifier there is indeed the ineffable jouissance of the *objet petit a'*.

5 See "Still Ethical Oil" in this volume for a more sustained discussion of this issue.

6 This is an interesting example of what Lacan terms the "subject supposed to know" where certain subjects are held up as having a direct relationship of knowledge to what these actual master-signifiers mean. Throughout the pro-oil sands promotional campaign, this figure of the subject supposed to know is regularly enlisted usually in the form of 'real' or 'ordinary' Albertan who testify to role of oil in bringing about greater prosperity and joy in their lives. See "'Know-Nothing Foreign Celebrity Millionaires': Celebrity, Authenticity, and the Sabotage of Civil Discourse in the Controversy of the Alberta Oil Sands" in this volume for a more sustained discussion of this.

References

Biesecker, B. 1998. "Rhetorical Studies and the New Psychoanalysis: What's the Real Problem? Or Framing the Problem of the Real." *Quarterly Journal of Speech*. 84: 222–259.

Canadian Association of Petroleum Producers. 2012. Accessed January 21, 2018. http://www.salmonguy.org/wp-content/uploads/2010/12/Oil-sands-ad.jpg

Cenovus. (August 29, 2016). *Cenovus Energy More than Just Fuel.* Accessed January 21, 2018. http://www.cenovus.com/news/more-than-fuel.html

Chaitin, G.D. 1997. *Rhetoric and Culture in Lacan*. Cambridge: Cambridge University Press.

Chaitin, G.D. 2017. "Rhetoric and Psychoanalysis." in *The Oxford Handbook of Rhetorical Studies*, edited by Michael J. MacDonald, 683–694. Oxford: Oxford University Press.

Das, S. 2009. *Green Oil*. Edmonton: Sextant.

Fink, B. 1995. *The Lacanian Subject: Between Language and Jouissance*. Princeton: Princeton Paperbacks.

Fink, B. 1997. *A Clinical Introduction to Lacanian Psychoanalysis: Theory and Technique*. Cambridge, MA: Harvard University Press.

Gailus, J. 2012. *Little Black Lies: Corporate and Political Spin in the Global War for Oil*. Victoria, Vancouver & Calgary: Rocky Mountain Books.

Guardian. August 16, 2016. *Oil Lobby Group Recruited Canadian Minister for Secret Strategy Meeting*. Retrieved from Guardian Unlimited: https://www.theguardian.com/environment/2015/may/28/oil-lobby-group-recruited-canadian-minister-for-secret-strategy-meeting

Hannah, L. 2016. *More 2 the Story: Why (and How) Cenovus Is Standing Up for Oil*. Accessed July 21, 2016. http://www.cenovus.com/news/speeches/2014/os101_speech.html

Kowalsky, N., & Hazula-Delay, R. 2015. "This is Oil Country: The Tar Sands and Jacques Ellul's Theory of Technology." *Environmental Ethics*, 75–97.

Lacan, J. 1992. *Seminar VII: The Ethics of Psychoanalysis*. Translated by Dennis Porter. New York: W. W. Norton.

Lacan, J. 1993. *Seminar III: The Psychoses*. Translated by Russell Grigg. New York: W. W. Norton.

Lacan, J. 1998a. *Seminar XI: Four Fundamental Concepts of Psychoanalysis*. Translated by Alan Sheridan. New York: W. W. Norton.

Lacan, J. 1998b. *Seminar XX: On Feminine Sexuality, the Limits of Love and Knowledge*. Translated by Bruce Fink. New York: W. W. Norton.

Lacan, J. 2006. *Écrits*. Translated by Bruce Fink. New York: W. W. Norton.

Lacan, J. 2007. *Seminar XVII The Other Side of Psychoanalysis*. Translated by Russell Grigg. New York: W. W. Norton.

Lacan, J. 2015. *Seminar VIII: Transference*. Translated by Bruce Fink. Cambridge: Polity.

Levant, E. 2005. *The War on Fun*. Calgary: Western Standard.

Lunan, D. March 2011. "What's in a Name?: Thorns by any other Names, Today's Green Grinches leave us a lot to Talk about." *Oilweek*, pp. 22–43.

Lundberg, C. 2012. *Lacan in Public: Psychoanalysis and the Science of Rhetoric*. Tuscaloosa: University of Alabama Press.

Morgan, G. September 19, 2010. *Leaders Must Counter Bogus Oil Sands Spin*. Retrieved from Globe and Mail Online https://www.theglobeandmail.com/report-on-business/rob-commentary/leaders-must-counter-bogus-oil-sands-spin/article4190330

Stastny, R. September 2013. "Changing the Message: How Cenovus and Others are Helping Counter Anti-oilsands Sentiments." *Oilweek*, pp. 22–28.

Stavrakakis, Y. 2007. *The Lacanian Left: Psychoanalysis, Theory, Politics*. Edinburgh: Edinburgh University Press.

Suncor Energy. 2016. *Suncor – What Yes Can Do*. Accessed January 21, 2018. https://www.youtube.com/watch?v=JtYJDxy2-SI

13 "Know-Nothing Foreign Celebrity Millionaires"

Celebrity, Authenticity, and the Sabotage of Civil Discourse in the Controversy of the Alberta Oil Sands

John Moffatt, Corey Owen, Debora Rolfes and Jeanie Wills

An Anecdote from the Front Lines of the Culture Wars

On any morning between 2011 and 2014, two Canadians open their morning newspapers. One lives in Fort McMurray, Alberta, or perhaps Calgary or Edmonton; they (and/or members of their family) are employed in the oil industry and believe that the oil sands are central to Alberta's and Canada's prosperity. The other may live in one of Alberta's cities, but for our purposes we may find it less ambiguous to imagine them in Vancouver or Toronto, and not in the employ of the oil industry.

Over the first coffee of the day, our readers scan the national news in the paper. They may learn that popular Canadian musician Neil Young, or American actor Leonardo DiCaprio, or South African Archbishop Desmond Tutu has described the oil sands as an environmental disaster, comparing it, as Neil Young did on Monday, September 9, 2013, to Hiroshima as a willful exercise in destruction, the effects of which will be felt in air and water pollution, global warming, and the erosion of First Nations sovereignty, to name but a few areas.

Turning to the op-ed pages, our readers may encounter voices in defense of the oil sands. Pundits as diverse as Ezra Levant and Rex Murphy return the fire, ridiculing the ignorance of wealthy celebrity environmental advocates, and the naivete of their supporters, none of whom can distinguish between celebrity and expertise, between the function of the entertainer and that of the advocate.

Stereotyping would have us assume that reader A in "Fort Mac" would simmer through the testimony of Young, DiCaprio, Tutu et al. in various stages of agitation, and nod in agreement at the responses of Levant, Murphy and company. Reader B in Vancouver would digest the observations of the celebrities with righteous approbation, and dismiss their opponents as troglodytic neocons motivated by the journalistic equivalent of road rage.

If A and B are on Facebook, perhaps they will encounter each other in cyberspace and consecrate part of their day to trading barbs like "Cuck" and "Neanderthal," while exchanging charges of ignorance and hypocrisy.

The scenario is generalized, but not grossly exaggerated, and is a reasonable snapshot of where the public controversy over Alberta's oil sands has bogged down for years, with no obvious way out of the impasse; it could serve as a representative anecdote (Burke 1969, 59) for the discursive gridlock containing the essential conflicting elements: "conservative" vs. "liberal"; rural vs. urban; Western vs. "Eastern" (with places like Vancouver perceived as liberal and urban and therefore consubstantial with the East rather than with the conservative, rural Prairies, and BC interior); blue-collar, working Canadians vs. elites (including experts, artists, and celebrities). On either side, rhetorical activity centers on attacking opponents as inauthentic; this inauthenticity frames opponents' arguments as invalid, which makes debate unnecessary, and thus renders the ideal of creating a public space for the solving of problems undesirable.

Warriors, Superheroes and Mudslinging over Dirty Oil

This situation represents the danger of the stalemate for public discourse in Canada. The rhetors engage in what Maurice Charland (1987, 137–138), following Louis Althusser, calls the interpellation of an audience, "the process of inscribing subjects into ideology" (138), which occurs when a discourse "recruits" a subject (cf. Althusser 1971, 174), calling upon that subject in such a way that they are "under some constraint to respond" (Charland 1987, 138/149 n 22). This interpellation is characterized, however, by discrepancy between the construction of an engaged audience of responsible/concerned citizens whose interests the public figures are understood to represent, and a covert or implicit address to an "ideal" audience, Black's "Second Persona" (Black 1970, 111), whose responsivity to the message depends on the maintenance of an attitude toward the conflict which embraces an immaturity of perspective as a point of identity. In an act of what Burke calls *secular prayer*, the audience is "coached" (1984a, 322) to respond to the conflict in a childlike manner in which they are not prepared to deal with the "forensic," the complex, negotiated engagement which Burke identifies with discursive maturity. (1984a, 254–256). Consequently, rhetors on both sides need to construct an ethos which empowers them to speak (ostensibly) on behalf of "ordinary" citizens. At the same time, that ethos makes those citizens an unreflective cheering section for their "heroic" combatants, rather than engaged participants in a debate to generate a solution. The interpellation corresponds to what Burke, using terminology derived from Thorstein Veblen, calls the audience's "trained incapacity" (cf. 1984b, 7) to engage with complexity. Audiences of these messages are constructed by the discourse as incapable of addressing the complexity of the issue in favor of a "naïve heroism" (1984a, 255) in which conflict is carried out by proxies. The rhetors position themselves in their role as performers as the event itself, heroes battling evil on behalf of a helpless, inarticulate citizenry.

While the sides seem opposed, we argue that the rhetors construct their audiences in similar ways. These discursive practices both perpetuate conflict and perform an entertainment function, coaching audiences to "buy into" the polarization without attempting to move the stagnant wrangle to a deliberative and reasonable discussion that seeks solutions through mature, reasoned public debate that sociologist Jürgen Habermas (1989, 176) associates with collective problem-solving in a functioning public sphere.

Dysfunctional Communication and the Heroic Struggle over Exigence in the Oil Sands Conflict

Bitzer tells us in "Functional Communication" that rhetorical communication is an attempt to bring about "harmonious adjustment" (1980, 29). Given the acrimonious tone of the debate and the repeated failure to engage at critical points of debate (stasis), it seems clear that this discourse is not intended to bring about agreement on the sustainability of the oil sands. On the contrary, the discourse serves two functions:

- establishing ethos for the speaker—the right to speak
- and establishing the lack of ethos in others—the need to remain silent.

Instead of bridging contrary positions, the discourse of the pundits and of the celebrities functions as rhetorical self-talk. While throwing non-productive invective at the other side of the oil sands issue, these discourses engage and support the mental landscape of the audience on the speaker's own side.

Bitzer states that speakers must convince an audience that the issue addressed by the discourse is real and also persuade the audience that it has an interest in that issue. Analysis of the discourses offered in this debate show that, often, the facts presented and the persuasion toward an *interest* are directed at the audience who already supports the position of the speaker.

For example, in a September 14, 2014 editorial in the *Financial Post*, Rex Murphy comments on Neil Young's "Honour the Treaties" tour and, specifically, on Young's comparison of Fort McMurray to Hiroshima. Ostensibly, Murphy's purpose is to refute the resemblance of oil sands territory to the devastated Japanese city. However, a closer look at the facts that Murphy offers and the interest that he assumes his audience has in the issue shows that he has no intention to engage those who might be swayed by Young's pronouncement. He intends to discredit Young as a speaker and so render irrelevant any arguments the celebrity makes. Murphy begins with an ironic reference to Young's past as a miner; Young's attempt to strike a heart of gold does not qualify as experience in the mining and natural resources field. The edge to this comment will signal to anyone sympathetic to Young's position that the following is not meant to sway them; the pro-oil sands supporters, on the other hand, will recognize what Black calls the symptomatic function of language (1970, 110). It is indisputable that composing a lyrical analogy comparing the search for love to the search for precious natural resources does not make one an expert in mining. Murphy makes this fact his starting point to embed a "verbal token of ideology" that "should be viewed as expressing a vector of influence" (Black 1970, 113) that is an ideological indicator of whom he believes he is speaking to. And what does Murphy suggest is the audience's interest in Young's analogy? Murphy expands Young's reference to the devastation of both Hiroshima and the area affected by the oil sands to include the people of Fort McMurray. It isn't just the environment that is devastated: "Does he really mean that he sees Fort McMurray and its citizens as somehow equivalent to the result of a war-ending atomic detonation and the instantaneous killing of tens of thousands?" By expanding (and misreading) Young's remarks to include the people employed in and serving the oil industry, Murphy tells his readers that they have an *interest* in the *fact* that an inexperienced celebrity is insulting (and threatening) the people of Fort McMurray; he tells them that they should feel threatened and respond with civic pride in the face of this attack.

The editorial discourse of pundits is not functioning to contribute to the understanding of opposite views. While Murphy points out Young's lack of qualifications, he makes no attempt to state his own qualifications. But the discourse itself acts as a display of Murphy's qualifications as superhero protector. This protector is one who rescues an innocent community, victimized by an evil enemy (who can only be defeated by the hero who acts outside the conventions of society). Murphy's argument is a demonstration of his power as the hero who is not hobbled by convention. And, by implication, his audience becomes the victims saved. The discourse of the pundit functions epideictically, speaking to the converted and constructing the situation as one in which the speaker is cast as the defender of this audience. The "heroic" combatants ensure that the audiences do not engage in fruitful discussion but are, instead, stalled and mired in the polarized name-calling.

The Avoidance of Stasis in the Public Discourse about the Oil Sands

In the controversy about the development of the oil sands, stasis theory reveals the various strategies and procedures pundits on both sides of the issue use to avoid meaningful public debate. Stasis theory asks arguers to discuss:

- The facts of a situation
- The meaning or nature of the issue (by definition strategies)
- The quality (or the significance of the issue)
- The plan of action (the next steps in policy).

Public voices in the controversy in the Alberta oil sands do their best to avoid discussing these issues, resulting in a paralysis in debate.

One of the techniques pundits use to avoid creating a public space for actual debate is the refusal to engage debates at the appropriate points of stasis. As Lawrence Prelli observes,

> In their advocacies rhetors encounter "contrary motions." When rhetors encounter contrary motions, a point of collision arises between disparate arguments when a line of argument is disturbed by a contrary argument. Advocates then make their stands relative to one another, at this point of *stasis* or at successive points of *stasis*. (1989, 45)

Points of stasis are thus issues in a debate that must be resolved, through rhetoric, for a debate to progress. In classical rhetoric, a point of stasis can pertain to conjecture (did something happen?), definition (what sort of thing happened?), quality (is such a thing harmful or beneficial?), and procedure (what action should be taken?), and an argument can proceed from any of these points, provided that the parties involved agree on the previous points.

With respect to the effects of the oil sands, a stasis procedure might flow in the following fashion:

1 Has the mining of the oil sands polluted the environment? (conjecture);
2 How do we define pollution of the environment? (definition);
3 Is such pollution significantly harmful? (quality);
4 Should we further regulate the industry, or simply allow it to continue with current regulation? (procedure).

Agreement on each point of stasis is important for the advancement of an argument: "Those rhetors who clearly and effectively address genuine points of *stasis* are more likely to resolve impasses and thereby induce favorable verdicts from audiences" (Prelli 1989, 46). In essence, the failure to advance an argument through addressing an appropriate stasis point is characteristic of demagoguery, which aims to end debate by inciting emotions.

The public discourses on the harms and benefits of the oil sands typically address three separate issues: the environmental effects, the social effects, and the financial effects. In such a debate, the question of the effects of oil sands mining on the environment should take priority. In other words, the question of procedure—that is, the question of whether we should continue to profit from oil sands mining according to current guidelines—can be pursued only if environmental concerns are thoughtfully addressed. As both the pundits who celebrate and environmentalists who attack the oil sands suggest, the environmental effects of the continued mining of the oil sands is ultimately a scientific discourse, and the scientific method is the appropriate approach for investigating the issue at the primary point of stasis. Yet, the responses from the pundits do not address environmental concerns, as if doing so would validate such concerns.

Although the question of environmental harms must be resolved before the debate can progress, the failure of critics of the oil sands to address the economic concerns of those whose livelihood relies on the industry is also a failure to address an essential stasis point, because oil sands employees and proponents either consider the environmental question to be resolved already, or because they consider short-term economic gains to have priority over projected long-term environmental damage. Thus, in addressing such a public, opponents to the oil sands need to emphasize the seriousness of the environmental damage while considering the economic effect the transformation of Alberta's economy would have on those who earn their living through the industry. Furthermore, because of the strong sense of identification experienced by oil field workers and their communities with the oil industry, those who work in the industry or live in communities whose economy is supported by the industry respond to an attack on the industry as though it were a personal attack. The consistent avoidance of establishing stasis is thus an attempt by each side to avoid valorizing the concerns of the other.

During the time frame we investigated (2011–2014), pundits, politicians, and industry representatives avoided addressing stasis points through the following five maneuvers: (1) attacking the ethos of celebrity critics while ignoring the question of ecological impact; (2) celebrating the oil sands without addressing their ecological impact; (3) briefly—yet dismissively—acknowledging their ecological impact while emphasizing the benefits they provide; (4) taking personal offense at the criticism of the oil sands; and (5) framing ecological concerns as anti-scientific.

Attacking Ethos of Celebrity to Silence Opposition

The main method oil sands advocates use to dismiss critics is casting doubt on their authenticity and engaging in *ad hominem* attacks designed to undermine their ethos. The most common form of *ad hominem* argument used by proponents of the oil sands and Keystone pipeline is *tu quoque* ("you too"), a fallacy that undermines the ethos of a rhetor by suggesting that the rhetor is guilty of the same behavior they are criticizing.

Many editorialists, politicians, and corporate representatives attack the ethos of celebrity critics by commenting on their high oil consumption and carbon footprint. Deliberately missing the point of a song he references, Rex Murphy, for example, writes,

> Neil Young's life is as oil-soaked and as oil-ripe as that of any of the rest of us. . . . He lives in cloistered fame because of the society fuelled by oil that supports him. There's quite a bit of hypocrisy, it turns out, in Neil Young's heart of gold. (Murphy 14 Sept. 2013)

Former Alberta Premier Alison Redford states, "I've got to question how people who are using energy, flying on planes, can make these sorts of comments and assume that they're going to have any credibility" (Wood September 18, 2013). Jason MacDonald, a former spokesperson for former Prime Minister Stephen Harper, states, "Even the lifestyle of a rock star relies, to some degree, on the resources developed by thousands of hard-working Canadians every day" (Lendon January 14, 2014). In an *Edmonton Journal* article dated August 29, 2014, G. Lamphier reflects on the large estates owned by Leonardo DiCaprio, and concludes, "I . . . resent the hypocrisy displayed by celebs like DiCaprio, who profess concern about the planet while refusing to impose restrictions on their own opulent lifestyles" (Lamphier August 26, 2014). Editorials replace reasoned objections with such *ad hominem* attacks.

Celebrities' criticisms are also rejected due to the nature of their profession as actors or musicians. In the *National Post* on January 16, 2014, Brian Ferguson, president and chief executive of *Cenovus*, is quoted:

> In Hollywood, everything is black and white, good or evil. It makes for a compelling story, but the real world doesn't work that way. And when it comes to energy, Hollywood stereotypes are unhelpful and often dead wrong. So it's time to inject a little reality into the energy debate. (Hussain)

According to this characterization, the concern for the ecological effects of the oil sands is the result of the simple psychology of Hollywood. Stasis theory requires that their opponents refute their specific claims, rather than simply attempt to sabotage their ethos.

At the heart of the debate about the oil sands is the struggle to establish an ethos of authenticity. According to Roger Davis Gratchet, "authenticity" is constituted through rhetorical practices. Its meaning is "often slippery and difficult to pin down," yet it is "always grounded in a given community's understanding of the term;" it is ambiguous, and this ambiguity "allows 'authenticity' to do the complex rhetorical work it does"—in essence, the concept is "negotiable, complex, changing, and wrapped up in symbolic struggle" (2011, 7). Authenticity is desirable—and useful in persuasion.

One of the fundamental challenges of the pundit, that is, of one who is outside of a certain community but presumes to speak on behalf of that community, is the need to establish authenticity that is recognized by the community. As Gratchet notes, theorists often discuss authenticity in its binary relationship with inauthenticity: "The concept of authenticity, whatever a given group of people come to understand it to be, requires the concomitant category of inauthenticity to legitimate it" (14). Pundits often portray themselves as righteously indignant commentators.

When rhetors are unable to project a persona the audience would regard as authentic, they shift the focus to the perceived inauthenticity of the opponent, and thereby enthymematically prompt the audience to regard them as authentic. Rex Murphy and Ezra Levant claim authenticity by denying the authenticity of others. Murphy aggressively interrogates the authenticity of Neil Young, a Canadian musician whose ethos projects authenticity to his legions of fans, and Levant raises questions about the authenticity of Archbishop Desmond Tutu, whom he portrays as "a sequel to the last know-nothing foreign celebrity millionaire to jet in and trash-talk us this year, namely Neil Young," who "for a presumed six-figure speaking fee . . . rent[s] out his reputation on demand" (Levant June 3, 2014). Both pundits act as debunkers,[1] and as debunkers they suggest that they are more authentic than those celebrities.

To create a contrast to the inauthenticity of the celebrities, pundits appeal to the authenticity of the working-class values of their audience. Murphy presents himself as a defender of the authenticity of the workers in Fort McMurray, whom he presumes Young has insulted:

> How superior Neil Young must feel. How high on the cloud of his own inflated esteem. How much better he is than the people of Fort McMurray, the workers and their families, how much better than those who keep the oil companies operating, do the building, handle the great equipment. (Murphy 14 Sept. 2013)

Murphy constructs the musician as a villain who harasses the people for egotistical purposes, and thus presents himself as the warrior-protector of this vulnerable group of common people.

Levant describes Archbishop Tutu's visit to Fort McMurray as the cleric blaming the oil sands for climate change, which Tutu describes as "the moral struggle that will define this century;" Levant responds to the charge, "Saying that puts us on par with what Tutu would likely say was the moral crime he knew best—apartheid" (Levant June 3, 2014). Throughout the article, Levant expresses solidarity with the oilfield workers of Fort McMurray through the use of the first-person plural pronoun: "Is this how Tutu repays us—by comparing us to racists, calling us filth?" (Levant June 3, 2014). Both of these responses strategically conflate the mining industry with the citizens of Fort McMurray, a discourse of authenticity that naturalizes the oil industry by asserting continuity between it and the citizens it employs. Young also contributes to this battle for authenticity:

> Those people who are the Fort McMurray people, either they're oil people or they're occupied by oil people. So of course they're going to be upset because I just said we don't want that. It's not good for our families. (Bains 10 Nov. 2014)

Here, Young questions the authenticity of those who defend the oil sands, while defending his own heroic authenticity as the essence of Canadianness: "There are some people who say that I'm not a true Canadian because I roam the earth. To me that's the most Canadian thing to do is roam the earth" (Bains November 10, 2014). The pundits, as well as the celebrities, establish their own authentic ethos through denying that of their opponents.

Celebrating the Oil Sands

Another approach that advocates take to avoid meaningful public discussion is to avoid addressing the ecological anxieties of critics and instead focus on the economic benefit of the oil sands. Chinta Puxley quotes Shawn Howard, a spokesman for TransCanada:

> It's unfortunate that people like Mr. Young want to mislead people about where Canadian oil goes and the benefits it creates . . . It has helped him create records and CDs, allows his tour buses to run, airplanes to fly . . . . (Puxley 16 Jan. 2014).

M.R. Coutu writes,

> For more than 2,000 years, human progress has been driven by our ability to harness and use energy. But not just any energy can power our modern civilization. It has to be affordable, plentiful, reliable and, yes, it should be produced in a way that mitigates environmental and social impacts. Oilsands [sic] meets the test.

After dismissing other sources of energy, he concludes: "Over time, we've become complacent to the fact that our use of oil has made life on this planet better for human beings—we live longer, safer, healthier, and more productive lives" (Coutu October 11, 2013). Coutu's not-so-epic sweep of the history of progress locates the development and maintenance of the modern world in oil, and one wonders whether he has read the scientific literature supporting current environmental standards with the same uncritical eye. Hussain's editorial quotes Russ Girling, CEO of TransCanada, who claims that "oil sands critics have erroneously labelled the oil sands as the world's largest carbon dioxide problem," and concludes, "If we get it right, this industry can be the single greatest drive [sic] of the Canadian economy" (Hussain January 16, 2014). Such epideictic rhetoric either ignores the charge that oil sands mining contributes significantly to various types of environmental degradation or dismisses the charge and alleges that those who express such concerns do not understand how the oil sands contribute to the production of goods and services and the local economy.

Briefly yet Dismissively Acknowledging Ecology

A few commentators make brief concessions to concerns about environmental harms while overshadowing concerns with statements about the economic benefits of such mining.

In a *Globe and Mail Press* article, Camille Bains writes, "Dave Collyer, president of the Canadian Association of Petroleum Producers, has said that while the industry needs to make environmental improvements, Young has used his rock-star status to mischaracterize oil sands development" (Bains November 10, 2014). Alison Redford, Alberta's former Premier said, "Alberta's oil sands development does impact the environment, but the province has come far in exploring new technologies such as carbon capture" ("Nothing New" September 18, 2013). G. Lamphier, who devotes much of his August 26, 2014 article to attacking the ethos of Leonardo DiCaprio, and refrains from commenting on the financial benefits of the oil sands, also acknowledges the legitimacy of environmental concerns related to the oil sands: "That's not to say the oil sands industry shouldn't do a better job addressing its own environmental issues. Criticism in this regard is justified, constructive and in many cases deserved" (Lamphier); nevertheless, his article trivializes environmental concerns about the oil sands by focusing only on its very small contribution to global carbon emissions. Another article frames its argument as though it were simply stating objective facts: "The simple facts, however, are these: Canada is a resource-rich country that needs to develop and export its products. Surface mining for oil is a dirty business, but it won't last forever and damaged land will eventually be reclaimed" ("Celebrity Activism" January 15, 2014). While these advocates for the oil sands ostensibly show environmental concern, by maintaining the emphasis on the prosperity derived from the natural resource, they imply that such environmental concerns must be subjugated to the needs of industry and the economy.

Both of the above strategies for avoiding stasis celebrate the wealth that the oil sands have created and treat environmental concerns as though they are a luxury created by the affluence the industry has afforded its critics, who are presented as extremists. For example, an editorial published on January 15, 2014 states, "Much [damaged land] has been [reclaimed], although not at a pace that satisfies environmentalists, who believe nothing can compensate for immediate damage" ("Celebrity Activism"). Murphy writes, ". . . there must be no end of industrial projects all over the world that do not rise to [Young's] standards of environmental aesthetics" (September 14, 2013), and just suggests that Young's concerns about pollution are merely aesthetic issues. Environmentalists are dismissed as extremists who cannot be satisfied, even when the pundits make concessions to environment concerns.

Taking Personal Offense at the Criticism of the Oil Sands

Pundits, editorialists, and interviewees deliberately or unintentionally misinterpret and take personal offense to poorly articulated criticisms of the environmental damage caused by mining.

After Neil Young compared Fort McMurray to Hiroshima, the musician received responses from angered Albertans. Melissa Blake, mayor of the regional municipality that includes Fort McMurray, states,

> When people say it's a wasteland, it really and truly isn't . . . When it comes to the community of Fort McMurray, you're overwhelmed frankly by the beauty of it. You've got an incredible boreal environment that's all around you. (Mertl 10 Sept. 2013)

Although she acknowledges that the area north of the city "will draw your attention" because of the "large chunks of land" devoted to mining, her interpretation of Young as though he were simply comparing the city of Fort McMurray to Hiroshima is a characteristic response to the musician's imprecise terminology. A similar sentiment appears in Camille Bains' article, which states, "'All our residents are outraged by the negative comments about our beautiful community,' said Fort McMurray resident Sheila Chartrand, who co-owns a local catering service with her husband Real in Fort McMurray . . . ."; the article also includes a Tweet from Kent MacKenzie. Bain underscores MacKenzie's authenticity by including the observation that he was "was born and raised on the prairies, according to his profile" (Bains November 10, 2014). As discussed above, Rex Murphy also takes advantage of the ambiguity of Young's terminology to dismiss his environmental concerns. He asks, rhetorically, "What does he mean here? Does he really mean that he sees Fort McMurray and its citizens as somehow equivalent to the result of a war-ending atomic detonation . . .?" (Murphy September 14, 2013). Instead of pondering the obvious answer, though, Murphy pursues a course of relentless literalism: "Only a mind-yodelling vacuous lyricist could dredge up this tasteless analogy—comparing a Canadian city and its inhabitants with a radioactive ruin" (Murphy). The outrage that these articles express effectively deflects attention from the question of environmental damage to the suggestion that Neil Young has lost touch with reality.

Framing Ecological Concerns as Anti-Scientific

Another tactic politicians, pundits, and editorialists use to dismiss concerns about the environmental effects of the oil sands is the accusation of what Leah Ceccarelli might regard as a manufactured scientific controversy. According to Ceccarelli, "A scientific controversy is 'manufactured' in the public sphere when an arguer announces that there is actually an ongoing scientific debate in the technical sphere about a matter for which there is actually an overwhelming scientific consensus" (2011, 196). While the work of Oreskes and Conway (2010), and of Ceccarelli, has argued that Global Warming Skepticism is a paradigmatic example of a manufactured controversy (in that proponents of the oil industry have emphasized uncertainty about the causes of global warning, even though there is a strong consensus in the scientific community), proponents of the oil sands accuse opponents of failing to recognize the scientific consensus.

An article published in the *Edmonton Journal* quotes former Alberta Energy Minister Ken Hughes, who comments on Robert Redford's video criticizing the oil sands: "These [celebrity commentaries] are not helpful to having an informed debate. They're not based on facts, they're not based on science" (Wood, September 17, 2013, "Iconic Actor"). Another article quotes Catherine Swift, the head of the Canadian Federation of Independent Business, who refers to Young as the "'Jenny McCarthy' of the 'anti-economic success anti-well-paying jobs movement'" ("Neil Young Concludes," January 19, 2014), thereby framing Young's environmental activism as resulting from the same sort of manufactured controversy as McCarthy's vaccine concerns. Also, Coutu writes, "Canada's oilsands are produced under world class environmental, social and regulatory standards, a fact supported by credible independent and scientific studies" (Coutu), a statement that is contradicted even by supporters of the oil sands such as G. Lamphier and David Collyer, who acknowledge the need for improvements. All of these proponents suggest that oil sands development is not a serious threat to the environment, and that those who think that it is have succumbed to anti-scientific celebrity alarmism that aims simply to enhance the public profile of the celebrity activists. Ultimately, the implication of such discourses is that regulatory agencies have, through adequate science, anticipated and monitored the effect of the extraction process on the environment, and that to oppose the environmental damage caused by the industry is both anti-scientific and anti-democratic, since a democratically elected government "spelled out clearly before it the environmental risks and uncertainties of an oil sands project, in all its gory detail, and decided it was worth it" (Leach January 15, 2014).

The framing of scientific research also contributes to this tactic for dismissing environmental concerns. In particular, a January 18, 2014 editorial challenges the assertion that the mining of the oil sands is responsible for the increased rates of cancer in Fort Chipewyan and claims that there is no connection between the oil sands and cancer:

> As for Young's false claims about the oilsands and cancer, that claim was already debunked by the Royal Society expert panel in 2010 . . . . Since 2010, some have attempted to discredit the report, but we will stick with a comprehensive scientific assessment from well-informed and objective scientists. ("Neil Young's Fantasy World")

This approach cherry-picks the Royal Society's observation that "there is no credible evidence of environmental contaminant exposures from oil sands reaching Fort Chipewyan at levels expected to cause elevated human cancer rates" (Gosselin et al. 2010, "Report Findings in Brief") but ignores the following line which states that "more monitoring focused on human contaminant exposures is needed to address First Nation and community concerns" and a host of recommendations, to suggest that there is nothing to debate. Otherwise put, the editorialist cites the 2010 study as conclusive, and ridicules those who, following the appropriate protocols of the scientific method, attempt to question the reliability of the report's findings, by accusing such investigators of being ignorant and partisan.

The analysis of articles shows the lack of engagement at points of stasis, demonstrating that there is no dialogue between opposing sides of the tar sands debate. However, the articles do help us understand how two opposing audiences are being called into being.

Of Oil and Actors

In his essay "The Second Persona," Black argues that discourse contains signs of both who the speaker believes his or her audience is and of who the author believes they should become. The arguments presented in the discourse and, just as importantly, the words used to formulate those arguments suggest an ideal audience for that discourse. This ideal audience (or auditor, to use Black's term) shares the worldview implied by the language choices and is influenced to embrace that ideology. Analysis of the ideological stances implied by the discourses of both pundits and celebrities reveals that speakers anticipate and facilitate an audience who is content to rest in a state of perpetual immaturity, gratefully accepting the intervention of mythic superheroes who fight on their behalf. Postman and Boorstin show that the ideology calls into being an audience looking for entertainment; Jewett and Lawrence help us identify what kind of entertainment the pundits and celebrities have on offer, influencing the audience to accept a passive, immature, and impotent role.

Neil Postman's *Amusing Ourselves to Death* notes that we are conditioned to look for entertainment in all of our communication sources including newspapers, which offer a variety of distractions between their covers, from comics and crosswords to sports and entertainment. Postman claims that "information derives its importance from the possibilities of action" (1985, 68). The culture wars about the meaning of Alberta's oil sands, which have played out in these artefacts, are a form of "information glut," in Postman's terms, in that residents of Alberta are barraged by these discourses every day. At the same time, Albertans are "faced with the problem of a diminished social and political potency" (68) that reduces the controversy to entertainment. The discourses do not encourage public debate but instead polarize discussions. The quarrels between pundits and celebrities are sensational and fragmented, conditions that Postman notes lead to news taking "the form of slogans, to be noted with excitement, to be forgotten with dispatch" (70). These discourses seem to exist for the public's amusement and pleasure, but not as a call to political or social action in the public sphere.

Both pundits and celebrities foil civil discourse that aims to solve a problem, in part because they can't agree on the problem (as our earlier stasis analysis shows). However, the wrangle does increase readership by creating what Daniel Boorstin calls "pseudo-events," which he defines as a "new kind of synthetic novelty which has flooded our experience" (1992, 9). Boorstin argues that modern attitudes expect that newspapers will "provide synthetic happening to make up for the lack of spontaneous events," noting that we seem to require that "something be fabricated to make up for the world's deficiency" (9). Boorstin outlines four characteristics of the pseudo-event, saying it is planned, planted, or incited; it is "planted primarily for the immediate purpose of being reported" and "its relation to the underlying reality of the situation is ambiguous;" lastly, Boorstin says, "Usually it is intended to be a self-fulfilling prophecy" (11–12). The editorials are designed to incite polarized opinions but not to foster discussion. The commentary by pundits such as Rex Murphy and celebrities such as Neil Young becomes news itself. The discourse's relationship to the controversies over the oil field are ambiguous, and the editorials then foster more editorials.

The resulting verbiage about what the pundit or the celebrity said are not conversations or dialogues but monologues performed for public consumption, leaving no room for audience participation or action and certainly no room for persuasion. None of the discussion is directed at changing minds, opinions, or lives but instead erects firm barriers between different interests. They perpetuate the conflict without elevating the discourse to debate.

Newspapers and other media exist to sell an audience to advertisers and to give their audiences what they demand. Spokespersons such as Levant, Murphy, Young, and DiCaprio seem to be what such audiences demand. These people are empowered by their audiences and stand in for experts. Rex Murphy or Neil Young's explanations of scientific phenomena are accepted seemingly because the men have earned reputations for success in the media. Boorstin's discussion of the conflation of celebrity and greatness sheds some light on the process of how these people are allowed to stand in for educated expert opinion. The public allows what Boorstin would call "human pseudo-events" to direct the patterns of the discussion because of the ease and simplicity of being a spectator rather an agent in the discussion.

"Captain Oilsands" versus the Four Horsemen: "Superhero" Discourse and the Citizen as Bystander

If the shadow boxing between pundits like Murphy and Levant and celebrities like Young and DiCaprio has become an entertainment pseudo-event (in the guise of reasoned debates between celebrities and pundits) that we passively consume and quickly forget, then Jewett and Lawrence help us decipher the particular genre of the *amuse-bouche* we are consuming. In their 2003 work, *Captain America and the Crusade against Evil*, Robert Jewett and John Shelton Lawrence interpret the American superhero tale, developed in the 1930s, as an attempt to reconcile the competing need for reasoned debate and compromise that is a hallmark of democratic society with the need to conquer and annihilate enemies perceived as threats to democracy. When the discourses of pundits and celebrities in the oil sands debate are analyzed using Jewett and Lawrence's description of the superhero genre, we see that these discourses contain verbal tokens that set the speaker up as superhero savior and the audience, by implication, as the impotent community in need of saving.

Many of the characteristics that Jewett and Lawrence identify as being integral to the modern superhero story can be found in the pundit/celebrity discourse genre. First, the superhero seems to reinforce democratic principles because he (and the superhero is almost always male) is, at least superficially, like everyone else. Jewett and Lawrence suggest that "this new myth system, which crystallized its conventions of plot and character in the axial decade of the 1930s, shows a democratic face in that the protagonist is an Everyman" (2003, 29). Although the superhero does great deeds, he can identify with the commoners he is saving.

Boorstin has traced the development of this need to see our heroes as like us. He notes that, until recently, famous men and great men "were pretty nearly in the same group;" they were imbued with divine purpose (1992, 46). Now however, fame can be manufactured and we are misled into believing that "well-knownness" is the hallmark of greatness. Boorstin distinguishes between men and women who are famous because they are great and those who seem great because they are famous. Pundits and celebrities alike use their well-knownness to enable their right to speak about any topic that catches their fancy. Boorstin links greatness to the heroic, defining the hero as "a human figure – real or imaginary or both – who has shown greatness in some achievement. He is a man or woman of great deeds" (49). He notes that the "belief in the power of the common people to govern themselves . . . has carried a distrust, or at least a suspicion of individual heroic greatness" and has contributed to people's lack of belief in the "power of the Great Leader" (49). Rather than believing expert opinion, audiences have come to rely on people whose well-knownness confers expertise even when that expertise is not supported by credentials or experience. Boorstin contends that "our most admired national heroes . . . are generally supposed to possess the 'common touch.' We revere them, not because they possess great charisma but because they embody popular virtues . . . [T]hey reveal and elevate ourselves" (50). Pundits claim to speak for blue-collar workers in the oil industry while celebrities claim to speak for the earth itself: both claim authenticity. They are able to be spokespersons in a scientific and economic arena with no expertise in these areas because, as Boorstin points out, "the great deeds of our time are now accomplished on *unintelligible frontiers*" (54) such as in the "laboratory, among cyclotrons and betatrons, whose very names are popular symbols of scientific mystery" (54).

A second characteristic of the superhero genre, identified by Jewett and Lawrence, and present in the culture war pseudo-debates, is a stark dichotomy between the good of the superhero and the evil of the supervillain. They note that, while the superhero can do no wrong (even while killing), "[t]he stereotype of the enemy is equally radical. ...Since they are irredeemable, their destruction is the single aim" (197). In the oil sands pseudo-debates, this attitude surfaces in the *ad hominem* attacks on the speakers from the other side of the debate, designed not only to discredit the opposition, but to deny the right of the opposition to exist as participants in the debate at all. Ostensibly, the focus of the discourse is not to destroy the argument of the opposition; it is to destroy the opposing side.

The irredeemable evil of the supervillain (and the unquestioned moral righteousness of the superhero) leads inevitably to the third characteristic of the genre: an unwillingness to compromise and seek middle ground. If the supervillain is purely evil, any compromise is a step away from righteousness. Just as Captain America is assumed not to need to consider that Red Skull may have a legitimate point of view, neither do the speakers in the culture wars consider their opposition as voicing legitimate concerns. The discourses of the pundits and celebrities close off debate rather than engage with ideas.

The superhero genre rose out of a period of anxiety about the need to protect democracy against totalitarianism, but, paradoxically, the superhero is anti-democratic when it comes to argument. No compromise is possible. Energy spent trying to reason with a supervillain is energy wasted. Although the superhero is identifiable as Everyman, while in the character of superhero, the Everyman is no longer bound by the rules of democratic society. The superhero is given license to violate the conventions of the community in need of being defended, "employing nondemocratic means to achieve democratic ends" (Jewett and Lawrence 2003, 28). The pundits and celebrities who engage in these pseudo-debates do not feel constrained by the conventions of debate. They violate debating procedures, setting themselves apart from the need to adhere to democratic principles of reasoned and reasonable debate. However, the weight of genre markers (the speaker as Everyman turned superhero, the dichotomy between the moral righteousness of the speaker and the absolute evil of the opposition, and the refusal to compromise) legitimizes the speaker's choice to violate the community's conventions of reasonable and respectful debate. These characteristics of the genre work as stylistic tokens that influence the audience to accept the speaker's claims.

Jewett and Lawrence make clear that a community needs a superhero only when the "community is ... incompetent at protecting itself against the evil predators who afflict it" (31). Largely, the impotence of the community stems from the constraints of democratic ideals, which require giving a hearing to the irredeemably evil villains. Democratic conventions force an engagement with evil that is best avoided. The role of the superhero is to intervene, protecting the community from engaging with the villain:

> The American monomyth betrays deep antagonism toward the creative exercise of reason on the part of the public as well as the individual. Careful deliberation, knowledge of law, and mastery of book learning are usually presented in monomythic materials as indicators of impotence or corruption. In the exercise of redemptive power, purity of intention suffices. ...The public and its representatives are pictured as too stupid to survive confrontations with evil. (42)

None of the pundits or celebrities explicitly tell their audiences that they are incompetent to engage with the villain; however, the genre tells the audience the role they are to play: "[A]s the artistic creators of popular entertainments respond to current events with mythic scenarios, they help to shape the public sense of what is appropriate in confronting the crises of national and international life" (Jewett and Lawrence 2003, 28). The ideology represented in these culture war debates between pundits and celebrities carries enough of the markers of the superhero genre that the audience understands the role it is to play and feels the enthymematic push to relax into the role of the innocent and incompetent community that must be saved by a superhero.

Talking Oil in the Rhetorical Marketplace

A further problem hindering the emergence of constructive discourse is the lack of alignment in the rhetoric of each side between the construction of audience and the goals of each side's rhetorical activity. Rhetors such as Young, on the one hand, and Murphy and Levant, on the other, respond to the oil sands controversy with a discourse which closes the door on any possible compromise or consensus with those holding opposing views, effectively foreclosing on a solution around which some future consensus might emerge.

There are two ways in which rhetorical theory reveals the capacity of these discourses to damage the conversation that the public, both within and outside Canada, needs to have. In a conflict where pro-environment discourse is attacked as idealistic and ineffectual, and where pro-extraction discourse is both attacked as soulless, both sides rely on their broken rhetoric to foreclose the dialogue itself.

The ideal audiences addressed by the opposing sides in the debate diverge. Young's Hiroshima analogy, for example, interpellates an audience for whom the end result of oil sands development is consubstantial with nuclear devastation; the analogy coaches the audience to fuse pro-environment and anti-war discourses (with which Young has been associated since the 1960s), to the point where human interference in the environment, identified with the extraction and burning of fossil fuels, becomes an aggressive act of war against the environment, a symbolic merger between fossil fuels and nuclear warfare. Young's analogy interpellates an audience who will respond to counterarguments as acts of war against the environment and by implication against innocent civilians. To engage with such counterarguments can only appear to legitimize those acts.

The same coaching of an attitude (in which hearing the other side of the argument is perceived as betrayal) occurs with destructive effect in Murphy, Levant, and others. The overt end of the pro-development/anti-protest discourse is an enhanced version of the status quo, in which life in the oil patch continues as it is. Opposing voices are silent, having apparently recognized the combination of inauthenticity, hypocrisy, and utopianism in their position. From the perspective of the pro-extraction rhetors, the relative inertia within their argument is evidence of the realism of their perspective. There will be no dystopic vision of the future. Instead, the audience will enjoy business-as-usual, as long as the old hippies and granola-crunchers shamefacedly fuel up their VW campervans and hit the road.

But the refusal to engage with dissent is not a victory for realism. Kenneth Burke offers us a model within which to approach this rhetoric critically. In the "Dictionary of Pivotal Terms" in *Attitudes Toward History*, Burke advances a theory of what he terms the "Forensic," positioned as an attitude toward reality that represents a standard of maturity necessary for constructive criticism. In doing so, Burke situates his use of the term *forensic* in a context quite distinct from the Aristotelian definition outlined in Chapter 3 of the *Rhetoric*, where Aristotle identifies it with judicial rhetoric, which "either attacks or defends somebody" (2004, 1358b 10f) and which "is concerned with the past ... with reference to things already done" (2004, 1358b 15f), as understood in the strict meaning of terms such as "forensic evidence."

Burke's account begins with the definition of *forensic* as "material supplied by the forum, the market place" (1984a, 254), and while the Aristotelian term likewise derives from *forum* as public space where judicial matters were decided, Burke carefully emphasizes his usage as more comprehensive than the traditional associations with law or justice; it includes "the materials of law, parliamentary procedure, traffic regulation, scientific-causal relationships evolved by complex and sophisticated commerce (of both the material and spiritual sorts)" (254). The emphasis on routine, even banal, administrative reality, and the association of spiritual life with such a fundamentally transactional perspective identifies Burke's forensic with the problem-solving, instrumental nature of rhetoric as an exchange of symbols (cf 1969, 43). As such, it is inalienable from Burke's insistence on rhetoric as a "realistic" use of language (43), where the term *realistic*, taken in the context of Burke's customary attention to a word's complete semantic range, conveys a sense both of language being used in a reasonable and practical manner, and of language being used to "realize" things, i.e., to make things real, with the latter meaning predominant. One uses rhetoric to make things happen "in the forum," and consequently, rhetorical acts/practices which fail to recognize the transactional nature of the forum as a constraint on actual problem-solving will likely fail to achieve concrete results.

The forensic, then, is both the complex details of daily life, and the appropriate attitude which one takes to dealing with them. Given Burke's definition of attitude as an "incipient act" (1984a, 42), his description of the forensic as a state of perceptual maturity is significant to an understanding of how the oil sands controversy is rhetorically constructed to resist and undermine actual debate.

The primary obstacle to an effectively forensic engagement is the "naïve heroic," which Burke associates with childhood:

> The child necessarily develops without much awareness of this forensic material. He is concerned with his immediate relatives and playmates, his toys and animals, material objects like food, chairs, tables, trees, cellar and attic. Even if you explicitly tell him of the complex situations involved in our broad social relationships, he does not grasp their relevance. He can, it is true, be taught a set of terms. But they remain essentially alien, since he has not yet earned them by his own experience. (1984a, 254–255)

In this passage, Burke describes a childlike perspective which has much in common with the attitude that Murphy and Levant seek to coach in their audience: the focus on the immediate and familiar as safe; the association of *complex situations* with being *alien*. Burke approaches this "pre-forensic" state as a natural part of development, which the individual consciousness normally, if not happily, outgrows:

> Often, when [the individual] becomes mature enough really to grasp something of their true significance, he is overwhelmed. This is particularly the case when he has been trained by a smattering of religious co-ordinates, with which the sophistications of the forensic lore can make a bad fit. But any naïve heroism, even of a purely secular sort, prepares him for the same disillusionment, as he gradually becomes mature enough to size up the ways in which people cash in on their moral assets, and as he discerns the same behavior in himself. Hence, the onslaught of the forensic must always come somewhat as a shock. (1984a, 255)

Burke's "naïve heroism" cuts two ways. On the one hand, it is what the pro-extraction rhetors accuse their opponents of not only exemplifying (the common pejorative use of the phrase "social justice warrior" comes to mind) but of encouraging the public to accept; it is the essence of "know-nothing foreign celebrity millionaires" (Levant; cf. page 12) and those who are bedazzled by them. Burke's phrase captures the whole problem of celebrity advocacy, in which the celebrity's persona is accepted as "real"; it also captures the disappointment that Murphy and Levant coach their audience to feel with Neil Young in particular for having "cash[ed] in on his moral assets" and having betrayed his "regular Canadian guy" AM/Oldies—radio hero persona.

At the same time, however, these rhetors position themselves as protecting their audience from "the complex situations involved in our broad social relationships," in other words, from the suspicion that there might be more to the controversy than misguided celebrities keeping honest people from making an honest living. On one level, they may thus be seen as attempting to manage "the onslaught of the forensic" to save their audience from "shock." Paradoxically, by painting opponents as immature and misguided, they ward off the intrusion of the forensic into the audience's secure world of "food, chairs, tables, trees, cellar and attic." In this regard, Murphy and Levant position themselves again as "superheroes," defending the values of the ordinary citizen again treacherous villains seeking to destroy their way of life.

On another level, however, this response locates the rhetors themselves within Burke's larger forensic continuum. Their attitude positions them as more worldly-wise than both their opponents and their own supporters; however, their rhetoric positions them as being only one step further down the forensic path. They have become what Burke calls "the Debunker" (1984a, 256). Burke describes this stage of development through a personal analogy involving suddenly having his vision corrected with eyeglasses:

> As he [Burke] emerged, with glasses, he came suddenly into a world of harsh outlines. He had not been immunized to the sight by small homoeopathic doses. It "hit" him. He saw the lines and blotches on peoples' faces, and the discomfiture was *alienating*. We submit that this same process prevails, in subtler ways, when one first begins really to understand the documents of the forensic. (255)

Burke further explains that "there is a natural tendency to rejection (the 'negation' of the childhood 'thesis'). The Debunker, no matter how mature his writing may be on the surface, remains at this stage [i.e., alienation and rejection]" (255–256).

The rhetors on both sides of the controversy fall into the category of "debunker." The pro-extraction rhetors place themselves more emphatically in this position in a rejection of idealism and in their anger at how Young and others "cash in their moral assets" in this situation. However, the general rejection of alternative viewpoints by both sides is evidence of a rhetorical attitude arrested in the Debunker stage.

Remaining in this stage is a problem because, for Burke, it retards or prevents the emergence of the kind of attitude necessary to engage in valid social criticism. For Burke, the act of criticism must necessarily be "comic" in orientation; his concept of the "comic corrective" (cf 1984a Chapter 6; Gusfield 1989, 25–26) involves articulating criticism of a situation in terms which at once communicate a constructive attitude and coach the same attitude in the audience. As Burke writes in *Attitudes Toward History*,

> Our philosophers, poets, and scientists act in the code of names by which they simplify or interpret reality. These names shape our

> relations with our fellows. They prepare us *for* some functions and *against* others, *for* or *against* the person representing these functions. The names go further: they suggest *how* you shall be for or against. Call a man a villain, and you have the choice of either attacking or cringing. Call him mistaken, and you invite yourself to attempt setting him right. Contemporary exasperations make us prefer the tragic (sometimes melodramatic) names of 'villain' and 'hero' to the comic names of 'tricked' and 'intelligent.' The choice must be weighed with reference to the results we would obtain, and to the resistances involved. (4–5, qtd in Farrell 1995, 41)

These observations allow us to see the rhetoric of both factions as failing on two scores.

Burke's "tragic (sometimes melodramatic) names" provides an accurate description of the attitudes motivating both Young's Hiroshima analogy and the attacks by Murphy and Levant et al. on celebrity intervention. Young keeps his opponents' hands on the lever dropping the bomb; Murphy and Levant cast Young in particular as an equally apocalyptic event jetting into Fort McMurray to shut down the town and turn its residents out onto the street. Moreover, their debunking of Young, DiCaprio, and perhaps especially Archbishop Tutu, embodies a tragic vision of celebrity itself, in which the platform which celebrity offers is a vehicle for corruption. The extent to which the pundits consider themselves exempt from/immune to the corrupting power of notoriety is part of the problem, contributing to a tragic frame of acceptance of a "heroic struggle." One could argue that the "silence" inherent in the pro-development entelechy[2] (the status quo minus dissent) implies an end to debate itself, and the elimination of the kind of public platform which celebrity represents.

Burke's account of the forensic serves as an antidote, or perhaps a therapy, for rhetorical attitudes stalled in the debunker state. For discourse to enable the forensic, and truly "enter the forum," the would-be critic must strive for, or at least be receptive to, "Transcendence," which "does not occur until the critic 'negates the negation'. This process, whereby he puts the pre-forensic and the forensic together, has also been called the state 'beyond good and evil', or 'beyond the opposites'" (1984a, 256).

Putting "the pre-forensic and the forensic together" would necessarily involve acknowledging the temptation to tragic discourse as a persuasive strategy, while ultimately seeking a critical vocabulary that approaches the exigence in the context of seeking common ground with the opposing discourse, seeking a "public voice" (Gastil 1994, 161)where fear of environmental disaster and fear of economic disaster might share a common vocabulary which might nurture the coaching of compatible attitudes in the exchange of views.

Burke stresses that participation in the forensic is not the end of dissent or dispute; although he associates it with the most fundamental acts of a society to "evolve an explicit verbalization and rationalization of the tribal acts, attitudes and policies," he also explains that, as it evolves, "it becomes more capable of sectarian stressing (on the part of 'specialists' who emphasize and logically extend one or another part of its ingredients)" (254). The forensic would thus, in situations of conflict, be a shared state in which the sides are aware of, and necessarily deal with, each new act of "sectarian stressing." Such a state is the equivalent of what Burke describes in the following section of the "Dictionary" as "the Good Life," when he writes of the desirability of "Construction, to channelize the militaristic by 'transcendence' into the cooperative. (The constructive, the creative, the cooperative being 'the moral equivalent of war')" (258). Here, we may take "militaristic" as consubstantial with a tragic attitude toward conflict in civil society.

Writing of the need to experience life unmediated by technology (and one can guess what he might have thought of the Internet as a vehicle for news), Burke writes, "There will be no better day until or unless a society at home in comedy will have been established long enough to lose their reverence for these exploitive playthings" (256). Burke was referring to the capacity of technological interaction to lead to a deferral of "real life," and there is no reason to suppose that he would have exempted information technology from his list of "exploitive playthings." The key phrase here, however, is "a society at home in comedy," which defines what Burke means by "the Good Life": a society which will communicate in the belief that a constructive language coaches constructive attitudes which lead to constructive interactions.

Engagement between Proponents and Opponents of the Oil Sands

While most of the artifacts promoted the breakdown of public debate, several provided examples of potentially constructive public discourse. An editorialist for the *Hamilton Spectator* concedes the dismissal of Neil Young's Hiroshima comments to encourage public discourse to return to the relevant stasis point: "If there is a downside to Young's comments . . . it's that the kerfuffle around Young might detract from the substance of his remarks. Some—including comparing the area to Hiroshima—are over-the top-silly" (Elliott). After disarming angry proponents of the oil sands, the editorialist returns to the exigence that has inspired the public controversy:

> The question isn't whether or not oilsands development should take place. It should, responsibly. The question is how fast growth should happen, and whether the regulatory and monitoring infrastructure

> is in place to make sure environmental damage is mitigated. Is it? Consider that in 2009 the Alberta government introduced legislation to reduce toxic waste in oilsands tailings ponds. But since then, not one oil company has met provincial requirements, and the government says it "does not believe that it would be appropriate to enforce compliance measures at this time." That's just one example. (Elliott 15 Jan. 2014)

Here, the editorialist focuses the critique on a specific environmental concern while conceding the proponents' position that the oil sands should be mined.

Another article, published in the *Globe and Mail* in January 2014, also concedes the critical stance towards Young's opposition of the oil sands: "[Young's] a rock star with a carbon footprint that is likely many times larger than that the average Canadian's; and he is prone to hyperbole, comparing the oil-sands capital Fort McMurray, to Hiroshima in 1945" (Berman January 21, 2014); however, the author also addresses the argument made by oil sands proponents that the oil sands is essential for the economy by arguing that Young's concerns are shared by investment strategists such as Jeremy Grantham: "[Young's] concerns are becoming increasingly difficult to ignore when they are supported by respected institutional investors—Mr. Grantham being near the top—who believe that the oil sands are probably doomed as long-term investments" (Berman January 21, 2014).

Finally, in response to the politicians, pundits, and editorialists who simply dismiss celebrity critics, an article published in Fort McMurray's *Connect* states,

> The development of an "us vs. them" mentality in the debate over oil sands development is a dangerous precedent. Setting it up as "taking sides" either for or against means there is no room for dialogue, discussion, or understanding, and I think it is only through that dialogue that we can find some sort of mutual respect ... Shutting down those who express concerns about the oil sands does nothing. It changes the mind of no one and adds nothing to the dialogue, and by doing so we risk looking like fools, particularly when we demean people who have caused tremendous change in the world like Desmond Tutu. It reflects poorly on us, our region and our industry. ("Wisdom of Voltaire," 6 June 2014)

This article, addressing the tendency of public discourse about the oil sands to simply dismiss any opposition out of hand, calls on like-minded proponents of the oil sands industry to engage in serious and respectful public discourse.

Conclusion: The Oil Sands as Rhetorical Disaster Zone

If the controversy over oil sands development is symptomatic of the larger culture wars, it is also indexical to the communication problems through which such conflicts perpetuate themselves, despite the efforts of a small number of voices on either side to achieve a more constructive level of debate. Approaching the conflict from the perspective of contemporary rhetorical theory is useful to demonstrate not only the failure of both sides to engage with their opponents, but also the damage that such failure is doing to public discourse in Canada. The problem is not mere proliferation, with the opposed voices growing louder and louder while the amount of information exchanged becomes smaller and smaller; rather, the problem is the cultivation of audiences for whom the act and art of listening to opponents is perceived as an act of concession or even submission.

Avoidance of appropriate points of stasis where viewpoints may be compared and exchanged is indexical to a public "conversation" unencumbered by a need to search for any truth beyond immediate beliefs, and uncommitted to any public processes through which to promote a constructive civil dialogue addressing the concerns of environmentalists and oil industry workers alike. Failure to pursue mutually well-informed and well-intentioned debate may strike an observer as unsurprising-if-regrettable, given the passions and pressures of twenty-first century economic and civic culture in Canada as elsewhere. However, this failure is combined with an addiction to tragic modes of discourse as Burke perceives them, in which the verbal framing of viewpoints points to rhetorical conflict as an end in itself. The rhetors' status as marketable "events" in the media economy depends on their ability to establish themselves as "superhero" combatants; their role demands that they destroy their opponents, rather than coming to an agreement with them; the entelechy of tragic struggle permits nothing less.

An audience required by the discourse to remain in an immature, pre-forensic state, the state in which one looks to superheroes and rigid lines between good and evil, is by definition inscribed within an entelechial construct where adult problem-solving strategies are denied them. When neither rhetor nor audience can transcend the negative, "debunking" mode of communication brought on by shock at the complexity of actual problem-solving, and when the act of debunking is construed as a heroic activity which the audience is coached to cheer, from a subordinate position at two removes from actual engagement, genuine rhetorical activity is effectively removed from the agenda. A rhetorical disaster of this magnitude can only exacerbate the two sides' alarm and hostility in the face of potential disaster, be that disaster environmental or economic.

Notes

1 According to Burke, a debunker is one whose criticism is predicated on maintaining a state of alienation toward the object of criticism, on the part of both critic and audience, thereby preempting any possible constructive criticism. Moreover, the debunker rejects the complexity of human experience and the discourses that represent it, both of which are elements of the Burkean forensic, which insists on critical engagement with imperfection and ambiguity (*Attitudes* 254–256). For more on Burke's idea of the forensic, see pages 30–32 below.

2 Lawson-Tancred (1986) translates and defines this Aristotelian term as "something like 'intrinsic possession of an end" and Burke (1969b) defines it as "classif[ying] a thing by conceiving of its kind according to the perfection (that is, finishedness) of which that kind is capable" (14).

Works Cited

Althusser, Louis. 1971. *Lenin and Philosophy and Other Essays*. Translated by Ben Brewster. New York: Monthly Review Press.

Aristotle. 2004. *Rhetoric*. Translated by W. Rhys Roberts. New York: Dover.

Bains, Camille. 10 Nov. 2014. "Neil Young says pipeline issues are "scabs" on the lives of Canadians." *The Globe and Mail*. www.theglobeandmail.com/news/national/neil-young-says-pipeline-issues-are-scabs-on-canadians-lives/article21518540/

Berman, D. 21 Jan. 2014. "Neil Young vs. Oil Sands: This is no Solo Act." *The Globe and Mail*. www.theglobeandmail.com/globe-investor/inside-the-market/neil-young-isnt-the-only-voice-on-energy/article16419139/

Bitzer, Lloyd F. 1980. "Functional Communication: A Situational Perspective." *Rhetoric in Transition: Studies in the Nature and Uses of Rhetoric*. University Park: The Pennsylvania State University Press, 21–38.

Black, Edwin. 1970. "The Second Persona." *Quarterly Journal of Speech* 56(2), 109–119.

Boorstin, Daniel. 1992. *The Image: A Guide to Pseudo-Events in American*. 25th Anniversary ed. New York: Vintage.

Burke, Kenneth. 1966. *Language as Symbolic Action*. Berkeley: University of California Press.

———. 1969a. *A Grammar of Motives*. Berkeley: University of California Press.

———. 1969b. *A Rhetoric of Motives*. Berkeley: University of California Press.

———. 1984a. *Attitudes toward History*. 3rd ed. Berkeley: University of California Press.

———. 1984b. *Permanence and Change: An Anatomy of Purpose*. 3rd ed. Berkeley: University of California Press.

Ceccarelli, Leah. 2011. "Manufactured Scientific Controversy: Science, Rhetoric, and Public Debate." *Rhetoric and Public Affairs* 14(2), 195–228.

"Celebrity Activism often Oily." 15 Jan. 2014. Editorial. *The Winnipeg Free Press*. www.winnipegfreepress.com/breakingnews/celebrity-activism-often-oily-240233351.html

Charland, Maurice. 1987. "Constitutive Rhetoric." *Quarterly Journal of Speech* 73(2), 133–150.

Coutu, Marcel. 11 Oct. 2013. "The Reality of Canadian Energy; Celebrity Critics Add Entertainment Value to Oilsands Discussion." *The Vancouver Sun.* http://www.vancouversun.com/opinion/op-ed/opinion+celebrity+critics+entertainment+value+oilsands/8998844/story.html

Elliott, H. 15 Jan. 2014. "We Should Hear Young's Worries." Editorial. *Hamilton Spectator.* www.thespec.com/opinion-story/4313376-the-spectator-s-view-we-should-hear-young-s-oilsands-worries/

Farrell, Thomas B. 1995. "Comic History Meets Tragic Memory: Burke and Habermas on the Drama of Human Relations." *Kenneth Burke and Contemporary European Thought: Rhetoric in Transition*, Edited by Bernard L. Brock. Tuscaloosa and London: The University of Alabama Press, 34–75.

Gastil, John. 1994. "A Definition and Illustration of Democratic Leadership." *Human Relations* 47(8), 953–975.

Gosselin, Dr. Pierre et al. 2010. *The Royal Society of Canada Expert Panel: Environmental and Health Impacts of Canada's Oil Sands Industry.* Ottawa: RSC-SRC. rsc-src.ca/sites/default/files/RSC%20Oil%20Sands%20Panel%20Main%20Report%20Oct%202012.pdf

Gratchet, Roger Davis. 2011. *The Struggle for Authenticity: Blues, Race, and Rhetoric.* Diss. University of Texas at Austin Grad. Sch. of Communication Studies. 25 Aug. 2016.

Gusfield, Joseph R. 1989. "Introduction." *On Symbols and Society*, by Kenneth Burke, Edited by Gusfield. Chicago, IL: University of Chicago Press, 1–49.

Habermas, Jürgen. 1989. *The Structural Transformation of the Public Sphere: An Inquiry into a Category of Bourgeois Society.* Translated by Thomas Barker and Frederick Lawrence. 1962. Cambridge, MA: MIT Press.

Hussain, Y. January 15, 2014. "Time to Inject Reality into the Energy Debate': Executives Lash out at Oil Sands Trash-Talk; Industry no 'Villain.'" Financial Post. business.financialpost.com/commodities/energy/time-to-inject-reality-into-the-energy-debate-oil-executives-hit-back-at-celebrity-trash-talk

Jewett, Robert, and John Shelton Lawrence. 2003. *Captain America and the Crusade against Evil: The Dilemma of Zealous Nationalism.* Grand Rapids, MI: William B. Eerdmans Publishing Company.

Lamphier, G. 26 Aug. 2014. "Hollywood Hypocrisy at its Best; DiCaprio Has a Seriously Large Carbon Footprint." *Edmonton Journal.* www.pressreader.com

Lawson-Tancred, Hugh. 1986. "Glossary." In Aristotle. *De Anima (On the Soul)*, by Aristotle, edited and translated by Hugh Lawson-Tancred. London: Penguin, 117–122.

Leach, Andrew. 15 Jan. 2014. "Neil Young, the Oil Sands and the Damage Done." *Maclean's.* www.macleans.ca/economy/economicanalysis/the-rock-star-and-the-damage-done/

Lendon, Brad. 14 Jan. 2014. "'Rock Stars Don't Need Oil,' Neil Young Says.'" *CNN* Wire. *Business Insights: Essentials.* www.cnn.com/2014/01/14/showbiz/neil-young-oil/index.html

Levant, Ezra. 3 June 2014. "Tutu Was Willing to Rent out his Reputation." *Toronto Sun.* . republicofmining.com/2014/06/05/tutus-oilsands-visit-raises-questions-by-ezra-levant-toronto-sun-june-3-2014/

Mertl, Steve. 10 Sept. 2013. "Neil Young Slams Oilsands, Compares Fort McMurray to Hiroshima." *Yahoo News Daily Brew.* ca.news.yahoo.com/

blogs/dailybrew/neil-young-slams-oilsands-compares-fort-mcmurray-hiroshima-190557100.html

Murphy, Rex. 14 Sept. 2013. "A Far Cry from 'Hiroshima.'" *National Post.* nationalpost.com/opinion/rex-murphy-a-far-cry-from-hiroshima

"Neil Young Concludes Anti-Oilsands Concert Series with Show in Calgary." 19 Jan. 2014. *Financial Post.* business.financialpost.com/commodities/energy/neil-young-concludes-anti-oil-sands-concert-series-with-show-in-calgary

"Neil Young's Fantasy World; Singer Conveniently Overstates the Viability of Alternatives to Oil." 18 Jan. 2014. Editorial. *Calgary Herald.* www.pressreader.com

Oreskes, Naomi and Conway, Erik M. 2010. *Merchants of Doubt: How a Handful of Obscured the Truth on Issues from Tobacco Smoke to Global Warming.* New York: Bloomsbury Press.

Postman, Neil. 1985. *Amusing Ourselves to Death: Public Discourse in the Age of Show Business.* New York: Penguin.

Prelli, Lawrence. 1989. *A Rhetoric of Science: Inventing Scientific Discourse.* Columbia: University of South Carolina Press.

Puxley, Chinta. 16 Jan. 2014. Neil Young's latest sour note over proposed Keystone XL pipeline

CTV News Winnipeg. winnipeg.ctvnews.ca/neil-young-s-latest-sour-note-over-proposed-keystone-xl-pipeline-1.1641956

"The Wisdom of Voltaire." 6 June 2014. *Connect.* (URL unavailable; newspaper no longer in operation)

Wood, James.17 Sept. 2013. "Iconic Actor Robert Redford Latest to Attack the Oilsands." *Edmonton Journal*. URL unavailable; link no longer active. 18 Sept. 2013. "Premier says Chinese enthusiasm high for Alberta energy, despite celebrity criticism *Calgary Herald.*http://www.calgaryherald.com/news/alberta/Premier+says+Chinese+enthusiasm+high+Alberta+energy+despite+celebrity+criticism/8922655/story.html

14 From Persuasion to Manipulation

Tracing Oil Sands Narratives in the *Calgary Herald*

Sibo Chen

Introduction

Over the past two decades, controversies concerning Alberta's oil sands industry have drawn domestic and international media attention. While the industry's proponents insist that its further expansion will bring economic benefits for both Alberta and Canada, opposition has been raised against the industry's devastating environmental impacts, especially its greenhouse gas emissions and toxic effects on local communities.

Although much has been written on the industry's influence over Canadian politics (e.g., Davidson & Gismondi, 2011; Stefanick & Shrivastava, 2015), only a few studies (e.g., Friedel, 2008; Gunster & Saurette, 2014; Raso & Neubauer, 2016; Remillard, 2011; Takach, 2013; Way, 2011) have explicitly addressed the communication aspect of oil sands debates. Thorough examinations of the discursive tactics employed by the industry remain scarce, and few claims have been connected to discursive legitimation theories.

This chapter takes a critical discourse analysis (CDA) approach to examine how the expansion of Alberta's oil sands industry is discursively constructed in the *Calgary Herald*, a major daily newspaper. As found in previous research (Gunster & Saurette, 2014; Raso & Neubauer, 2016), the *Herald* has promoted the oil sands industry in a relentless manner, portraying it as besieged by well-funded and aggressive environmental lobbyists. Given the newspaper's ties with the oil sands industry, the current study focuses less on the objectivity or truthfulness of its coverage on the oil sands; instead, the primary concern here is how it legitimizes the expansion of the oil sands industry discursively. The broader interest of this chapter lies in the interactions between discursive constructions and sociopolitical issues in environmental politics.

The chapter is organized as follows. Section II reviews controversies surrounding Alberta's oil sands and previous research on communication practices in this booming sector. Section III overviews the relationship between public discourse and legitimation. Section IV introduces the current study's empirical data and research methods. Section V elaborates micro semantic prosodies and macro discursive tactics found in the *Herald*'s oil sands coverage during 2015. This section aims to demonstrate that in response to the mounting public doubts on the future of the oil sands, the promotional narratives orchestrated by the fossil fuel sector were leaning toward adopting more covert manipulative strategies. Finally, Section VI concludes by assessing the significance of discursive struggles in environmental politics.

Communicating Oil Sands

Technically known as bitumen, Alberta's oil sands are primarily located in three deposits: Athabasca, Cold Lake, and Peace River. Alberta's reserves of bitumen are estimated at 1.7 to 2.5 trillion barrels of oil, making the province the largest single deposit of crude in the world (Davidson & Gismondi, 2011; Remillard, 2011; Takach, 2013). Although the extraction of the oil sands was initiated in the 1960s, it was not until the 2000s that the industry began to experience unparalleled growth. Two major factors initiated this boom. First, high oil prices during the first decade of the twenty-first century made the oil sands industry extremely profitable. A 2011 report (Honarvar et al., 2011) estimated that the growth of Alberta's oil sands sector between 2010 and 2035 would generate 830,000 new jobs, $2.1 trillion GDP, and $311 billion tax revenue for Canada (including $105 billion for Alberta). Second, the oil sands present a viable means for countries like the United States and China to meet their energy needs and reduce their reliance on Middle Eastern sources.

Unlike conventional oil, the oil sands exist in a natural mixture of sand, clay, and rock. During a typical bitumen mining process, this "synthetic" crude is surface-mined, and then crude oil is extracted through an energy-intensive process using either water or steam. The extraction and refinement of the oil sands come with significant ecological costs. As Nikiforuk (2010) summarizes, the extraction of the oil sands is accompanied by the destruction of virgin boreal forest and wildlife habitats, air pollution, groundwater contamination, and high energy consumption and greenhouse gas emissions. Furthermore, these ecological effects lead to social costs. Since many oil sands extraction sites are set up near First Nations communities, their toxic effects directly threaten public health and traditional Aboriginal lifestyles in these communities. These issues have led to local, national, and international opposition to the industry's further expansion.

Thus, the public controversies over Alberta's oil sands industry present "an emerging, international flashpoint in the rising tension between economic development on the current, global model and its ecological costs" (Takach, p. 212), which has drawn attention within the field of environmental communication. There has been a growth of communication scholarship engaging with the public controversies around the oil sands industry (e.g., Friedel, 2008; Gunster & Saurette, 2014; Raso &

Neubauer, 2016; Remillard, 2011; Takach, 2013; Way, 2011). Briefly speaking, these studies can be divided into two research strands. The first strand, represented by Friedel (2008), Remillard (2011), and Takach (2013), addresses visual representations of the oil sands, especially the rebranding efforts by the industry and the Alberta government. Takach (2013) examined a rebranding slideshow produced by the Alberta government and concluded that the images used in the slideshow, despite their apparent "romantic gaze" toward nature, reproduced the oil sands industry's anthropocentric and extractive stance toward nature. Similarly, Friedel's (2008) analysis of industrial advertising revealed how First Nations' bodies and landscapes were used as semiotic tropes for promoting transnational energy companies' neoliberal agendas. The second strand, including studies by Gunster and Saurette (2014), Raso and Neubauer (2016), and Way (2011), focuses on how the oil sands industry and the Alberta government are discursively represented and contested in the public sphere.

Collectively, these studies highlight the key stakeholders orchestrating the narratives of the oil sands, notably politicians, corporations, and think tanks. Another finding shared by these studies is the crucial role played by news media in setting up a disproportionately structured discursive space that neglects the voices of scientists, environmental groups, and concerned citizens. As revealed in Gunster and Saurette (2014), conservative newspapers such as the *Calgary Herald* have been involved in constructing a convincing story line depicting the oil sands industry as a victim under constant and aggressive attacks from environmental groups, which thus effectively undermines the environmental critiques of the industry. Industry proponents and conservative think tanks facilitate construction of this story line by functioning as the primary voices in media texts, relegating oil sands oppositions to secondary positions (Raso & Neubauer, 2016).

Yet, despite previous studies' insights on oil sands communications, the sociopolitical context shared by these studies has been undergoing a profound shift since 2015. The year 2015 witnessed fluctuating oil prices, the surprising victory of the New Democratic Party (NDP) in the Alberta general election, a majority government led by the Liberal Party following out of a federal election, and, most importantly, the historical Paris Agreement on carbon reduction in the 2015 United Nations Climate Change Conference. All of these changes have contributed to an unfavorable discursive environment in 2015 for the oil sands industry's blunt promotion of oil dependency and oil prosperity. Thus, as the industry's proponents strive to legitimize further expansion of oil extraction, public concern over the oil sands' future keeps growing.

Discursive legitimation is a central concept for explaining the oil sands conflicts. Following, I first discuss the processes of discursive legitimation (as part of framing my own research methods) and then report on an exploratory study that addresses how the *Herald* continues its discursive legitimation of the oil sands industry in light of the recent domestic and international changes in environmental politics.

Discursive Legitimation and Its Implications for the Oil and Gas Sector

Legitimation has been one of the most discussed concepts in CDA, addressing how institutions seek explanations and justifications for their actions and established order (Beetham, 1991; Giddens, 1984). Legitimation can be defined as "the process by which the exertion of power by one person, group or political body over another is made to be – and maintained as being – acceptable to those over whom power is wielded" (Mackay, 2015, p. 325). A legitimation process' central outcome is the creation or reproduction of collectively accepted and recognized "common sense" that serves as the basis of political obedience and power (Beetham, 1991). In pragmatic terms, legitimation answers two essential questions within public debates: "why should we do this" and "why should we do this in this way" (van Leeuwen, 2007, p. 108).

To a large extent, legitimation cannot exist without language use since social values and norms are established through discourse and disputes over values and norms during legitimation processes are conducted linguistically (Fonseca & Ferreira, 2015; Vaara, 2014). Fairclough and Fairclough (2012) distinguish between legitimation and justification, noting that the former is an argumentative process involving a public exchange of reasons. Only when the reasons presented are collectively accepted and recognized can a justificatory practice be considered as a (successful) legitimation act. In other words, legitimation is a particular type of justification built upon public deliberation. As such, public discourses generated by noninstitutional stakeholders (e.g., corporations, news media, and NGOs) also play a role in illuminating legitimation processes since these discourses shape the "common sense" held by the public.

Concerning discursive tactics used in legitimation processes, van Leeuwen (2007) proposes a framework including four legitimation strategies: authorization (reference to authoritative opinions), moral evaluation (value systems), rationalization (reference to knowledge claims or arguments), and mythopoesis (constructing compelling narratives). Another framework, proposed by van Dijk (2006), identifies how legitimation, delegitimation, and re-legitimation are accomplished through binary constructions at lexical, phrasal, and discursive levels. Legitimation, van Dijk argues, is often implemented through comparing positive self-presentations and negative other-presentations. In recent years, empirical research has adopted both frameworks to identify discursive underpinnings of legitimizing statements. For instance, Vaara (2014) focused on Finland media's coverage during the Eurozone's legitimacy crisis and identified how discourses of financial capitalism, humanism, nationalism, and Europeanism were adopted by pro-Eurozone discussions. His analysis further revealed how these commonly held values were embedded into media discussions through knowledge-based authoritarian voices, economic arguments, moral evaluations, and mythopoesis involving alternative future scenarios of Europe. In a similar vein, Fonseca and Ferreira (2015) demonstrated the intensive discursive efforts by the Portuguese government for legitimizing its austerity policies between 2011 and 2014, with binary constructions being frequently found in the government's "state of exception" narrative and blame allocation strategies.

One trend in recent research on discursive legitimation is that growing attention has been paid to the discursive efforts by institutional or corporate actors after perceived controversies when legitimacy crises considerably threatened the existence of involved stakeholders. In some cases, the perceived controversies spread into an entire sector, leading to collaborative discursive campaigns. As shown in Breeze (2012), after the Deepwater Horizon catastrophe in 2010, BP was joined by other oil companies to defend the fossil fuel industry's safety records and to calm the angry public.

Following this trend, the next section examines oil sands proponents' narratives in the *Herald* during 2015, when negative speculations concerning the future of fossil fuel drove the oil sands sector to summon up a range of justificatory narratives to depict itself as the only viable option for Canada's economic future.

Decoding the *Calgary Herald*'s Story Lines

The current study focuses on how the *Calgary Herald* utilizes micro semantic prosodies and macro discursive tactics to construct and strengthen its promotional story line of the oil sands industry. The *Herald* was selected for its connection with the oil and gas sector and its status as the leading regional news provider in Alberta. In 2015, the newspaper had an average daily circulation of 113,579 and its website attracted approximately 718,000 unique visitors per month (Calgary Herald Fast Facts, 2016). The newspaper's parent corporation, Postmedia Network, is a major Canadian media chain specializing in newspaper and website publishing. The Postmedia newspaper chain owns many large regional newspapers across Western Canada, making it a powerful provider for cross-platform advertising and storytelling. According to a leaked Postmedia presentation to the Canadian Association of Petroleum Producers (CAPP), Postmedia is eager to "work with the Canadian oil and gas industry to bring energy to the forefront of our national conversation and engage executives, the business community and the Canadian public to underscore the ways in which the energy sector powers Canada" (cited in Gunster & Saurette, 2014, p. 335). According to previous research (Gunster & Saurette, 2014; Raso & Neubauer, 2016), this agenda has been spearheaded by the *Herald* and other Postmedia-owned media outlets such as the *Calgary Sun* and the *Edmonton Journal*. Unlike direct sales pitches from the fossil fuel sector, however, the *Herald* still has a mandate to appear to be following basic journalism principles such as truthfulness and objectivity, which makes it an ideal venue for examining the ideological and political efforts underlying discursive legitimation.

The data used here include stories published by the *Herald* during the year 2015 since a series of unfavorable sociopolitical changes for the oil sands industry occurred during this period. CDA was adopted as the analytical framework for data analysis. The tradition of CDA is to engage with a relatively small set of texts through close reading and interpretation (Wodak & Meyer, 2016). Despite the prevalence of quantitative corpus-driven approaches in CDA for handling a large set of texts, qualitative interpretation and explanation remain crucial for uncovering the existence of bias and manipulation in discourse (Baker & McEnergy, 2015). Thus, although the current study engaged with a broad set of texts, it was qualitative in nature, focusing on macro discursive features appearing across multiple texts. The analytical framework was derived from Gunster and Saurette's (2014) identification of the crucial role of storytelling in cultivating and reinforcing our values, norms, and political preferences regarding controversial issues. The power of storytelling lies in its ability to generate coherence and moral certainty: by offering recurring patterns of meaning and emotion, persuasive stories naturalize their embedded ideologies to provide the public with particular views of the world. As such, this study sought to offer an indicative glimpse into the *Herald*'s compelling "meta-narrative" on the oil sands, especially its recent changes in 2015 compared with previous research (Gunster & Saurette, 2014; Raso & Neubauer, 2016).

For the data collection and analysis, I used the string "oil sands OR tar sands AND energy" to perform a search in LexisNexis for gathering all oil sands-related texts published by the *Calgary Herald* in 2015. I filtered out items that addressed the oil sands peripherally. The final data set consisted of 168 items, including four genres: news articles, editorials, op-eds, and reader letters. The data analysis was a bottom-up and two-step procedure. First, keywords such as "oil sands," "energy," and "environment" were searched to identify recurring semantic prosodies at the phrasal level. Then, I attended to discursive tactics appearing in multiple texts. I used van Leeuwen's (2007) discursive legitimation framework (authorization, rationalization, moralization, and mythopoesis) to code the media texts and this rough coding was then refined for (1) identifying additional legitimation strategies and (2) elucidating the key discursive features of the *Herald*'s defense of the oil sands industry.

Oil Sands Narratives in the *Calgary Herald*

Deriving from pioneer research in corpus linguistics, the term "semantic prosody" refers to the fact that certain expressions tend to collocate with each other and people unconsciously remember these reoccurring prosodies (Baker & McEnery, 2015). Previous research has found that a specific concept's public perception is influenced by its semantic prosodies found in everyday discourse. For instance, Baker, Gabrielatos, and McEnery (2013) examined the representation of refugees in the British press and found that the media consistently associated refugees with negative expressions, which at least partially contributed to the public's hostile attitude. Given the media texts' focus on energy issues, the semantic prosodies of the following terms are identified and analyzed: oil sands, energy, renewable energy, and environment.

We begin with "oil sands." How to refer to Alberta's bitumen deposits as a contested issue in Canadian politics (Davidson & Gismondi, 2011; Stefanick & Shrivastava, 2015). Environmental critics prefer "tar sands" because it highlights the dirtiness of bitumen. By contrast, the industry and the Alberta government use "oil sands" as a counter linguistic strategy. In the analyzed media texts, bitumen is referred to as "oil sands," which distanced it from the dirtiness invoked by "tar sands." In fact, only when the texts address "environmental lobbyists" does the term "tar sands" appear. In other words, the texts generally avoid discussing the dirtiness of bitumen until they link "tar sands" with their antagonists to delegitimize their claims. For instance, when reporting how the Wild Rose Party (the official opposition after the 2015 provincial election) opposed the newly elected NDP government's appointment of Graham Mitchell as chief of staff to the Energy Ministry, the *Herald* wrote:

Excerpt 1

> On Thursday, the Wild Rose managed to land a solid jab against the government, not in the assembly, but in a news release revealing a curiously troubling fact about Graham Mitchell, the newly appointed chief of staff to Energy Minister Marg McCuaig-Boyd. Turns out Mitchell was a federal lobbyist with a firm fighting against proposed pipeline projects for Alberta's energy industry. On its webpage, the lobbying firm - Lead Now - refers to the oil sands as the "toxic tar sands" and says the National Energy Board's upcoming study of the proposed Energy East pipeline project is a "sham review process". (Thomson, 2015)

The above excerpt is built upon the assumption that anyone with a history of environmental advocacy cannot work for the Energy Ministry of Alberta. By driving the public attention toward how "federal environmental lobbyists" fabricate the term "toxic tar sands," the text implies a conflict between Alberta and outsiders, with the province's right to economic growth (through the proposed Energy East pipeline) being "unfairly" impaired. Such binary construction is found at the discursive level, which will be discussed later.

If bitumen is not the "toxic oil sands" described by environmentalists, then what is it, according to the *Herald*? Through coverage on the oil sands industry, from its everyday issues to its struggles against falling oil prices, the newspaper strives to emphasize the oil sands as a source for crucial energy projects that provide economic prosperity and employment growth. While the argument for economic growth is shadowed by the falling oil prices, it remains the central rationale of the media texts' promotional narratives. Compared with previous research (Gunster & Saurette, 2014; Raso & Neubauer, 2016), however, the current texts present the economic rationale in an implicit way: rather than directly addressing the benefits of the oil sands industry, these texts highlight Alberta's economic dependency on the industry and then use this fact to call for support from the governments of Alberta and Canada. The following is a typical example framing the significance of the oil sands industry for Alberta:

Excerpt 2

> Low oil prices that are threatening the Alberta economy have prompted Suncor Energy Inc. to eliminate 1,000 people from its workforce of about 14,000 and cut its 2015 capital spending budget by $1 billion. [...] "Cost management has been an ongoing focus, with successful efforts to reduce both capital and operating costs well underway before the decline in oil prices," said Steve Williams, president and chief executive, in a news release. "However, in today's low crude price environment, it's essential we accelerate this work. Today's spending reductions are consistent with our commitment to spend within our means and maintain a strong balance sheet. We will monitor the pricing environment and take further action as required." The news came as Alberta Premier Jim Prentice rejected a Conference Board of Canada report suggesting Alberta is headed for a recession because of falling oil prices. [...] While acknowledging that low oil prices have severely dented the provincial budget, Prentice said the board's report is at odds with the projections of chartered banks and other forecasters. [...] Suncor spokeswoman Sneh Seetal said the job reductions will be felt throughout operations in Calgary, Fort McMurray, Eastern Canada and in the United States but cuts may be deeper in certain areas. (Healing, 2015)

Here, the excerpt discusses Suncor's decision to cut 1,000 jobs in response to the low oil prices in January 2015. It depicts a sense of crisis by engaging the voices of stakeholders and providing details of the scale of the job cut. Yet, this sense of crisis does not challenge the logic of oil dependency. The focus is still on how the oil sands industry can survive the current crisis and then flourish again. The logic of oil dependency becomes clearer when examining the use of the term "energy" in the texts. Except for referring to the Energy Ministry of Alberta, the term "energy" almost exclusively refers to fossil fuels (the oil sands and electricity generated by coal plants). The term "renewable energy" is only mentioned 59 times in the texts, with most instances depicting the government's *future plans* of developing renewable energy production. When summarizing the NDP government's release of climate change strategies in November 2015, the *Herald* claimed:

Excerpt 3

> In many ways, Alberta's plan to retire coal-fired plants represents an opportunity to invest in the province's renewable energy potential. Environmental groups, such as the Pembina Institute and Canadian Wind Energy Association, have called on the province to legislate a set of renewable-energy requirements to encourage investors to build wind farms and solar power stations, rather than replacing coal strictly with natural gas. Currently, about nine per cent of Alberta's electricity comes from renewable sources. The panel discussion document says wind energy is expected to be the least costly option for new power by 2026 and solar power could take that spot by 2030. But challenges such as preventing skyrocketing electricity prices remain. How the province will tackle them is still unclear. ("After final deliberations", 2015)

By highlighting the limits of renewable energy, the excerpt undermines the urgency of reducing greenhouse gas emissions through renewable energy. The discussion of renewable energy, by no means, challenges the oil sands' dominance in Alberta. Many coal-fired plants are built for powering up oil sands production. Replacing them with wind farms and solar power stations will make little contribution to reduce greenhouse gas emissions overall if oil sands production continues to expand in Alberta. The *Herald*'s critical stance toward renewable energy is revealed in columns questioning the cost of renewable energy infrastructure. Following the NDP government's release of its climate change strategies, one columnist commented:

Excerpt 4

> Current estimates are between $4 billion and $12 billion for early retirement of these coal plants alone. Then there's the cost of replacing them with new hugely expensive plants for the unreliable renewables,

> their transmission lines, and backup systems that will have to be built - paid for by the taxpayer or the consumer; either way, that's you and me. How many billions will that be? (Klassen, 2015)

The delegitimation of renewable energy is argued via economics. Combined with the ways the oil sands are described in the texts, such argument creates an ideological closure that denies the possibility and necessity of a shift toward a post-carbon economy.

Finally, let us consider how environmental issues are addressed in the texts. Searching the term "environment" suggests that in most cases the term refers to the Environmental Minister of Alberta. A closer look at the minister's statements on the oil sands industry, however, reveals his unwillingness to criticize the industry. In one article titled "I'm no enemy of the oil sands, environment minister says," the standpoint of Environment Minister Shannon Phillips was presented as follows:

Excerpt 5

> Stand back. Environment Minister Shannon Phillips has something to say about claims that she's out to shut down the oil sands. "I categorically reject this charge that I'm somehow against the oil sands," says Premier Rachel Notley's most forceful minister, who heads to Paris in just two weeks for the international summit on climate change. "It is false. I, like the rest of my cabinet and caucus, know that we are - and will be for the foreseeable future - an energy economy. I've said this every single time I speak publicly on the matter. . . we are going to build economic diversification on the back of a strong energy industry. I've never felt any differently on the matter." (Braid, 2015)

This excerpt represents the media's reoccurring coverage of the Environmental Ministry's assurance of its support for the oil sands industry, which reproduces the notion that environmental protection should go along with the oil sands industry, instead of obstructing it. By contrast, there is no discussion of the oil sands' environmental impact throughout the year of 2015 in the *Herald*. According to previous research (Davidson & Gismondi, 2011; Gunster & Saurette, 2014), such neglect conceals two facts about the oil sands: first, the oil sands are an unconventional fossil fuel and their refinement generates more greenhouse gases than conventional crude oil; second, the toxic effects of oil sands production often disproportionately influence First Nations communities.

So far, this section has identified two legitimation strategies implemented through semantic prosodies in the analyzed media text: (1) binary constructions that reaffirm the irreplaceability of the oil sands for Alberta's economy (positive self-presentation) and suppresses environmental movements (negative other-presentation); (2) appeal to inevitability that justifies the oil sands industry by emphasizing the instability of renewable energy and invoking the fear of loss. Both strategies are also found in the texts' meta-narratives constructed by intertextual story lines.

To be specific, the binary construction is developed through reader letters. Compared with previous research (Gunster & Saurette, 2014; Raso & Neubauer, 2016), the binary argumentation in the current texts is more covert, with ideological flak conducted by "concerned readers" and independent columnists instead of editors themselves. The adoption of covert argumentation serves two goals. First, it aims to mobilize the Alberta public emotionally by accentuating the "public anger" caused by unfair critiques of the oil sands. Second, there is a clear intent to ostensibly maintain the *Herald*'s "objectivity" by involving third parties in the public debates on the oil sands. Nonetheless, the covertness does not weaken the ideological effects of negative expressions of environmentalism. In one letter responding to the idea that "the oil sands industry is unsustainable," for instance, the author wrote:

Excerpt 6

> Phil Elder says that by developing the oil sands, Albertans would be contributing to "the inundation of thousands of kilometres of low-lying coastal areas," and also states we need a "crash program for renewable energy" and that the alternative is worldwide chaos. Elder has completely bought into the climate hysteria promoted by Al Gore and various groups, like the radical environmental NGOs, the UN and IPCC. According to these doomsayers and the IPCC's computer models, low-lying areas like Bangladesh are by now supposed to be under water because of global warming, Instead, we have had global cooling for 18 years. Elder also quotes various sources calling fossil fuels a sunset industry. Maybe so, but if Elder would drive around Calgary and observe the hundreds of thousands of fossil-fuelled vehicles busily going to and fro, I think the reality would be we have a long way to go to replace fossil fuel as an energy source. (Gehl, 2015)

The excerpt employs harsh accusations of environmentalism to delegitimize environmentalists' critique of the oil sands being unsustainable. Although such one-sided and aggressive attack is unacceptable according to journalistic standards, its appearance as an independent opinion letter justifies its publication. Davidson and Gismondi (2011) argue that oil sands proponents have engaged in "diversionary framing" through which attention to the oil sands' health and ecological risks is distracted by the exaggeration of economic benefits. The excerpt reproduces the logic of diversion by covertly hiding the industry's interests behind the "concerned public."

Meanwhile, the "appeal to inevitability" strategy is associated with two meta-narratives constructed in the texts. The first meta-narrative focuses on the seemingly unproblematic connection between fossil fuel and modern life. In essence, this narrative champions the idea that anyone enjoying the prosperity brought by fossil fuel has no right to criticize it. In one article with the provocative title, "You can't have your cake without the power that heats the oven; we enjoy the good life oil pays for yet we still protest energy development," the author argued:

Excerpt 7

> So, will the obstreperous aboriginal bands, who cry foul on any proposed development through their lands, accept in return fewer and slimmer federal cheques in the mail as tax receipts flowing to Ottawa from energy companies are severely chopped? Will the protesting university students in Quebec do a grand bargain where not a single shovel will touch the earth on a pipeline project in their province if, in return, they actually pay close to the full cost of their education and don't rely on transfer payments from Alberta to help grease those squeaky wheels? Will the fervent Greenpeace lot find funding for and successfully implement a grand post-industrial strategy that will, in turn, provide ample work above the level of bottle picking for all those who have mortgages but no job with which to pay them? And will the premier of Ontario declare that such are the inherent evils of carbon emissions that never again will she or her federal playmates expect taxpayers to bail out the sputtering auto industry in her province? (Nelson, 2015)

The excerpt delegitimizes environmentalism by equating it to other "hypocritical" political movements and the sense of hypocrisy is further reinforced by the adoption of parallel construction. Built upon the assumption that prosperity is built up by the consumption of fossil fuels, this strategy delegitimizes alternative choices. Media framing plays a central role during the above delegitimation process. Although the *Herald* may not convince its readers directly by celebrating the oil sands' economic benefits, the appeal to inevitability constrains what we *think about*, which offers crucial leverage to oil sands proponents.

The second meta-narrative supporting the appeal to inevitability concerns the losses of the oil sands industry during 2015. Rather than avoiding coverage of low oil prices and job cuts, the media texts use these issues to highlight the irreplaceability of the industry for Alberta and Canadian economies. This narrative strategy is repetitively used by the *Herald*'s coverage on the industry's confidence in responding to the low oil prices.

Excerpt 8

> For Blake (Mayor of Fort McMurray), today's low oil prices aren't the biggest worry. "I'm more concerned about what happens when this turns around and whether we're going to be prepared adequately." [...] "We had so much growth in such a short time, that we were already behind the 8-ball," said Blake. "And so getting caught up now, it's actually a good place for us to take that reflection time and make sure that we have what we need for the people that are here without overshooting." Like Sanders (President of Fort McMurray's chamber of commerce), Blake sees some potential benefits now that the pace has slowed a bit, such as more contractors to bid on projects. The slowdown means "maybe a little time to regroup" but "no doom and gloom," said Catherine Koch, vice-president academic at Fort McMurray's Keyano College. About a third of the college's 2,500 students are pursuing careers related to oil and gas, whether that be welding, operating heavy equipment or power engineering. Koch said she's finding that, if anything, those courses are in higher demand. As things slow down, companies can free up employees to upgrade their skills, she said. Bryan Lutes, who leads Wood Buffalo Housing Development Corp., said rents aren't climbing as rapidly as they did in boom times, but they're not falling, either. "We anticipate a levelling off," he said. (Krugel, 2015)

As shown in Excerpt 8, such stories often feature a variety of industry voices, from experts to ordinary workers to illustrate that "the oil sands industry is too important to lose for Albertans." In light of the ongoing political debates on the industry across Canada, narratives like this also implicitly champion the idea that the Alberta government should function as a "petro-state" (Gunster & Saurette, 2014) to protect the industry's interests on behalf of Albertans. Compared with the "job versus environment" argument previously used by the industry, the current narrative strategy seems to be more effective since it invokes the cognitive mechanism of "loss aversion," that is, people's tendency to prefer avoiding losses over acquiring equivalent gains.

Conclusion: From Persuasion to Manipulation

This chapter has elucidated the discursive tactics employed by the *Calgary Herald* in its coverage of the oil sands industry. By doing so, the chapter makes a contribution to our understanding of discursive legitimation in environmental debates. Working with data in a synergic way, the analysis has demonstrated how a favorable story line regarding the oil sands industry was fabricated across different linguistic levels. At the phrasal level, the economic benefits and the centrality to provincial and federal politics of the concept "oil sands" were emphasized extensively, yet little reporting addressed important issues such as this energy source's unconventional nature and its disproportionate negative effects on First Nation communities. The analysis identified two manipulative strategies (i.e., binary construction and appeal to inevitability) in framing the oil sands industry as too important for Albertans and Canadians to lose.

Although the findings may not come as a surprise, given the *Herald*'s known association with the oil sands industry, they still invite us to consider the differences between "persuasion" and "manipulation" in discursive legitimation. According to van Dijk (2006), discursive manipulation is "a form of illegitimate influence by means of discourse in which manipulators make others believe or do things that are in the interest of the manipulator, and against the best interests of the manipulated" (p. 360). The crucial factor distinguishing manipulation from discursive persuasion is that the former tends to be a one-sided practice, which is built upon abuse of discursive power. Through discursive manipulation, recipients are turned into passive victims instead of active discussion participants.

Viewing from this perspective, the justificatory discourses found in the *Herald*'s news become problematic since their ideological enclosure on alternatives to the oil sands fundamentally weakens the deliberative aspect of a valid legitimation process (Fairclough & Fairclough, 2012). What makes such manipulation even worse is its covertness, which allows the oil sands industry to easily embed their ideological standpoints in seemingly unproblematic news stories. In an age when climate change has become a global priority, fossil fuel corporations adopt strategies like this to maintain existing unsustainable social and economic structures. In this regard, struggles over discursive power and space have become a frontier of environmental politics. However, the notable trend of media concentration nowadays is corroding the spaces for dialectical public conversations.

The need for thorough research on the discursive dynamics of environmental politics has been proposed as terrain for communication studies. The growing public concern on climate change is driving the oil and gas sector's discursive promotion into a new era, with overt persuasion being gradually replaced by covert manipulation. Although it is still too early to comprehensively assess the impacts of this discursive shift, the shift adopted by the oil and gas sector for prolonging their dominance in current and future environmental politics should be contested by critical communication scholarship.

References

After final deliberations. November 2, 2015. *The Calgary Herald*, p. A5.

Baker, P., Gabrielatos, C., & McEnery. T. 2013. *Discourse Analysis and Media Attitudes: The Representation of Islam in the British Press*. Cambridge: Cambridge University Press.

Baker, P., & McEnery, T. (eds) 2015. *Corpora and Discourse: Integrating Discourse and Corpora*. London: Palgrave.

Beetham, D. 1991. *The Legitimation of Power*. Basingstoke, Hampshire: Macmillan Education.

Braid, D. 12 November 2015. "I'm No Enemy of the Oil Sands, Environment Minister Says." *The Calgary Herald*, p. A4.

Breeze, R. 2012. "Legitimation in Corporate Discourse: Oil Corporations after Deep-Water Horizon." *Discourse & Society*, *23*(1), 3–18. doi:10.1177/0957926511431511

Calgary Herald Fast Facts. 2016. Retrieved from http://www.postmediaadvertising.com/

Davidson, D. J., & Gismondi, M. 2011. *Challenging Legitimacy at the Precipice of Energy Calamity*. New York, NY: Springer Press.

Fairclough, N., & Fairclough, I. 2012. *Political Discourse Analysis: A Method for Advanced Students*. London: Routledge.

Fonseca, P., & Ferreira, M.J. 2015. "Through 'Seas Never Before Sailed': Portuguese Government Discursive Legitimation Strategies in a Context of Financial Crisis." *Discourse & Society*, *26*(6), 682–711. doi:10.1177/0957926515592780

Friedel, T.L. 2008. "(Not So) Crude Text and Images: Staging Native in 'Big Oil' Advertising." *Visual Studies*, *23*(3), 238–254. doi:10.1080/14725860802489908

Gehl, J. August 17, 2015. "Climate Hysteria." *The Calgary Herald*, p. B7.

Giddens, A. 1984. *The Construction of Society*. Cambridge: Polity Press.

Gunster, S., & Saurette, P. 2014. "Storylines in the Sands: News, Narrative, and Ideology in the *Calgary Herald*." *Canadian Journal of Communication*, *39*(3), 333–359.

Healing, D. January 14, 2015. "Suncor Cuts 1,000 jobs; Premier Rejects Suggestion Alberta Headed for Recession." *The Calgary Herald*, p. A1.

Honarvar, A., Rozhon, J., Millington, D., Walden, T., Murillo, C.A., & Walden, Z. 2011. "Economic Impacts of New Oil Sands Projects in Alberta (2010–2035)." Calgary, AB: Canadian Energy Research Institute and University of Calgary. Retrieved from http://www.api.org

Klassen, K. November 3, 2015. "Notley Owes us the Numbers for Climate Action." *The Calgary Herald*, p. B5.

Krugel, L. February 3, 2015. "Pause, but not Panic, in Fort Mac; Low Oil Prices Haven't Halted the City – Instead, it Has a Chance to Regroup." *The Calgary Herald*, p. A6.

Mackay, R.R. 2015. "Multimodal Legitimation: Selling Scottish Independence." *Discourse & Society*, *26*(3), 323–348. doi:10.1177/0957926514564737

Nelson, C. July 23, 2015. "You Can't Have Your Cake without the Power that Heats the Oven; We Enjoy the Good Life Oil Pays for Yet We Still Protest Energy Development." *The Calgary Herald*, p. A18.

Nikiforuk, A. 2010. *Tar Sands: Dirty Oil and the Future of a Continent* (Rev. ed.). Vancouver, BC: Greystone.

Raso, K., & Neubauer, R.J. 2016. "Managing Dissent: Energy Pipelines and 'New Right' Politics in Canada." *Canadian Journal of Communication, 41*(1), 115–133.

Remillard, C. 2011. "Picturing Environmental Risk: The Canadian Oil Sands and the *National Geographic*." *International Communication Gazette, 73*(1–2), 127–143. doi:10.1177/1748048510386745

Stefanick, L., & Shrivastava, M. 2015. *Alberta Oil and the Decline of Democracy in Canada*. Edmonton, AB: Athabasca University Press.

Takach, G. 2013. "Selling Nature in a Resource-Based Economy: Romantic/Extractive Gazes and Alberta's Bituminous Sands." *Environmental Communication, 7*(2), 211–230. doi:10.1080/17524032.2013.778208

Thomson, G. June 13, 2015. "Honeymoon almost over for Motley's NDP; Wild Rose Lands Solid Jab against Government and its New Hires." *The Calgary Herald*, p. A25.

van Dijk, T. 2006. "Discourse and Manipulation." *Discourse & Society, 17*(3), 359–383. doi:10.1177/0957926506060250

van Leeuwen, T. 2007. "Legitimation in Discourse and Communication." *Discourse & Communication, 1*(1), 91–112. doi:10.1177/1750481307071986

Vaara, E. 2014. "Struggles over Legitimacy in the Eurozone Crisis: Discursive Legitimation Strategies and their Ideological Underpinnings." *Discourse & Society, 25*(4), 500–518. doi:10.1177/0957926514536962

Way, Laura. 2011. "An Energy Superpower or a Super Sales Pitch? Building the Case through an Examination of Canadian Newspapers Coverage of Oil Sands." *Canadian Political Science Review, 5*(1), 74–98.

Wodak, R., & Meyer, M. 2016. "Critical Discourse Studies: History, Agenda, Theory, and Methodology." In R. Wodak & M. Meyer (eds.), *Methods for Critical Discourse Analysis* (3rd ed., pp. 1–22). Thousand Oaks, CA: Sage Publishing.

15 How Not to Stop a Pipeline

A Critique of Activism in the Burnaby Mountain Protests

Sean Zwagerman

On December 16, 2013, the Kinder Morgan corporation filed an application with the National Energy Board (NEB) of Canada seeking to triple the capacity of the Trans Mountain pipeline, allowing it to carry 890,000 gallons per day of mixed petroleum products from the Alberta tar sands to Burnaby, British Columbia (BC) for export to China (2016). Declaring that the project is in the public interest, the NEB on May 19, 2016 recommended federal approval, subject to 157 conditions (Morgan). The Canadian government approved the pipeline in November, 2016, and Kinder Morgan plans to complete the project in December 2019. Proponents of the project cite the benefits of job creation and tax revenues (2016), while opponents—including Burnaby Residents Opposing Kinder Morgan Expansion—argue that the project will result in "the degradation of our city, our neighborhoods, and the natural habitat" (BROKE, 2016). Kinder Morgan's preferred route for the pipeline runs under a corner of Burnaby Mountain, site of a city park, unceded First Nations land, and Simon Fraser University. This corner of the mountain has been the site of protests receiving national and international media coverage. In 2014, over one hundred protesters were arrested, and two SFU professors, my colleague Stephen Collis from the English Department[1] and Lynne Quarmby from Molecular Biology and Biochemistry, were among five activists named in a $5.6 million civil suit, wherein Kinder Morgan accused them, as leaders of the protest, of costing the company millions of dollars in delays by interfering with survey crews. On November 26, 2014, Justice Austin Cullen dismissed the arrests "because of GPS errors in the injunction specifying the exact location of the no-go zone" (2014). Quarmby declared Cullen's decision a "fabulous victory" (Uechi, 2014), as did the "Burnaby Mountain Updates" Facebook page, which credited the protesters with driving away Kinder Morgan's surveyors:

> Hundreds of people are expected to arrive at Burnaby Mountain on Saturday and Sunday to celebrate a significant victory against Kinder Morgan, and to resolve to continue the years-long campaign to stop the pipeline. . . . After three months of presence by caretakers

> on Burnaby Mountain, hundreds of residents showing up every day for two weeks of protests against Kinder Morgan drilling activity, and 125 arrests, the pipeline company removed their equipment and stopped their survey work. (2014)

A closer look at the judge's decision and the surveyors' departure challenges this causal claim (and thus the use of the word "victory"), while a consideration of polling data challenges the wisdom of resuming the protest when construction begins.

Citing Kinder Morgan's own testimony, Justice Cullen ruled that the company had no need to remain on Burnaby Mountain because surveyors had already obtained "a sufficient level of information from geotechnical and engineering studies to meet the [NEB's] information requests" (Uechi, 2014). The protesters did not expel Kinder Morgan's surveyors: the surveyors left because they had what they needed. And though it was no doubt a huge relief for the protesters to have the criminal charges dismissed, the dismissal was not a victory for civil disobedience but the procedural result of Kinder Morgan's GPS error. To his credit, Collis does not join the chorus declaring victory; "so far, no pipeline has been stopped" (2015).

Unquestionably, the Burnaby Mountain protest has succeeded in drawing attention to the pipeline project. What the protest has not done—and, I will argue, has almost no chance of doing in the future if it continues in its present form—is stop the pipeline. A poll shows Canadians in overwhelming agreement: 88% predict that the pipeline will be built despite protests (Hager, 2014). My purpose here is to explain why the Burnaby Mountain protest has not accomplished, and will not accomplish, its goal. Achieving this goal involves influencing public opinion and motivating people to act, which requires participants to try to understand the opinions, values, and motives of nonparticipants. But activists leading the protest have shown little effort—or even interest—in such understanding. So, my initial question is a simple one: why are activists saying these things? Since we can expect more protests on Burnaby Mountain, and since it is important from an environmental perspective to reduce or, ideally, eliminate extraction from the Alberta tar sands, this environmental exigence is also a rhetorical exigence.

After describing the activists and the audience of the Burnaby Mountain protest, I employ speech-act theory and Burkean rhetoric to categorize the protesters' speech acts and analyze three key terms which appear throughout their discourse, terms which activists invoke as fundamental to their ideology and their choice of tactics: "direct action," "diversity," and "non-hierarchy." Motivated by their belief in these principles, activists engage in civil disobedience I call "expressive protest," which privileges the beliefs and desires of the speaker while showing minimal interest in an audience other than the like-minded. I argue that this prioritizing of ideology and belief over pragmatism and persuasion shows the activists to be working in what Burke calls the "ultimate order" (1966), rather than in the dialectical order where policy is made. Finally, to put this critique of a particular protest into the larger context of rhetoric and writing, I identify the continuities between expressive protest and expressivist pedagogy, the former sharing the latter's emphasis upon the authentic individual voice at the expense of collective, dialogic, and pragmatic speech acts.

The Protesters and the Public

First, I shall try to characterize the attitudes and desires of both the Burnaby Mountain activists and the public. I want to distinguish protesters from activists and focus primarily on the latter. "Protester" is a temporary position: after the protest is over, the protester is no longer a protester. But an activist never stops being an activist—in part because the protest, or as they are more likely to call it, the struggle, is never over. Activists tend to inhabit the political extremes; I am not aware of any group called, say, "Activists for Compromise." Collis, Harsha Walia, and David Graeber identify as activists rather than as protesters. Describing himself as an activist and an anarchist, Graeber is on the far left, while over on the far right are people like Joseph Scheidler, founder of the Pro-Life Action League and also a self-described activist. I focus on the words and actions of the activists because they tend to be the ones interviewed as spokespeople (Collis, 2015) and are the ones writing books, blogs, tweets, and Facebook updates about their activism. These are the documents I analyze.

"From the motivational point of view," Kenneth Burke writes, "there is implicit in the quality of a scene the quality of the action that is to take place within it" (1945: 6–7). If the scene is Burnaby Mountain, then the protesters' actions have followed a certain scenic logic. Conforming to the scripts of the campus free speech movement of the 1960s and West Coast anti-logging protests of the 1970s and 1980s, Burnaby Mountain protesters have blocked survey crews, chained themselves to equipment, occupied trees, cooperated with police for noisy confrontations and arrests, and attempted—on the scenic logic of geographic proximity—to get Simon Fraser University to officially oppose the pipeline. Given the establishment of Burnaby Mountain as the scene of protest (and given the political inclinations of participating activists), it is not surprising that the activists' argument against Kinder Morgan has relied so heavily on the claim that Burnaby Mountain is unceded First Nations land. Collis (2015) includes "issues relating to Aboriginal title" among topics he believes people are "increasingly concerned about," and Walia cites "encroachment onto Indigenous territories" as part of the "broader context" within which "standing with the caretakers of Burnaby Mountain becomes even more crucial" (2014). "No pipelines on stolen native land" has been a popular chant and protest sign (Wheatley, 2016), and, in a concentrated distillation of activist "god terms" (Weaver, 1985)—those words which, like Burke's "ultimate" terms, connect one's actions and utterances to powerful and positive symbols and beliefs—the Burnaby Mountain Facebook page identifies itself as "Timely updates from so called Burnaby Mountain, on unceded Coast Salish Territories, in the struggle against Kinder Morgan" ("Burnaby Mountain Updates," 2014).

But the scope of what J.L. Austin calls "the total speech situation" (1975: 148) is a matter of opinion. While some activists see aboriginal land claims—along with climate change, capitalism, gender discrimination, and war (Walia, 2015)—as the context for, and inseparable from, the Trans Mountain pipeline controversy, most of the public does not. While 61% of Burnaby residents oppose the project, 93% list oil spills as a primary concern, and 84% list increased tanker traffic (Insights West, 2014: 11). First Nations land issues and climate change do not even warrant their own line in these poll results, though these are perhaps included in the 12% "other" category (Insights West, 2014: 11). So too on the national level, where even opponents of pipelines rank "aboriginal and treaty rights" as their lowest concern (Walia, 2014). On the pipeline expansion itself, polls show Canadians almost evenly split. A November 2014 poll shows 51% in support of the pipeline—47% in BC, 75% in Alberta (Harrison, 2015). A 2016 poll again shows 51% approving, with 35% disapproving, and 14% unsure—41%, 52%, and 6% in BC (Forum Research, 2016). Another 2016 poll of BC residents found 45% supporting the pipeline, 36% opposed, and 19% unsure (Insights West, 2016). Regarding the protest, Canadians are again more or less evenly divided, with 53% supporting the demonstrations (Harrison, 2015). It seems obvious that activists should be addressing the potentially persuadable—the 35% of people in BC unfamiliar with the project, the 24% only moderately in support, and the 19% undecided (Insights West, 2016)—while de-emphasizing issues of little or no public concern, and weighing the likely impact of their words and actions in light of how they might be represented by the media and perceived by the Canadian audience, only 53% of whom support the protest in the first place. As Kathryn Harrison says, "the people that need to be convinced don't look like the activists" (2016). Nor, in many ways, do they think like the activists. So, why have activists been so misattuned to the beliefs, values, and concerns of the people who should be their primary audience?

Key Terms in the Speech Acts of Protest: Direct Action, Diversity, and Non-Hierarchy

I find the terminologies of speech-act theory and of Burkean dramatism useful in analyzing what the Burnaby Mountain activists are doing and saying. Burke observes how well they cooperate: "I would equate an utterance's illocutionary force with its role in explicitly or implicitly symbolizing an attitude" (1975, 154–155). John Searle (1979) speaks to this cooperation, noting that the attitude participants take toward a collective, linguistically constructed, social phenomenon largely determines the ontology of that phenomenon (33). Both Searle and Austin distinguish between illocution ("the performance of an act *in* saying something" [1975, 99]) and perlocution (the fact that "[s]aying something will often, or even normally, produce certain consequential effects upon the feelings, thoughts, or actions of the audience" [101]). Significantly, Austin notes that while illocution is "conventional" in the sense that it can be successfully uttered in explicit, idiomatic form, perlocution is not; that is, one can argue by saying "I argue that," but cannot persuade by saying "I persuade you that." Burke finds Austin's passing observation of persuasion's asymmetry "quietly jolting" (1975, 157); "This is a radical matter," Burke writes, since "traditionally, 'persuasion' is the term of terms in texts on rhetoric" (1975, 157).

The upshot of persuasion's resistance to the explicit, first-person, performative formula is that while one can, as long as certain necessary conditions are met (1975, 14–15), use myriad "scripted" utterances as successful illocutionary acts ("I promise," "You're fired," "Class dismissed"), successful persuasion—i.e., rhetoric in the narrow sense—must be approached strategically; it cannot be declared because the agency and will which primarily determine the speech act's success reside not in the speaker but in the audience. Aristotle recognizes the perlocutionary essence of rhetoric when he states that something is persuasive "because there is somebody whom it persuades" (1959, I.2); as Burke puts it, "In light of Austin's clear distinction [between attempting an illocutionary act and succeeding], we realize that a wholly accurate title for Aristotle's text would be something like 'The Art of *Trying* to be as Persuasive as One can'" 1975, 158). Thus, Burke does connect Austinian speech-act theory with rhetoric generally and with his own dramatistic rhetoric in particular:

> in the course of using speech acts to be persuasive, to the best of my ability I would so design my speech as to form, in the audience, the kind of attitudes that would lead them to adopt the policies or judgments I am advocating (1975, 158).

Burke articulates precisely what Burnaby Mountain activists have *not* done: selected their illocutionary acts based on purpose and audience, while mindful of what perlocutionary effects are even possible for a particular illocutionary act.

An analysis of the terministic screen of contemporary leftist activism reveals why the protest has been rhetorically inept and misattuned.

Three terms that recur in contemporary activism are “direct action,” “diversity,” and “non-hierarchical.” These terms support a civil disobedience which I call “expressive protest”—one which, by privileging the beliefs and desires of the speaker while showing little interest in audience, inhibits its own effectiveness.

“Direct Action”

David Graeber uses “action” to refer to “anything from leafleting in front of a supermarket to shutting down a global summit” (2009, 359). Collis endorses Graeber’s definition of “direct action” as involving confrontation (“After . . . Part 3”), immediate and physical acts of protest: vandalism, human blockades, confrontations with police, and chaining one’s self to things are all examples of direct action, with the implication that working for change through legislative or judicial channels or using other nonphysical means of persuasion is indirect, passive, and inferior. Graeber endorses this hierarchy of tactics: his belief that the goal of activism is a world “without capital or state” makes it hypocritical to seek change through state institutions. Collis seems less dogmatic, granting that “there are some contexts in which our current system ‘works,’ or can be made to ‘work,’ and many others in which it very clearly does not” (February 12, 2015). On the other hand, the contrast between “some” and “many” and his selective use of scare quotes around ‘works’ indicate that Collis’ position is close to Graeber’s. And like Graeber (2009, 420ff) and Walia (2013, 182), Collis imagines power as monolithic, embodied in “the state” and “the system,” thus making power abstract, inhuman, and unassailable.

What Quarmby (2014) calls “a mounting sense of desperation” justifies direct action. “The most pressing issues we face,” Collis writes, “require us to take direct action outside of the electoral and representative apparatus of governance” (October 14, 2015). We see this same logic—that urgency precludes seeking change through conventional democratic processes—in Scheidler (1985, 1): “Pro-life activists cannot wait for the legislative and judicial process that will make abortion illegal. The activist has to save lives now.” The importance of the issue compels us to take matters into our own hands, to physicalize democratic participation—against, paradoxically, a disembodied conception of institutional power.

Activists are making a mistake in how they define “direct.” For now, the fate of the Trans Mountain project has been determined by a declarative illocutionary act: its approval in November, 2016 by Trudeau’s cabinet. Since the federal government is the scene of decision-making authority, it is also the primary scene of direct public influence—of direct action. Only a large and stable social institution—the Canadian government—has the authority and the power to stop a 1,000 km, $5.4 billion infrastructure project. The outcome of the protest at Standing

Rock in North Dakota should serve as a cautionary example. Though a compelling event, Standing Rock was, practically speaking, a failure; protesters did not achieve their goal of preventing construction of the Dakota Access Pipeline. Here in Canada, Kinder Morgan will build the pipeline in spite of the protesters; they will not build it in spite of the government. Nor will physical acts of delay, disruption, or sabotage make the pipeline sufficiently unprofitable; the protesters will not be able to significantly affect the bottom line of a huge, diversified, international corporation in the way that boycotts decimated the profits of the Montgomery Bus Lines. No, if the conflict is physical, the state will win. The state has far more legal and physical power—and if need be, violence—at its disposal than does a group of protesters with a 53% popularity rating.

If the goal of activists and protesters is stopping the Trans Mountain pipeline, they need to recognize that the truly direct acts of protest are speech acts. The primary scene of direct action is participatory democracy, via the conventional channels for influencing the decisions (and the membership) of the federal cabinet, and so the act of protest must say to Canadian citizens, "to stop the pipeline, make cabinet members fear that approving it will cost them their jobs." (Now that this particular pipeline has been approved, the scene of direct action moves to the courts). Only in those institutional scenes do words of protest "count as" something other than just themselves.[2] Putting a bumper sticker on my car that says "Vote Trump" and marking a ballot next to the name "Trump" express the same attitude. But whereas the bumper sticker is purely expressive, marking the ballot actually counts as a vote for Trump. There is a context in which "we object to the pipeline" counts as an official objection among the people actually empowered to make that decision. On the ground in Burnaby Mountain is not that context. The decisions already handed down by the NEB and the Canadian government and any current and future legal challenges are such contexts. Searle calls such decisions declarations (1979, 16), a powerful type of performative utterance which brings about that which is uttered, as the baseball umpire's "You're out" does not just describe the batter being out but *makes* the batter out. As institutional, language-dependent facts, state policy (and the state itself) are "made of"—and remade through—democracy and language. So linguistic, performative acts of democracy are direct, while obstructing surveyors, confronting the police, and getting arrested are indirect. Regarding Enbridge's controversial Northern Gateway pipeline, Jon Gordon writes, "To be successful, opponents will need to speak in a context in which they have institutional authority" (2015, 124). Effective protest, then, should inform people about the pipeline and try to persuade them to oppose it in the contexts where that opposition counts. Voters in the Burnaby-Lougheed riding elected NDP newcomer Katrina Chen in 2017, in part because of her opposition to Trans Mountain. But unless this victory for local opposition results in political action at the national level, Kinder Morgan will have its way. So, to the argument that perhaps Burnaby Mountain activists are thinking locally and aren't trying to persuade a national audience,[3] I say that that is precisely the problem. Effective protest does need to motivate at the micro level—appealing to a specific audience, based upon their concerns—but then must mobilize that interest as civic engagement at whatever institutional level determines policy. But effective protest appears unlikely if activists are in charge, since activists, as Graeber (2009) says, see "existing structures of authority as illegitimate" (359).

Instead of a declaration, the protesters' primary illocutionary act has been the expressive speech act (Searle, 1979, *15*) "we protest." Like "agree" or "deplore," expressives communicate a psychological state—in this case, an opinion—of the speaker. Whether waving a sign, crossing a police line, or occupying a tree, the protesters' words and actions all have had the illocutionary force "we protest." Where declarative illocutions can change minds and change institutional reality, expressives don't necessarily or reliably change anything. First, all that are required for the success of an expressive are the sincerity of the speaker and literal comprehension by the audience. I believe most of the Burnaby Mountain protesters are sincere, and since their protest has followed the conventional protest script, it has been obvious that protesting is what's going on. Thus, the protest *as a protest* has been a success, because the illocutionary act "we protest" is self-satisfying; by *saying* "we protest," the protesters *do* protest, and participants can go home each day satisfied that they have done what they set out to do: protest.

That expressive protest is self-satisfying—that to say "we protest" is to protest—makes any goal or purpose unnecessary. On Burnaby Mountain, the direct object of "we protest" has evolved from the specific and (at least potentially) achievable—we protest the expansion of this pipeline because it may threaten the local environment (BROKE, 2016)—to the more divisive and less tangible—we protest climate change—to the increasingly divisive and unpopular—we want all land which we consider unceded returned to First Nations control—to the improbable and uncompromising—"We will accept nothing less than leaving coal, gas and oil in the ground!" ("Burnaby Mountain Updates," 2014)—to the delusional: we want the end of capitalism and of Canada. (Walia [2014] can't even bring herself to say "Canada," instead using the First Nations name "Turtle Island," a place of the mind with no institutions of performative civic engagement). Expressive protest concerns itself with the expression of disapproval. Among protesters, the globalizing of the Burnaby Mountain protest may be the result of losing control of the argument. But among activists, it has been purposeful and ideological. Walia opposes "reformism" (2013, 182)—focused, pragmatic actions—citing Ng'ethe Maina's opinion that "We should not be doing campaigns that cannot be connected to a broader ideological conversation" (2013, 184). Walia offers this stunning example:

> If . . . we restrain ourselves from fully *expressing* [emphasis added] our systemic analysis, for instance, on prison abolition within a neighborhood meeting about increased school tuition, we are losing critical opportunities to engage with others about the interconnections in the school-to-prison pipeline. (2013, 180)

Note that Walia's rhetorical motive here is not addressing tuition increases—the stated purpose of the meeting—but rather appropriating that scene as a platform to expound what she elsewhere calls her "political vision." In like manner, Walia does globalize the Kinder Morgan pipeline by connecting it to the U.S. "military industrial complex" (2014). As an example of what Searle calls "a holistic ideology," leftist activism imagines "the structure of power [as] a seamless fabric" (1972, 23) unifying Canada, capitalism, Kinder Morgan, racism, sexism, and the U.S. military.

"Diversity"

The second counterproductive god term is "diversity," as in "diversity of tactics:" "in different moments, different tactics are productive and effective," Walia says (Polychronakos, 2015). As with "direct action," I believe activists are misusing "diversity." For the question arises— "productive and effective" for what?—Walia's answer is, "in meeting strategic goals" (2013, 185). But activists' writings celebrate unfettered self-expression as the most valued form of free speech, more than they advocate the use of speech performatively to change institutional reality. For as Romantics, Searle recognizes, activists fail "to see freedoms (and when you use the plural, you force yourself to look at concrete examples) as necessarily presupposing stable and established institutions," instead seeing "freedom (the unmodified singular is a largely meaningless abstraction) as being constantly at war with authority and institutions" (1972, 156). Like Walia (2013, 177ff), Collis (February 12, 2015) promotes "diversity" of tactics and "respect" for "a range of tactical approaches." But this ecumenical attitude of allowing each to protest in his or her own way must reject as heresy the rhetorical reality that some tactics might be more effective than others in achieving any goal other than unfettered expression or protest itself. Walia writes about the effectiveness of various tactics, concluding that "the question of whether a tactic is effective or not is entirely contextual" (2013, 187). Walia's context includes the range of possible tactics, the participants' "goals and purpose," and their long-term ideological "vision." But never once does Walia recognize that audience is part of that context, that acts of protest are *addressed*.

Instead, she answers the question of how one decides among tactics by saying that "those engaging in the action are best suited to decide" (2013, 187). Collis (February 12, 2015) seems to concur, writing of the importance of "allowing room, and even respect, for our different experiences—communicating and coordinating together—even when this means those differences seem (depending on your position) more 'radical,' or more 'liberal,' than you'd normally be comfortable with." So, Collis' "our" is Walia's "those engaged in the action" (2013), with no mention of extending respect—or even curiosity—to the opposition or the undecided. "The point, to me," Collis continues, "is not . . . whose tactics are better, or more likely to succeed, and whose are doomed to failure. . . . The question to me is how a diversity of tactics . . . might actually function" (February 12, 2015). Collis' error is separating these two topics and thinking that one can functionally mobilize a diversity of tactics without asking which tactics work better than others. If we don't ask that question, then we're not really even talking about tactics; it's just a bunch of like-minded people doing stuff simultaneously.

Nowhere in his blog entries (2015) about tactical debates does Collis show an interest in using, as a measure of assessment, the reception of tactics by the protest's audience. For Collis, the debate about tactics on Burnaby Mountain is entirely internal and about figuring out how all the participants can find a space to do their own thing. "But I'm not so deluded," he writes, "that I think . . . we are going to find the silver bullet tactic we can all get down with here and now" (February 12, 2015). It is extremely telling that the "silver bullet tactic" is not the one which stops the pipeline, but the one which satisfies the individual desires of each participant. Harrison (2015) argues that the impacts of civil disobedience on a democratic audience will occur at the margins, in swing ridings (i.e., districts) and among swing voters and new voters. The average Canadian swing voter is in his or her early 1950s and considers climate change a low priority (Harrison, 2015). These swing voters should be a target audience for the Burnaby Mountain protest. But to these potential allies against the pipeline, the television news broadcasts scenes from Burnaby Mountain of activists baiting and clashing with the police.[4] According to a 2012 poll, 70% of swing voters have a moderate or high level of trust in the RCMP (Harrison, 2015). Again, is the goal of protest to express one's self or to stop the pipeline? If it's the latter, participants must be selective about the former. But selection has been absent on Burnaby Mountain and is contrary to the ideology of direct action, diversity, and non-hierarchy. Why have activists been so misattuned to the beliefs, values, and concerns of the public? Perhaps persuading the public is not the goal at all.

One objection to my critique of diversity is that the protest looks the way it does—tactically heterogeneous—because it's a grassroots, bottom-up phenomenon.[5] But the fact that a collective action is bottom-up does not preclude coherent, organized, and collective intentionality. A pickup basketball game is a bottom-up phenomenon, but it's guided by a shared understanding and acceptance of the norms by which everyone must conduct themselves if they're going to have a functional basketball game. What's missing on Burnaby Mountain is a shared acceptance of the norms by which everyone must conduct themselves if they're going to stop the pipeline. Furthermore, to the extent that it's governed by ideology and—as I will describe later—by ultimate terms (Burke, 1950, 183ff), this protest is a top-down phenomenon. To the extent that activists have served as spokespeople, the protest has been governed by political—in this case, leftist—ideology, *a* protest recast as a moment in the historical trajectory of *the* struggle. The particularities of the pipeline—and even of climate change—are lost amid, or made subordinate to, the sweeping context of "climate justice," a political position characterized by (as Walia describes it) anti-capitalism, economic isolationism, and ethnic nationalism (2015). The further the context of the Burnaby Mountain protest expands beyond the specific issue of the Trans Mountain pipeline, the smaller the number of people it will appeal to—in both senses of "appeal." As a practical suggestion for future protests, I will here propose a simple equation: if the ultimate goal of a protest is the overthrow of the state and/or capitalism and if the scene is present-day Canada (or the United States, for that matter), then the explicit association of a specific protest with that ultimate goal will result in the failure of the protest. Without a clear, achievable thesis and some specific, valid, audience-sensitive, persuasive reasons supporting it, "we protest" does what expressives do—it expresses the mental state of the speakers—and other impacts will be unpredictable and likely coincidental.

"Non-Hierarchical"

A participant in the Burnaby Mountain protest describes "an impromptu moment of peace-making in this non-hierarchical group of protectors. People united in a circle of prayer. We repeated a 'hum' in a spiritual practice" (Mathias, 2014). The third god term, "non-hierarchical," refers to a vision of social movements without leaders, imagined in opposition to "the system" which activists perceive themselves battling (Polychronakos, 2015). Mia Nissen, one of the activists sued by Kinder Morgan, says, "They're singling out Lynne [Quarmby], Stephen [Collis], myself and Adam. They think we operate under the same hierarchical system that they do, but we don't" (Prystupa, 2014). Exemplifying non-hierarchy is Graeber's "autonomous march":

> [T]he experience of taking part in an autonomous march—in which anyone can try to start a chant, or improvise a new chant, and then, if it catches on, experience their own individual initiative suddenly

> become a moment of collective dissolution of individuality, as all speak in a collective voice, then follow along as others start new ones—is a kind of democratization of effervescence. (2009, 485)

Graeber measures the value of a protest by the experience of those participating in it, with success characterized as a sudden moment of feeling, a spontaneous collective epiphany—*for the protesters*, for those already moved and convinced by their own words. This is not an argument addressed to other people; it is a hymn of solidarity. Graeber does ask the essential rhetorical question, "What [message] does get through?", and gives the promising answer, "The question is one of the intended audience" (2009, 489). But the promise goes unfulfilled. Admitting that he has "not conducted any actual surveys," Graeber instead quotes the "N30 Black Bloc Communiqué" to discuss what property destruction means *to those doing it*: "When we smash a window, we aim to destroy the thin veneer of legitimacy that surrounds private property rights" (qtd. in Graeber, 2009, 489). On Graeber's reading, "Smashing windows and spray-painting is . . . a smashing of the surface of the Spectacle" (2009, 490). Note that both Graeber and the author(s) of the "Communiqué" seem interested solely in the significance of the act *for the actor.* The rhetorical effect of property destruction for the audience goes unremarked, while the expression—the activist's "externalizing of himself" (Burke, 1941, 6)—is all-important. So too may residents of Burnaby—63% of whom oppose Kinder Morgan's project—be reluctant to support a protest which declares that their homes are on stolen native land (Angus Reid Public Opinion, 2012). But faith in non-hierarchy, in concert with diversity and direct action, precludes participants from thinking that perhaps someone should be orchestrating the various acts of protest, or critiquing and selecting among the diversity of spontaneous effervescences.

The ideal of non-hierarchy is rhetorically disempowering in that it disqualifies *ethos*: it negates the deployment, or even the recognition, of expertise. On Burnaby Mountain, what counts as credible and persuasive has been determined by looking inward to the participants' own beliefs and values. Embodying the protest's emphasis on First Nations land claims, Grand Chief Stewart Phillip and Tsleil-Waututh Elder Ta'ah Amy George allowed themselves to be arrested on Burnaby Mountain, in a solemn and visually powerful scene. But as stated earlier, the First Nations angle is not salient for most Canadians, so the elders' *ethos* is unclear—especially given the equally honorable behavior of the RCMP: "Ok, sir," said the arresting officer, "I'll let you make your decision, I'll be standing here in person to take you into custody, and obviously I want to do that with as much dignity as possible" (Prystupa and Uechi, 2014).

If the non-protesting opponents of the pipeline are not much concerned with First Nations land claims (or with climate change), what are they concerned with? Oil spills. An article in the *National Post* notes that "A broader public concern than greenhouse gas increases is safety, and the belief is that the public can be persuaded transporting oil by pipeline is preferable, and safer, than shipping by rail" (Ivison, 2016). This belief is likely correct: "Three times as many voters say pipelines are the safest way to transport crude oil (61%) as say this of rail (20%)" (Forum Research, 2016). Now, "We should support the pipeline because oil trains are even more dangerous" is a laughably bad argument. But there's no denying that, with its invocation of apocalyptic images of the 2013 oil train explosion which killed forty-seven people in Lac-Megantic, Quebec, this argument gives pipeline proponents the upper hand on the issue most important to the people who can influence the outcome: actual and potential Canadian voters. Meanwhile, activists' focus on climate change deflects their attention from an argument right under their feet, one which would require them to consider scene a bit more deeply, as geology and not just politicized geography. People are concerned about oil spills; Kinder Morgan wants to expand storage at their Burnaby Mountain tank farm from 1.4 million to 5.4 million barrels; and several recent studies indicate the potential for earthquakes under Burnaby Mountain (see Clague, 2014; Jones, 2014). But these reports are ignored in activists' speeches, interviews, and blogs. While Kinder Morgan wages a savvy and consistent campaign across multiple platforms, the Burnaby Mountain Facebook page features protesters fighting amongst themselves over whether the people tending the sacred fire at the protest site have to be First Nations. Protesters who want to accomplish their goals would do well to renounce—or at least critically reconsider—their god terms, and to seek leadership from somewhere other than the ranks of self-identified activists.

The Ultimate Order

The infighting among protesters exposes a fundamental problem with non-hierarchy. Hierarchy is intrinsic to language, since to make distinctions is to invite comparisons. And judgment—in all its meanings—is central to rhetoric. Since we cannot (nor should we) avoid assessment and judgment, and since protest is a rhetorical act of address and appeal, then participants must pragmatically assess, judge, and hierarchize their words and gestures. So, it is with discourse in what Burke (1950) calls the "dialectical order:" "Here are words that belong, not in the order of *motion and perception*"—which Burke calls "positive terms," words for "things having a visible, tangible existence" (1950, 183)—but rather in the order of *action and idea*. Here are words for *principles*," Burke's examples including "capitalism" and "socialism" (1950, 184). In arguing that Canadian political institutions are the primary scene of public influence on the fate of Trans Mountain, I am arguing that the issue is a "parliamentary conflict" best resolved in the dialectical order (1950, 187), where each participant may "remain somewhat unconvinced by any solution which does not mean the complete triumph of his partisan interests. Yet he may have to compromise" (1950, 187). Activists' tactics, however, are designed "to maximize the adversary relationship with authorities," and "precisely not designed to produce cooperation or manifest a spirit of conciliation or compromise" (Searle, 1972, 20). In terms of rhetorical orders, the third and final aspect of my critique, Burnaby Mountain activists are operating within the "ultimate order," which differs "from the 'dialectical' . . . in that there would be a 'guiding idea' or 'unitary principle' behind the diversity of voices" (Burke, 1950, 187). To cite Burke's particularly apt example, "Precisely by reason of this ultimate order, a spokesman for the proletariat can think of himself as representing not only the interests of that class alone, but the grand design of the entire historical sequence, its final outcome for all mankind" (1950, 190–191). In an ultimate framework, since the present "moment" is part of "a universal movement," each situation is "simultaneously the concrete thing it is, in its own unique combination of conditions, and a participant in the perfection of the total sequence" (1950, 191).

Since contemporary leftist activism is, by its adherents' own admission, committed to bringing about "a universal movement" (1950, 187), it must seem natural to activists to extend the context of the Trans Mountain "moment" to include climate change, First Nations rights, globalization, and capitalism, to support opposition to the pipeline with an "argument from transcendence" (Stewart, 2001, 274), locating this moment of protest within the historical "struggle." Since in the ultimate order opposing stances are seen as successive rather than dialectical, the attitudes of others are not something to be negotiated but something to be transcended; progress does not involve compromising among perspectives, but leaving one perspective behind as we rise to a more enlightened one. Sometimes, this is exactly what should happen, as was the case during the Civil Rights Movement. Similarly, stopping the pipeline will involve, in part, persuading some of its current supporters to leave a perspective behind. Quarmby makes an effort in this direction when she writes, "We want plans to assist those currently working in fossil-fuel industries so they can move to healthier, well-paying jobs." But she cannot resist the trajectory of her ultimate terms, undermining this overture to the opposition by writing in the same editorial, "Pipelines and coal ports are about as backward as one can get" (Quarmby, 2014).

Conceptualized in the ultimate order, Burnaby Mountain activism has been an appeal not to an audience, and certainly not to an audience who may disagree, but to an ideology. Activists place the various aspects of, and the competing positions on, the pipeline issue in "an arrangement whereby each can be said to participate . . . in the ultimate perfection of the series" (Burke, 1950, 189–190). "How," Collis writes, "are we going to stop a pipeline, begin the transition to renewable energy, and ultimately *do something* about climate change?" (February 12, 2015). Such is the impulse of ultimate terms. To his credit, Collis is up front about his ultimate motives: "Personally, I want the revolution tomorrow" (February 12, 2015). But the vast majority of people, both for and against the pipeline, do not want the revolution tomorrow. By no means is there anything wrong with invoking ultimate terms, especially if they refer to principles shared with one's audience, a rhetorical opportunity where *ethos, pathos*, and *logos* can be invoked as one. Earthquakes and oil spills, pipelines and houses, waterways and parks are terms in the positive order, some with powerful associations in the dialectical and ultimate orders: the positive term "house," for example, can—as it does for Burnaby residents opposed to the pipeline and many Canadians of various opinions—connote the dialectical term "property," and the ultimate concept of "home." To shift the associations away from those persuasive to the audience and toward those persuasive to activists—for example, linking "house" and "property" to stolen land and the evils of capitalism—serves the activists' ideology but not the goal of stopping the pipeline.

As a physical fact, "climate change" too should be a positive term. But as Harrison (2015) points out, it is "a tougher order" to protest climate change with civil disobedience than to protest, say, the logging of old-growth forests. The latter is more "palpable and local," and easier to visualize. Also, the persistent (if decreasing) denial of climate change keeps the term at least somewhat in the dialectical order, and—most importantly for the present issue—the extent to which attitudes toward climate change have come to align with oppositional and rigidly held political ideologies invokes the ultimate order in a way which obstructs rational dialectical discourse. A recent study by Marquart-Pyatt et al (2014) indicates that "political orientation has the most important effect in shaping public perceptions about the timing and seriousness of climate change," while "objective climatic conditions . . . only have a negligible effect on [such] perceptions" (246). A study by Campbell and Kay (2014) finds that skepticism on issues like climate change "is not necessarily [motivated by] an aversion to the problem, per se, but an aversion to the solutions associated with the problem" (809). Campbell and Kay show that attitudes toward climate change policies can be shifted by aligning or opposing proposed remedies with people's preexisting political orientations. Recognizing these tendencies, some canvassers will not even mention climate change when seeking signatures for a petition opposing oil tankers or pipelines; that association tends to drive people to their hardened political position and away from a reasoned assessment of the petition (Harrison, 2015). Which brings me to a crucial point: if stopping the pipeline is a positive response to climate change, *we get that benefit whether we mention climate change or not.*

So, if it is rhetorically counterproductive to express it, then don't. But by associating Trans Mountain with the radical ideology of climate justice, Burnaby Mountain activists are, if anything, making it *less* likely that their audience will support policies that ameliorate climate change. Collis (October 26, 2014) is on the right rhetorical track when he says, "There is simply no benefit to the citizens of Burnaby to have this pipeline here": 63% of Burnaby residents oppose the pipeline. But remember, they oppose it primarily because they are worried about oil spills. Instead of taking this group of allies as they are and respecting their values and opinions, Collis states in a TV interview that most Canadians are, "quite frankly, concerned about climate change." But the majority are not highly concerned, and perhaps Collis' modalized assertion (Biber and Finegan, 1989, 119)—his use of the certainty adverbial "quite frankly"—suggests that he knows this, since, paradoxically we tend to "express certainty when we are not sure about something" (Downing, 2015, 380).

As it does with climate change, the ultimate order of terms compels activists to condemn capitalism. An ExxonMobil television ad features the slogan, "You don't need to think about the energy that makes our lives possible . . . because we do." In critiquing this ad, Jennifer Wenzel writes, "Our task in the energy humanities is to reclaim that thinking from the industry, a task made harder because capitalism understands the workings of the imagination and desire better than we would like" (2016, 33). ExxonMobil's message to consumers is almost shocking in its directness: "Stop thinking." But Wenzel's response is problematic because her claim about capitalism is erroneous. As Sharon Crowley observes, "Since antiquity rhetorical theorists have understood the centrality of desires and values to the maintenance of beliefs" (2006, 4). In claiming that capitalism understands imagination and desire, Wenzel is in effect claiming that capitalism understands rhetoric. But capitalism doesn't understand *anything*. Capitalism is an institutional fact;[6] it can no more understand than traffic laws, polygamy, or diplomas can understand. This is not a trivial objection. Capitalism's influence, of course, is profound and pervasive, but Wenzel's anthropomorphizing of capitalism is like activists' misunderstanding of power as monolithic. To grant capitalism the power of understanding renders invisible its actual human agents in the dialectical order—in the case of ExxonMobil or Kinder Morgan, people who work in advertising agencies and public relations departments. If arguments about oil, in general, or Trans Mountain, in particular, involve an understanding of, and competing appeals to, imagination and desire, then the engagement is seen more productively as rhetors vs. rhetors than as capitalism vs. anti-capitalism. Protesters need to come down from the ultimate order to the parliamentary, where it's not a struggle for the minds of the public between capitalism and Wenzel's "we" (really an "it": anti-capitalist ideology), but citizens opposed to the pipeline trying to persuade other citizens, most of whom may have some complaints about capitalism, but are not categorically and ideologically opposed to it. As with climate change, protesters would do well to leave capitalism out of the conversation, and focus instead on *pathos* appeals that matter to the audience.

But it seems activists *must* move a discussion into ultimate terms, not only because those terms speak to the "ultimate" goal, but because it's the ultimate context that makes discreet local actions meaningful, as steps toward the fulfillment of a vision. Activists on the left can no more avoid proclaiming the ultimate goal of a post-capitalist world than evangelical Christians can avoid proclaiming the vision of a world which has accepted Jesus Christ as lord and savior. Now, an alliance between protest and religion is not necessarily a bad thing, as many social movements have effectively invoked faith and mobilized religious communities. Nor do I identify the continuity between activism and evangelism in order to be inflammatory, but to recognize a rhetorically problematic inevitability when ideology and idealism overrule pragmatism. The ultimate of ultimates, Burke writes, would be prayer—an address to God (1950, 276). And indeed, activism as performed on Burnaby Mountain is *ultimately* a religious movement: the protest's symbols are derived from First Nations spirituality; the earthly kingdom—i.e., the capitalist state—is corrupt and illegitimate, and a revolution will usher in a new order where the last shall be first; and the urgency of the coming apocalypse justifies any means for bringing about the revolution.

Searle's description of the religious character of the Free Speech Movement is so relevant to Burnaby Mountain that I will quote it at length:

> They did not use, nor did they respond to, the rhetoric of political effectiveness. On the contrary, effectiveness be damned, what they offered their audiences and what they wanted for themselves was a whole new set of values and a new way of life. Their rhetorical style was not one of saying "Here is our platform and here is how we intend to achieve our objectives", but rather, in effect, "Here is our style and it is itself the objective, for it offers you meaning, fulfillment, and community, . . . a chance to avoid the hideous and bankrupt materialism of the world around you." (1972, 61)

With a telling choice of words, Walia (2015) claims that "Capitalism has put everything that's sacred—all of our natural resources—onto the market." Walia does not place capitalism in the dialectical order, where it would be merely problematic or unethical; she places it in the hierarchic ultimate order, where it is developmentally inferior and sacrilegious. In the ultimate order, negotiating agreements with industry on environmental issues—as was done successfully in the Clayoquot Sound logging protest (Harrison, 2015)—is not compromise but heresy. Catherine Welsh writes on the Burnaby Mountain Facebook page, "Why in the hell is [sic] Joyce Murray and Tzeporah Bermann allowed to speak on Burnaby Mtn. today?" ("Burnaby Mountain Updates," 2014). As a Member of Parliament, Murray is part of the system and the state. The hostility toward Bermann, a prominent activist on Clayoquot Sound, results from her current environmental work in the dialectical order, negotiating agreements with industries on logging, hydroelectric projects, and carbon output (Hampson, 2011). The antidemocratic, antidialogic attitude that Murray and Bermann should not be "allowed to speak" derives from the religious zeal of ideology in the ultimate order. Note the missionary motive in Walia's description of her activism: gaining people's "confidence and trust" provides an opening to "share our own analysis," and working to make a "tangible impact" is an opportunity to inform "oppressed communities" about "long-term revolutionary change" (2013, 183). Walia cites the following from Joshua Kahn Russell's "New Radical Alliances for a New Era:"

> A genuine radical imagination holds space for those who have not yet come to adopt the entirety of our worldviews, and sees those close to us as potential allies, rather than enemies. . . . Learning how to work together is part of the process that births a new world (qtd. in Walia, 2013,177).

Walia reads this excerpt as stressing the need to reach "beyond our echo chambers to unite as many people as possible" (177). But Russell says nothing of the sort. Note how limited the radical "space" really is, open not to people with different opinions and beliefs but only to those who have "not yet" accepted "the entirety" of our views.

This is not rhetorical work as classically understood, since the goal of activists' speech is not persuasion but conversion, to change the audience's mind to a way of thinking already determined to be unequivocally right—and for everyone's own good. As Searle writes,

> Like most religious truth, radical truth is revealed to the elect. . . . The forces of evil conspire to conceal the real truth, and radicalization is the process whereby the veil of illusion that has been woven by the Establishment is torn from one's eyes, and one sees how the world really is (1972, 62).

In Burke's terms, the pragmatic rhetorical motive is subordinate to the motive of "pure persuasion," directed not toward other people but toward the gods. As the idealist Plato writes in the *Phaedrus*,

> a wise man ought not to undergo [learning the art of speech] for the sake of speaking and acting before men, but that he may be able to speak and to do everything, so far as possible, in a manner pleasing to the gods (1966, 274).[7]

Why, I've asked, has Burnaby Mountain activists' rhetoric been so misattuned to the beliefs, values, and concerns of the people who should be their primary audience? Because, I've argued, activists are not particularly interested in audience. As idealists, their speech is not directed to a worldly audience at all, but "to the gods."

Protest as Expressive Composition

As a collective rhetorical act, the Burnaby Mountain protest can be seen as a group project in composition—specifically, Neo-Romantic or expressivist composition. Expressivism is marked by a "radical individualism" in which "self-expression is exalted" and "public discourse is devalued" (Winterowd, 1994,36, 37). It may seem odd to claim that a protest devalues public discourse. But as I've argued throughout, activist discourse on Burnaby Mountain has not been directed at an actual public other than the like-minded. And "without an audience," Winterowd explains, "the writer (for I cannot now say 'rhetorician') can be absolutely true to him- or herself, uncorrupted by the exigencies of genre, institutions, or, certainly, audience expectations" (1998, 182). With its commitment to individual expression and its disinterest in audience, expressivist composition results in "the death of pathos" (1998, 182) and the death of "identification" in the Burkean sense: the recognition of effective persuasion as involving the identification of one's cause with other (not just like-minded) people's interests (1950, 24). Collis writes:

> Our democratic system is vulnerable and has been slowly dismantled by those in power. . . . Citizens today must wrestle with the contradiction of participating in a broken system—voting, supporting parties and candidates, participating in public debate, even running for office—at the same time, recognizing that the most pressing issues we face (such as climate change, the geographical displacement of populations, and Indigenous rights and land claims), require us to take direct action outside of the electoral and representative apparatus of governance. (14 Oct. 2015)

But remember, polls show that Canadians are roughly split on both the Trans Mountain pipeline and the NEB's decision: nationally, 41% believe "the NEB made the right decision," 24% disagree, and "the rest weren't sure." Even in British Columbia, the numbers are similar: 41% approve, 34% disapprove, and 25% are unsure (Insights West, 2016). So, in this instance, Canadian representative government *is* working: we who oppose the pipeline just didn't get our way. So, the protest should not primarily be an expressive act against all ills, but an invitation to the unconvinced.

The ideology of expressivism, Winterowd writes, does away not only with *pathos* but with "semantic intention," the question which guides the rhetorician through every decision in the composing process: what do I want this composition to *do*? (1994, 182). Since a participant in expressive protest necessarily succeeds the moment she gives voice to her opinion, the question of semantic intention need never arise. As in expressivist composition, activist protest places great value on each individual's voice, as exemplified in Graeber's vision of the autonomous march. But the "democratization of effervescence" (Graeber, 2009, 485) is not necessarily the democratization of effective protest, since, as Carla Kaplan succinctly puts it, not every "instance of 'speaking up' will work as an instance of 'talking back'" (2001, 74). Winterowd cites as another legacy of Romantic rhetoric the fact that "imagination (genius, creativity) replaces invention" (1994, 37). One of the major shifts from Romanticism in its own day to Neo-Romantic composition pedagogy was the democratizing of genius, the belief in the creative genius within each of us. Diversity and non-hierarchy bring this belief into the theory and practice of activism, where these terms do to *ethos* what expressivism does to *pathos*: expertise and credibility are democratized out of existence, instead leaving as spokespeople for the protest those proclaiming themselves to have the greatest understanding of the spiritual/ideological vision and the "ultimate" context of the struggle: on Burnaby Mountain, that would be First Nations elders and leftist activists.

In summary, Burnaby Mountain activists have focused on the global level even though most citizens' concerns are local, disputed the legitimacy of the state institutions within which actual civic power resides, and emphasized cultural and political agendas opposed by the majority of those who also oppose the pipeline. The ideological commitment to direct action, diversity, and non-hierarchy precludes a practical conversation about what will likely work and what won't and privileges every individual's voice above the collective voice actually accomplishing a goal. It is as nonsensical to say, in the name of diversity, "Protest the pipeline in whatever way feels right to you" as to say, "Use any words you want to officiate a baseball game," or "Use whatever gesture you want to cast a vote." In fact, successful acts of protest are far more difficult than either of these because persuasion cannot be accomplished via declarative utterance—I can't do it by saying "I persuade you"—and because it's the audience who determines success. If the Burnaby Mountain protest resumes and is to succeed, participants need to recognize their words as rhetorical speech acts, and renounce their commitment to non-hierarchy and tactical diversity. What's needed is focused, realistic, audience-aware, carefully considered, rhetorically savvy political engagement: which speech acts by which people in which scenes will most likely get the job done? Recall from the Introduction Salvaggio's description of oil as a "spectral substance" (2014, 386).

Kinder Morgan's reassurance of safety is a reassurance that the oil will remain invisible, that it won't leak or explode. If environmentalists' rhetoric is to effectively "intervene in this process," then its role is quite literally expository: to expose to the public the physicality of oil and its potential negative consequences. Protesters should thus ask themselves some basic rhetorical questions:

- What is the scene of engagement, and what kinds of speakers and illocutionary acts are (and are not) recognized there?
- What are we trying to do, and what sorts of illocutionary acts and rhetorical choices are most likely to affect that?
- Conversely, what should we *not* say or do?
- Who is our audience, and what do they think, feel, believe, value, fear, etc.?
- How do these aspects of *pathos* compare to what we think, feel, believe, value, fear, etc.?
- What kinds of evidence should we muster to support our position?
- What are the potential areas of agreement, negotiation, and compromise?

One could say I'm being instrumental, that the purpose of protest is largely symbolic. But the deployment of symbols is a pragmatic rhetorical act. Participants in protest must consider goals, strategies, audience, etc. If the protest is "just" symbolic (if that's even possible), expressivism *publicly performed* will be *taken as* rhetorical, and is thus likely to have perlocutionary effects, real-world impacts on the attitudes and actions of those who witness it. Either way, it's clear that protesters should be in control of those effects by selecting their rhetorical materials. Thus far, the Burnaby Mountain protests have demonstrated that the heterogeneous performance of generalized discontent is not an effective strategy for change. The protest gets attention, and participation *feels* empowering, but, if it resumes in its current form, the protest will continue to be but a sideshow to the actual decision-making process.

Notes

1 Notes: I should state here my unease regarding what follows: an argument highly critical of the words and actions of a valued member of my own department. But we academics are in the argument business, and despite their vehemence, my criticisms are not personal.
2 See Searle (1995, 28ff).
3 I thank Sibo Chen for posing this argument.
4 See https://www.youtube.com/watch?v=wCspnAKUfjk.
5 I thank Sibo Chen for this and other constructive counter-arguments.
6 See Searle (1995, 27ff).
7 I thank Peter Cramer for the reference to the *Phaedrus*.

References

Angus Reid Public Opinion. Oct. 2012. "Opposition to Northern Gateway Remains High in British Columbia." 11 Oct. 2012. *Angus Reid Public Opinion.* 30 Aug 2016 http://angusreidglobal.com/wp-content/uploads/2012/10/2012.10.11_Pipelines_BC.pdf.

Aristotle. *Rhetoric.* 1959. Trans. W. Rhys Roberts. New York: Oxford UP.

Austin, John Langshaw. 1975. *How to Do Things with Words.* Cambridge, MA: Harvard UP.

Biber, Douglas and Edward Finegan. 1989. "Styles of Stance in English: Lexical and Grammatical Marking of Evidentiality and Affect." *Text* 9(1), 93–124.

BROKE. 1 Jan. 2016. "Mission Statement." 30 Aug. 2016 http://brokepipelinewatch.ca/category/mission-statement.

Burke, Kenneth. 1945. *A Grammar of Motives.* Berkeley: U of California P.

———. 1966. *Language as Symbolic Action.* Berkeley: U of California P.

———. 1941. *Philosophy of Literary Form.* Berkeley: U of California P.

———. 1950. *A Rhetoric of Motives.* Berkeley: U of California P.

———. 1975. "Words as Deeds." *Centrum* 3, 147–168.

"Burnaby Mountain Updates." 29 Nov. 2014. *Facebook.* 30 Aug. 2016 https://www.facebook.com/burnabymountain#.

Campbell, Troy, and Aaron Kay. 2014. "Solution Aversion: On the Relation between Ideology and Motivated Disbelief." *Journal of Personality and Social Psychology* 107(5): 809–824.

Clague, John J., Doug Stead, Allison Westin, and Mirko Francioni. 2014. "Engineering Geology of Burnaby Mountain: A Preliminary Report." *Trans Mountain Pipeline ULC TMEP Westridge Tunnel Investigation – 2014 Site Investigation Data Report.* Vancouver: BGC Engineering Inc. 31 Aug. 2016 www.neb-one.gc.ca/fetch.asp?language=E&ID=A4F5F0.

Collis, Stephen. 1 Feb. 2015 "After Burnaby Mountain (Part 1)." *Beating the Bounds.* Blog. 30 Aug. 2016 https://beatingthebounds.com/2015/02/01/after-burnaby-mountain.

———. 12 Feb. 2015. "After Burnaby Mountain (Part 3)." *Beating the Bounds.* Blog. 30 Aug. 2016 https://beatingthebounds.com/2015/02/12/after-burnaby-mountain-part-3.

———. 26 Oct. 2014. "The Last Barrel of Oil on Burnaby Mountain." BROKE (Burnaby Residents Opposing Kinder-Morgan Expansion). 26 July 2018 https://beatingthebounds.com/2014/10/26/the-last-barrel-of-oil-on-burnaby-mountain.

———. 14 Oct. 2015. "When Democracy Becomes Controversial." *Beating the Bounds.* Blog. 30 Aug. 2016 https://beatingthebounds.com/2015/10/14/when-democracy-becomes-controversial.

Crowley, Sharon. 2006. *Toward a Civil Discourse: Rhetoric and Fundamentalism.* Pittsburgh: U of Pittsburgh P.

Downing, Angela. 2015. *English Grammar: A University Course.* 3rd ed. New York: Routledge.

Forum Research. 17 Mar. 2016. "Majority Approve of All Three Controversial Pipelines." *Forum Research.* 30 Aug. 2016 http://poll.forumresearch.com/post/2480/most-see-pipelines-as-safer-than-rail-for-moving-crude.

Gordon, Jon. 2015. *Unsustainable Oil: Facts, Counterfacts and Fictions.* Edmonton: U of Alberta P.

Graeber, David. 2009. *Direct Action: An Ethnography*. Oakland: AK Press.

Hager, Mike. 19 Dec. 2014. "Most Canadians Support Anti-Kinder Morgan Protesters: New Online Poll." *Vancouver Sun*. 30 Aug. 2016 http://www.burnabynow.com/news/most-canadians-support-anti-kinder-morgan-protesters-new-online-poll-1.1689868.

Hampson, Sarah. 3 Oct. 2011. "Activist Tzeporah Berman Steps Out of the Trees and Into the Boardroom." *Globe and Mail* 31 Aug. 2016 http://www.theglobeandmail.com/life/relationships/news-and-views/sarah-hampson/activist-tzeporah-berman-steps-out-of-the-trees-and-into-the-boardroom/article2189407.

Harrison, Kathryn. 29 Jan. 2016. "The Impact of Civil Disobedience on Public Policy." President's Dream Colloquium on Obedience and Disobedience: Taking Action on Climate Change, Simon Fraser University, Vancouver, BC.

Insights West. Sept. 2014. "Public Opinion Poll: Kinder Morgan's Trans Mountain Pipeline. Wave #2" 30 Aug. 2016 https://www.burnaby.ca/Assets/TMEP/Public+Opinion+Pool+Wave+2.pdf.

———. 2 Mar. 2016. "Fewer British Columbians Would Endorse Pipeline Projects." *Insights West*. 30 Aug. 2016 http://www.insightswest.com/news/fewer-british-columbians-would-endorse-pipeline-projects.

Ivison, John. 11 April 2016. "Trudeau Convinced That Pipeline Strategy Must be Top Priority." *National Post*. 31 Aug. 2016 http://news.nationalpost.com/full-comment/john-ivison-trudeau convinced-that-pipeline-strategy-must-be-top-priority.

Jones, Russ. 2014. *Catastrophic Earthquake Preparedness*. Victoria, BC: Office of the Auditor General of British Columbia.

Kaplan, Carla. 2001. "'Talk to Me': Talk Ethics and Erotics." *Talk, Talk, Talk: The Cultural Life of Everyday Conversation*. Ed. S.I. Salamensky. New York: Routledge, 63–76.

"Kinder Morgan Loses Bid to Extend Injunction." 27 Nov. 2014. *CBC News*. 30 Aug. 2016 http://www.cbc.ca/news/canada/british-columbia/kinder-morgan-loses-bid-to-extend-injunction-1.2852222.

Marquart-Pyatt, Sandra T., Aaron M. McCright, Thomas Dietz, and Riley E. Dunlap. 2014. "Politics Eclipses Climate Extremes for Climate Change Perceptions." *Global Environmental Change* 29, 246–257. 31 Aug. 2016 https://www.researchgate.net/publication/268526184_Politics_eclipses_climate_extremes_for_climate_change_perceptions.

Mathias, Eric. 16 Nov. 2014. "Love, Not Anger, Motivates Burnaby Mountain Protest Against Kinder Morgan." *Vancouver Observer*. 30 Aug. 2016 http://www.vancouverobserver.com/opinion/love-not-anger-motivates-burnaby-mountain-protest-against-kinder-morgan.

Plato. *Phaedrus*. 1966. Trans. Harold North Fowler. Cambridge, MA: Harvard UP. http://www.perseus.tufts.edu/hopper/text?doc=Perseus%3Atext%3A1999.01.01 74%3Atext%3DPhaedrus%3Asection%3D227a.

Polychronakos, Helen. 2015. "Harsha Walia on the Principles of DIY Activism." Interview. *Room* 38(3). 30 Aug 2016 https://roommagazine.com/interview/harsha-walia-principles-diy-activism.

Prystupa, Mychaylo. 5 Nov. 2014. "'We are Not Radicals' – Kinder Morgan Lawsuit Defendants Speak Out." *Vancouver Observer*. 30 Aug. 2016 http://www.vancouverobserver.com/news/we-are-not-radicals-kinder-morgan-lawsuit-defendants-speak-out.

Prystupa, Mychaylo and Jenny Uechi. 27 Nov. 2014. "RCMP Responds with Respect as Grand Chief Arrested on Burnaby Mountain." *Vancouver Observer.* 31 Aug. 2016 http://www.vancouverobserver.com/news/grand-chief-stewart-phillip- prepares-arrest-burnaby-mountain.

Quarmby, Lynne. 19 Sept. 2014. "March for the Climate." Opinion. *Vancouver Sun.* 30 Aug. 2016 http://www.vancouversun.com/technology/Opinion+March+climate/10215292/story.html

Salvaggio, Ruth. 2014 "Imagining Angels on the Gulf." *Oil Culture.* Minneapolis: U of Minnesota P.

Scheidler, Joseph. 1985. *Closed: Ninety-Nine Ways to Stop Abortion.* San Francisco: Ignatius Press.

Searle, John R. 1972. *The Campus War: A Sympathetic Look at the University in Agony.* London: Penguin.

———. 1995. *The Construction of Social Reality.* New York: Free Press.

———. 1979. *Expression and Meaning: Studies in the Theory of Speech Acts.* Cambridge: Cambridge UP.

Stewart, Charles J., Craig Allen Smith, Robert E. Denton, Jr. 2001. *Persuasion and Social Movements.* Project Heights, IL: Waveland.

Uechi, Jenny. 27 Nov. 2014. "'Fabulous' Victory for Burnaby Mountain Protesters as Court Rejects Kinder Morgan Contempt Charges." *Vancouver Observer.* 30 Aug. 2016 http://www.vancouverobserver.com/news/huge-victory-burnaby-mountain-protesters-court-rejects-kinder-morgan-contempt-charges.

Walia, Harsha. 4 Nov. 2014. "Burnaby Mountain: Latest Wall of Opposition against Tar Sands." *Harbinger.* Blog. 30 Aug. 2016 https://nbharbinger.wordpress.com/2014/11/07/burnaby-mountain-latest-wall-of-opposition-against-tar-sands.

———. 5 Mar. 2015. "The Climate Justice Movement." President's Dream Colloquium on Obedience and Disobedience: Taking Action on Climate Change. Simon Fraser University, Vancouver, BC.

———. 2013. *Undoing Border Imperialism.* Oakland: AK Press.

Weaver, Richard M. 1985. *Ethics of Rhetoric.* Davis, CA: Hermagoras Press.

Wenzel, Jennifer. 2016. "Taking Stock of Energy Humanities." *Reviews in Cultural Theory: Special Issue on Energy Humanities.* Eds. Jeff Diamanti and Brent Ryan Bellamy. 6(3), 30–34.

Wheatley, Michael. 30 Aug. 2016. "No Pipelines on Stolen Native Land." Photograph. *Alamy* 2 Dec. 2014. http://www.alamy.com/stock-photo-no-pipelines-on-stolen-native-land-sign-burnaby-mountain-anti-pipeline-76051915.html.

Winterowd, W. Ross. 1998. *The English Department: A Personal and Institutional History.* Carbondale: Southern Illinois UP.

———. 1994. *A Teacher's Introduction to Composition in the Rhetorical Tradition.* Urbana: NCTE.

Index

Note: *Italic* page numbers refer to figures and page numbers followed by "n" denote endnotes.

www.ingramcontent.com/pod-product-compliance
Ingram Content Group UK Ltd.
Pitfield, Milton Keynes, MK11 3LW, UK
UKHW022003180926
475701UK00003B/177
* 9 7 8 1 0 3 2 1 7 8 2 8 8 *